BEYOND FORMALISM

Beyond Formalism

Literary Essays 1958-1970

by Geoffrey H. Hartman

New Haven and London, Yale University Press

Published with assistance from the Kingsley Trust Association.
Publication Fund established by the Scroll and
Key Society of Yale College.

Library of Congress catalog card number: 79–115371
ISBN: 0–300–01327–2 (cloth), 0–300–01515–1 (paper)

Designed by John O. C. McCrillis,
set in Times Roman type,
and printed in the United States of America by
the Murray Printing Company, Westford, Massachusetts.

Published in Great Britain, Europe, Africa, and Asia
(except Japan) by Yale University Press, Ltd., London.
Distributed in Australia and New Zealand by Book & Film
Services, Artarmon, N.S.W., Australia; and in Japan
by Harper & Row, Publishers, Tokyo Office.

Copyright information concerning the original appearance of these essays
is included in the acknowledgments.

For
HAROLD BLOOM

Contents

The essays collected here have a varied subject matter: the state of literary criticism, the novel, poetry, and literary history. Yet there is a unity of concern. I try to combine literary history—the discerning of large, continuous, and highly speculative patterns—with literary criticism—a daily, discontinuous, and very pragmatic effort. The theoretical difficulties of this are not resolved in the present book, which remains essayistic, though my last paper suggests the mutuality of criticism and historiography in a more sustained way.

What, after all, is *criticism?* Corpses of ideas, a self-dissolving or purgative series of reflections. The natural positivity of the mind is engaged only to be chastened, as the literary work, whether richly obscure or puzzlingly simple (a sonnet by Mallarmé or a Wordsworth lyric), teases the reader out of thought. This purgation of the interpretive mind resembles literature's constant flight from literariness: its wish to dissolve as a medium or, at the very least, to renounce romantic props and to intuit things directly. That truth is found to be stranger than fiction, that to tell things as they are produces a highly mediated art, simply renews the condition which started the protest.

If literature joins in the quest for a truth or objectivity transcending it, the critic becomes something of a philosopher. He considers literary works as an engaged reflection on personal myths and communal dreams, consciousness of consciousness in its mixed state of freedom and dependency. I hope bringing literary criticism closer to philosophy (in its most liberal aspect) meets no objection: in order to respect the formal study of art I had also to go beyond formalism and to define art's role in the life of the artist, his culture, and the human community.[1]

1. *Formalism* is used here in a more general sense than in socialist thought, which opposes to it art's direct or "progressive" contribution to social issues.

I do not lay claim, however, to a special theory of consciousness: of how one achieves that degree of self-awareness firm enough to be called an identity or authentic enough to be honored as destiny. Perhaps these very ideas of identity, destiny, etc. are among the beliefs a mature mind renounces. But Yeats comments on the difficulty of such a step: having demythologized ourselves, "the last kiss is given to the void." Our illusions lead cunningly into reality, and literature is part of this Negative Way. It is not the contemporary mind alone which takes that road. Though Lionel Trilling sees Thomas Mann's Mme. Chauchat, for whom freedom is "se perdre et même . . . se laisser dépérir," as a Muse of modernism, some such beguilement to "the very heart of loss" (Shakespeare)—some such "desolation of reality" (Yeats), in which the multiplying secondary aims of civilized life are stripped off and we touch essentials again—is a master-illusion of more than contemporary art. It is a northern enchantment, part of the continuous poem of our climate.

Illusions can be of many kinds. Shelley suggests that there are "generous superstitions," and perhaps it is art that makes them generous. If we denominate as Romance the field of all strong illusions—of all myths that have charmed, for good or bad, the mind of man—then art cultivates that field, bringing forth food out of the eater and sweetness out of the strong. With the Romantic poets the purification of Romance moves into the center of the literary enterprise. Though they belong to the Enlightenment and believe in a progress of consciousness, they were not for bigger and better minds but for a finer magic, a more liberal participation of all in the imaginative life. Without imagination, no soul-making. When we are young, we have projects for sun and moon, as for everything. Born into romance, we replace one illusion with another, until the pain of being is the pain of imagination. Only one myth, perhaps, proves inexhaustible. A poet, says Keats, "has no Identity; he is continually in for—and filling—some other Body." There will always be an Other, or the dream of Otherness. Literature is the form that dream takes in an enlightened mind.

Many of these essays converge on Continental modes of thought where a purifying reflection engages artist and critic alike. The interpreter reconstructs a journey that passes through a deeply negative moment: solipsism or despair, self-emptying or the brooding dark. Much depends on where, in this journey, we place the zero point. Does the artist become his own iconoclast and, like Descartes, methodically question his world to achieve an authentic cogito? Or is the zero point a cataclysm like the Black Death, Protestantism, the French Revolution, the German "Kahlschlag"? Does our creative despair come from the fullness of the past, or is each man sufficiently subversive to himself? Can we even tell whether it comes from within or without? Is not the realization of one's mortality enough? Such questions arise in every wholistic consideration of art.

Despite an allegiance to the Continental style of criticism, I feel strongly what James called "the coercive charm of form." Continental criticism can be a lesson in how to subvert the specificity of literature. In attacking "the naive, egotistical ideal of the work's unity" (Gaston Bachelard), it often neglects literary form and dissolves art into a reflex of consciousness, technology, or social process. In Anglo-America, respect for literary form is a priori, but not necessarily deeper. A more radical difference between the two approaches centers on the presumed objectivity of the work of art: for us the reader in his selfhood is the problem, and he needs historical, philological, or similar correctives (I. A. Richards' *Practical Criticism* lies totally within that perspective); but for the Continental critic it is the objective form of art which seems problematic, and he seeks to liberate it, to release a hidden or repressed content. Not our subjectivity is to be feared but our overreaction to it, those pseudo-objective criteria which imprison both the work and ourselves.

Though some essays are directly patterned on the Continental model ("Virginia's Web") and others blend that approach with an attempt to understand precritical modes of exegesis ("Adam on the Grass with Balsamum"), I do not reject the notion of literary form as organic or unified. Yet I think we have used it too reductively. The domain of art is as tricky and dualistic as human life: "Beauty is Truth, Truth Beauty" inculcates no absolute correspondence but a "fair attitude" that tells us not to sacrifice present joy by nervously rationalizing it. Let the mind have space to breathe, free of teleologies; let it enjoy a fine surmise, the run of an interpretation, a greeting of the spirit, a weather.

"Oneness makes war, and the obsession of oneness." Or, as Lawrence also says, echoing the book of Job, "there is no reconciliation in the flesh." In *Studies in Classic American Literature* he sees through formal reconciliations to the world of conflict without denying the necessity of a transcendence *in allo genere*. Our desire for at-one-ment is engaged by the cunning of art more than by the cunning of reason.

When rhetoric becomes bloody and the intellect opportunistic, philology's "still, small voice" is not heard. To these external dangers we must add one internal to the discipline. The New Criticism, which arose in the 1930s and gained its major influence after World War II, did a great service to the schools. Rejecting literary gossip and half-hearted historical knowledge, it called for a return to the text and a new trust in the lights of a growing body of students drawn from all levels of society. It retained, however, many parochial and even aristocratic elements. Born in an era of "the bewitchment of the mind by words" (Wittgenstein)—when techniques of vulgarization and propaganda confused archetype and stereotype, logos and cliché—it concentrated all its attention on teaching a methodical suspicion of the word, on demanding even of poetry an ironic or tensional structure, and on establishing by that criterion a new and exclusive line of modern classics. Judiciousness is always needed, and the abuse of words has not diminished. But the New Criticism proved to be dangerously narrowing. An emphasis on words is discriminatory as well as discriminating unless it guides us to larger structures of the imagination: to forms like drama and epic, but also to what Northrop Frye calls "archetypes" and Lévi-Strauss "mythèmes." Since these structures are present in popular as well as learned poetry, no special acculturation or very refined training is required to observe them. Indeed, somewhat like Molière's M. Jourdain, we see we have been mythologizing all the time. This discovery is hopeful if it revives our sense of community and leads to an understanding of the intrinsic role of the arts in all culture. It may, in fact, lead beyond the restricted vision of particular societies by revealing the schematic or "archetypal" basis of all social mythologies. A new, less culture-bound, judiciousness could emerge from this.

Many imitators of the New Criticism have, moreover, become formalists, hunting structures by means of what they believe to be value-free techniques and confusing art with ideas of order. We witness today the pedagogical triumph of the auxiliary science of exegesis: of the repetitive, compulsive analysis of works of art in terms of theme or formal relations. Great exegetes, however, have always, at some point, swerved from the literal sense of the text. This text, like the world, was a prison for Rabbinic, Patristic, or Neoplatonic interpreters, yet by their hermeneutic act the prison opened into a palace and the extremes of man's dependence and of his capacity for vision came simultaneously into view. I feel the poverty of our textual imaginations compared to theirs. The very idea of interpretation seems to have shrunk. If books are not prophetic, if they do not reveal "the voice of the shuttle" as well as "the figure in the carpet," they are expendable. I hope these essays broaden the idea of interpretation by remaining text-bound, and that of literacy by not abandoning the mediation of words.

New Haven, Connecticut
October 1969 G.H.

Acknowledgments

"Structuralism: The Anglo-American Adventure" and "Camus and Malraux: The Common Ground" were first published in *Yale French Studies* 36–37 (1966): 148–68 and 25 (1960): 104–10; they are reprinted here by permission of the editors.

"Ghostlier Demarcations: The Sweet Science of Northrop Frye" was originally published in *English Institute Essays* (1966) and is reprinted here by permission of Columbia University Press.

"Beyond Formalism" originally appeared in *Modern Language Notes* 81 (1966): 542–57; copyright © 1966 by The Johns Hopkins Press, and is reprinted here by permission of the Johns Hopkins Press.

"The Heroics of Realism" appeared in *The Yale Review* (Autumn 1963), copyright © 1963 by Yale University, and is reprinted here by permission of Yale University.

"Virginia's Web" first appeared in *Chicago Review* 14 (Spring 1961): 20–32. Copyright © 1970 by Geoffrey Hartman.

"Maurice Blanchot: Philosopher-Novelist" was originally included in *The Novelist as Philosopher,* edited by John Cruickshank (London, 1962), copyright © 1962 by Oxford University Press, and is reprinted here by permission of Oxford University Press.

"Milton's Counterplot" appeared in *ELH* 25 (March 1958): 1–12, "Adam on the Grass with Balsamum" in *ELH* (March 1969), and "Marvell, St. Paul, and the Body of Hope" in *ELH* 31 (June 1964): 175–94, all copyright © by The Johns Hopkins Press and reprinted here by permission of The Johns Hopkins Press.

" 'The Nymph Complaining for the Death of Her Faun': A Brief Allegory" was originally published in *Essays in Criticism* 18 (1968): 113–35 and is reprinted here by permission.

"Blake and the Progress of Poesy" is from *William Blake: Essays for S. Foster Damon,* edited by Alvin H. Rosenfeld (Brown

University Press, 1969), copyright © 1969 by Brown University Press, and is reprinted here by permission of Brown University Press.

"Wordsworth, Inscriptions, and Romantic Nature Poetry" was originally included in *From Sensibility to Romanticism: Essays Presented to Frederick A. Pottle,* edited by Frederick W. Hilles and Harold Bloom. Copyright © 1965 by Oxford University Press, Inc. Reprinted by permission.

"Hopkins Revisited" was included in Geoffrey H. Hartman, editor, *Hopkins: A Collection of Critical Essays,* © 1966. Reprinted by permission of Prentice-Hall, Inc., Englewood Cliffs, New Jersey.

Portions of "The Maze of Modernism: Reflections on Mac-Neice, Graves, Hope, Lowell, and Others" first appeared in *Kenyon Review* 22 (Autumn 1960); 691–700, 23 (Spring 1961): 354–61, 25 (Spring 1963): 374–79, and 25 (Autumn 1963): 751–57; portions were also included in *Partisan Review,* vol. 31, no. 1 (Winter 1964), pp. 110–16, and vol. 32, no. 1 (Winter 1965), pp. 135–40, copyright © 1964 and 1965 by *Partisan Review.* They are reprinted here by permission of those journals.

"False Themes and Gentle Minds" is from *Philological Quarterly,* vol. 47, no. 1, The University of Iowa, and is reprinted here by permission.

"Romanticism and Anti-Self-Consciousness" was originally published in *Centennial Review* 6 (Autumn 1962): 553–65 and is reprinted here by permission.

"Romantic Poetry and the Genius Loci" is from *The Disciplines of Criticism,* edited by Peter Demetz, Thomas Greene, Lowry Nelson, Jr., pp 289–314. Copyright © 1968 by Yale University. Reprinted by permission of Yale University Press.

"The Voice of the Shuttle: Language from the Point of View of Literature" first appeared in *The Review of Metaphysics* (December 1969) and is reprinted here with permission.

"Toward Literary History" is reprinted by permission from *Daedalus,* Journal of the American Academy of Arts and Sciences, Boston, Massachusetts, vol. 99, no. 2.

Structuralism: The Anglo-American Adventure

Structuralism is a complex and many-faceted intellectual movement: born in Russia and Switzerland, confirmed in Prague, sowing a wild and fertile seed in France, but respecting the separation of disciplines and keeping to linguistics in America. It is not suited for monogamy, however, and is about to form a dangerous alliance with literary criticism. In France that alliance has already begotten a vast and sophisticated offspring. If, as Claude Lévi-Strauss demonstrated, the new method for studying language could yield a Structural Anthropology, it should also be transferable to the study of literature. Having made the term *social sciences* respectable, structuralism becomes more ambitious and holds out the hope that even literary criticism might be counted one day among the *sciences humaines.*

New movements win out over old by their purity, or simplicity —by removing a burden of unnecessary assumptions and freeing the energy released for a more integral purpose. It is easy to predict that structuralism will have an era, a genuine and lasting influence. The purity of the structural method results from the central place accorded to the idea of mediation. We usually think of mediation as give-and-take, barter, interpretation, dialogue, or ritual. Its basic formula is *do ut des,* or the converse. A whole group of related notions, such as parity, equity, balance of power, and compensation, also enter. The structuralist, inspired by the Saussurian principle that language has a systematic (synchronic) as well as historical (diachronic) form, tries to gain a conspectus of all these relations or institutions—of which speech is indeed the paradigm case. Aristotle defined soul as the form of forms: the structuralist seeks the relation of relations. If we take Mauss's essay on gifts and Lévi-Strauss's on kinship as the classic examples, structural theory comprises the following theses: (1) that societies are systems, and that there is a totality of these systems

3

which makes the structure of the societal visible; (2) that to clarify this structure is to clarify the form of "mediation," where mediation is always a total social phenomenon and always intersubjective, i.e., an I-Thou and not I-it relation, a relation of persons or personae, even when the thing mediated seems to have the "it" character of property, money, the past, etc;[1] (3) that there is always a *contrat social* (see 1 above) whether or not the participants are conscious of it—indeed they cannot be fully conscious of it, since it is so complex, concrete, and comprehensive, with an almost Kafkaesque extension. The structure of society is therefore latent rather than manifest.

Thus structuralism is a "unified field" theory. Its subject is not this or that culture (a corpus of texts, a geographically or historically delimited area) but the very process of mediation and how rites, values, meanings, and all such recurrent currencies relate to it. But to turn now to the study of literature. The struc-

---

1. See M. Mauss on gifts and E. Cassirer on language:
What they [the Polynesians] exchange is not exclusively goods and wealth, real and personal property, and things of economic value. They exchange rather courtesies, entertainments, ritual, military assistance, women, children, dances and feasts; and fairs in which the market is but one element and the circulation of wealth but one part of a wide and enduring contract. [Mauss, *The Gift* (Glencoe, Ill., 1954)].

In speech and art the individuals not only share what they already possess; it is only by virtue of this sharing process . . . that individuals have attained what they possess. This can be observed in any living and meaningful conversation. It is never simply a question of imparting information, but of statement and response. It is only in this twofold process that true thought emerges. Plato has said that "questioning and answering each other in discourse" is our only access to the world of the "idea." In question and answer "I" and "you" must be distinguished, not only that they may understand each other, but even if each is ever to know himself. Here both factors are in continual interplay. The thought of one partner is kindled by that of another. And by virtue of this interaction each constructs for himself a "shared world" of meaning within the medium of language. [Cassirer, *The Logic of the Humanities* (New Haven, 1961)]

Compare also: "They will give each other a hundred new names, and take them away again, as quietly as one takes off an earring" (Rilke); and "Lass die Sprache dir sein, was der Körper den Liebenden. Er nur/Ist's, der die Wesen trennt und der die Wesen vereint" (Schiller).

turalist asks, What is the status of words in society? Is literature to be compared to ritual, or does it mediate in a distinctively different way? At the most general level, are not social systems best defined by analogy to language systems? With respect to the special role of literature, we have case studies and brilliant general hints, but no one with the scope of a Lévi-Strauss. De Saussure, for instance, in unpublished notebooks recently brought to light, suggests that certain types of religious poetry are created out of a primal or cultic name which is covertly (anagrammatically) "distributed." Grammar, language, and poetry might then be looked at as a purposive *sparagmos,* as a second mode and second power of naming.[2] We could think of literature as a hoard of sacred or magical words which the poet, as secular priest, makes available. This is pure speculation. In the absence of a more definitive essay on literary mediation, it is best to be content with the brief eulogy of a famous rabbi by his disciple: "He changed my gold into silver coins." *La monnaie de l'absolu;*—words reveal the individual talent and make it negotiable.

It may still seem, however, as if structuralism were a foreign import, especially in literary studies. This is because Anglo-American tradition is endemically suspicious of systematization. We remember Dr. Johnson on Bishop Hurd: "Hurd, sir, is one of a set of men who account for everything systematically"; and he proposes "scarlet breeches" as a worthy topic for the Bishop's interest in origins. Now Richard Hurd, Bishop of Worcester, author of *Letters on Chivalry and Romance* (1762), is one of our first structure-minded critics. He justified the peculiarities of gothic romance (Spenser's *Faerie Queene)* by grounding it in the manners and rituals of an earlier age. He is not as yet the perfect structuralist, for his interest is strongly antiquarian. But there is an important English tradition of structuralist analysis which emerges here as part of a movement to put native sources on a par with the classics. The interest in native poetry goes hand in hand with a body of criticism seeking to justify that poetry's eccentric, nonclassical form; and the idea that art is to be seen in its relation to social institutions (which became a nineteenth-century cliché) helps this end.

2. "Les anagrammes de Ferdinand de Saussure," Textes présentés par Jean Starobinski, *Mercure de France* (Février 1964).

5

The idea of a formal relation between literature and social institutions does not in itself define a structural approach. It may even obscure it if "relation" implies the priority of the societal and the purely mimetic or documentary status of art.[3] A naïve sociological assumption of this kind is not removed till the beginning of the present century. Then the renewed study of oral tradition reveals the archetypal rather than archaic, and universal rather than local, character of convention. W. P. Ker's investigations of epic and romance, E. K. Chamber's research into the origins of medieval drama, and F. B. Gummere's theories on the ballad showed that all literature was governed by similar conventions. At least all literature with a source in oral tradition; and the strength of these scholars lay in uncovering that source. But this meant that the formal features of Romance could no longer be explained, as in Hurd, by the institutions of an age of chivalry, since they are found in literature from the beginning. It cleared the way for a new kind of criticism, which could view literature as an institution with its own laws or structural principles, yet relate these laws to both local traditions and to the societal as such. Any interpretation that can respect these aims is rightly called structural.

Consider C. L. Barber's *Shakespeare's Festive Comedy* (1959). It is surely inadequate to think of it only as myth criticism. Subtitled, "A Study of Dramatic Form and its relation to Social Custom," its affinity to Hurd is apparent. The eccentricities of Shakespearean comedy are attached to a "saturnalian pattern" whose ritual origin F. M. Cornford had described, but which came to Shakespeare through such native holiday customs as the May Games and the convention of the Lord of Misrule. Like Sartre or Lucien Goldmann, Barber is interested in the local mediations by which a social structure comes to the artist. Yet his perspective reaches beyond Elizabethan England. The saturnalian pattern, present both in Greek and Shakespearean comedy, expresses a

3. There is, however, a "structuralisme génétique" of Marxist inspiration, based on the theory that art reflects, in its structure rather than content, the collective vision of certain social groups, "whose consciousness tends toward a total vision of man." Lucien Goldmann identifies these groups with the classes of orthodox Marxism. A problem here is the casuistry needed to distinguish between structure and content as well as, on occasion, between structure and form.

problematic human need which must last as long as society is society—hierarchic, repressive, in conflict with itself. Malinowsky would have said that it resolves a social tension.

The reason why studies like Barber's are not recognized for what they are is that they remain obstinately naïve in point of theory and shy away from explicit social criticism. The opposite is true of Kenneth Burke, but his theorizing is so thick and unpurified that its influence can only gradually filter into literary studies. Francis Fergusson's *Idea of a Theater,* on the other hand, is exemplary in its combination of theoretical and practical criticism. It is only fair to acknowledge, however, that in Anglo-American practice a brilliant method is often accompanied by an undeveloped theory. Barber holds no less than three variant views concerning the relation of social to artistic structure: that social forms are translated into artistic, that it is peculiarly significant that Shakespeare manages to translate social forms into artistic, and that the social is not so much prior to art as it is a mixed form created by the conflict of ludic and legal—a form, therefore, in which art participates constitutively. But to transcend antiquarianism—to become genuinely critical—we need a firm idea of the role of art in the light of which the particular work can be judged.

Literary theory has been striving for exactly this: a firm and adequate conception of the role of art in human life. The modern increase in literary criticism suggests, in fact, that art is now subjected to greater expectations than ever. Since the early part of this century, and already since the Romantic period, we have turned to art in order to sustain our diminishing sense of "the common nature" of man.[4] There is no need to discuss in detail why the individual should feel a loss in his sense of communal identity, and why he should now turn to art for a saving hypothesis. It is enough to point out that Bergson, writing at the time of crisis, views art as an instinctive defense against social disintegration. Also during this time myth criticism arises, encouraged by new evidence concerning the communal or ritual origin of art. Our first modern and inspired structuralists are Jane Harrison in

4. See chapter 1 in Maud Bodkin's *Archetypal Patterns in Poetry* (1934), and the conclusion of F. B. Gummere's *The Beginnings of Poetry* (1901). Cf. W. Wimsatt, Jr. *Hateful Contraries* (Lexington, Ky., 1964), pp. 16 ff., for a highly critical account of these developments.

Themis (1912), F. M. Cornford in *The Origins of Attic Comedy* (1914), and a great breed of classicists and orientalists indebted to Frazer (Gilbert Murray, Jessie Weston, T. H. Gaster, G. R. Lévy).

Part of the crisis, clearly, is that the classics have lost their power to be models for communal behavior. What follows is an upsurge of individualism but also a deepening insight into the nature of model-making. The realization gradually comes that society is always based on some form of social lie or vital myth; indeed that myths, however barbarous in content, serve the same purpose in their society as the classics in ours. Borrowing a term from biology, one can say that all myths are analogous, that they show a correspondence of function if not of structure. But this recognition, which still allows myth to be criticized for its primitive content (Frazer stops here), is followed by the recognition that myths may also be homologous, or of the same structure. The first recognition can lead to the view that each society has its own classics, which are mortal or gradually purified, but the second disparages a naïve historicism of this kind. Since all models productive of social cohesion are basically of one structure, the reason they become obsolete must lie in a modification of that structure. The literary cliché and popular stereotype exemplify disabling change of this kind. By the same token, however, the dead convention can be restructured and revived, as it is in all authentic art. We recover its nature by an act of historical or artistic sympathy—in short, by some sort of hermeneutic engagement. In Paul Ricoeur's words, "Le symbole donne à penser." When Nietzsche sees Dionysus behind Apollo, when Jane Harrison sees the Daimones behind the Olympians, when Yeats talks of "grounding mythology in the earth," they not only revive an ancient model, but reveal something of the structure of every myth. The recognition that myths are homologous entails a theory of the life cycle of myth.

In the final analysis, then, structuralism is based on two important and related discoveries. The first, that myths are models productive of social cohesion, grants myth and art an exemplary role in society. The second, that all such models are myths, homologous in structure as well as analogous in function, enables structuralism to become a science of all social-systemic behavior.

8

This *nova scienza,* however, is always faced with explaining the difference between the manifest content of myths and their latent structural identity. Here two developments play a crucial role: one is psychoanalysis, with its technique for uncovering latent meanings; the other is structural linguistics, with its discovery that meaning resides not in the sounds themselves but rather in their combination at a phonemic (latent) level. A structural interpretation of literature may utilize categories which appear abstract because they are the equivalents to phonemes and their laws of combination.[5]

Such interpretation, however, must never become so formalistic as to forget its origin. The aim of myth criticism from Jane Harrison to Northrop Frye, and of anthropology from Durkheim to Lévi-Strauss, is to save the common nature of man—despite fragmentation, specialization, and ideological wars. Structuralism cannot follow this aim unless it exerts a genuine historical consciousness vis-à-vis itself. To learn with Lévi-Strauss that primitive thought is as logical as our own leads to a humanizing recognition, one that both comforts and disconcerts. We turn now to examine the progress of structuralism in England and America, choosing a few central figures but inevitably neglecting others of importance.

The refinement which allowed myth criticism to become a form of literary criticism had almost no connection with the rise of structural linguistics.[6] It came about as a natural development of

5. There remains, however, an unresolved conflict between the depth-analysis of linguists and of Freudians. Psychoanalytic technique represents the latent entities as symbols or archetypes; i.e., they are, if anything, overdetermined, and the consciousness of the individual is a context that limits or objectifies their meaning. The entities of structural linguistics, however, are underdetermined or arbitrary without an a priori, systematic, and intersubjective context that generates meaning like a Kantian unconscious.

6. A rival theory of linguistics does, however, influence Anglo-American criticism. It is set forth in C. K. Ogden and I. A. Richards, *The Meaning of Meaning* (1923), to which Malinowski contributes a supplement on "The Problem of Meaning in Primitive Languages." Malinowski stresses what he calls the "context of situation" (Ogden and Richards's "sign-situation") in addition to the "linguistic context." A problem common to this theory and structuralism is the role of the meta-verbal

the basic theory. The latter, adjusted to the study of literature and extended from archaic society to all cultures, converted archaeology into anthropology. Gilbert Murray is less advanced in this than Northrop Frye, but the direction is already apparent. Murray, F. M. Cornford, and Jane Harrison are contemporaries; and Murray had contributed an important "Excursus on the Ritual Forms preserved in Greek Tragedy" to Harrison's *Themis*. He expands Aristotle's description of the plot structure of tragedy, treating it as a reflection of the ritual acts of a hypothetical *sacer ludus*. Aristotle's anagnorisis and peripety are expanded as agon, pathos, threnos, theophany, etc. A few years later, in a famous lecture on "Hamlet and Orestes" (1914), Murray established the similarities between the Hamlet and Orestes stories and, not finding a direct historical explanation for them, fell back on something like the Jungian theory of a collective unconscious. According to this theory a primal pattern is inscribed on the memory of man and acts as an a priori determinant of his experience. This pattern not only reflects our racial history but remains vital to it, vital to our continued communal life. It is the communal or social whose locus is being widened; we are clearly in the midst of a general effort to save the common nature, to revalue the claim of tradition vis-à-vis individual talent. (Jane Harrison, strongly conscious of Durkheim and Bergson, called her book *Themis* because of her conviction that god-making and society-making were deeply related.) But though Murray realized that collective representations are the structural principles of literature, he was unable to dissociate poetics from the historical study of ritual and religion.

The progress of structuralism centers in good part on this dissociation. Aristotle had achieved it almost as a matter of course. But the *Poetics* remains a limited field theory: it deals with only one culture in its maturity. T. S. Eliot, however, says in his first essay that "the historical sense compels a man to write not merely with his own generation in his bones, but with a feeling that the whole of the literature of Europe from the time of Homer, and

---

(context of situation, social reality, sacred mime, *praxis* as distinguished from *lexis*) in a verbal system. A recent attempt to resolve the "referential-contextual" dichotomy is Murray Krieger's *A Window to Criticism* (Princeton, 1964).

within it the whole of the literature of his own country, has a simultaneous existence and composes a simultaneous order." These circumstances compel a wider, even universal, field of vision and lead us beyond special historical redemptions of the past and toward archetypal rather than archaic principles of structure. Northrop Frye, a new Aristotle, says in the opening chapter of the *Anatomy of Criticism* (1957) that his book will annotate that sentence of Eliot's.

Though Frye's theory is unified only for literature, it has larger implicit ambitions and is concerned with the "fables of identity" latent in all cultural or symbolic forms. The difference between his work and earlier myth-criticism can be illustrated by inventing a new subtitle for the *Anatomy*. In 1903 Durkheim and Mauss published one of their most famous essays, "De quelques formes primitives de classification: contribution à l'étude des representations collectives." This could be adapted to Frye's *Anatomy* by means of few changes: "De quelques formes générales de classification littéraire: contribution à l'étude des archétypes." Yet Frye's work is misunderstood if its classifications are taken too rigidly. Culture aims to do away with classes, as Matthew Arnold says; we are all spiritual Marxists. The *Anatomy* is a carnival rather than a scholastic Summa: its multiplication of terms and phases has a promiscuous aim, that of unification. The millennial hope which makes of Frye our most energetic critic is that the arts are one, that even science is a sister art with its mythical matrix and social purpose, and that literature reveals this unity best.

Close to half a century, however, separates Frye's work from Murray's. Before we enter more deeply into our *terminus ad quem* an intermediate figure should be mentioned. This is G. Wilson Knight, whose *Miracle and Myth* (1929) and *Wheel of Fire* (1930) were radical steps forward in Shakespeare interpretation. They anticipate Frye and enunciate clearly certain structuralist tenets. The strangest of these is a distinction between criticism and interpretation. *Criticism* is "a judgment of vision"; *interpretation,* "a reconstruction of vision." But Knight insists on a distinction he admits is impractical only to introduce a new concept of holism. The greater the artist, says Knight, the more purely interpretive our judgment; we must accept the artist's vision in its entirety. In practice this means that we should con-

sider Shakespeare's plays as a totality and a "Progress": a visionary whole, a complex of characterization (Knight calls it "personification" to diminish the idea of external reference), atmo-
spheric suggestion, and continuities of theme. "Each incident,"
writes Knight, "each turn of thought, each suggestive symbol . . .
radiates inwards from the play's circumference to the burning
central core without knowledge of which we shall miss their
relevance and necessity: they relate primarily, not directly to each
other, nor to the normal appearances of human life, but to this
central reality alone." Many years later, when *The Wheel of Fire*
was reissued (1949), Knight saw that his method had an analogy
in physics and that he had replaced "character" and all such
"rigid particles" by a field theory. His hero is not "an isolated
'character' rigidly conceived, but in direct and living relation to
his own dramatic environment . . . it is precisely such a 'relationship' that lies regularly behind Shakespeare's use of symbolism as
distinct from persons."

It is hard to think of a more important development for modern
criticism than this change from particle to field theory. True, there
had been an organicist postulate of this kind, at least since Coleridge; but now the naïve dichotomy of mechanical versus organic
is broken down, and the word *organicism* is seen to stand for the
fact that the whole is greater than its parts, and that the whole is
a system. A dream, a plant, a work of art, a machine, are all systems; the common factor being that they separate, ecologically,
what is outside from what is inside and so impose, within limits,
their form on whatever passes into them.

Knight, unfortunately, having modified the biological metaphor,
introduces one of his own. "A Shakespearian tragedy is set spatially as well as temporally in the mind. By this I mean that there are
throughout the play a set of correspondences which relate to each
other independently of the time-sequence which is the story." We
know what experience he is describing: the greater a work of art,
the greater our sense of something that conditions every element in
it. Is that something an *arche* or a *telos?* The concept of spatial
form, like structuralism itself, evades that question. By reducing
time to mere sequence of events and making it, as it were, a
dimension of space, Knight is able to cross from the single work

to the corpus of the artist and from that to all literature as "correspondent." His concept of spatial form is thus related to what Frye will call "total form"—the synoptic vision of all works of art as composing a simultaneous order.

But Frye carries Knight's position a step further. He argues that whatever literary structure is in itself, it must be spatial *to the critic*. Interpretation, to grasp the work as a complete and simultaneous pattern, must ignore its movement in time. The spatial is now a form that enables the understanding of art and makes criticism possible as a progressive science. This Kantian turn in the philosophy of literary structure is remarkable, but its explanation lies less in Kant than in technology. For the concept of total form is unimaginable while the artifact is still attached to sacred place or sacred time. As long as the work of art participates in its place of origin as a kind of *genius loci* it cannot enter that ideal museum—the "museum without walls"—foreseen by Eliot and Malraux. Technology must first deliver art from originality by allowing it universal duplication and distribution. Only then can art yield its aura and become a secular property. The spatial relation of critic to art thus reflects a change in the temporal relation of the work of art to its source in ritual or sacred history.

Frye's criticism can be seen as an attempt to value positively the influence of technology on culture, and especially on the appreciation of art. His subject is not the quality of art but the quality of our attitude toward it, which alone can be improved. He claims, as we saw, to be writing about the structure of literary recognition and not about the work of literature in itself. To be transitively understood, to be understood in such a way that it can play its role in society, the work must be placed among other works, and finally among that ideal order of existing monuments which Eliot mentioned. "You cannot value the artist alone; you must set him for contrast and comparison among the dead. I mean this as a principle of esthetic, not merely historical, criticism." Technology breaks the exclusiveness of canon or cult: Frye is anything but a formalist in this respect.

Still, these optimistic Magi of the North, Frye and McLuhan, surprise me. A generation after Eliot, and in the full swing of the technological revolution, they do not seem to be afflicted by the

13

darker insights of Ortega y Gasset, Erich Auerbach, Walter Benjamin, and Günter Anders.[7] Nor by the instinctive and general feeling that too much criticism, too much appreciation, is, if anything, dangerous to the unmediated element in art. As Keats knew, "The creative must create itself." The loss of originality, already mentioned, and which has prompted critics like Gaston Bachelard, Georges Poulet, and Maurice Blanchot to emphasize anew poetry's *valeur d'origine,* cannot be seen only as a gain for the consumer.

We approach here a critique of Frye. His archetypes are defined primarily as communicable symbols. They are neo-Kantian forms that serve to objectify our experience of art. Unlike the archetypes of Jung, which have too much content and may therefore overwhelm consciousness, those of Frye have as little content as wavelengths.[8] But media are not mediations: their structure is quite different. Whereas mediation is always precarious, media have the fixity of Kant's synthetic a priori. "The medium is the message," as one slogan puts it. The term *archetype,* however, like *principle,* is in etymological tension with the meaning Frye imposes. Both words suggest a *valeur d'origine,* and our distance from it. Whether we think of Plato or Jung, *archetype* infers a radical discontinuity between firsts and seconds, between original and copies. Mediation is, as it were, a "third" which allows us to return to an origin, to recover, if only at moments, some link between second and first. Technology's Midas touch, however, has turned all things into duplicates; and media, as distinguished from mediations, prevent the possibility of transcendence.

Now myth, ritual, and art are clearly mediations rather than media. They presuppose a discontinuity, a separation from the presence they seek. Theophany, epiphany, and parousia are formal concepts defining that presence. The actors become gods, the word becomes flesh, the figure is fulfilled. Ritual seeks this "fulness of Time" by a rediscovery of the origin. Ritual is The

7. Frye strongly criticizes McLuhan, however, or the belief that technology can of itself bring an increase in human freedom, in *The Modern Century* (Toronto, 1967), pp. 38 ff.

8. In theory only; as a practicing critic, Frye vacillates fruitfully between the positions distinguished in note 5 above. His archetypes are underdetermined as principles of structure and overdetermined as poetic symbols.

Way Back.[9] Organic form is already, therefore, a more difficult concept to apply to art, for the organic seems always in touch with the origin, instead of having to seek it by one fateful method. In nature there is no Single Way except what leads to death; and as long as the organism can modify itself, that is, change its ways, it avoids death. Seed becomes petal, petal blossom, blossom fruit, fruit seed. As to spatial form (field theory), that seems to deny the very idea of origin, to the point where nothing is "here and now" yet everything "there."[10] Spatial form emphasizes the co-presence of all creative human acts, as if they were *gesta* of a single culture. "The four *mythoi* that we are dealing with," says Frye "may . . . be seen as four aspects of a central unifying myth. *Agon* or a sequence of marvellous adventures is the basis or archetypal theme of romance, *pathos* or catastrophe, the archetypal theme of tragedy; *sparagmos,* or the sense that heroism and effective action are absent, the archetypal theme of irony and satire; and *anagnorisis,* or recognition of a newborn society, the archetypal theme of comedy" *(Anatomy of Criticism,* p. 192). Frye's "total form" is a strange and problematic equivalent to the Presence evoked by ritual and myth.

But we never, of course, encounter historically Frye's total or unifying myth. No more than we meet our own anatomy. It remains the potential vision of a potential Albion. Hence it is said that Frye is a gnostic, who prefers myth to the scandal of a historical revelation. But Frye actually neglects myth rather than history: he omits a vital structural aspect of mythic thought. A myth mediates a discontinuity—winter, death, paradise lost, *temps perdu*—and its very movement, the narrative, is a series of bridges over a gulf. Myth participates in what Van Gennep has called a rite of passage; and since literary rites have at least one character in common—that they are words or, more exactly,

9. Cf. Mircea Eliade, *Myth and Reality* (1956; English, 1963).
10. As, for example, in the copy of an original. The significance of spatial form has been variously explored by Joseph Frank, "Spatial Form in Modern Literature" (1945), Georges Poulet, *La Distance Intérieure* (1952), *Les Metamorphoses du Cercle* (1961), and *Explorations in Communication,* ed. E. Carpenter and M. McLuhan (Boston, 1960). But terms are deceptive: Lévi-Strauss, in the "Ouverture" to *Le Cru et Le Cuit* (1964), sees musical form as the proper analogue to the structure of myths.

15

timely words—we infer that the discontinuity is temporal (like winter) and logological (like Moses's stutter).

The difference between Frye's theory of literature and a true theory can be stated most simply as the difference between two particular myths: that of Ceres and Proserpina, and that of Orpheus and Eurydice. The former is Frye's favorite, but both contain identical elements. There is the quest, the descent into the underworld, the theme of death and revival. The persons in the one are gods, in the other humans; which indicates, for Frye, the difference between myth proper and Romance. This is the right distinction to make, for poetry, or the sympathetic powers of the human voice, enter the latter story far more strongly. The quest of Ceres, to be sure, is already associated with images or acts of the voice, with crying, lamenting, beseeching, and within or behind these the sense of sudden transition, the sense of being swallowed, of going from light, "the fair field of Enna," to darkness, or "gloomy Dis." All this is there, although it is not used by Frye. But the story of Orpheus, more tragic than myth and less associated with a natural cycle, centers on poetry itself, on the mediation of the human voice. Orpheus is much closer to the figure of a mediation that failed, of a presence not brought back, of "mortal power frozen at its source." The difference between the two myths is also that between Frye and Maurice Blanchot and represents one of the great divides separating Anglo-American and European criticism.

Yet Frye's theory is not so much faulty as incomplete. For he does, to some extent, respect the nexus of myth with discontinuity. By means of Blake's concept of imaginative states, which holds that we cannot rise directly from innocence to perfection, he introduces a dialectical principle and modulates from one (seasonal) mythos to another. This factor, however, is not truly dialectical: it does not reveal at what point the mediation failed. It is more like a natural law of the order "what goes up must come down." In fact, the seasonal cycle and the dying god archetype are used to affirm that poetry seeks the typical and recurring:

> The sequence of seasons, times of day, periods of life and death, have helped to provide for literature the combination of movement and order, of change and regularity, that is

needed in all the arts. Hence the importance in poetic symbolism of the mythical figure known as the dying god, whether Adonis or Proserpina or their innumerable allotropic forms, who represent the cycle of nature. [*Fables of Identity,* p. 58]

What we need is a theory of recurrence (repetition) that includes a theory of discontinuity. Rites center on a periodic discontinuity in the mediatory process, but what corresponds in art to this "seasonal" awareness? This is the question badly resolved by Frye's important work; and even Lévi-Strauss, who comes closest to an answer, does not succeed in defining the true *agon.*

Lévi-Strauss proposes that myths are logical techniques to resolve the basic antinomies in thought or social existence. The Oedipus myth, for example, expresses the inability of a culture to reconcile the belief in man's autochthony with the knowledge that he is born of man and woman. Barely stated, this may not seem convincing; and I must refer the sceptic to Lévi-Strauss's key essay on "The Structural Study of Myth." But even without that fuller exposition, we can see that myth, for Lévi-Strauss, is fundamentally conservative—that it tries to respect an older theory (in the Oedipus story a cosmological belief) in the face of a knowledge irreconcilable with it. It might therefore be better to call myth a hermeneutic rather than logical technique, but this is not the place to quarrel over terms.

One should point out, however, that to call myth a logical tool *(outil logique)* reflects more than the Gallic *faible* for reason; it shows that Lévi-Strauss is in the functionalist tradition. He holds that human thought is bound to run into perplexities serious enough to obstruct the progress of the mind or even of society. In this he is not different from Freud, Malinowsky, or Wittgenstein. Language, social structure, and mental life are systems that must be cleared of blockages, pseudo-problems, or scleroses. The function of myth is to allow man to keep on functioning, and the originality of Lévi-Strauss is to show that myths resolve their antinomies not by some special logic but by the universal and common logic we use for any problem. The antinomies may change, but the logical forms remain constant.

17

How do these logical forms deal with the antinomy they are to resolve? Here structuralism becomes technical and may resort to mathematical language. But I gather the following: the original problem is made to expand its context until it is brought into association with other problems which are moral and social rather than metaphysical—in short, for which a socially structured solution exists. The Oedipus myth establishes the following linkage, according to Lévi-Strauss: "The overrating of blood relations is to the underrating of blood relations as the attempt to escape autochthony is to the impossibility of succeeding in it." Social life validates the cosmological belief; and we notice again that nothing is actually dissolved or eliminated, but rather conserved by being put into this larger and specifically social context of relations.

I hope this somewhat slanted summary has suggested certain of my doubts. Do we need the dignification of an appeal to logic or mathematics? Does Lévi-Strauss say more than that certain existential paradoxes, or ontological discomforts, which might indeed perplex and even destroy the untutored mind—the paradox of love, for example, phrased memorably both by Augustine and Yeats, "For love has pitched his mansion in/The place of excrement"—must be integrated into life and society? In other words, that they need mediation? What myths do, then, is to provide that mediation, not so much by their apparent content, which is often a naïve and jumbled story, but by a latent meaning for which a degree of initiation or at least historical sympathy is required.

Now initiation is itself an integrative and socializing procedure, so that the difference between manifest and latent meaning, if not carried too far, would itself be functional. But let us leave this possibility aside. If we wish to respect surfaces as well as depths, and so to trust our immediate impression of myths, would we not have to say that what is most obvious in them is the instability of the story line, or of the mediator found for a particular problem? Is not the structure of myths, and especially of folklore, precisely that of the American movie cartoon, where, as soon as one impossible problem is resolved by the ingenuity of the hero, another supervenes? The labors of Loupy de Loup or of Jerry the Mouse are not unlike those of Hercules, or of the young boy in this Bororo legend which serves as one of Lévi-Strauss's "myths of reference" in *Le Cru et Le Cuit* (I abridge considerably):

Once in ancient times, when the women went to gather palms for the male initiation rites, a boy followed his mother and raped her. The boy's father finds out and decides to take revenge. He sends his son three times to the kingdom of the souls, asking him to bring back various musical instruments. The boy succeeds each time with the help of his grandmother and three animals. Furious, the father invites his son to go parrot catching. Since parrots build their nest high in mountain sides, the boy has to climb up a long pole to reach them. As soon as he is up, the father takes the pole away, and the boy, dangling in the air, holds on in the nick of time with a magic stick provided by his grandmother. By using a liana he gets to the top of the mountain, where he survives by killing lizards. He eats some of them, and tucks the others in his belt. But they rot and start asphyxiating him. Vultures come and eat the lizards, and wake the boy up when they start eating him too. Being sated, however, they save him by conveying him in their beaks down the mountain. [p. 43–45]

The instability of established social relations is most remarkable here. If the story reveals a structure it is clearly that of the *unreliable mediator:* those vultures, for instance, which by eating the lizards save the boy from asphyxiation, but then start eating him too. (I find this an especially appealing instance of black humor.) We easily perceive how tenuous the thread of the tale is, as tenuous as existence itself. It is almost as if the narrative line were the lifeline. Thus we find a direct structural equivalent to that "periodic discontinuity in the mediatory process" previously mentioned.

Lévi-Strauss does nothing to explain the simplest, most formal characteristic of myths or stories: their tendency to run on and their repetitiveness. Or rather, he simplifies this characteristic of repetition by saying its function is to make the structure of the myth apparent. But repetition is itself the structure we are interested in; and here we have Kierkegaard, Hegel, and Freud behind us. Lévi-Strauss does realize that some story extension of time is necessary, but only, according to him, to allow the social integration of a basically antisocial dilemma. By this he omits the link of repetition with miming, with strong religious or emotional participation, and also with a compulsive element which Freud empha-

19

sized in the phrase *repetition-compulsion.* Repetition, in other words, is a venture, an incarnation, an assault: anything but a *logical* operation. *Teleological* or even *soteriological* would be better terms.

And so we realize our aim: a theory of repetition that would include a theory of discontinuity. Story extension of time suggests that time is not the reliable mediator Kant thought it was. The mind cannot know or resolve itself except by a temporal run, but we are unsure how much time we have, or whether we will be allowed, morally, any number of runs. We are always in the situation of Sheherezade, whose life depends on telling a different story each night and so, in a very real sense, on "making time." Perhaps language is also more precarious than we have the power to acknowledge. Perhaps the very existence of literary as distinguished from nonliterary discourse shows that we "make language" as we make time. Yet language too is raised by structuralism to the dignity of a Kantian form or an a priori mediation. Here Ernst Cassirer and I. A. Richards have been equally influential. Their optimistic view of the symbolic or therapeutic powers of language makes it a medium and a method rather than a mediation to be renewed by the vulnerable genius of each single poet. "Genius," says Blake, "dies with its Possessor, and does not rise again until Another is born." Everything turns on the individual, on his saving power of address, though with it he calls into being something greater—a society, a world.

A theory of literature should be able to distinguish between literary and nonliterary discourse, but it should also tell us the difference between literature and other forms of symbolic action, such as ritual. The difference between ritual and literature, in particular, is defined neatly by the school of Frazer as one between source and derivation: *ritual* is prior, and *myth* is the middle term between the *dromenon* of ritual (the sacred mime, the thing acted in distinction to the thing said) and literature. But structuralism discounts the genetic or historical assumptions of Frazer. As Frye puts it: "The *Golden Bough* . . . reconstructs an achetypal ritual from which the structural and generic principles of drama may be *logically,* not chronologically, derived. To the critic, the archetypal ritual is hypothesis, not history."[11] This is methodologically sound, but it does not help us to state how art differs from myth or ritual.

What *can* help us? I think we must first accept something like Frazer's hypothesis, but explore it in a phenomenological rather than logical (à la Frye) way. When Georges Poulet determines the beginning position of a poet's consciousness, or when the analyst seeks to discover the primal scene expressed obliquely and repetitively in a writer's work, he respects the structure of art even if he cannot prove the historical, or more-than-imaginary, reality of this first event. Even the formalist, who has renounced depth analysis, cannot deny that art evokes the sense of something hidden which teases the mind like Keats's "Bride of Quietness." This hermeneutic character of art is quite apparent and always contains a hint of the muteness of the things to be interpreted. Thus the plot of *Hamlet* is set going by a spectacle, an apparition that demands to be deciphered (it is "a questionable shape"); while in the play itself we have Hamlet's mime to catch the conscience of the king. The mime is the *dromenon* of sacred drama in vestigial form, but is there a literary work without the quality of a charade? Poetry has often been defined as "a speaking picture."

Art, in short, discovers something that corresponds on the level of society or history to the movement from esoteric to exoteric and from sacred to secular. Perhaps we can differentiate art from ritual by determining how it structures this movement. It is of the utmost importance to overcome naïve antinomies of sacred and secular. They prevail not only in historiography but also in personal and even national psychoses. Anthropology has helped to overcome them by showing that the sacred is not a class of special things but rather a special class of things. Every kind of content can be found in this class of the sacred; what differentiates one society from another, or one historical stage from another, is the change in what is classified as sacred and what as profane. But art seems generically and ambiguously involved with sacred and profane. Its relation to myth and romance has persisted; it is always inauthentic vis-à-vis the purity of ritual and vis-à-vis a thor-

11. "The Language of Poetry," in *Explorations in Communication,* ed. Carpenter and McLuhan. Cf. Frye, *Anatomy of Criticism* (1957) pp. 108–10.

21

oughgoing realism. This generic impurity is the best clue to its nature.

A Kafka parable may help us to define more closely art's mixed essence:

> Leopards break into the temple and drink the sacrificial chalices dry; this occurs repeatedly, again and again: finally it can be reckoned on beforehand and becomes part of the ceremony.

Profanation enters the inner sanctum and becomes part of the holy. From a purist or ritual point of view there is contamination. The sense that the holy is contaminated is one of the views that emerges from Kafka's work as a whole. Not the death of God, but his impurity. Yet as soon as we read the story as a parable, which refers beyond the special case of ritual to life as such, a new meaning emerges. Does not every society, every relationship, every system have its necessary and permitted profanations? We think of the Greek satyr play, the Roman Saturnalia, and the "holy profanation" of the body in the daily institution of marriage. Is not art itself an institution of this kind?

To begin with words as words. They can be viewed as on the side of profanation. The ineffable is expressed; they are intrinsically a movement from esoteric to exoteric, or beyond solipsism. But there are solipsistic societies as well as solipsistic individuals. If words expose the private dream, they also expose public illusions—the solipsistic on the level of society is the sacred, and literature is a kind of loyal (though not always legal) opposition which opens the sacred to scrutiny, and so at once profanes and purifies it. But it is less a matter of destroying than of demystifying whatever is held to be sacred. Philosophies that consider secularization as a fall from some holy age and golden clime are infected by the very mentality which art criticizes from within. The secular is the sacred integrated, rather than degraded or displaced.

In some writers we feel the trespass of words directly. Henry James comes immediately to mind. Myth is not only the open form of ritual, the "leaf-fring'd legend" which "haunts about" an "unravish'd" event; myth is a necessary and precarious profanation of a "sacred secret." And so is literature—but now speech itself becomes vulnerable and open to violation. Poetry moves us toward a new sense of the profaned word. The history of literature, in its broadest aspect, appears to be a continual breach of levels of style (high style being profaned, low style elevated), or a history of metaphorical transference (sacred attributes being secularized, and vice versa).[12] Thus literature and myth are not mere accretions to a central mystery but involved in its very nature. They penetrate and become part of the structure of the sacred event, as in Kafka's parable. Great art is always flanked by its dark sisters, blasphemy and pornography. What Yeats says cannot be bettered, and I conclude with it. The soul must become "its own betrayer, its own deliverer, the mirror turn lamp." Without an exemplary trespass of this kind there would be no self-transcendence, no heroism, no myth, no literature— indeed, no regeneration.

12. This emerges not only from the synoptic work of Erich Auerbach, Northrop Frye, M. H. Abrams, André Malraux, and others, but also from the simple if important criterion of stylistics (popularized by the Russian formalists) that in literary as distinguished from normative discourse language is "deformed," "estranged," "rebarbarized." The poet subjects language to an "organized violence." Yet, as Mukarovsky pointed out, it is the essence of the aesthetic norm to be broken. Cf. the brilliant and neglected article of Walker Percy, "Metaphor as Mistake," *Sewanee Review* 66 (1958): 79–99.

Ghostlier Demarcations: The Sweet Science of Northrop Frye

The dark Religions are departed and sweet Science reigns.
—Blake

Commenting on Aristotle's *Poetics,* the first systematic criticism known to us, S. H. Butcher remarks that its author is preeminently "a Greek summing up Greek experience." Northrop Frye, the latest and most ambitious exponent of a systematic criticism, can hardly be described as a Canadian summing up Canadian experience, or even as a scholar summing up the experience of English literature. His situation is so different from Aristotle's that to express it it is tempting to use Copernicus's image of the "virile man standing in the sun . . . overlooking the planets." I do not intend this image to suggest a premature deification, but to describe a new vantage point with its promise of mastery and also its enormously expanded burden of sight. Certainly no literary thinker, systematic or not, has attained so global a point of view of literature. The nearest parallels to this achievement come from other, though related, disciplines: there is Mircea Eliade's work in comparative mythology, or André Malraux's in the history of art.

It is the question of point of view, or of the critic's situation, with which I shall be initially concerned. For although Frye has said that his system exists for the insights and not the other way around, the excitement, the liberation, the play, as well as the most serious claim he makes, is the possibility of system. Frye is an overreacher, a man with hubris, but it is a methodical hubris, a heuristic and applied attitude. There is, in other words, a more-than-intellectual aspect to system-making on such a scale. Literary criticism remains an expressive act, and, despite its claims to objectivity, its moral and intellectual ends mingle. If Aristotle is a Greek summing up the experience of his culture, we should be able

24

to discern the *polis* of Northrop Frye, and what visionary politics are his.

THE SITUATION OF THE CRITIC

Literature has not always been the property or interest of the many. Some, even today, think that the *paidea* of the New Criticism, the attempt to open literature to the direct understanding of students of any background, is undesirable or doomed to failure. It may not please those who know the great differences in pedagogical method between the New Critics and Northrop Frye to have me begin by suggesting that Frye is part of a single modern movement to democratize criticism and demystify the muse. I would go further and say that Frye is our most radical demystifier of criticism, even though his great achievement is the recovery of the demon or of the intrinsic role of romance in the human imagination. His importance to literary history proper is as a topographer of the romance imagination in its direct and displaced forms. But in his service to the ongoing need to have greater numbers of persons participate in the imaginative life, to open the covenant of education until the difference between persons is really "ghostly," only a matter of more intense or lesser participation, he continues the vision of those first struck in the nineteenth century with the possibility of universal education, and who felt with Victor Hugo that the multiplying of books was comparable to the multiplying of loaves of bread.

Demystification begins in Frye with the very concept of system. This concept should be distinguished, at first, from the particular system furthered. To systematize criticism is to universalize it, to put its intellectual or spiritual techniques into the hands of every intelligent person, even every child. To imagine children of the future performing little anatomies as easily as they now do basic operations in mathematics may not be everyone's utopia, but we should recall that Frye is ambitious only with respect to the possibility of system and not to his particular version of it. Yet it must be pointed out that he fuses, or confuses, two notions of universality. One is the scientific, and holds that the criticism of literature should be pursued as a coherent and systematic study, which, like mathematics, has elementary principles explainable to anyone.

The other is the evangelical, and holds that critics have stood like priests between literature and those desiring to participate in it, whereas even a child should be able to be instructed in the principles that make art nourishing. When Frye says "the only guarantee that a subject is theoretically coherent is its ability to have its elementary principles taught to children,"[1] it is hard to tell the scientific from the evangelical notion. Frye's scientism is therefore the opposite of exclusionary: he does not seek to overdignify criticism or scholarship but to place its basic principles and their creative development in the hands of every earnest reader. "What critics now have is a mystery-religion without a gospel . . . they are initiates who can communicate, or quarrel, only with one another."[2]

But who put the mystery Frye wants to purge into criticism? Nobody: Frye is indicating that unorganized innocence falls prey to the latest compulsions in taste—to casual, sentimental, or social value judgments. This is the more likely as the assumption of innocence, in literary scholarship, takes the form of an appeal to pragmatism, common sense, or impartiality. The unsystematic critic considers his lack of system proof that he cannot possibly be prejudiced. Frye, I think, would hesitate to go further and to accuse specific groups of surrounding the study of literature with a mystique. Yet the feature of his system that has caused most protest is precisely his relegation of certain kinds of value judgments to the history of taste and his resolute exclusion of them from criticism. If there is a mystique, it lies here—in the conviction challenged by him that literature is to be used as a training ground for the elite judgment.

Such a conviction is a carry-over from the time when classics were at the center of humanistic studies, and English did not exist as an academic field. The classics were studied not for themselves but as part of the proper education for the upper classes, composed of administrators, churchmen, and statesmen. When English, a mere baby among academic disciplines, won its freedom in the 1920s and 1930s (Tillyard's *The Muse Unchained* records

1. "The Developing Imagination," in *Learning in Language and Literature* (Cambridge, Mass., 1963), p. 33. Cf. Frye, *Anatomy of Criticism* (Princeton, 1957), p. 14.
2. Frye, *Anatomy,* p. 14.

vividly part of that emancipation), it engendered its own protective and self-dignifying mystique. It did this by assuming the mantle of classical studies and claiming for English literature the same function of training the judgment. It also insisted that this training was best provided by the immediacies of vernacular literature. We may admire the careful scrutiny, the chaste inquisition brought to bear on the vernacular status of words or on the consciousness organizing them, which now for the first time enters literary studies, and still acknowledge that the object of the new discipline was not a total or synoptic conception of literature but the training, through literature, of a specific and judicious sensibility. And it is hard not to feel the breath of a mystique in the following recommendation of the "English School," which shows how thoroughly Leavis, who wrote it, adapted and refined the classicist emphasis on the importance of judgment:

> The essential discipline of an English School is the literary-critical; it is a true discipline, only in an English School if anywhere will it be fostered, and it is irreplaceable. It trains, in a way no other discipline can, intelligence and sensibility together, cultivating a sensitiveness and precision of response and a delicate integrity of intelligence—intelligence that integrates as well as analyses and must have pertinacity and staying power as well as delicacy.[3]

Whether or not Frye's expulsion of rationalized taste from the history of criticism is viable, its purpose is to cleanse that discipline of a sporadically chauvinistic cult of culture. His "categorial criticism" is a direct challenge to the English mystique of English Studies. It bypasses personalistic judgment and the tutorial approach to literature. Instead of the tutor there is the system; instead of judgments reposing on a precarious blend of moral, verbal, literary sensibility, there is the extroversion of archetypes and the free yet controlled establishment of a criticism without walls. The act of appreciating literature has its private pleasures, but it becomes criticism by becoming extramural—by interpreta-

3. Quoted by Fred Inglis, "Professor Northrop Frye and the Study of Literature," *Centennial Review* 9 (1965): 325–26. On the importance of the "Vernacular Matrix" for modern criticism, see W. J. Ong, s.j., *The Barbarian Within* (New York, 1962), chap. 10.

tions that link the classics to English literature and all literature to a total form that reveals archetypal features. Frye's concern is with a point of view determined by culture as such, rather than by a particular culture, tradition, or line.

This raises the question of what Frye means by total form and obliges us to turn from his concept of system to the system itself. The intellectual problems here are very great, but ours are greater: for Frye is an eloquent man who somewhere has provided an answer to every question. What must therefore be judged is not his comprehensiveness, which is extraordinary, or his intentions, which are the best since Matthew Arnold, but how well he has dealt with problems every literary critic faces whatever his attitude toward systematic thought. These problems must center, at some point, on how the individual literary work is related to art's general function in consciousness or society. "No discussion of beauty," says Frye, "can confine itself to the formal relations of the isolated work of art; it must consider, too, the participation of the work of art in the vision of the goal of social effort, the idea of complete and classless civilization."[4]

If we were to apply the technique of extracting the myth to Frye himself, we would come on a pastoral motif: "The hungry sheep look up, and are not fed." His critical system moves in the same direction as the history of art it seeks to liberate—away from the closed culture, the closed society, the priest-interpreter, the critic's critic. Properly understood he appears as a knight in a continuing quest: that of removing the dragon from the hoard, or mystery from communion.

THE CONCEPT OF TOTAL FORM

In saying that Frye aims at a "criticism without walls," I was implicitly adapting a phrase used by André Malraux. He remarked that modern techniques of reproduction had created in the visual arts a "museum without walls," and made the world's master-pieces available to every viewer. But he also noted that this had changed profoundly our conception of the uniqueness of the arti-fact which is now universally distributed and no longer in a special relation to its place of origin. The more transportable the sacred

4. Frye, *Anatomy,* p. 348.

objects of a culture, the more abstract our notion of art tends to be. "You do not put gods in a museum," says Malraux, "the gods there become paintings." Modern photography converts all historical artifacts into free works of art. It robs them of their original context and reveals through synopsis and juxtaposition a more coherent or self-referring entity.

Frye, whose concern is chiefly with the verbal arts, where the revolution of which Malraux is talking began with Gutenberg, does not stress the technological factor. "The revolution," he writes, "is not simply in technology but in spiritual productive power."[5] Yet we have seen that his very concept of system combines a technological result with an evangelical purpose. If the Bible had not been unchained by Gutenberg and the Reformers, and if this liberation had not continued until the gods sat as books in our libraries, the kind of analysis Frye calls archetypal might not have come about.

For there is no mystery about archetype. The archetype is simply the typical at the highest power of literary generalization. The typical was valued in the eighteenth century for its universality within the context of polite society; and the archetypal emerges when the concept of a literary universe, made possible by technology, is substituted for that of polite society. And just as the world of the typical is society perfected, with its hieratic structure, its vertical line of authority; so the world of the archetypal is not some primitive communion but Arnold's and Malraux's "complete and classless civilization" with its intersubjective structure and its authority derived purely from a continuing vision transmitted by the arts.

Thus art contributes to a supreme fiction, an archetypal or total form, which is the forerunner of a new, demystified theory of participation. The Marxist concept of types, the Western historians' concept of topoi, the renewal of interest in biblical typology, the attempt to see art as an especially concrete sort of universal—as well as the varieties of myth criticism—show how deeply modern literary theory is implicated in transcending the view that art is a private or elitist enterprise.

Historically the new theory of participation was given its most radical statement by the Romantics. "Would to God that all the

5. Frye, *Anatomy*, p. 344.

29

Lord's people were prophets," writes Blake, quoting the reply of Moses to those who wished him to restrict the divine vision.[6] Art must be freed from mystery, from the very thing Mallarmé cultivated as "le mystère dans les lettres." It is to be within the reach of all and practically a biological inheritance: "The mystery in the greatness of *King Lear* or *Macbeth* comes not from concealment but from revelation, not from something unknown or unknowable in the work, but from something unlimited in it."[7]

The emphasis on demystification also helps with the curious flatness of archetypes as Frye conceives them. Archetypes are not hidden but almost too open—if we do not easily spot them it is because we expect the wrong kind of mystery. Frye does not practice depth criticism or depth psychology; in this he differs absolutely from Jung, and it is impossible to attach an occult or, simply, ontological virtue to the structures he derives from mythology. This flattening out of the mythic substance is like transforming a landscape into a map, but also like opening a closed book. Archetypal analysis brings art into the public domain and makes it what nature was to Sir Thomas Browne, a "manuscript expans'd unto the eyes of all."

When we recall the rejection of myths of depth in contemporary literature and phenomenology, and when we think of how Wallace Stevens tries to return to a fundamental insight of the Romantics obscured even in him by traces of Symbolist cultism, we easily perceive Frye's link to the modern movement which insists on demystification. The "virile man standing in the sun" begins to merge with Stevens's virile poet and central man who declares he has outlived the esoteric muses: "No longer do I believe that there is a mystic muse, sister of the Minotaur. This is another of the monsters I had for nurse, whom I have wasted. I am myself a part of what is real, and it is my own speech and the strength of it, this only, that I hear or ever shall."[8]

Yet archetypes, unmysterious as they are, cast a shadow. It has often been remarked that the particularity of the literary work may be obscured by too great or synoptic an angle of vision. Archetypal analysis can degenerate into an abstract thematics

6. Num. 11:29, quoted in Blake, Epigraph to *Milton*.

7. Frye, *Anatomy,* p. 88.

8. "The Figure of the Youth as Virile Poet," *The Necessary Angel* (1951).

where the living pressure of mediations is lost and all connections are skeletonized. These faults appear clearly in the little book on T. S. Eliot and the essay on Milton's "Lycidas," inexpensive world tours of myth. Yet what we are facing here is not merely the weaker side of a method but something inherent in any response to a dilemma posed by the very promise of technology. "What we have to defend today," Marshall McLuhan has said, "is not the values developed in any particular culture or by any one mode of communication. Modern technology presumes to attempt a total transformation of man and his environment. This calls in turn for an inspection and defense of all human values."[9] The need for a global perspective is evident.

Every greater critic has recognized this situation, which demands the rejection or else redemption of technology, but in any case a total rather than piecemeal approach. Yet few have accepted the challenge so optimistically as Northrop Frye. Ortega y Gasset writes of the dehumanization, and not humanization of modern art; and Walter Benjamin, in "The Work of Art in the Era of Its Technical Reproduction," sees more sharply than anyone the estranging influence of technology on culture. Technology, he asserts, will transform works of art into exhibition pieces and consumer goods, and so destroy what he calls their *aura*.[10] And Erich Auerbach, toward the end of *Mimesis,* a book almost the obverse in temperament to Frye's *Anatomy,* foresees the withering away of those fully individuated civilizations of which he has just written as if already their last historian. What, then, is the future of historical criticism? Can the aura of the individual work be saved? Or is Frye's totalizing approach, which looks more and more Olympian, the true alternative? The theory of literature, like literature itself, seems to have entered the crisis stage in its attempt to find the relation of the particular, the "dreadful sundry of this world," to any authentic concept of totality.

THE COURSE OF THE PARTICULAR

The possibilities of myth as a structural principle were brought to light by the practice of certain writers in the Symbolist era.

9. "Sight, Sound and the Fury," *The Commonweal* 60 (April 9, 1954): 11.
10. "Das Kunstwerk im Zeitalter seiner technischen Reproduzierbarkeit," *Schriften* (Frankfurt a.M., 1955), 1: 366–405.

Yeats and Joyce, T. S. Eliot said in a famous essay of 1923, substituted "the mythical method" for the "narrative method." Eliot
had resolved the problem of the "dreadful sundry" by similar
means. The new method, according to him, "is simply a way of
controlling, of ordering, of giving shape and significance to the
immense panorama of futility and anarchy which is contemporary
history."[11] It is clear that the substitution of mythical for narrative method, in literature or criticism, expresses the difficulty of
finding ideas of order within secular history.

Frye, however, does not emphazise the heuristic character of
the new method. Although his system is frankly speculative, it
rarely allows for counterpoint or opposition between the historical
and the mythical. Supremely eclectic, Frye melts what many
would consider as contraries into one system of alternative yet
concordant approaches. What counterpoint exists is for the richness of the melody: he does not make us feel the problematic
situation of either writer or critic, or any sign of that divided consciousness which the mythical method affirms by remaining an
artifice in Yeats and Joyce.[12]

To bring out the discords between Frye's mode of criticism and
a more historical one, let us consider a model of the act of interpretation furnished by biblical hermeneutics. When Donne, in
his Sermons, uses the expression "the intention of the Holy Ghost
in that place," the word *place* refers to one or more of three things:
topos, or figure of speech; context; locality. These relations of
word to *place* also situate secular literature in its particularity.
Thus the question of verbal or internal context can be equated

11. "Ulysses, Order, and Myth," first published in *The Dial*. Eliot's
practice may also be indebted to the rediscovery of the ritual origin of
literary forms by the Cambridge anthropologists. See his somewhat condescending remarks on Jane Harrison and others in "Euripides and Professor Murray" (1920).

12. Frye's strength lies in that grammar of imagery, or morphology of
myth, derived from Blake and Yeats, which has allowed literary criticism
to be—for the first time—truly systematic (synchronic) rather than historical (diachronic). He is better, in other words, at respecting the identity
of mythical and systemic (an identity glimpsed by Vico and elaborated by
French anthropologists from Durkheim to Lévi-Strauss) than the difference between mythical-systemic and historical. He is closest to Plato, for
whom, as he observes in the *Anatomy*, "the ultimate acts of apprehension
were either mathematical or mythical."

with that of the temporal medium of the literary work; the question of topoi or figures with that of the authenticity of myth or figures derived from myth; and the question of the relation of words to native place with the aim of conventional histories to understand the literary work *in situ* by recovering its lexical and social ambiance.

What does Frye have to say on these matters which are essential to any historically based criticism? His attitude toward the fact that literature unfolds in time rather than quasi-simultaneously in space is puzzling. It would be possible to apply his type of analysis to the visual arts as well as to the verbal, for he stands back from poem or play as from a picture. A full-fledged example of the pictorial stance is his book on the development of Shakespearean comedy *(A Natural Perspective),* where he identifies structural similarities by removing himself to a "middle distance." In fact, as is well known, Frye's concept of literary structure is consciously spatial. It depends on a disjunction between our immediate experience of literature, which is guided by the tempo of the work, and criticism, which lays out the completed pattern spatially. "When a critic," he writes, "deals with a work of literature, the most natural thing for him to do is to freeze it, to ignore its movement in time and look at it as a completed pattern of words with all its parts existing simultaneously."[13] In the *Anatomy,* this disjunction is presented as fundamental to the establishment of criticism as a progressive body of knowledge.

Unfortunately it is also an evasion of the whole problem of temporality. With the related question of the unity of the literary work, this problem has been the single most important topic of poetics. It is true that systematic thought on temporality, starting with Lessing and renewed by Heidegger, is mainly German. Yet Helen Gardner expresses the identical concern when she says that "the discovery of a work's center, the source of its life in all its parts, and response to its total movement—a word I prefer to 'structure,' for time is inseparable from our apprehension of works of literature—is to me the purpose of critical activity."[14]

13. "Myth, Fiction, and Displacement" (1961), in his *Fables of Identity: Studies in Poetic Mythology* (New York, 1963), p. 21.

14. *The Business of Criticism* (Oxford, 1959), pp. 23–24. One wonders why Frye has not made greater use of Mircea Eliade's argument that

One of the most formal differences of literature is omitted if we cannot encompass by reflection its moving power in time.

Frye's practice here is preferable to his theory. In his concern not to isolate the work of art, but to let it flow into a larger realm of discourse, he often perfects the example of G. Wilson Knight, who first applied a spatial analysis to Shakespeare in the *Wheel of Fire* (1930).[15] Frye on Beckett, Shakespeare, or Wallace Stevens can be compared with such critics in Europe and America as Bachelard, Poulet, Lucien Goldmann, René Girard, J. Hillis Miller, and *(sui generis)* Leslie Fiedler. Also in search of the total form, they insist that the boundary lines of the individual work are to be subordinated to larger patterns revealed by decomposing those outlines. But for them this form cannot finally be expressed in literary or mythical terms: it merges with an analysis of society, consciousness, and language. Although Frye posits the goal of society and art's drive toward it, he does not specify what has separated man from his vision or into what temporal errors the vision has fallen. The European-trained philosophical critic might therefore say that Frye looks at literature from the point of view of the Hegelian end-state. It would

---

literary time remains basically mythical, because literature submerges us in a "strange" time, and it is the character of myth to cure or at least purify temporality by a ritual "going back" to the origins (anamnesis). The spatializing habit of all structuralist analysis of the imagination has been ably defended by a French work devoted to "archetypology." See Gilbert Durand, *Les Structures Anthropologiques de l'Imaginaire,* 1st ed. (Paris, 1960).

15. "One must be prepared to see the whole play in space as well as in time. It is natural in analysis to pursue the steps of the tale in sequence, noticing the logic that connects them, regarding those essentials that Aristotle noted: the beginning, middle, and end. But by giving supreme attention to this temporal nature of drama we omit what, in Shakespeare, is at least of equivalent importance. A Shakespearian tragedy is set spatially as well as temporally in the mind. By this I mean that there are throughout the play a set of correspondences which relate to each other independently of the time-sequence which is the story. . . . Now if we are prepared to see the whole play laid out, so to speak, as an area, being simultaneously aware of these thickly-scattered correspondences in a single view of the whole, we possess the unique quality of the play in a new sense." From Knight's first chapter, "On the Principles of Shakespeare Interpretation."

seem to him as if Frye were replacing mystery with obscurity—unless he knew that Frye's analysis of error is identical with Blake's, and that his book on Blake, *Fearful Symmetry,* must be read in conjunction with the *Anatomy.*

The second topic of any historical inquiry—the authenticity of myth and of poetic language—is involved with religious doctrine. All disputes, for example, concerning the use of pagan or indeed any mythology in literature belong as much to the history of religion as to that of art. To resolve such disputes, scriptural and secular hermeneutics may differ in approach. The former depends almost totally on the principle of accommodation for its criterion of authenticity, but criticism is free to develop other criteria. Since Frye develops his own principle of accommodation, it may be useful to recall here the gist of the original doctrine.

It states that what is said or written may be a limiting form of what is meant, the limit being determined historically by the capacity of the hearers.[16] Interpretation, therefore, is essential not only to prevent wrong conclusions arising from the limiting form but also, in the presence of more capable hearers, to translate the intended thought into its true form. Criticism, however, as distinct from exegesis, may decide that the original form in its very concreteness or obscurity is more authentic than any supposed translation of it. Thus we often say that a metaphorical expression is not really translatable.

Frye's system rests on a tacit assumption of the authenticity of myth, but we are in some difficulty if we ask how this authenticity is revealed. By what process do we accept the Romantic element in Shakespeare's comedies? According to Frye it is authenticated by being placed in a context of totality. The individual myth or isolated play reveals its archetypal features by the mutual association of a great number of works of art. What Frye proposes is, in effect, a hermeneutic translation of literature into a clarified form or "reconstructed mythology." Yet the absence of an official or dogmatic theology must always leave the authen-

16. This does not imply that the speaker himself knows what is meant—he may be inspired, or the hermeneutic paradox which Dilthey emphasized may obtain—that we understand the author better than he understands himself. The speaker can be one of his hearers, sharing their limited historical situation.

ticity of that form in doubt. Keats, for example, appreciated romance and certainly understood the Romantic element in Shakespeare, yet he felt, like Wordsworth, that the modern vocation was to surpass it. Myth, whether used substantively or merely as a narrative device, remains a problem for the Wordsworthian tradition. The literary counterpoint of mythical and secular in Eliot and others is a method reflecting this problematic yet insistent presence of myth.

There is, however, a concept in Frye which corresponds to the principle of accommodation and contributes to literary history because it reveals the difficult relation of poetic to ordinary discourse. I refer to what Frye calls *displacement* and defines as the "adaptation of myth and metaphor to canons of morality or plausibility."[17] So defined it is a restatement of the doctrine of accommodation. Frye supposes that there is such a thing as a pure myth (archetype), the displacements of which can be traced through history. The displacements have a specific direction which his first essay in the *Anatomy,* on historical criticism, describes. There he classifies all fiction in terms of the status of the hero who moves from a mythic or supernatural to an ironic or all-too-human mode of being. Thus Shakespeare's use of the Proserpine story shows a twofold displacement: as well as being an oblique version of the myth of death and revival, it had to be accommodated in Shakespeare's time to a high mimetic level of plausibility; i.e., it could no longer be a mythic story about gods, or a romantic fable, but only a tale of heroism in which the order of nature is not violated.

The concept of displacement enables us to revalue what grosser histories of literature sees merely as secularization. For the movement from myth to realism does not imply the sad decline of hero into antihero or of an ancestor's great seal rings into Belinda's hairpin. We discover that secular man is not devoid of mythical attributes.[18] Except for Frye's hint of a cyclical return of realism to myth, the notion of displacement is empirically sound: it works,

17. *Anatomy,* glossary; cf. p. 136.

18. So Hawthorne's Hester Prynne, Melville's Billy Budd, Hardy's Tess, and Mrs. Woolf's Septimus seem to assume the role of *pharmakos* or scapegoat—an observation carried into modern American fiction by Ihab Hassan's study of the "Radical Innocent."

it is teachable, and above all it reveals the permanence of romance. One can no more remove the romantic element from art than natural instincts from man. It is eternal, as Freud discovered the instincts to be eternal and therefore gave them the name of gods, Eros and Thanatos.

I suspect, however, that Frye has shown not that myth is displaced but that it is historical. It is never found in that unaccommodated state he posits when he mentions "the pure myth of death and revival" or when he claims that literature is a reconstructed mythology. One can make such a claim only by reducing myths to archetypes in the strictly Platonic sense of simples rather than complexes. But anyone who has read the *Anatomy* will agree that there are no simples in it. Or what simples there are, are hooked simples in the sense in which Lowes's *Road to Xanadu* explained Coleridge's fantastically assimilative mind by memories that are "hooked atoms." We do not find myth pure of religion or literature; it comes to us institutionalized from the beginning, and, though it may also be a body of structural principles, there is no point in underplaying the war in the members of that body.

For, historically, some structural principles seem to exclude others: the realistic writer, as Frye notes, "finds that the requirements of literary form and plausible content always fight against each other. Just as the poetic metaphor is always a logical absurdity, so every inherited convention of plot in literature is more or less mad."[19] What is true of the realist is true of any writer, as Frye's own theory of displacement has shown: reality is never more than the plausible artifice. But in that case the notion of displacement becomes unnecessary except to indicate the direction of human credibility—credibility defining that realm in which contraries are no longer felt.

To Frye's total myth we must therefore add a historical account of the war that myth has waged with myth. Just as the redactors of the Book of Genesis had to reconcile several divergent formulas of the "myth" of creation, so it is in non-oral tradition: a writer does not confront a pure pattern, archetype, or convention, but a corpus of tales or principles that are far from harmonized. The pressure bringing unity out of diversity may indeed come from a

19. "Myth, Fiction, and Displacement," *Fables of Identity,* p. 36.

latent archetype in the competing stories; but this raises the question of artistic unity and its necessary relation to a dialectical principle, such as the reconciliation of opposites or the harmonizing of variant traditions.

Temporality and authenticity are aspects, finally, of the largest topic of historical criticism: the relation of words to place of utterance. The metaphor of situation, used several times in this essay, suggests that there is a determinable ground of presuppositions on which a writer stands consciously or unconsciously. Even the divine word, according to Angelus Silesius, could not exist without place—the world which it creates:

> Der Ort und's Wort ist eins, und wäre nicht der Ort,
> Bei ewiger Ewigkeit; es wäre nicht das Wort.
> [Word and place are one, and if place did not exist
> By all that is eternal, the word could not exist.]

The sense that art is addressed, that it is always in dialogue, is what historical criticism furthers.

Although Frye increases significantly our knowledge of the structural presuppositions of the literary work, he neglects the one presupposition which is most affected by place of origin: the verbal. He seems relatively unconcerned with the exact dialogue or status of words in the individual consciousness and the particular society. Such apt remarks as, for example, that Emily Dickinson's poetry was a form of personal correspondence ("This is my letter to the World") remain undeveloped or linked to theses on the general nature of poetry that diminish her peculiar paradox. Instead of examining the verbal, Frye immediately subsumes it in what is called the "verbal universe." But this concept prevents a definitive description of the very element after which it is named.

For the concept of a verbal universe does not agree with what we know of the place of words in society. The opposition of science to art has always centered on the relation of words to things, which is another way of stating that words compete with conventions claiming to be better than verbal. Every writer in society is therefore concerned with the alternatives to the word. There has been fruitful conflict even among the arts themselves on the question of alternatives (musical, pictorial, hieroglyphic) to the verbal. This *paragone* may simply express the fact that all art aspires to the condition of totality; it remains, even so, a force in the writer's consciousness. Is there room in Frye's system— which has many chambers, and not all opened—for that radical doubt, that innermost criticism which art brings to bear on itself? Or does his system circumvent the problematic character of verbal fictions?

Since the verbal, in Frye, is a larger category than the literary or the mythical, he may have intended to say that literature itself is always in dire need of being humanized. It becomes an institution easily infected by *ratio* and must be led back to its source in *oratio*. This surely is what the great work of fiction (or criticism) achieves: it recalls the origin of civilization in dialogic acts of naming, cursing, blessing, consoling, laughing, lamenting, and beseeching. These speak to us more openly than myth or archetype because they are the firstborn children of the human voice. Myth and metaphor are endued with the acts, the gesta, of speech; and if there is a mediator for our experience of literature, it is something as simply with us as the human body, namely the human voice. It is here that one possibility of progress lies: in honoring the problematic relation of words to a reality they mediate rather than imitate. To envision "ghostlier demarcations," a poet must utter keener sounds.

Thus Frye's criticism and a historical approach differ more than we are led to believe. Yet the reservations I have expressed should not be taken as a plea for conventional literary history, for that either does not face the question of the mission of art or is content to show that art, like any cult or closed society, has a self-authenticating range of allusions to be decoded only by the priest of the cult: the historical expert.

CRITICISM AND THE ORAL TRADITION

In conclusion, I recall ruefully Aristotle's remark that unity of plot does not consist in the unity of the hero. The plot was criticism; the hero, Frye—and in case my reflections have been too picaresque, I would like to end with a firm and even didactic estimate of Frye's importance to contemporary criticism. The more we read in him the more we understand how essential the romance tradition is, both in itself and in its modern afterlife.

Poetry is inconceivable without it; even Shakespearean drama and the vast majority of novels conform to a romance poetics, or are significantly clarified by it. Frye's permanent achievement is as a theorist whose recognitions favor romance rather than tragedy; had he no more than rescued for us the spiritual form of William Blake and then the spiritual form of romance, it would have been sufficient.

Frye will not be grateful to me for considering him as the fulfillment of Bishop Hurd. And indeed he is much more, as I hope to have shown; yet his claim to provide the basis for a universal criticism remains less convincing than his anatomy of romance. His discoveries reflect on unity of design rather than unity of plot, and on the unity of art rather than the unity of the work of art. Even his style, a constant pleasure, is a romance multiplication of recognitions; its symmetry, an allegorical layering of the levels of recognition.

But this revival of a romance poetics is of more than professional literary interest. It is romance which mediated the themes and structures of the oral tradition, so that the revival of the one is linked to an interest in the other. Frye reverses the preference of Aristotle, who attempted to modify the predominance of oral tradition by esteeming unity of action more than the variegated energies of epic. The *Anatomy of Criticism* re-- turns to the values implicit in the multiple design of epic and romance. The archetype as a structural principle resembles nothing so much as the *formula* of oral poetry, while Frye's system is in quest of a community as universal as that which oral poetry may have reached.

There is of course no question of a return to oral tradition. But there is some hope that its renewed appreciation will change our narrow concepts of originality in art and permit us, in reading a book, to touch the central man and through him the life of generations. There is some hope that reading can become once more an encounter of imagination with imagination, as in Blake. But if Frye's purpose is to contribute to this encounter and to recover for literature its widest audience, his emphasis on system remains a stumbling block. Systems are the inkhorn children of bookcraft and erudition: they arise whenever humanists warm themselves on the ashes of myth. Despite Frye's return to a criticism nourished by the values of oral tradition, he has not escaped the ethos of the printed word. That "virile man standing in the sun" belongs to the Gutenberg Galaxy and is scanning the Milky Way of Romance as if it were an alienated part of his —and our—imagination. I cannot wish he were standing anywhere else or that he should descend to that "lower flight" which Raphael in *Paradise Lost* urged on Adam.

Beyond Formalism

Some years ago F. W. Bateson attacked what he called "Yale formalism." His main targets seem to have been Cleanth Brooks, René Wellek, and W. K. Wimsatt, and he has recently added Yale's "pseudo-gothic Harkness Tower" to this distinguished list. Bateson defined *formalism* as a tendency to isolate the aesthetic fact from its human content, but I will here define it simply as a method: that of revealing the human content of art by a study of its formal properties. This definition does not say that form and content are separable; nor does it imply that the human and the formal could not be caught and exposited as one thing by a great interpreter. It does suggest that the literary scholar establishes a priority which has procedural significance and which engages him mediately and dialectically with the formal properties of the work of art. I do not know whether the mind can ever free itself genuinely of these procedural restraints—whether it can get beyond formalism without going through the study of forms. I am sure, though, that the faults of those whom Bateson calls formalists are due not to their formalism as such but rather to their not being formalistic enough; and that, conversely, those who have tried to ignore or transcend formalism tend often to arrive at results more abstract and categorical than what they object to. My argument on these points will develop in a twofold way: I want first to take up an interpretation by Mr. Brooks, and a comparable one by Mr. Bateson, to suggest that their faults are alike (that neither critic is enough of a formalist); and I will then consider an essay by an avowed antiformalist, Georges Poulet, to suggest that he is more formalistic than he thinks, and that where he is less so his work may fail to situate the writer. My conclusion is a sceptical one, or else critical in the Kantian sense: to go beyond formalism is as yet too hard for us and may even be, unless we are Hegelians believing in absolute spirit, against the nature of understanding.

In "Irony as a Principle of Structure" (1949), Mr. Brooks interprets two of Wordsworth's lyrics on Lucy: "She dwelt among the untrodden ways" and "A slumber did my spirit seal." The essay is well known, and I can limit myself to recalling what it says about Wordsworth. Mr. Brooks is anxious to show that irony is a general aesthetic structure, that it is found variously in the poetry of every school or period. Wordsworth, as in the Lucy poems, is a challenge to his thesis: common feeling as well as common verbal usage prevent us from thinking of such poetry as ironic. Yet Mr. Brooks's armed vision, examining poems as clear as water, reveals to us new animalcules of structure. The following comment on the second stanza of "She dwelt among the untrodden ways" is representative of his argument for the presence in the Lucy poems of something comparable to witty contrast:

> The violet and the star . . . balance each other and between themselves define the situation: Lucy was from the viewpoint of the great world, unnoticed, shy, modest, and half hidden from the eye, but from the standpoint of her lover, she is the single star, completely dominating that world. . . . The implicit contrast is that so often developed ironically by John Donne in his poems where the lovers, who amount to nothing in the eyes of the world, become, in their own eyes, each the other's world—as in "The Good Morrow" . . . or as in "The Canonization," where the lovers drive into the mirrors of each other's eyes the "towns, countries, courts"—which make up the great world; and thus find that world in themselves. It is easy to imagine how Donne would have exploited the contrast between the violet and the star, accentuating it, developing the irony, showing how the violet was really like its antithesis, the star, etc.

To this let me add a quotation from Mr. Bateson's analysis of what he calls the dreamlike or unreal quality of the same poem:

> Wordsworth's method here is to combine positive and negative ideas so that they cancel each other out. . . . A simple example of the method is the paradox propounded by the last two words of the poem's first lines. How can *ways* be *untrodden?* . . . There are two similar verbal contradictions in lines 3–4 and 9–10. . . . If it is possible to use language so

43

loosely that *untrodden* need not mean 'not trodden,' that *love* cannot connote *praise,* and that *unknown* obtains a positive sense ('known to a few'), *and yet be completely intelligible,* the neighbouring oppositions and collocations of grammar and logic also tend to become discredited. Both the private and the public worlds retreat into a common unreality for the reader, who emerges with the impression that the boundaries between them are less absolute and perhaps less important than the surface meaning of these three sentences had suggested.

The same structure of contradictions is said to appear in the antithetic yet merging images of violet and star.[1]

The two interpretations have a problem in common. Both puzzle over a style that is felt to be, in some sense, no style. Bateson recalls Matthew Arnold's comment that nature itself seemed to have written Wordsworth's poems for him. Yet Bateson interprets this as involving an attack on language as such: "In order to get at meaning behind language he has had to discredit and break down the ordinary apparatus of language." Hence those subversive qualifications. Yet to Wordsworth himself it surely seemed as if he were returning to, not breaking down, ordinary language: poetic diction is discarded for a natural diction. Unless "She dwelt among the untrodden ways" is a special case in Wordsworth's canon, Mr. Bateson's view is nonhistorical in that his understanding of the poet does not harmonize easily with the poet's understanding of himself.

Mr. Brooks's view is also nonhistorical in that no effort is made to relate the new and subdued style to the more overt style it replaced. Mr. Brooks suggests that there are at least two poetic modes centering on the art of contrast, and that Wordsworth's art differs from that of Donne or Marvell in favoring "simple juxta-

1. *Wordsworth: A Re-Interpretation,* 2nd ed. (London, 1956), pp. 31–33. As a curiosity I might add that the first person to draw attention to contrast implicit in the violet-star image was Mary Shelley in *The Last Man* (1826). "[Wordsworth's] lines," her narrator says, "always appeared to me rather a contrast than a similitude." He goes on to compare two women: Perdita, "a violet . . . cowering from observation," and Idris, "the star set in single splendor ready to enlighten and delight the subject world."

position with no underscoring of the ironical contrasts." But he does not connect these modes, or read one of them out of court by means of an Act of Uniformity. Thus we are left with two essentially unhistorical descriptions of Wordsworth's style. Mr. Bateson's is perhaps less formalistic and more historical, in going directly from a formal feature to a generalization about the engagement of the poet in his society and in the language moulded by it. But we cannot check whether it goes genuinely from the one to the other. The only kind of ideal or objective interpretation is that in which we can cross-check our terms (rather than particular exegeses or conclusions) by relating them to the poet's own or to those prevalent in the poet's milieu. Interpretation is bringing the poem forward into the present, which is acknowledging its historicity, which is grounding our terms in history. To do this we must go beyond both Bateson and Brooks and describe as historically as possible the difference between the Wordsworthian "no style" and the stylish style it challenged.

Wordsworth's subtler mode serves to free the lyric from the tyranny of point. To recover what the pointed style implied is to review a considerable segment of literary history. The pointed style as it developed in seventeenth-century England is witty and antithetical: everything in it is sharp, nervy, à pic, and overtly like a hedgehog. Metaphysical poetry, on which Brooks's poetics are ultimately based, although he has extended its range with the help of Coleridgean theses, is a particular development of the pointed style: indeed, its freest and richest efflorescence, even in prosody where point and roughness unusually combine. Neoclassicism pruned the hedgehog and smoothened the prosody. But both metaphysical and neoclassical style are essentially epigrammatic, and each mediates between two recognized, divergent traditions of the epigram. Scaliger had classified these as *mel* and *fel;* and tradition varied these terms as *sweet* and *sour, sugar* and *salt; naïve* and *pointed.*[2] As Robert Haydn wrote in his *Quodlibets* (1628):

2. See J. C. Scaliger, *Poetices Libri Septem* (Lyons, 1561), p. 171, Appendix pro Epigramnate. Scaliger associates the "honey" type of epigram with Catullus and lists no less than four anti-types characterized by the terms "gall," "vinegar," "salt," and one that is outlawed, "in qua foeditas est." He seems to distinguish further between a continuously

> Short epigrams relish both sweet and sour,
> Like fritters of sour apples and sweet flour.

This may also, of course, reflect the Horatian *utile dulci*. Yet the condiments were not always so deliciously mixed. Because the sonnet had become identified with petrarquising poetry, or the sweet and honeyed mode, epigram was often contrasted with sonnet, as specialized in gall and the sour. Sir John Harrington, in his *Elegant and Witty Epigrams* (1618), sees it this way:

> Once by mishap two poets fell a-squaring,
> The sonnet and our epigram comparing,
> And Faustus, having long demurred upon it,
> Yet at the last gave sentence for the sonnet.
> Now for such censure this his chief defence is,
> Their sugared taste best likes his lick'rous senses.
> > Well, though I grant sugar may please the taste,
> > Yet let my verse have salt to make it last.

Those final lines, of course, are supposedly pointed and salty, like the concluding couplets in Shakespeare's sonnets—sonnets which, though essentially "sugared,"[3] attempted to marinate the style of love. By a natural development, since epigram and sonnet were not all that distinct, the pointed style often became the honeyed style raised to a further power, to preciousness. A new opposition is consequently found, not between sugared and salty but between pointed (precious, overwritten) and plain. Samuel

---

pointed epigram ("consertam, densam, multiplicem") and a finer, more naturally developed kind ("species quaedam nobilis ac generosa . . . aequabilitate plena . . . ut sit venustas cum gravitate & acumen cum lenitate"). For echoes of Scaliger or further evidence of the prevalence of these categories, see Ben Jonson, *Epigrams* (1616), 2, 49; also John Peter, *Complaint and Satire in Early English Literature* (Oxford, 1956), p. 297; and the valuable introductions in James Hutton, *The Greek Anthology in Italy* (Ithaca, 1935) and *The Greek Anthology in France and in the Latin Writers of the Netherlands* (Ithaca, 1946).

3. "The sweete wittie soule of Ovid lives in mellifluous and hony-tongued Shakespeare, witnes his *Venus* and *Adonis,* his *Lucrece,* his sugred Sonnets among his private friends, &c." Francis Meres, *Elizabethan Critical Essays,* ed. and reprinted by G. G. Smith, 2 (Oxford, 1904), 317.

Rowland gives us a bumbling sketch of that opposition at the turn of the century, when he describes an English *précieux ridicule* ordering his servant to fetch him his cloak:

> He utters speech exceeding quaint and coy:
> Diminutive, and my defective slave,
> Reach my corps couverture immediately.
> My pleasure's pleasure is the same to have,
> T'ensconce my person from frigidity.
> His man believes all's Welsh his master spoke,
> Till he rails English, Rogue, go fetch my cloak![4]

Wordsworth redeems the mother tongue from such precious and foreign artifice—but without railing. The Lucy poems, Lucy herself, are directed against something non-English: Lucy is no German-Gothic spook or French coquette. The style of the poems is a new and gentle plain style. Following Ben Jonson's example, English poetry had tried to marry plain style to the sinew and maleness of point. The poems of Herbert, and especially those of Marvell, are an exceptionally successful blend of the naïve and the pointed epigram.[5] Ben himself had chosen plainness as most appropriate for the epitaph, where things were to be expressed at once pithily and simply. Yet precisely the epitaph succumbed most often to the tyranny of point. Eighteenth-century elegiac verse is at best smooth antithesis and elegant turn; at worst, striving for the simplicity of pathos, as in the verses on the Lady who passed away at Bath ("She bowed to the wave, and died"), the expectation of point leads to splendid instances of the art of sinking. Lyttleton's epitaph on his wife illustrates the usual and perverse smoothness of eighteenth century elegiac lyricism. Here is Lyttleton's Lucy:

> Made to engage all hearts, and charm all eyes,
> Though meek, magnanimous; though witty, wise;

---

4. *Letting of Humor's Blood* (1600). See the highly instructive section on epigrams in J. W. Hebel and H. H. Hudson, *Poetry of the English Renaissance 1509–1660*.

5. I have tried to broach the question of Marvell's epigrammatic style in "Marvell, St. Paul, and the Body of Hope," pp. 163–64.

> Polite, as all her life in Courts had been;
> Yet good, as she the world had never seen . . . [6]

And here is Wordsworth's:

> A Maid whom there were none to praise
>   And very few to love
> Fair as a star, when only one
>   Is shining in the sky
> She lived unknown, and few could know
>   When Lucy ceased to be. . . .

Is this not a tender parody of Lyttleton's pointed inanities? Instead of a *catalogue raisonné* of mutually qualifying and even alliterative antitheses, Wordsworth's statements are almost tautological, or with a second clause so simple as not to qualify the first in any calculating (plus or minus) fashion. Lucy is in her grave, subtract one; but the difference, as Wordsworth says, is incalculable. His verbal style purifies the mannered lyric and particularly the elegiac epigram.

In the light of this abbreviated history of lyric style, what Brooks calls irony or paradox is not an independent structural principle but is mediated by literary traditions developing in contradistinction to each other. The sharper epigram, often satirical but not inevitably so, prided itself on a continuous fireworks of pointed sentiments and phrases, while the honeyed epigram had to justify itself by parallel yet finer devices. These devices, when they are truly fine and not merely dainty, are hard to describe because they grow naturally out of language or thought. To define them by terms drawn from the rhetoric of the copious style is futile, since we have to do with relatively brief and intensely personal verses—with lyric poetry. The one historical procedure open to us is to see how the modern lyric liberates itself from the tyranny of the witty style. The quarrel of the epigrammatists is especially intense at the beginning of the seventeenth century,

6. See also Wordsworth's *Essay on Epitaphs,* where this poem is quoted. For Dr. Johnson, on the road to Romantic sensibility, elegy and epigram came to stand in opposition. His *Dictionary,* 1st ed. (1755) defines *elegy,* inter alia, as "a short poem without points or affected elegancies," where *point* is defined as "a sting of an epigram; a sentence terminated with some remarkable turn of words or thought."

when the vernacular art-lyric is freeing itself from its subordination to music, emerging as an independent genre, and so finding its own resources, both of the mellifluous and the pointed kind. The initial dominance of that pointed style we are accustomed to call metaphysical is probably due to this war of independence, since point, combined with roughness of verification, was at farthest remove from the musicality of music. Both Sidney's and Shakespeare's sonnet series participated in this battle of sugar and salt. The battle did not cease with the independence of the lyric: the two modalities remained, now mixing, now antagonistic. We begin to recover in this way the historical terms that validate Brooks's description of Wordsworth's style as "juxtaposition without an underscoring of the ironical contrasts," and Bateson's more specialized observation on the subversive antitheses in "She dwelt among the untrodden ways."

Our conclusion was reached, however, by a formalistic exercise in literary history. While existential issues are not excluded, they remain closely associated with literary technique. Whatever ideas a composer may have must be translated by a set of equivalences into musical phrase: so it is here with human concerns that express themselves as modifications of style. I would not be so naïve as to equate formalism with an understanding of the history of style, but I do not see whatever else may be added, that it can do without this understanding. And only now, I feel, are we in position to ask the kind of question that might indeed lead beyond a primary concern with style or form or even poetry. The history of style itself seems to urge us beyond formalism by asking, What is the point of *point?* Conversely, what is achieved by Wordsworth's creation of so pointless, so apparently simple a style?

The question may serve to clarify the modern and recurrent aspiration toward a natural style. It can be charged that neoclassical poetry, or lyricism Old Style, was a didactic and digital poetry—calculating, pointing, computing too much by fingers and feet. It knew its weakness, certainly; and much of the theory of the time cautions against false wit and excessive *pointe*. (Marjorie Nicholson has written about "The Breaking of the Circle"; it is also useful to consider "The Breaking of the Point.") Perhaps Wordsworth comes to reveal rather than teach, and so to free poetry of that palpable design which Keats still charged him with. All truth, said Coleridge, is a species of revelation.

Revelation of what? The question cannot be answered without a certain kind of pointing, as if truth were here or there, as if life could be localized, as if revelation were a property. Yet Wordsworth's concepts of nature, of natural education and of poetry, are all opposed to this reduction. Who knows, Wordsworth asks in *The Prelude,*

> the individual hour in which
> His habits were first sown, even as a seed?
> Who that shall point as with a wand and say
> 'This portion of the river of my mind
> Came from yon fountain?'

The error in such pointing is not only intellectual, due to that "false secondary power . . . by which we multiply distinctions," but it is also spiritual. Pointing is to encapsulate something: strength, mind, life. It is to overobjectify, to overformalize. It implies that there is a fixed locus of revelation or a reified idolatrous content.

Yet pointing in this larger sense cannot be avoided: it seems inextricably tied to the referential nature of signs or the intentional character of thought. All Wordsworth can do is to emancipate the direction of the reference. The Lucy poems, taken as a sequence, remove the mimetic dependence of imagination on reality, or on any fixed order of 'this then that.' We cannot tell whether the poet is reacting to an imaginary thought or to an actual death, or which of the two came first. Lucy's death is reflective rather than reflected; it is, in fact, so strongly linked to the awakening consciousness as to be coterminous with the latter.[7] Lucy is a fiction integral to the mind: if she did not exist, she would have to be invented. Her mode of being, therefore, cannot be reduced to the imagined or the real by a temporal principle of anteriority or an ontological one of priority. Between the imagined and the real there is, in Merleau-Ponty's words, a "modulation of coexistence." Reflection becomes revelation and alters so

7. To interpret this link as expressive of the primacy of consciousness is to reintroduce the (now causal) notion of "this then that" and with it the magical view that Wordsworth's thought is symbolically killing Lucy off. See Bateson's thesis in *Wordsworth: A Re-interpretation* (1954).

radically the relation of consciousness to itself that Wordsworth sometimes denies primacy to his point of departure. Thought "hath no beginning." This is something Georges Poulet, to whom we now turn, and who loves beginnings, should interpret.

If it is hard to be a thorough formalist, it is equally hard to be a genuine antiformalist. Georges Poulet's work may help to illustrate this. What I say is critical of him, but I take it for granted that his work is sufficiently esteemed to withstand my barbs.

Poulet has not written on Wordsworth, though a long essay on Romanticism refers to him as well as to Coleridge. I prefer to choose for analysis his essay on Henry James in *Les Métamorphoses du Cercle* (1961). Poulet's method is to place himself in a writer's consciousness. He can do this by ignoring all formal distinctions, as between part and whole or preface, novel, journalistic comment, *obiter dicta.* He may be sacrificing lesser forms to greater, but this would have to be proved, not assumed. Chronological distinctions are also ignored: the method, in truth, approaches that of the synoptic reading of the gospels. In the case of the gospels there is of course a central event, a common mythos responsible for the clustering of the original stories and which outweighs their divergencies. It is not surprising that something similar to this center is assumed by Poulet as common to the biblia of the individual writers. This center is the artist's *cogito,* a continuously generated relation linking thought to the world, the *I think* to the *I am.* This is the crux relation, as it were. It precedes or constitutes all other relations of time, space, imagery, action.

Henry James's *cogito* is defined in the following terms: "To become conscious of oneself and the world is to be conscious of a double expanse whose borders are impossible to reach and whose parts cannot be separated out. Everything is connected, continuous and growing, everything stretches out as an illimitably growing web. We search in vain to discover something that might be isolated." The problematics of the Jamesian consciousness derive from this situation in which form is impossible except as a self-constituted and always illusory act. In James the formalization of consciousness is the very center of the literary activity, and there are no forms to be transcended except those imposed by the individual consciousness on itself.

Poulet aims at nothing less than the rewriting of literary history as a history of human consciousness. (He acknowledges as masters Marcel Raymond, Paul Hazard, the Abbé Bremond, and Gaston Bachelard, among others.) But are there not as many consciousnesses or cogitos as there are individuals? Poulet admits the difficulty and proposes a solution. The only way to emerge from this infinity of individuals and to gain something that can be called history is to postulate a period consciousness in which contemporaries participate.[8] The problem faced is similar to that of Dilthey, who also wished to respect the uniqueness of the individual and was obliged to postulate a typology of world views which subsumed, as a genus does its species, types of great men. In the absence of an explicit comment by Poulet it is difficult to decide whether his period consciousness is a heuristic device, or whether it is grounded in a Hegelian view of the development of the human spirit.

Poulet's predominantly thematic method helps him to periodize the cogito of each writer. The themes chosen by him are well known: space, time, center-and-circle. It is less obvious, perhaps, that these themes play the same role in the periodization of consciousness as Lovejoy's unit ideas in the history of ideas. Lovejoy sees the development of the history of ideas as the continuous attempt to reconcile an original paradox or antinomy in the idea of God. Time and space yield similar paradoxes for Poulet, who traces the reconciling strategies of individual writers. His work illustrates and enriches rather than revises the accepted historical outlines; and his history remains a history of ideas with expanded materials and a finer method. I do not mean to suggest that a critic must rewrite literary history, but it is a curious antiformalism which strains at the gnat of genre distinctions and is obliged to swallow the camel of periodization. I am not sure that Poulet gives us more than a subtle and expanded Great Chain of Inner Being. A considerable achievement, certainly; but is it what Poulet intended?

The need to periodize, which I take as a residual formalism, can seriously and detrimentally influence Poulet's studies. Many observations on James, acute and interesting as they are, would be more appropriate to someone else: to Butor, or Virginia Woolf, or

8. Cf. J. Hillis Miller, "The Literary Criticism of Georges Poulet," *MLN* 78 (1963): 471–88.

Valéry. They rarely reach to the quick of James's consciousness, to that which makes him unmistakably Jamesian. Take this remark, for instance, on the passage of time: "Time," says Poulet, "is realized by substitution, not of one moment for another but of one place for another. It is as 'localized' a time as possible. James's novel becomes a succession of changes of locale." This is certainly true, and Butor in *La Modification* may only exploit the technique, yet the remark omits something more primitive and essential in James—his refinedly superstitious response to spirit of place. The fact is that there are few neutral places in the world of his novels: place is always impregnate with spirit, and spirit is characterized by intentionality. The displacement of a person, as from America to Europe, is the start of a spiritual adventure involving a gothic traversing of unknown areas of influence—not necessarily forbidden rooms, recesses, and gardens, yet analogous to these. Place has presence or is an extension of a presence: and if people fall under the spell of others, it is because they cannot escape an intentionality that extends to place and haunts imagination like a ghost.

If Poulet loses by the formalism he must retain, does he gain by what he rejects? It is part of his antiformalism to make no distinction between Coleridge's primary and secondary imaginations. The *I am* implicit in every act of consciousness is also the *I am* revealed by art. In art as elsewhere, consciousness feels out or I-am-izes the world; and the relation, in the original cogito, of "I think *therefore* I am," is shown to be phenomenological rather than logical. All knowledge is personal knowledge, a construction putting us in relation to the world and to ourselves. It is as if Cartesianism were the trauma or primal scene of the history of consciousness which the individual mind progressively repeats. The structure of this repetition is what concerns Poulet, but he does not link it explicitly to the manifest form of the work of art. This omission, however fatal, gives him a certain initial advantage over the formalist critic. By looking through form, as Blake claims to look through rather than with the eye, Poulet gains his unusually intimate access to the writer's mind. It does not matter to him whether he enters that mind by door or window or through the chimney: he tells us what he finds without telling us how he got in. Yet one thing he cannot properly describe—the essential latency of what he finds, the quality of art's resistance to intimacy. Art, says Wallace Stevens, *almost* resists the intelligence. In Poulet the differential relation of form to consciousness is lost. Yet form represents the Other to the practicing artist; it is form he must I-am-ize. And the stronger his concern with form, the more difficult his task: here, if anywhere, is "the seriousness, the suffering, the patience, and the labor of the Negative."

The essay on James shows how interesting yet unsatisfactory Poulet can be on the subject of form. We have already noted his remark that since, in James, life gives no single or definitive clue for its organization, the artist himself must cut the tangle and find a limiting view. Thus point of view is not a technique to achieve interiority but a way of limiting introspection in order to make character and plot possible. Consciousness as such appears to be no problem; the only problem is how to represent it.

A difficulty of representation, however, is not yet a difficulty of being. Poulet either assumes or does not make the connection. He writes as if everything were a procedural rather than substantive matter, and he is probably misled by James's casual style of self-commentary. It is admirable that James should talk in such an objective if engaged fashion about his art, but this will deceive no one truly respectful of his realized art: of verbal style, plot as story, plot as pressure of story leading to discoveries, and thematic structure. Of these Poulet respects only one kind of thematic repetition, the imagery of point and circle, and there he misses the fact that point is by no means divested of sting and wavers between its neutral and its wounding sense. Things come to a point with difficulty in James because that point is knowledge and knowledge is still under its old curse: it is an originative wound, a seeing of the evil mixed in with the good. Consciousness is the place at which being reveals itself as wounded. James's problem is not that of facing as a writer the plenitude of things and having arbitrarily to limit it: his problem is not to be able to think of consciousness as disinterested, as a free and innocent appetite. Its appetitiveness is what is curbed by the self-imposed convention of point of view, though the momentum of James's novels erodes all such curbs.

That the difficulty is one of being rather than of representation is reflected by everything so naturally excluded from Poulet's essay. He does not mention the central importance of marriage, and a Jamesian marriage, or an analogous contract, is what principally generates as well as imposes form on consciousness. If we respect the simplest themes and structural features of James's novels, we must describe his cogito as follows. In the beginning the mind is conscious of a plot or secret marriage of some kind. Eventually, the mind is conscious of itself—of its own complicity or secret marriage. Consciousness, in other words, is not at all free or disinterested. It is knowingly or unknowingly the result of a contract, as in *Faust,* of a conspiracy, as in the Fall, or of a covenant like the crucifixion. Such *liaisons dangereuses* implicate us, make us historical, and create in us a new and powerful awareness. From this perspective each novel is seen to be a story that exacts from its hero and often from the storyteller himself a contractual quid pro quo. Consciousness must be paid for, and the usual wages are sacrifice and death. Thus whatever stands greatly against consciousness is drawn into a plot whose acquisitive and inquisitive purposes blend; the plot tests, until it destroys, the illusion that there is innocence or disinterestedness. I find no way to reconcile this view with Poulet's benevolent conclusion: "The astounding peripheric activity of multiple consciousnesses has, in James, the effect of inflating reality by charging it with all the possibilities it implies. Truth is a center surrounded by a luminous halo of both infinite and finite possibilities." No wonder that Bachelard commended phenomenology as "une école de naïveté"! This is the expanse, not the expense, of vision. Consciousness here is purely a good, and its triumph a matter of mental technology. The shadow side of James is elided.

It is not that Poulet cannot respect this side of a writer (see, for example, his important study of Pascal[9]). Perhaps his error might have been avoided by considering the form of the novels and of their sequence, yet I doubt that it is directly caused by the absence of this check. The flaw seems to reside in too optimistic a view of the progress of consciousness. Poulet is certainly too optimistic regarding James. By unperplexing James's "consciousness of consciousness" or substituting a perplexity of representation for one of being, he harmonizes James with a stage in the history of consciousness that might have been reached. As long as the artist,

9. *Études sur le temps humain* (1949), chap. 3.

moreover, is in phase with a supposed historical progress, the problem of evaluation need not arise, and Poulet prefers it that way. His view of history is too formal, and his understanding of the writer not formal enough. He has not been able to situate James either in history or in the realm of values.

I conclude with the following observation. The case against formalism was stated eloquently in Trotsky's *Literature and Revolution* (1925). "Having counted the adjectives," says Trotsky of the formalist, "and weighed the lines, and measured the rhythms, a Formalist either stops silent with the expression of a man who does not know what to do with himself, or throws out an unexpected generalization which contains five per cent Formalism and ninety-five per cent of the most uncritical intuition." Our modern formalist is more sophisticated than this literary quasi-scientist, but the remedy would seem to be the same. What is needed for literary study is a hundred percent of formalism and a hundred percent of critical intuition. Like all counsels of perfection this one sets an impossible ideal. But I do not see why the study of forms should distract from genuine critical intuition, or why there should be competition between virtues. There are many ways to transcend formalism, but the worst is not to study forms. Even multiplying distinctions in the manner of Northrop Frye helps to free literary study because it frees the mind vis-à-vis literature. Categories and forms are man-made before they are authenticated by tradition, and if we think Frye proposes too many terms and Brooks too few, we may have to rethink the whole question of terminology in an arduous, perhaps philosophical way—in fact, to examine the *term* aspect of terms.

Lest these comments seem too unobjectionable, I should add that there is good reason why many in this country, as well as in Europe, have voiced a suspicion of Anglo-Saxon formalism. The dominion of Exegesis is great: she is our Whore of Babylon, sitting robed in Academic black on the great dragon of Criticism, and dispensing a repetitive and soporific balm from her pedantic cup. If our neo-scriptural activity of explication were as daring and conscious as it used to be when Bible texts had to be harmonized with strange or contrary experience, i.e., with history, no one could level this charge of puerility. Yet our present ex-

plication-centered criticism is indeed puerile, or at most peda-
gogic: we forget its merely preparatory function, that it stands to
a mature criticism as pastoral to epic. Explication is the end of
criticism only if we succumb to what Trotsky called the formalist's
"superstition of the word." To redeem the word from the superstition of the word is to humanize it, to make it participate once
more in a living concert of voices, and to raise exegesis to its
former state by confronting art with experience as searchingly as
if art were scripture.

The Heroics of Realism

> "I embrace ALL," says Whitman, "I weave all
> things into myself.
> Do you really! There can't be much left of *you*
> when you've done. When you've cooked the awful
> pudding of One Identity.
>
> —D. H. Lawrence

The contemporary novelist displays an immense faith in the original right of all data. Sense and nonsense are both admitted; little distinction is made between public matters and private; no restricted or insignificant events remain. "The 'proper stuff of fiction' does not exist," wrote Virginia Woolf after seeing the first fragments of *Ulysses,* "everything is the proper stuff of fiction, every feeling, every thought; every quality of brain and spirit is drawn upon; no perception comes amiss."

Such ranging or expansive sympathy is not new to literature. According to Wordsworth the only infallible sign of genius is "a widening of the sphere of human sensibility for the delight, honor and benefit of human nature"; and there is no proof that Homer felt less widely than James Joyce. Yet whether or not the modern writer has a broader range of feelings, he is somehow nearer or more acutely receptive to them. "He can no more cease to receive impressions," to quote Virginia Woolf again, "than a fish in mid-ocean can cease to let water rush through his gills." This is, to say the least, a rather uncomfortable state of existence.

For though no person is capable of responding infinitely to impressions, the writer labors today under that a priori charge. He expects himself to be constantly aware. Like Dostoevsky's Lebedyev, he becomes a blend of visionary and voyeur: a know-all, a sense-all, a satanic kind of spying character, "walking up and down in the earth." By the passkey of fiction he lets himself into every door and most minds. His novels exfoliate in a leafy riot

61

of impressions and indiscretions. But they also prove that art will die where the focus of sensibility is, on fixed principle, too wide.

The difficulty is usually stated in a different way. It arises as a question of how form may be imposed on modern (limitless or chaotic) experience. But this is a deceptive formulation with a touch of hysteria in it, as in Virginia Woolf's further comment. "Life is subjected [by the novelist] to a thousand disciplines and exercises. It is curbed; it is killed. It is mixed with this, stiffened with that." We recognize here the dogmatic factor in realism: its assumption that a direct contact with life—with things themselves —is always available. Forms are therefore a betrayal of life. A necessary evil, they stand arbitrarily yet nobly between the novelist and life, to curb and kill.

Does life whelm the novelist in this manner? It is doubtful that we are as directly in touch with life as we would like to be. And the modern novelist does like to be: he suffers, more than ever, under an ideal obligation to the totality of experience. Yet though it is only ideal, it is no less an obligation, for the spirit of the time does not allow him to restrict his focus willfully. Everyone acknowledges, of course, that art cannot do without form and that forms restrict; but the sanction for those forms is no longer spontaneously social or religious: the sanction now rests almost completely with the individual artist. We hold him responsible whether he accepts the forms of his society or rejects them and makes his own. Whatever the forms, and whatever the subject, he is judged only in the light of that largest and most difficult abstraction—life itself.

Past novelists did not have to keep up with life. Change and novelty, before the industrial and technological revolutions, were rejected rather than accepted a priori. Despite this particular conservatism, art has always fostered larger perceptions; and the contemporary novel merely continues its general momentum toward a freer human sensibility. The coldest work of art still has its reversals and shocks: a falling of veils as in the Racinian *tu,* the illegitimate sympathy evoked by the Satan of *Paradise Lost,* the rare moments of almost physical illumination in the novels of Henry James. What we value in ancient as in modern art is precisely this power of sympathetic trespass: trespass against the society circumscribing the artist's range of feeling. The only difference, in this respect, between the two kinds of art is that this trespass previously coexisted with a narrow and now coexists with a broadening range of experience.

This difference, however, is more substantial than first appears. One might assume that literature before the present century had greater difficulties in transcending conscious or permitted limits. Are not social imperatives more persistent, and do they not prevent strange alliances of thought or feeling? Yet the truth is that the difficulty lies all on the side of modern literature. Not that the contemporary writer finds it harder to transgress; on the contrary, he finds it too easy. The reality of trespass is disappearing with the reality of convention; and the repressions on which great literature battens, from which it shapes the pressure of its scenes, is weakened. A generation's freedom to give its feelings away obviates that shuddering, magnanimous breakthrough of the conventional sensibility to excluded parts of life. When we know in advance that everything is permitted, what is there to reclaim? Just because his sensibility is (in principle, not always in fact) permissively open, the modern writer is faced with having to renew the image of a redemptive transgression.

A trespass presupposes something to be breached, some strong convention between characters, or author and character, or author and audience. Though the novelist, before the present era, is allowed a potential omniscience, he will not use it beyond a certain point: he leaves many things unsaid or presents them obliquely. The ultimate reason for this may be aesthetic as well as social; but it is difficult, in the traditional novel, to separate these motives. There is, moreover, a good deal of flexibility and ambivalence in the conventions: a breach of style, for example, a trespass of author against audience, may occur without breaching other conventions, as between characters—but this is a subject we do not have to consider at this point. What is generally true is that the author is restrained by social norms that affect directly his sensibility or the canons of his art; and this restraint, a narrowing of focus and subject, makes every breach of appearances significant and allows a real emergence of dangerous sympathy.

Jane Austen's restraint is of the older kind. In *Persuasion,* two estranged lovers meet accidentally after many years, and we never doubt that their reconciliation will occur, any more than that Odysseus will reach home. They are kept, however, in tense separation and have to navigate social barriers and serious obstacles of self-esteem before they reach a new mutual accord. To collapse the space of separation too soon would be to collapse the novel, to sin at once against art, society, and some deeper sense of the necessity of a slow redemption, of having to buy back what is estranged or wasted. Jane Austen's art is, in fact, so honest that we feel her to have ultimately written a fairy tale, something mellow and miraculous like *The Tempest*. So deeply does she make us perceive the gulf that might have been between the lovers; so careful is she to respect a reality of time which love might not have overcome.

The contemporary novel, however, precisely because its realism is a priori or formal, runs the danger of inducing too quickly a sense of intimacy with person and place. The initial or founding distance is gone. The heroine may lose her virtue or a character his mystery in a few pages. The novelist just can't help himself: the promiscuity is less in him than in the genre. Its impetus is demonic. Instead of proceeding toward intimacy, the writer must somehow manage to go from intimacy (Virginia Woolf's "mid-ocean") to that natural estrangement which is Jane Austen's donnée. He must reveal the inauthenticity of every assumption of intimacy or find, as John Crowe Ransom once said, "techniques of restraint" to replace the force of convention. To make lightning you must have charged poles and a distance to traverse; the conventions provided the distance, and the emotions did the rest. What provides that distance now?

Malamud's *The Assistant* can illustrate the problem. It falls patently into two parts, of which the first shows the distance between the main characters being destroyed, and the second a new distance being carefully realized. Like *Persuasion,* the novel's subject is a buying back, a redemption. Despite the gulf between Frank and Helen, one an Italian on the prowl and the other a Jew—a gulf made up of prejudice but also of genuine cultural difference—the two draw closer together. At the critical moment, however, Frank rapes Helen; and, in the catastrophe that follows, the assumption that a common humanity binds them together is removed. Frank is now at a much truer yet also more hopeless distance from Helen. It is only from this deeper estrangement that he can really win the "Jewish" as well as "human" Helen and redeem what he has lost.

Malamud also shows that the contemporary novelist is not naked of all social or inherited forms. He still has some access to traditions firmly held or to archaic cultures. He may also use the common rituals of his society; party, church-going, dinner, excursion, caucus, dating, interview. It is rather rare, moreover, that he chooses a perspective which so destroys the norm of distance that, as in Kafka, the relations between man and man become as precarious as those between believer and God after Protestantism had voided the intermediaries. Yet many of the rituals retained by the novelist—retained without anachronism—are no longer conventions of restraint. They are more in the nature of conventions of unrestraint, rapid transit communions. The modern picaresque is a flourishing genre because it recognizes this fact candidly: it is *the* genre of unrestraint. Sublime energies, said Thomas Mann, appear today only in the guise of the grotesque; but "today" is a large category, one that stretches from *Don Quixote* to a Saul Bellow novel or to Mann's own finale, *Felix Krull*. The picaresque, however, breaches realism in so far as the hero is not altogether of the world in which he moves. He is a knight, a god of sorts; we cannot entirely draw him to our level.

Even when a writer stays entirely within realism his novel must still estrange us, like the picaresque, from the intimacy of its mode. Malamud's Frank is no picaresque hero, yet he belongs to the archetype of the stranger, the man without a visible past, who is almost a fixture of the novel; and he is also, perhaps too obviously, a suffering servant figure. One can say that the writer's trespass is now against realism itself. If the novelist's mode commits him to the position that "nothing real is alien to me," his works break through to the fact that "nothing real is familiar to you." Realism being as great a tyranny as supernaturalism, a vital antithesis of mode and work appears, so that the author tends to beget otherness rather than intimacy, vision rather than common sense. How visionary Balzac's realism was is only clear today.

The reachieved distance, in other words, whether aesthetic or mythical, is not established only to be annihilated again. It is a more positive, vital, visionary thing. To gain the world truly, one must first learn the measure of one's distance from it; and the dehumanization of art, noticed by Ortega y Gasset, is a general symptom of this necessary recreation of distance. Ortega's highest praise was to say, as of Proust, that he invented a new discrepancy between reality and ourselves. Dehumanization, however, is the wrong word. In the abeyance of self-justifying conventions, which limit the contact of persons and encourage a language intrinsically veiled, the artist makes room in the "all too human" for a necessary angel (sometimes, a necessary devil):

> I am the necessary angel of earth
> Since, in my sight, you see the earth again,
> Cleared of its stiff and stubborn, man-locked set.
>
> —Wallace Stevens

This humanistic attack on the anthropomorphic ("man-locked") intelligence fosters techniques of perception which are dissociative rather than associative in nature. They do not make the strange familiar but rather estrange the familiar. One such technique (there are a great many) is Faulkner's and Robbe-Grillet's use of the "estranged consciousness." Even where it depicts an abormal state of mind it does so by projecting reality as irreducibly, troublingly, *other*. Consciousness, for these writers, is little more than a rape, a wrong or premature intimacy. It is a moral labor to reach the innocence of things or realize their independence vis-à-vis ourselves. Our narcissism is endless and essential, and only by various methods of dissociation that disrupt ordinary perception can we get beyond the self to a sense of the other.

In France, the surrealist movement, which had its effect on the novel, began a programmatic search for techniques of estrangement. "La surréalité," said André Breton, "sera . . . fonction de notre volonté de dépaysement de tout." The Parnassian coldness, the art for art's sake attitude, and Rimbaud's call for sensory experiments, were general forerunners. Much may even be attributed to the Romantics, especially the German branch, and that addition of strangeness to beauty in which Pater saw the characteristic of their art. But to discuss the relation of the modern novel to poetry is not my purpose, though this relation is clearest in France. Let it suffice to say that the figure of the angel, used by both Rilke and Stevens, has a certain bearing. It tells us that the human, at a time like this, when sympathies are socialized and spread so wide as to become abstract, is often a fog of intimacy hiding the genuine difference; and that art must then make room for the other and even the divine. Art refuses to let us fall into one circumference.

I conclude with an example from the modern novel of how this genuine sense of difference, or otherness, is kept alive. It is related to what we have said about the mythic dimension of certain characters in the realistic novel. There is a highly complex kind of distancing that has recently come under attack. A new, self-generated convention, it is often considered the distinguishing mark of realistic fiction after Flaubert and Henry James. In objective or impersonal narration, as this convention is sometimes called, the author intrudes as little as possible, developing the story by means of reflectors (centers of consciousness) or some other dramatic method. Wayne Booth has made the first comprehensive and systematic critique of this mode in *The Rhetoric of Fiction*. He examines the impersonal novel with great patience and insight and discovers a flaw never before so carefully described.

This flaw he calls "confusion of distance." We know Jane Austen's attitude toward her characters, but who can say precisely how an impersonal novelist stands in relation to his hero? How does Joyce consider Stephen Daedalus? Where does the truth lie in *The Turn of the Screw*—with the governess or the children? The author's attitude, of course, is complex. But should it not be sufficiently resolved, after due respect to mystery, so that contradictory answers (Joyce thinks Stephen is an ass; Joyce is deeply in sympathy with him) cannot be offered as they have been in a deluge of exegeses? Mr. Booth holds that this uncertainty about the author's true judgment is not due to any insufficiency of understanding in his critics, except as they are willing to tolerate an intolerably ambiguous author, but is an inevitable result of the impersonal mode of narration. Explicit judgments are not necessary, but no author may fail to provide an implied standard without throwing his work to the winds of opinion.

Yet is there really a confusion of distance in the greater modern novel? Perhaps the author does not stand in a relation of judgment to his characters? How then could he (or we) approve or disapprove? The reply that the author in creating, and we in reading, cannot but weigh the characters constantly, is not very convincing. Do we really judge Macbeth? Only by faint analogy can "judging" be applied to what our minds do on confronting certain exceptional figures like Lear, Macbeth, Vautrin, or even Felix Krull. Tradition provides us, moreover, with a definite term for the man who is so much greater than we are, not morally perhaps but in mode of being—Nietzsche would have said he stands beyond good and evil—that our familiar, democratic judgment is suspended, if not disabled. He is the *hero*.

Stephen Daedalus, I believe, is a hero in that sense: he embodies a special fate. The confusion of which Mr. Booth is aware arises when we see a character put almost beyond our judgment who is realistically portrayed as in no essential way superior to us. Camus's *étranger* is the extreme example of the hero who is only one of us, or even less, yet shakes off our judgment by simply being what he is, as the trial at the end of the novel probably makes too explicit. By now such radically innocent characters are almost a convention. Between E. E. Cummings's *The Enormous Room* (enormously neglected) and John Cassavetes's film *The Shadows,* there lie two generations, a second world conflict, and a medium strongly challenging the novel, yet the characters in both have the same resilience, the same basic innocence, the same status beyond good and evil.

In fact, modern realistic fiction, with the exception of some eighteenth- and many nineteenth-century English novels (they provide *The Rhetoric of Fiction* with its truest ground), has kept its attachments to romance and myth, to characters that bear a daimon which cannot be morally or psychologically reduced. In Dostoevsky's *The Idiot,* Prince Myshkin exerts a disastrous influence. He destroys the two women he might have saved, and it would be impossible to say whether he is a saint, an idiot, an impotent, or all three. Yet if his character (a moral and psychological entity) is unclear, his mode of being (ontological) is transparent: he is human in all respects, and judgeable, except for his pity. That is his daimon, as anger is Achilles'. By that he is divine and disastrous, like Christ. The love others attribute to him is not love at all but a more-than-human pity, directed toward all suffers and therefore unable to make the exclusive love-judgments that Nastasya and Aglaya demand.

In what sense, however, is Daedalus a hero? Though he has no attribute as clear as that of Myshkin, Joyce's *Portrait* shows him moving toward the realization of his special fate. By the end of the book he has rejected all existential choices except that of being an artist. But this choice is not on a par with choosing love, the priesthood, patriotism. It means a fatal break with these. "Silence, exile, cunning" is Stephen's motto henceforth. To be an artist has become a special fate involving the severance of familiar human ties. It may not have been so always; it could be argued that Stephen's act, however correct, does not reflect more than an unfortunate historical situation, one that forces the artist into exile. Even so, at this point in history, whether it has passed today or not, the artist is the form that the heroic takes. Like heroes of old Stephen moves from a matriarchal realm (family, church, Ireland) to the patriarchal aegis: "Old father, old artificer, stand me now and ever in good stead."

Something of course remains dubious about Stephen. The hero is always a problem. Especially the realistic hero not separated from us by signs or status: we cannot escape double thoughts, and we try to bring him to our level by moralism and psychology. Nor can the hero himself escape them: he differs from his royal prototypes by being not only a problem to others but also to himself. His destiny may lift him beyond our final judgment, but he is not beyond self-judgment. In the *Brothers Karamazov,* Zossima, instead of adjudicating the case brought to him by Dmitri and his father, bows down before Dmitri. The novel begins in a withdrawing from, and leads into a miscarriage of, judgment. Yet Dmitri, like all Dostoevsky's characters, deeply and incessantly judges himself. Stephen, likewise, is quite self-critical. The hero is not abstracted from all judgment or in all respects. Joyce does, however, suggest a limit beyond which we should not go—unless we criticize his hero's daimon in the light of a religious concept. So a Christian might judge Achilles adversely as part of a world which still connects divinity and great wrath. Yet is not any religious criticism tantamount to setting up one daimon against another? Achilles gives way to Myshkin and a new fatality.

Impersonality in art can allow illicit sympathies or evade the problem of judgment. This is the threat of passivity, the opiate acceptance of monstrous fact secreted in novel or movie. It is the very thing that caused us to raise the question of the modern

69

novelist who is (to quote Virginia Woolf once more) "terribly exposed to life." Yet confusion of distance—or, to speak less pejoratively, twofold vision—though often found together with impersonal or ironic fiction, is also a separate phenomenon, as the case of Myshkin shows. It is joined to impersonal narration not as an effect to its cause but as one method of self-generated distancing to another. They are both responses to a common problem, a serious contemporary exigency of realism.

When empathy becomes conventional, and the new or alien loses its aureole of sacred danger, it is increasingly difficult to admit transcendent personality or real difference. But art retains its power of making room for the strange, the different, and even the divine. It is the familiar world that must now be saved—from familiarity. Only in this light does impersonal narration find its reason. The author, staying within realism, must keep from too easy an intimacy with creation. The body of the world, the body of other persons, is a strange fact; their thoughts are a mystery; every relation includes shock and unveilings. The impersonal mode is clearly an effort at distance, one of many. It is an effort to hold back—by placing true imaginative obstacles before—the leveling and inquisitive mind. James obstacles himself; he refuses simply to know. Every mind tends to be viewed through another, and the desire to know positively (and can even the artist escape it?) is always presented as a vampirish act. A great novel does not breed familiarity; a bad novel is simply one that betrays the mystery, rapes the past, and lets us possess too quickly another person or mind.

Virginia's Web

This goddess of the continuum is incapable of continuity.

—Valéry, on the Pythoness

Transitions may well be the hardest part of a writer's craft: Virginia Woolf shows that they are also the most imaginative. One remembers, from *Mrs. Dalloway,* the inscrutable motor car proceeding toward Piccadilly, and the way it serves to move the plot with it. Or, in the next episode, how the skywriting plane moves different minds, each guessing at the slogan being dispensed and then dispersed. The wind stealing the smoky letters before any guess is confirmed is the same that, fifteen years later, miscarries the players' words in *Between The Acts.* Suppose now that these letters or words or glimpses are divided by years, by some indefinite or immeasurable gap. We know that years pass, that words are spoken or spelled, and that cars reach their destination; yet the mystery lies in space itself, which the imaginative mind must fill, perhaps too quickly. The dominant issues in the study of Virginia Woolf have been her solipsism and her treatment of time and character; I propose to suspend these and to see her novels as mirrors held up primarily to the imagination.

Let us consider a fairly simple passage from *To the Lighthouse.* To look at it closely requires a concern, a prior interest: in our case, how the novelist goes from one thing to another. The context of the passage is as follows. Mr. Ramsey and his two children, Cam and James, are being ferried to the Lighthouse. The weather is calm, and it seems the boat will never get there; Cam and James, moreover, do not want it to get there, resenting the tyrannous will of their father. In the first section of the novel, with Mrs. Ramsey still alive, it is he who dampens the childish eagerness of James to go to the Lighthouse; and now (many years later) he insists on this outing as a commemorative act.

The sails flapped over their heads. The water chuckled and slapped the sides of the boat, which drowsed motionless in the sun. Now and then the sails rippled with a little breeze in them, but the ripple ran over them and ceased. The boat made no motion at all. Mr. Ramsey sat in the middle of the boat. He would be impatient in a moment, James thought, and Cam thought, looking at her father who sat in the middle of the boat between them (James steered; Cam sat alone in the bow) with his legs tightly curled. He hated hanging about.

The continuity is kept on the verbal as well as visual plane by echo and repetition (flapped, slapped, drowsed, them, them, boat, boat). This is an intensifying device any writer might use, but one is hardly aware with what skill the sentences lead inward, to that parenthesis and fine slowing-up that encompasses boat, man, and children. Mrs. Woolf's style is here at its best, and the continuities going from the freest to the stillest part of the scene (from the sail to the middle of the boat) do so with an almost humorous resistance. It is interesting to think that the rhythm should be generated by an avoidance; there is, in any case, a stop and go pattern to it, magnified perhaps by the subject of the passage. In terms of plot or subject we have a pause; in terms of the prose that describes it, a sustained if not augmented interest in continuity. As the description reaches the inside of the boat, and then the inside of the mind, the rhythm slows, and as the rhythm slows the continuity is made more obvious as if to counterpoint the pausing. This pattern, however, may be found elsewhere too and cannot be purely an intensifying or descriptive device. It may originate in the writer prior to the particular subject.

I am suggesting that continuity is a deeper matter here than craft or style. In his first important essay Valéry remarked that the extension of continuity by means of metaphor, language, or other means was the common gift of genius. His thesis implied two things: that there is "space" or apparent discontinuity, and that the genial inventor can project his mind into it. If we identify this ability to project (or better, interpolate) with imagination, then the crucial question is what this space may be. There can be only one answer which is not a gross generalization, and this is—anything We are dealing, it must be remembered, with appearances, and there is nothing that may not succumb to blankness.[1] Art respects appearances so much that everything may become questionably blank, even the continuities firmly established by science. For though science has shown them to exist, it has not shown why they should exist so unapparently, and the formula that proves them also proves the coyness of nature.

To the Lighthouse begins with a sense of fullness and continuous life as we are led in and out of Mrs. Ramsey's mind. There are few apparent pauses to threaten the continuity of thought or existence. The dark space between the beams of the Lighthouse does, however, penetrate consciousness. "A shutter, like the leathern eyelid of a lizard, flickered over the intensity of his gaze and obscured the letter R. In that flash of darkness he heard people saying—he was a failure—that R was beyond him. He would never reach R. On to R, once more. R—" Mr. Ramsey's intellectual ambitions are described, and there are other fine sequences of the same kind.

These darker intervals, rare in the first part, consolidate as the encroaching and live darkness of the second part, which traces the gradual abandonment of the Ramsey house and its last minute rescue from oblivion. Then, in the last section of the novel, a horrid calm moves directly into the heart of the characters. The becalming of the boat is part of a larger sequence, in which all are involved with death, present as distance or the sea's calm or the absence of Mrs. Ramsey. Each person is compelled by a stilling glance, like the wedding guest by the Mariner. They must suffer the suspense, endure the calm, and ultimately resist it—its intimations of peace and of a happy death of the will.

Resistance is the major theme of this novel. The lighthouse itself is a monitory object, warning off, centered in hostile elements. Mr. Ramsey, an enemy of the sea that becalms his boat, is a stronger resister than Mrs. Ramsey, who lives toward the sea. Resistance is a matter of imagination which can either actively fill space or passively blend with it and die. Imagination could also die to itself and become pure will, as in the case of Mr. Ramsey, who wishes to

1. For a strictly philosophical account, see Hegel's *Phenomenology of Mind* (1807), introduction and opening section on "Sense-Certainty"; Heidegger's *What is Metaphysics* (1929); and Sartre's *L'Imaginaire* (1940).

cross the sea, or from Q to R, by force. He denies space and violates the privacy of others. Yet to keep imagination alive involves staying alive to space, to the horrid calms of Virginia Woolf's ocean.

The imagination itself neither acknowledges nor denies space: it lives in it and says to every question "Life, life, life," like Orlando's little bird or Blake's cricket.[2] Affirmation, not meaning, is basic to it, and the problem of meaning cannot even be faced without considering the necessity or fatality of some primary affirmation. Religious belief is such a primary act, but a special form of it. The founding of fictional world is such a primary act. Fiction reveals something without which the mind could not be, or could not think. The mind needs a world, a substantialized Yes.

Yet every great artist rebels against this, and today his rebellion is conventional. By beginning to question the necessity of fiction, i.e., the inherently affirmative structure of imagination, he joins the philosopher who seeks a truth greater than that arbitrary Yes. The more Henry James seeks the definitive word, the more his mind shrinks from affirmation. It is, similarly, Mrs. Woolf's resistance, her continuous doubting of the continuity she is forced to posit, that we are interested in. At the end of *To the Lighthouse,* Lilly Briscoe's "It is finished," referring in turn to the reaching of the Lighthouse and to her picture, is deeply ironic. It recalls a suffrance greater than the object attained by this last term, by any term. Each artist resists his own vision.

This resistance, however, cannot take place except in the space of fiction and requires the creation of a work of art which is its own implicit critique. The reason that an artist's critique cannot be discursive, or purely so, is that it still involves an affirmation—the new work of art. It is therefore quite proper to put our question in strictly literary terms: What kind of novel does Mrs. Woolf write? And how does it criticize its origin in the affirmative impulse?

I shall try to define Virginia Woolf's novel as the product of a certain kind of prose and a certain kind of plot. This dyad should justify itself as we proceed, but what I say is experimental and may

2. *Orlando,* chap. 6; *Auguries of Innocence:* "A Riddle or the Cricket's Cry/Is to Doubt a fit Reply."

lead to some undue generalizing. The reason for omitting character should also appear: there is only one fully developed character in Mrs. Woolf's novels, and that is the completely expressive or androgynous mind.

Her concern for the novel is linked everywhere with that for prose style. She often remarks that prose, unlike poetry, is still in its infancy, and her first experimental novel, *Mrs. Dalloway,* matures it via the peregrinations of a woman's mind. It may be said with some truth that the novel is, for Virginia Woolf, simply the best form of presenting a completely expressive prose.

A Room of One's Own (1928) illustrates in slow motion how this mature prose came to be. Mrs. Woolf's "sociological essay" is about the future of fiction and woman's part in it. But we are not given a straight essay. She refuses to separate her thought from certain imaginary accidents of time and place and writes something akin to the French *récit*. Her mind, porous to the world even during thought, devises a prose similar to that of *To the Lighthouse,* which makes continuities out of distractions. It is as if a woman's mind were linked at its origin, like the novel itself, to romance; and one is quite happy with this natural picaresque, the author walking us and the world along on the back of her prose.

Still, prose in a novel is different from prose in some other form. Its function can be determined only within a particular structure, and a novel or story requires some finite series of events necessary to produce suspense and move the reader toward the resolving point. This raises the question of the relation of plot and prose.

In the modern novel there are at least two significant ways of making prose subsume the suspense previously offered by plot. One is to structure it as highly as the verse of the seventeenth-century classical drama in France, so that even the simplest conversation becomes dramatic. Henry James's prose has affinities to this. The other is to have the plot coincide with the special perspective of a character. Faulkner and many others (including James) may use this method, which creates a kind of mystery story, the mystery being the mind itself. Mrs. Woolf's prose has some affinities here, but it is not made to issue from a mind limited or peculiar enough to make us suspect the darkness it circles.

The curious fact is that neither the prose nor the plot of Mrs. Woolf's novels can explain the suspense we feel. Perhaps suspense is the wrong word, since we are not avid for what happens next but fascinated by how the something next will happen. To understand this let us take *Mrs. Dalloway*. Its plot is simple and realistic, as is always the case with Virginia Woolf (*Orlando* is only an apparent exception). The suspense or fascination cannot come from that source. Nor does it come, in isolation, from the rich prose woven by Clarissa's mind, since the plot often parts from her to present other people or views, yet our attention does not flag at those points. But if Mrs. Woolf goes at will beyond Clarissa's consciousness, it is on condition that some line of continuity be preserved. There are no jumps, no chapters; every transition is tied to what precedes or has been introduced. The first line of the novel, "Mrs. Dalloway said she would buy the flowers herself," presupposes some immediate prior fact already taken up in consciousness and is emblematic of the artist's mood throughout the novel. Our fascination is involved with this will to continuity, this free prose working under such strict conditions.

The plot, however, does play an important role. Clarissa waiting to cross the street, then crossing, is part of the plot; her thoughts while doing so effect many finer transitions. A tension is thus produced between the realistic plot and the expressive prose; the latter tends to veil or absorb the former, and the former suggests a more natural continuity, one less dependent on mind. We know that certain things happen in sequence, that a play will go on, that people fall in love or cross streets, that a day moves from dawn to dusk. The simpler continuity of the plot tempts the mind forward, as a relief form the essential prose, or as a resting place in something solid.

This tension between two types of continuity also makes the mind realize the artificial or arbitrary character of both. It is moved to conceive the void they bridge. A void is there, like the pauses or thoughts of death in Mrs. Dalloway. But the mind conceives it joyfully, rather than in terror, because of the constant opening up of new perspectives, and the realization through this of its connective power. The continuities we have labeled "plot" and "prose" are, moreover, not unrelated or without special value. I would now like to show that they stand to each other dialectically as major types of affirmation, the plot line coinciding mostly with what we call nature, and the prose line intimating something precarious but also perhaps greater—the "Nature that exists in works of mighty Poets." To do so I return to *A Room of One's Own,* in which Mrs. Woolf (or her persona) is thinking about women writers, and the last of her thought sequences suggests the structure of her novels in microcosm.

Mrs. Woolf looks from her window at London waking for the day's business in the fall of '28. She looks out, not in, allowing herself to be distracted. The city seems to be indifferent to her concerns, and she records the fact strongly:

> Nobody, it seemed, was reading *Antony and Cleopatra* . . . Nobody cared a straw—and I do not blame them—for the future of fiction, the death of poetry or the development by the average woman of a prose style completely expressive of her mind. If opinions upon any of these matters had been chalked on the pavement, nobody would have stooped to read them . . . Here came an errand-boy; here a woman with a dog on a lead.[3]

Something is wrong. Can a writer be so calm about indifference, especially when it threatens art? But Mrs. Woolf is hastening the end. Not her own, but the end of a civilization which had exalted one part of the soul at the expense of the rest. The twenties are reaching their close; the first world war is not forgotten; Proust, Bergson, and Freud have advertised human possessiveness and male arbitrariness, the subtlest workings-out of the patriarchal will. The bustle she welcomes has, at least, the arbitrariness of life rather than of the will: an errand boy here, a funeral there, business men, idlers, shoppers, each going his way.

But her thought does not stop at this point; she lets it found its dialectic. The mind, to begin with, accepts a life indifferent to itself. The affirmative movement is not overcome, though what Virginia Woolf affirms is life rather than her will. Yet she is less interested in life as such than in the life of the mind, which can only appear if thought is left as apparently free as the goings and comings beneath her window.

That this freedom may be an illusion does not matter. It is still a

3. The thought-sequence from which I quote in this section is found in the last chapter (6) of *A Room of One's Own.*

window to the truth and, in any case, lasts a short time. As Mrs. Woolf continues to look, the life disappears, and only the indifference remains: "There was a complete lull and suspension of traffic. Nothing came down the street; nobody passed. A single leaf detached itself from the plane tree at the end of the street, and in that pause and suspension fell." Her mind, however, will not accept this pause, this emptiness. The affirmative movement attaches itself the more strongly to the slightest sign. "Somehow it was like a signal falling, a signal pointing to a force in things which one had overlooked."

What the mind has overlooked seems at first to be nature, an impersonally and constantly active principle of life. This certainly has a presence in Mrs. Woolf's novels. It is much more important to her than the spice of illusionistic realism. In her wish for a purer affirmation, one which does not merely go toward the male will, she often has her characters go toward nature. Their direct relationships are diverted by a second one: "human beings not always in their relations to each other but in their relation to reality; and the sky too, and the trees or whatever it may be in themselves." No human being, she adds, should shut out the view.

Yet it becomes clear, as Mrs. Woolf continues, that the mind had also overlooked something in itself. The falling leaf reminds her, it is true, of a natural force—but in the artist. It is the artist, the person at the window, who affirms a world where there is none. She imagines that the signal points to "a river, which flowed past, invisibly round the corner, down the street, and took people and eddied them along." In *Mrs. Dalloway* the author's consciousness is precisely this: a stream of prose that moves people together and apart, entering at will this mind and that. Nature, as she now conceives it, is one in which the artist participates, so that Shakespeare, poetry, and the finding of a new prose style become once again vital issues.

The artist, at this point, is clearly a Prospero figure. She stages an illusion whose object is a marriage: the mind coming together outside of itself by means of the world or the stage. Nature and art conspire for this illusion or prothalamion; the river, we notice, is a natural and artificial image of rhythm and leads directly to the closing event. As if the river had eddied them together, a girl in patent leather boots and a young man in a maroon raincoat meet a taxi beneath Virginia Woolf's window and get in. "The sight was ordinary enough," she remarks; "what was strange was the rhythmical order with which my imagination had invested it."

Only now does she withdraw from the window, reflecting on the mind. Because of her topic—the woman as writer—she had been thinking intensely of one sex as distinct from the other. But, seeing the couple, the mind felt as if after being divided it had come together again in a natural fusion. Perhaps, she goes on, a state of mind exists in which one could continue without effort, because nothing is required to be repressed and no resistance develops. Interpreting the event literally as well as analogically, she concludes that the fully functioning mind is androgynous.

There is much fantasy in this. What remains is a sustained act of thought, a dialectic that comprises certain distinct types of affirmation. *Dialectic* is not, at first glance, the right word, since all we see is an affirmative movement increasing in scope. There comes, however, a critical pause, a moment of discontinuity, in which the *negative* almost appears. "Nothing came down the street; nobody passed." Such "power failures" are not rare in Virginia Woolf and not always so lightly overcome. They assume a cosmic proportion in her last novel. Miss La Trobe, the illusionist, cannot sustain her country pageant. The wind is against her, life is against her, the rhythm breaks. She learns the depth of space between her and her creation; the vacuum, also, between it and the audience. "Miss La Trobe leant against the tree, paralyzed. Her power had left her. Beads of perspiration broke on her forehead. Illusion had failed. 'This is death,' she murmured, 'death.'" At this very moment, as in the scene beneath Virginia Woolf's window, nature seems to take over and reestablish the rhythm in an expressionistic passage revealing the complicity of art and nature: "Then, suddenly, as the illusion petered out, the cows took up the burden. One had lost her calf. In the very nick of time she lifted her great moon-eyed head and bellowed. All the great moon-eyed heads laid themselves back. From cow after cow came the same yearning bellow. . . . The cows annihilated the gap; bridged the distance; filled the emptiness and continued the emotion."

Between the Acts reveals the same voracious desire for continuity as *Mrs. Dalloway* and *To the Lighthouse,* yet in this last work the novelist has dropped all pretense as to the realism of her transitions. She is outrageously, sadly humorous. "Suddenly the cows stopped; lowered their heads, and began browsing. Simultaneously the audience lowered their heads and read their programmes." This is how she gets from the cows to the audience, with the result, of course, that one feels the space she bridges more intensely. Yet does not the whole novel turn on what is between the acts, on the interpolations of the novelist who continually saves the play for Miss La Trobe? As in the example from *A Room of One's Own,* it is finally irrelevant whether the continuities discovered by Mrs. Woolf are in nature or in the artist.

Our question as to the kind of novel Virginia Woolf writes can now be answered. There is a line of development which goes from the realism of *The Voyage Out* (1915) to the expressionism of *Between the Acts* (1941), and passes through the experimental period of 1925–31 containing *Mrs. Dalloway, To the Lighthouse, Orlando,* and *The Waves.*[4] Mrs. Woolf sought to catch the power of affirmation in its full extent, and her effort to do so includes this shuttling between realistic and expressionistic forms of style. She never abandoned realism entirely because it corresponds to an early phase of affirmation. It is realism of the simple and illusionistic kind which guides our powers of belief toward the world we see, when we see it most freely. We can call this world nature, understanding by that a continuous yet relatively impersonal principle of life, even when (as in the bustle beneath Virginia Woolf's window) it assumes a more human shape. The next phase, more complex, raises the problem of "interpolation." The falling leaf is a signal from Nature, but it points to the artist who sees or affirms a nature persisting through the negative moment. Art, therefore, becomes interpolation rather than mimesis.

4. I am probably unfair in omitting *Jacob's Room* (1922) from the experimental novels. The link between imagination and interpolation is gropingly acknowledged: "But something is always impelling one to hum vibrating, like the hawk moth, at the mouth of the cavern of mystery, endowing Jacob Flanders with all sorts of qualities he had not at all—for though, certainly, he sat talking to Bonamy, half of what he said was too dull to repeat; much unintelligible (about unknown people and Parliament); what remains is mostly a matter of guesswork. Yet over him we hang vibrating."

Though Mrs. Woolf retains a realistic plot, everything of importance tends to happen between the acts, between each finite or external sign. *Mrs. Dalloway* and *To the Lighthouse* are distinguished by this indefinite expansion of the interval, of the mind-space, for example, between the beams of the lighthouse. The realistic plot is sustained by an expressionistic continuity.

Let us provisionally omit *The Waves* and go to Virginia Woolf's last novel. Though its plot is as realistic as ever, we cannot any longer tell with complete certainty what really happens between the acts that make up the action. The novel has a movement like that of Zeno's arrow: we know it flies continuously, and will reach some end, yet are still amazed it does not break in mid-flight. The author, another La Trobe, might fail the continuity, and history, the subject of the play, might fail likewise and not reach the present moment. But life and the novel continue in the same country manner because the artist's interpolations are imaginative enough.

In the case of *The Waves* we cannot even tell what happens. It is not that the plot line is unclear, but now everything is interpolation, even the characters who are simply their speeches, and these speeches interpret acts that might and might not have been. What happens is what the speeches make happen. The purple prefaces alone, describing a day from dark to dark, seem to be founded in reality, or rather nature: the human parts are pushed between as a supreme interpolation standing against the impersonal roll of time.

Considered as notes toward a supreme fiction the novels of Virginia Woolf say "It must be affirmative." They suppose a mind with an immense, even unlimited, power to see or build continuities. It is almost as if the special attribute of the unconscious, that it does not know the negative, belonged also to mind in its freest state. The artist is either not conscious of the negative (i.e., his unconscious speaks through him), or fiction is generically the embodiment of the negative—and whatever dialectic characterizes mind—in purely affirmative terms. The reader, of course, may reconstitute the negative; this task is one of the principal aims of interpretation. We have done a similar thing by pointing to the precarious and interpolative character of Virginia Woolf's continuities. In parts of *To the Lighthouse,* in the last chapter of

Orlando, and in *The Waves,* the novel is brought to the limit of its capacity to show death, decay, repression, and discontinuity in terms of thought, speech, and prose rhythm. Irony is no longer a device; art becomes irony, and the reader sees that the extreme eloquence of *The Waves* hides silence and incommunicability, or that Mrs. Ramsey thinking to affirm life really affirms death.

I wish to make this irony more cogent by a last glance at Mrs. Ramsey. The first section of *To the Lighthouse* is called "The Window." Mrs. Ramsey (like her creator in *A Room of One's Own*) sits near a window and knits. Her hands knit—so does her mind. Every strain that comes from without is absorbed by the regularity of her hands and the continuity of her mind. The strains are endless; she is besieged by eight children, by memory, by nature, and above all by a husband who constantly if surreptitiously demands her attention. Yet, as if another Penelope, apart from the clamoring suitors, she sits and weaves an interminable garment.

Is it a dress or a shroud? A reddish brown stocking, of course, in expectation of visiting the Lighthouse Keeper and his son, though we will not see her arrive. She dies suddenly one night, and her death reveals what she has woven. Darkness and decay creep over the house, which even now is none too tidy. Mrs. Ramsey alive keeps the disorder vital and prevents it from overrunning. She is the natural center, the sun, and however confused relationships get, all come back to her and are resolved into simplicity by her word or presence. But when she dies, impersonality, waste, and vagueness flood the house like a delayed judgment.

The second part of the novel, "Time Passes," describes the near-ruin of the House of Ramsey. It reverts to the sea, to nature; and the human events breaking that slope are reported parenthetically, as interpolations. The structure of *The Waves* comes directly out of this second part. What can the author be saying but that there existed a strange (perhaps unavoidable) correspondence between the mind of Mrs. Ramsey and the will of nature? Although most open to life, sitting by the window, knitting every impulse into a fabric of thought and feeling, what she worked proved finally to be a shroud. But the male will survives in the form of Mr. Ramsey, a sparse, old, domineering man still feeding on the sympathy of others.

It is, therefore, a tragic choice which confronts us. Mrs. Ramsey is the feminine part of the soul, with its will to bypass the will, its desire to let things be and grow in their own time, and above all with its frightening power for mystical marriage, that refusal to sustain the separateness of things in an overly great anticipation of final unity. This last is her most profound trait (she is also literally a matchmaker), and it reveals her identification with death:

> Not as oneself did one find rest ever, in her experience (she accomplished here something dexterous with her needles) but as a wedge of darkness. Losing personality, one lost the fret, the hurry, the stir; and there rose to her lips always some exclamation of triumph over life when things came together in this peace, this rest, this eternity; and pausing there she looked out to meet that stroke of the Lighthouse, the long steady stroke, the last of the three, which was her stroke, for watching them in this mood always at this hour one could not help attaching oneself to one thing, especially of the things one saw; and this thing, the long steady stroke, was her stroke. Often she found herself sitting and looking, sitting and looking, with her work in her hands until she became the thing she looked at—that light for example. And it would lift up on it some little phrase or other which had been lying in her mind like that—"Children don't forget, children don't forget"—which she would repeat and begin adding to it. It will end, it will end, she said. It will come, it will come, when suddenly she added, We are in the hands of the Lord.

This is Mrs. Ramsey's mind knitting, and she knows she has gone too far, hypnotized by her own rhythm. It was not she who said, "We are in the hands of the Lord." "She had been trapped into saying something she did not mean." It is curious how at this moment Mrs. Ramsey echoes a mood which breaks into Shakespeare's tragedies imminently before the end. Do we not hear Desdemona's "All's one" and Hamlet's "If it be now, 'tis not to come; if it be not to come, it will be now; if it be not now, yet it will come"?[5] Despite her great longing for privacy, she cannot but help the reconciliation of all things—she plots to marry off Paul and Minta, William Banks and Lily Briscoe, subdues her judgment, and always finally gives in to her husband, betraying her soul and others for the sake of peace.

Virginia Woolf's use of a realistic plot and an expressionistic continuity seems to me as deep a solution to the structural problems of prose fiction as that found in *Ulysses*. Though the form cannot be said to originate with her, she gave it a conscious and personal perfection, and it remains a vital compromise with the demands of realism. She learned, of course, a great deal from (and against) Joyce, and to mention her in that company is itself a judgment. Her weakness, bound up with her virtues, lies less in any formal conception than in her subject, which is almost too specialized for the novel. I suspect that it is her subject, not her form, which is poetic, for she deals always with a part of the mind closest to the affirmative impulse. We do not find in her great scenes, passionate and fatal interviews with the characters restricted to and revolving about each other. For however complex her characters may be, they are caught up essentially in one problem and are variations of the "separatist" or "unifier" type. The one lives by doubting, and the other by affirming, the illusion of a divine or childhood nature. Poetry gives us this nature more vividly than Virginia Woolf, but it is she who makes us aware of its daily necessity and deception.

5. Similar echoes and rhythms weave through the thoughts of Mrs. Dalloway ("Fear no more the heat o' the sun") and play an interesting part in *Between the Acts*.

Camus and Malraux: The Common Ground

In 1936 Camus produced his first play, an adaptation of Malraux's *Days of Contempt*. His contacts with the older writer have always been of this symbolic and open-hearted kind.[1] For us *Days of Contempt* is Malraux's most contrived novel, but for Camus and many Europeans it was more than a book, it was an event. Malraux's novel confirmed less a particular thesis than a certain idea of the writer's function in a time of crisis, when literature gave way to journalism and writing to politics.

Malraux was faced with a situation in which speed was of the essence. His was the first novel to recognize and broadcast the danger of Nazism. Yet he sacrificed nothing to propaganda. His book, neither an indictment nor a cry of hate, was concerned with the sources of man's resistance, and hate did not figure among them. This refusal to sit in judgment, its most significant omission, is also its deepest point; and it recalls Camus's own, lifelong refusal to judge his epoch "from above."[2] The real enemy for both Malraux and Camus was something more universal than Fascism, something in the nature of man, even of the man writing. In their hands fiction became an act of resistance, not an act of judgment.

Malraux defined quite clearly what had to be resisted. He saw that the "unformulated individualism" of his contemporaries would prove utterly ineffective against the ruthless ideological

1. Hearing of his Nobel Prize he is said to have remarked: "I would have voted for Malraux." In *The Myth of Sisyphus,* while using a theme of Dostoevski's to support his analysis of "la création absurde," he adds a note that Malraux is equally relevant. But he never, as far as I know, fulfilled this promise of a confrontation. Camus's *absurde* has no real relation to that which Malraux talks of in *La Tentation de l'Occident.* Another early essay of Malraux's "D'une jeunesse européenne" *(Ecrits* [Paris, 1927])* seems to me to have a greater bearing on at least the spirit of Camus's inquiry.

2. Cf. K. Bieber, *L'Allemagne vue par les écrivains de la résistance française* (Genève, 1954).

techniques portrayed in *Days of Contempt*. Propaganda, subtle or violent, all those attempts to "engineer the soul" which he also attacked at the Moscow Writers' Congress of 1935, imply a radical contempt of the individual. No vague individualism can oppose this contempt: a man must be sure of his intellectual and personal worth, sure of what nourishes, even in extreme situations, his identity as a man.[3] Kassner, the Communist hero of the book, discovers in the absolute solitude of his prison that only the primitive artist, his will to memory and communication, keeps his reason alive. He deciphers a prison language of knocks against stone and establishes, through this drive for shared intelligence, an unforgettable moment of human contact. Through Kassner we learn that all warfare is, at its base, psychological, and all defense is related to man's artistic nature. Fascism, in particular, sought to destroy less the man than the idea of man in him.

Despite Trotsky's assertion, therefore, resistance—not revolution—is the modern, at least European, theme; and it is as an analysis of the sources of resistance—and of complicity—that Malraux's writings affect "les enfants d'un demi-siècle."[4] Camus joins Malraux in this analysis. He could hardly avoid doing so, with the historical facts growing ever more oppressive. At the time of Malraux's novel (1935), the Nazi terror had not been consummated, and the Moscow purges were still under the horizon. The full extent of Russia's complicity with Stalin and of Germany's with Hitler was unimaginable. Camus's literary career starts, symbolically, with *Days of Contempt,* but reaches its height in a terrifying "Confession d'un enfant du siècle"—the portrait in *The Fall* of Jean-Baptiste Clamence, *the* portrait of complicity. Yet most English and American writers remained unaware of the mystery, at least in its political aspect.

For Camus, even style is an act of resistance. It goes against the confessional urge of speech, against the telltale heart. When he writes in his own person, it is with the stutter of a man lifting a

3. What Malraux depicts in stylized fashion has recently found a confirmation in Victor Frankl's *From Death-Camp to Existentialism* (Boston, 1959).

4. On this, see the strong testimony of Gustav Regler, *Das Ohr des Malchus* (Cologne, 1958), who calls him "Der ehrlichste Freund aller, die vor der Tyrannei flüchteten. Der Unbestechliche. *Le torturé et le pur.*"

stone, and the "terrible fluidity of self-revelation" comes only in the subversive confessional toccatas of *The Fall*. He always resists too easy a love for man, too great a desire for communion with him, that "horrid sympathy" depicted by Poe and Baudelaire with such curious rational delight. His most horrible story, "The Renegade," is the monologue of a priest whose tongue is cut off by savages he wants to missionize. Camus has not used this gory detail as a masking symbol for castration, but through it he punishes two equivalent things: the treacherously easy communion of sex, and that of religious fervor ("l'éloquence de la chaire"). All his stories are, directly or indirectly, about true muteness, about a measure of solitude in man. To respect the latter is to create the very space of communion. The electrical contacts of, for example, d'Arrast and his new friends ("La pierre qui pousse") and of the workers and their boss ("Les muets") occur in this space.

Seen as a whole, Camus's work is a critique of communion, of which the major types are religion, politics, sexuality, work, and speech (art). As religion weakens and leaves a vacuum, that "between man and man" which haunts modern thought, the other modes become more essential, at least more obsessive. It is clear that Camus, in his concern with communion, must stand on religious ground without being thereby religious. *L'Exil et le Royaume* and *La Chute* are, as their titles indicate, aware of a religious world. But it shows a strange distortion. To go back for a moment to the question of speech, religious speech is related to prophecy, and prophecy to some concept of final judgment. Yet today we have to find a way of speaking clearly without speaking from above, and how difficult this is Camus shows by two portraits—one of a penitent and one of an artist, both of whom substitute a form of complicity with man for real judgment. John the Baptist, prophet-precursor of Christ, "clamans in deserto,"[5] becomes in *The Fall* Jean-Baptiste Clamence, refusing the desert and clinging to man with the insidious voice and confessions of a drunkard. To his victims he holds out the fruit of knowledge or of complicity, the impossibility of innocence. He baptizes them with guilt, not with faith in a second, redemptive life. Jonah, who flees

5. John Cruickshank has an excellent page on this in his *Albert Camus and the literature of revolt* (Oxford, 1959).

from God into the sea in order not to prophesy against the city, becomes in *L'Exil et le Royaume* Jonas the modern artist, fleeing serenely into the compromises of life. When ultimately forced to seek solitude, he produces after long labor a blank canvas, inscribed with the mouse of a word: it could be *solitaire* or *solidaire*. Jonas, like Jean-Baptiste, has refused a desert, which, beginning with *Noces,* plays so great a part in Camus's imagination; and he enters it only to escape the baptismal powers of real human contact. His silence and Jean-Baptiste's fluency reveal the same dilemma: man fleeing from the desert voice of man, from duties of prophecy and judgment.

This parody of religious themes does not imply that religion was originally a false type of communion, any more than Pope's use of the epic style in "Rape of the Lock" implies Homer's dishonesty or Baudelaire's use of religious eloquence Bossuet's. Yet the abyss left by the decay of religion, an abyss in which man should learn to realize himself, is constantly bridged by false religion, by perversions of the original need for communion. The very truth of Christianity, its emphasis on the unity of man, on a universal communion, engenders now its worst enemy. Camus derives from it the tyranny of totalitarian attitudes. "Totality," he writes in *The Rebel,* "is, in effect, nothing other than the ancient dream of unity . . . projected horizontally onto an earth deprived of God." We recall that the landscape of *The Fall* is characterized by its horizontals, and the house of the artist Jonas by mock verticals. In this purely horizontal world only complicity, the secular form of original sin, links men together. "In the universe of trial . . . a race of culprits will endlessly shuffle toward an impossible innocence, under the grim regard of the grand inquisitors."

The Fall is Camus's most savage portrayal of this condition of man. It has behind it Gide's concern with sincerity and Sartre's with authenticity, but its fundamental subject remains distinct from these. "Je n'ai plus d'amis," says Jean-Baptiste, "je n'ai que des complices. En revanche, leur nombre a augmenté, ils sont le genre humain." This is *The Rebel* in a nutshell, and the colloquial "en revanche" may retain here its stronger etymology: Satan is taking the only revenge he can, the revenge of seduction. With *The Fall* a particularly French and self-conscious genre, that of the *human* fable, achieves its maturity. Man is represented not under the mask of animals but under the mask of man, and the moral consists in distinguishing human from too-human. That the serpent has a human voice does not make him man. It is an extreme irony that we must refuse Jean-Baptiste's *de te fabula narratur,* his mirror technique of complicity, and see in him the inhumanity of the too-human. To raise in the reader a strong no, a no which makes him refuse to identify with man at the expense of all men, is Camus's deepest intent as early as *Caligula* and *The Plague,* where we can hardly bear the blindness and provocation involved and become as a child at a puppet show, shouting and jumping at the lurking yet so obvious devil—a very human mephisto-devil, of course.

We have said that the concern with complicity has a clear contemporary basis: it is unavoidable after the Moscow "confessions" of 1936, and the consent of entire peoples to the hegemony of a few men of blood and propaganda. Yet literature anticipated the overt historical facts by almost a century. The eyes of the modern writer are sharpened by the intuitions of a Baudelaire, a Nietzsche, a Dostoevski—the last being certainly the most important of all the sources common to Camus and Malraux. The conception, for instance, of the "judge-penitent" (Jean-Baptiste) is taken from Dostoevski's *Diary of a Writer,*[6] while Camus's spirit of exposition and subornation recalls Baudelaire's sly "Hypocrite lecteur, mon semblable, mon frère!" The nineteenth-century writer had foreseen both man's lack of communion and the tyrannies of new, apparently antireligious modes of communion. What does Camus add, in the theatre of European voices, to the irrevocable nature of the historical fact or the forceful anticipations of it from Dostoevski to Kafka?

6. See the entry for October 1876. Camus happens to quote it in *Le mythe de Sisyphe,* the section on Kirilov, although confusing it with the entry of December 1876. The entry deals with logical suicide, and the soliloquist imagined by Dostoevski argues: "En ma qualité indiscutable de plaignant et de répondant, de juge et d'accusé, je condamne cette nature qui, avec un si impudent sans-gêne, m'a fait naître pour souffrir—je la condamne à être anèantie avec moi" (Camus's text). The substitution of "juge-pénitent" for "juge et accusé" is important in one respect: Dostoevski's reasoner has the courage to kill himself, because he cannot get at nature, but Camus's reasoner condemns himself only to be able to also condemn the world. His nihilism is more total and consequent.

His virtue was to not accept the historical fact as an absolute. He refused, like Malraux, to be on the side of history. This refusal is expressed in several ways—some going back to Malraux, some deeply personal. His distinction, in *The Rebel,* between historical and metaphysical rebellion gains a special persuasiveness in the light of *Man's Fate,* a novel which reveals the personal and metaphysical bases of a "historically inevitable" revolution. Camus defined the metaphysical rebel by the cogito "I rebel, therefore we are—*alone,*" and this *alone* is the precise tragic denouement observed by Malraux. His rebels begin by dreaming of an absolute communion in and through revolutionary ardor. But most end in solitude, watching others die or being taken to die, acting out Pascal's parable on the human condition. The heroes of *Man's Fate,* moreover, are specifically tempted, just before their death, to replace a fraternity based on the unity of man by one based on complicity. Chiang Kai-shek's police chief, to seduce his man, even stages a neat little communion ceremony—coffee, milk, two cups, slices of bread . . .

One line of resistance, therefore, followed by both Camus and Malraux, is to show that revolution has no purely objective or historical necessity but is caused as much by an irreducible metaphysical anguish as by a specific political motive. To try and solve a metaphysical problem by political means is to take the path of the Inquisition, to substitute totality for unity, complicity for communion, history for man. And, history against them, both writers rely on art for an image of man's inviolability: "Art," writes Camus, "teaches us that man cannot be explained by history alone and that he also finds a reason for his existence in the order of nature. For him, the great god Pan is not dead."

But a second line of resistance is Camus's own, a deeply original and unconsummated thought. It already appears in the words just quoted, for Malraux rarely links art to a restitution of the sense of nature.[7] Yet the nature to which Camus refers is a special experience, the mediterranean nature of Cézanne, Picasso, Matisse, and, among poets, of Rilke and Valéry. In it the sun strips the artist of the carnality of hope. "If there are landscapes which are states of soul, they are the most vulgar ones" *(Noces).* What man recovers at the meridian is the vigor to look at himself without

7. The last pages of *Les Noyers de l'Altenburg* are a significant exception.

Maurice Blanchot: Philosopher-Novelist

The seriousness, the suffering, the patience, and the labour of the Negative.

—Hegel

Blanchot's work, says one of his few interpreters, offers no point of approach whatsoever. Today, twenty years after his first novel,[1] he is still the most esoteric writer of contemporary France. There have appeared only three or four essays on his fiction; his novels remain untranslated. This is the more remarkable as Blanchot is also a prolific and well-known critic: beside his three novels, a number of *récits,* and a dyad of short stories, he has published five thick volumes of criticism. But then his criticism has its difficulties too.

One could draw on his criticism to illumine his novels. Such an inquiry, however, though helpful, would also be reductive. I will only use one clue provided by it: Blanchot, as critic, always goes from the work under discussion to the problematic nature of literature. He illumines, therefore, the literary activity in general as well as in this or that text. Literature, for him, is problematic in that it cannot be taken for granted; it is an activity hedged with contradictions, plagued by philosophic doubt, and shadowed by prophecies of obsolescence. This establishes a presumption that his novels will also deal with this area of concern, with the problematic status of literature.

They certainly tease us with the question of whether they are novels, or even literature. The difficulty is not in the prose, which is eloquent, or in the characters and world, which are physically (if not entirely) ordinary. It is, as in Kafka, the atmosphere and action that puzzle, yet all deceptive realism is absent. There is little plot, little characterization, and the ordinariness may be breached by the fantastic. If Blanchot must be attached to a

1. This essay was first published in 1960.

93

tradition, it involves rather than derives from Kafka and goes back to the rebirth of romance and the beginnings of surrealism in the Romantic period. Between Flaubert's *réel écrit* and Blanchot's *irréel récit* there is a distance as great as between Mlle de Scudéry and Flaubert. It has recently been argued that the change from the romance to the novel proper had a distinct philosophical cause; and I will eventually suggest that there is also a philosophical analogue to the apparent reversal of direction, the return of the novel to a romantic or surrealistic form. The German Romantics encouraged it by bringing the novel closer to fairy tale and novella, and the reverse development passes via Novalis, Poe, Nerval, and Baudelaire, to Mallarmé's *Igitur* and the quasi-confessional literature of Gide, Breton, Leiris, and Bataille.

The ranging of Blanchot within a certain tradition is a comforting but hardly illuminating state of affairs. For that tradition and what it intends are still somewhat obscure. It may be that Blanchot, understood, will focus it more sharply, but one cannot begin with it. A last extrinsic resort lies with the interpreters of Blanchot, and these too do not take us beyond our starting-point: that the novels somehow have themselves, or the activity of art, as their subject. Sartre, for example, calls *Aminadab* (1942) a new type of fantasy and secular ghost story. He notes in it an evasive mood of finality and identifies this as the ghost of transcendence floating loose in a world deprived of transcendence.[2] What Sartre means by *evasive finality* I can best show via a short passage from a later novel, *Thomas l'obscur (nouvelle version,* 1950):

> The book rotted on the table. Yet no one moved about the room. His solitude was complete. And yet, as surely as there was no one in the room and even in the world, so surely someone was there, who occupied his sleep, dealt intimately with him, was around him and in him. Naïvely, he sat up, and tried to eye the night . . . but nothing would let him catch this presence as a form or as an other. . . . It was a modu-

2. "*Aminadab* or the Fantastic Considered as a Language," *Literary Essays* (New York, 1957), pp. 56–72. Another interesting critic is Georges Bataille, "Ce monde où nous mourons," *Critique* 13 (1957): 675–84. On Blanchot and Kafka, cf. M. Goth, *Kafka et les lettres françaises* (Paris, 1956), chap. 3.

lation in what did not exist, a different mode of being absent, another void in which he came alive. Now, for certain, someone was coming close, who stood not nowhere and everywhere, but a few feet away, invisible and sure. By a movement which nothing stopped yet which nothing hastened, a power was coming toward him whose contact he could not accept. [pp. 36–38]

I leave aside the question of whether an English or American mind can tolerate even Blanchot's most mature prose. The French have a higher level of sympathy for experimental philosophical fiction, and I shudder to think what F. R. Leavis might say. But we can, on the basis of the later novels, move beyond Sartre's rather professional insight. The subject here is clearly art and its relation to consciousness. The dilemma rendered is the artist's own, that of a mind that seeks to overcome itself from within, to pass into reality rather than into more and more consciousness; and it is through art that it intends to become real rather than more conscious. The evasive, ghostly finality Sartre has noted is projected by the mind while seeking to confront itself as a real body. Something of the agony of its quest to get out of itself without ceasing to be itself is given by this further passage from *Thomas l'obscur,* in which the hero

felt himself bitten or struck, he did not know which, by a thing that seemed to be a word, but resembled rather a gigantic rat, with piercing eyes, pure teeth, an all-powerful animal. In seeing it a few inches from his face, he succumbed to the wish to devour it, to make it the most intimate part of himself. He threw himself on it and, digging his nails into its entrails, tried to make it his own.

The melodious horror of this combat is sustained for another page, at the end of which we realize that Thomas is fighting, like the writer, with the nature of consciousness.

This quest to make the mind real rather than more conscious involves, as the above passage shows, an attempted self-estrangement. The old question of whether the artist is more conscious or less conscious than the thinker is resolved in an interesting manner. Art, Blanchot suggests, is consciousness in search of an unselfconscious form, consciousness estranging itself as in a dream, which is still a dream of itself. In a beautiful phrase he describes the movement of his characters, and perhaps of his novels as a whole, as that of a strange and burning wheel without a centre: "l'étrange roue ardente privée de centre."

I need hardly add that this attempt to transmute consciousness always fails, that success is only its asymptote, and that, according to the image of the wheel, the effort is continually renewed. But there is an inner principle of progression. The writer's failure increases, by a kind of peripety, his burden of consciousness, so that the ghost figure, or the mind thirsting for concreteness, exercises a constantly stronger allure. This ghost figure, just like its avatars, demands flesh and blood; yet being consciousness, being "ce refus d'être substance," it cannot be incarnated and therefore actually haunts some characters to their death. To die may become a ruse for giving a body to its void (see *Thomas l'obscur*, p. 130).

The most puzzling as well as the most imaginative features of Blanchot's novels are linked to this dialectic of emanation, of strange intimacies and intimate estrangements. The distance between any two human beings in his novels is infinite and yet nothing. The magic of chance crystallizes and dissolves relationships. The shifts between familiarity and estrangement, or, occasionally, life and death, are so quick and pervasive that they affect the very nature of the symbols used and put the essence (the ontological status) of words in doubt. Blanchot is difficult to interpret because we can never say that here he reflects the world we know and here an imaginary world. He endows his symbols with a middle and unresolved quality, and he does this in part by a judicious use of the improbable and an only exceptional use of the sheer fantastic. His latest *récits,* in fact, move purely in the realm of the improbable and contain no fantastic incursions or overt breaches of the tenuous realism. The improbable, being a special case of chance, keeps the mind within the story, teasing it with the hope that all details together might solve the mystery, since no single event is quite absurd. But no resolution occurs, and the reader is obliged to take the mystery as an integral rather than resolved part of the whole. And since the whole is simply the novel, he thinks of the latter as the space in which a mystery is revealed, but *as* a mystery.

Sartre has interpreted the improbabilities to which we refer as depicting a revolt of means against ends and so constantly inciting, yet denying, the idea of finality. There is a labyrinth of corridors, doors, staircases, and messages that lead to nothing. Locked doors open, a person summoned to appear is asked why *he* requested the interview, and characters or narrator find themselves returning to the point they started from. But if these and similar improbabilities keep us fascinated, it is because they point obliquely and inexhaustively to a specific mystery. They could be explained by positing an all-pervasive forgetfulness. And this seems to be a part of the general pattern of self-estrangement. Blanchot's personae never walk the straight line between two points—they seem imbued, physically and mentally, with a spirit of oblivion—and his novels strike us as being the most un-Aristotelian ever written: they are all *middle*. To be in Blanchot's world is to err: to follow something, to be involved in a maze of words or passageways, to encounter chance openings, to be attracted and distracted continually, to forget to remember, to remember to forget.

With this we come to our first substantive philosophical link. Blanchot's emphasis on forgetfulness harmonizes with what Heidegger calls the mystery of oblivion. Heidegger himself has sources in Hegel and the Romantic period, and it is quite possible that Blanchot assimilates Heidegger through the perspective of a common literary tradition reaching from the German Romantics to the French Symbolists and Rilke. The mystery of oblivion is described by Heidegger as follows.[3] Historical existence, or man's attempt to live fully in the here and now, would not be possible without an intrinsic oblivion on his part. He learns about the earth by being practical, by attending to each

3. My summary is drawn primarily from "On the Essence of Truth" (1943), "What is Metaphysics" (1929 and 1943), and the various essays on Hölderlin published between 1937 and 1943. I present Heidegger's thought as homogeneous, but this is a simplification: the writings on which I draw postdate *Sein und Zeit,* and there is evidence that both in them and again in recent years Heidegger has modified certain of his views. Some concepts mentioned below, e.g., error, have an acknowledged source in Nietzsche and other Romantics and post-Romantics. For Blanchot's own summary of Heidegger's thought, and in relation to Hegel's, see esp. *L'Espace littéraire* (Paris, 1955), pp. 263 ff.

thing as it appears necessary or interesting to him. Yet to do this he must forget the possible wholeness of things and rest content to substitute continually the part for the whole or being for Being. But how, asks Heidegger, can he forget the whole? There must be, first of all, a dissimulation in Being itself, one that offers him the possibility of mistaking the part for the whole. The part comes to be or appear only in so far as the whole sets it off, but invisibly, without overshadowing. Man's turning toward the part or anything apparently open to him (Heidegger plays on the Greek for *truth,* a word cognate with *unhidden)* means a turning away from the whole; yet he is attracted to the part precisely because it also promises a whole, albeit a different one: the earth in its fullness. Thus the direct search for wholeness (the metaphysical quest) is displaced by a historical appropriation of the earth (the existential quest) and by means of a movement which Heidegger calls "error," because it is an erring, a wandering from part to part, and because it is erroneous, the mistaking of being for Being.

But beside this dissimulation of the whole there must also be a dissemblance of the dissimulation. A mere veiling of the essence of things would only spur us to pierce the veil, to become mystics rather than existentialists. To accept our human nature we must become freely blind and dissemble the original dissimulation. And when our eyes are occasionally opened, it is to the existence of dissimulation rather than to Being itself. The mystery of oblivion is an oblivion of mystery, and this alone enables us to live humanly and dynamically and to keep making errors and so gradually to explore and possess the earth.

It will already be clear that Heidegger is giving a very subtle version of Plato's mythically expressed theory of reminiscence, but shifting the emphasis to an involved process of discovery and forgetfulness. Plato's myth is revived in all its potency in the Romantic period; there is hardly a great writer, from Novalis to De Quincey, who does not explore both the existential and metaphysical implications of—shall we say—sleep. I mention this because, though I think Blanchot is indebted to Heidegger, his understanding of the latter's philosophy is likely to have been mediated by a larger and predominantly literary tradition. If there is any one trait that unifies literary movements since the Romantic period, it is their quest for an adequate theory of unconsciousness or creative self-oblivion.

Blanchot certainly gives Heidegger's concepts a rather exact presence. The oblivion that besets his characters alienates them from various finalities, intensifies their erring motion, and brings them into a freer contact with life, a contact having the surprise, sharpness, and inconsequence of chance. Yet his novels' endless estrangement of every final term raises a double nostalgia which Heidegger also describes: a nostalgia for the concrete, the here and now, and for something greater than every here and now. The first, a tenacious holding on to the part as if it were the whole, Heidegger names insistence (in contrast to existence); and the second is the revived metaphysical desire for the vision of the whole. Heidegger shows, however, that the latter cannot be attained other than by first passing through and standing outside everything; or projecting, as he also expresses it, into Nothing. Human life in its freedom is a transcendence toward Being, but always as this Nothing, this eclipsed or veiled form. Certain passages in Blanchot seem to translate Heidegger's dialectic of finitude almost word for word:

> I saw immediately [says the narrator in *Celui qui ne m'accompagnait pas*] that I must stay in this place. Perhaps the insight did not teach me anything I had not known. Perhaps in showing me the only point by which I could hold to something real, it screwed the anxiety of the void tighter on me, as if, these words being the only ones I could live in, I had felt them slipping away, as if they were the last abode from which I could control this errant coming and going ['le va-et-vient errant']. I understood well enough, or seemed to understand, why I had to take root here. But, here, where was I? Why near him? Why behind everything I said and he said was there this word: 'Surely everything, where we are, is dissembling?' I heard and did not hear; it was beyond being understood. [pp. 98–99]

If the realistic novel puts man wholly into a physical setting, then the "irrealistic" novel may be said to put him wholly into Nothing. A good part of the action of the *récit* quoted above is the narrator's attempt to describe his physical setting and his inability to do so. The narrator cannot embody himself. In *Thomas l'obscur*, similarly, Thomas seeks various embodiments, and in vain. The sea and earth reject him, and one is reminded of the Old Man in Chaucer's "Pardoner's Tale" who knocks on the gate of his mother earth, seeking death, imploring her to let him in. Yet Blanchot's value is not in the transcription, however imaginative, of a philosophy such as Heidegger's. This would make his novels a kind of allegory, which they are not. What is perhaps hard to understand is that they participate in the dilemma they describe. They are a passion imitating an action. Blanchot does not represent Nothing, or the dissimulation of Being as dissimulation. He endures it, and fiction is his durance. In one of the *récits* this is given literal form by the author moving self-divided through his pages, seeking to attain unity of Being yet questioning the symbols that promise it. But all his novels create a void rather than a world, an *espace littéraire* as ontologically equivocal as mind itself and which neither reader, author, nor characters can cross to reach Being. What Ortega y Gasset said of Proust can be applied, with a slight though important change, to Blanchot: "He stands as the inventor of a new distance between symbols and ourselves."

But how, exactly, do Blanchot's novels participate in what he calls, in *La Part du feu*, "the realization by literature of its unreality" (p. 306)? Let us consider shortly certain conventional carriers of meanings, such as book, genre, character, and plot. It will be seen that Blanchot uses these to criticize the very realism from which they spring and which, as part of literature, they must retain.

A book is a portable and condensed experience. For Blanchot it involves the questioning of the idea that portable and condensed experiences are possible: the *œuvre* of an artist is the path he takes to realize his *désœuvrement* (see *Le Livre à venir*, p. 253). It is true that Blanchot's books are separate entities, individualized by title. Yet he has written two versions of *Thomas l'obscur* (1941 and 1950), and in a note prefacing the second version he says that a work has an infinity of possible variants. This multiplication (by the modern painter also) of sketches and states, though perhaps linked to Balzac's retake of characters, to the *roman-fleuve* and devices of perspective, may also have an opposite intent. The difference turns on whether the mimetic power of the artist is strengthened or questioned. Balzac's novels add up, they increase the depth and realness of his world, but Blanchot's novels stand in an abstractive relation to one another. What the second *Thomas l'obscur* removes from the first is analogous though not identical to what Cézanne subtracts from Delacroix. Rather than a literary and exotic realism Blanchot purges a literary and exotic irrealism, or, to give it the more popular name, surrealism. He is concerned only with the unreality in reality itself.

That is also why Blanchot uses the *récit,* a form strongly associated with Gide. The *récit* is a first-person confessional narrative, a kind of dramatic monologue in prose, and through it Blanchot attacks the Achilles' heel of realism, the notion of the sincere and even of the authorial "I." Like the soul, the I is not a simple substance. In the case of the alienated man, who suffers from the "disease of consciousness" (Dostoevski), the I is one of many faces, and at most a dialectical component of the whole man. "The whole history of fiction since Arnim," writes Breton, pointing once more to the Romantic origins, "is that of liberties taken with the idea of 'I am.'" Blanchot, however, is less interested in personality as such than in the personality of words, their deceptive dual character of veil and revelation. His *récits* in their essence are simply (or not so simply) a critique of word notions that at once motivate and seduce the artist: the *je,* the *ici,* the *maintenant,* the *nous,* the *fin.* To resist them is to restore the space (between the artist and words, between him and the world) which art seems expressly created to deny.

To illustrate this questioning and distancing power of Blanchot's I choose a passage from *Celui qui ne m'accompagnait pas* (1953), similar in some respects to the one quoted previously from this book. The narrator is reflecting, as he does throughout, on the words of an interlocutor, who has no presence except through cryptic replies, echoing silences:

> It is true that from his mysterious word of encouragement I could draw another persuasive idea, namely, that I need not fear a false approach, the itineraries of error; I did not have one way, I had all, and this should have served to put me on my way with exceptional confidence. "All! but on condition

that I have time enough, all the time I can bear." He did not demur, for of course the essence of a way is to furnish a short-cut across "time"; it was this short-cut I sought, with the unreasonable idea that I should find thereby not a continued length of wayfaring but the shortest interval, the soul of brevity, to the point that on taking the first steps, it seemed to me, refusing to go further, that I had the right to tell myself: "This is where I stand, this is what I'll stick to," and to him this is what I said with increased firmness: "This is where I stand, this is what I'll stick to," which he happened to answer with a kind of élan and without my being able to resent it: "But you have all the time you want!" [pp. 16–17]

This is part of a development still hinging on the first line of the book, "I tried, this time, to approach him directly"; and practically everything in the sentence—the I, the him, the notions of time, way, and directness—are questioned by the *récit,* which moves forward by the force of its questions. The opening (to which we shall return later) expresses an attempt at immediacy, and, as in Kafka, the narrative ironically unfolds in the space that shows immediate contacts to be impossible, though the hope for them cannot die. But while Kafka draws us into his world, giving it circumstantial and symbolic flesh, Blanchot uses fictional counters that are as literal as words, and as abstract. Though we ask, Who is the narrator? Who is his companion? When does it happen? we never reach more than the conclusion that the narrator is the one who narrates, his companion someone inseparable from the act of narration, time and space simply that of narration itself. As such everything remains unreal or virtual, and the theme itself points to the perplexity of living in such a condition, again called error. It is, in fact, a comedy of errors, but one that draws us into it insidiously. Though the novel, by its inherently negative progress, leaves us with as little at the end as we started with, it does make the *void* of thought visible as the *space* of art—a space, of course, anything but spacious; rather an effort of distance, as if the writer were constantly in danger of being tricked by the nature of words or crushed by some endless automatic process of mind murmur, of mental conjunction.

To suggest the unreality of his characters—who are like the

space they inhabit—Blanchot sometimes uses a word with a strong neoplatonic flavour. They are said to lose *resemblance:* "He saw them lose under his eyes all resemblance, manifesting a small wound on their foreheads whence their faces escaped" (*Thomas l'obscur,* p. 57). It is as if the idea, whose image they are, suddenly disappears. The characters lose their transcendence, are unable to reach an *au-delà,* whether this is nature, supernature, or symbolic existence. Shades doomed not to rest, they wander through the author's pages as if neither his nor any world would receive them. But they gain therefore a caricature of immortality. They cannot die. Thomas the Obscure digs his own grave and hangs a stone about his neck as if to drown himself in the earth. Yet he is forced to "exist," to stand outside himself till the end of the novel.

It would be untrue, however, to say that Blanchot's characters exist only in art; at least they do not "live" in art any more than in reality. They have no inn to live in; they are literally outsiders. They are shown not as alive but rather as deathless, or as afraid of being deathless and so seeking death. I hope to find a fuller explanation for this later; here I can only say that art for Blanchot is intrinsically linked to the quest for and impossibility of realizing the self via symbols. What does not have real body, and yet is, must be a species of ghost. "The symbol," he writes in *La Part du feu,* "has no meaning . . . it is not even the embodied meaning of a truth otherwise inaccessible, it surpasses every truth and meaning, and what it gives us is this very transcendence which it seizes and makes felt in a fictional work, whose theme is the impossibility of fiction to realize itself" (p. 86).

In following through, finally, the plot or action of one of these ghostly novels, we come upon a second philosophical link, this time primarily with Hegel. If my description of Blanchot's theme is correct, and he shows consciousness seeking to be real rather than conscious (and failing in this), we already have a Hegelian *donnée.* For that the mind should need to realize itself shows it is estranged from reality, and this estrangement is then seen to be in its very mode of existence: it desires to have itself external or opposite or invested with reality. The starting point, therefore, seems to be what Hegel calls the unhappy consciousness (which craves complete consciousness of reality and cannot attain it) or the self-estranged consciousness (whose true self seems split or

103

estranged as if of necessity).[4] Yet we have said that the novels are problematic and have themselves or the activity of art as their subject rather than consciousness per se. The distinction may seem slight but can now be explored further. It is of some importance to determine exactly what the relation of art to consciousness may be. For religion, according to Hegel, shows a higher state of consciousness than art, and philosophy the highest. The great challenge, in fact, to the autonomy of literature, and hence the real enemy to any *rapprochement* between philosophy and art, is Hegel's prediction of the end of art. Only if the two activities are thought co-substantial is the true dignity of either assured. I will now seek to show that Blanchot wants to negate this prediction of obsolescence, that his *récits* are conceived as an answer to it.

Hegel, though he considers it necessary for the mind to suffer a long history of self-estrangement, yet insists that progress can be made which affects not only the quantity but also the quality of consciousness, and that the philosopher, coming toward the end of this history, will conceive the real as the rational and so overcome the felt difference between the real world and the world of the mind. Art, however, is a product not of the philosophical but rather of the phenomenological imagination: it is an exile form of consciousness and cannot realize its truth. Blanchot, accepting this characterization of art, will argue that art must, if necessary, work against the grain of history. Even should the real approach the ideal, art must remain unreal. It is inherently a project of self-alienation.

With this in mind, let us trace the action of *Celui qui ne m'accompagnait pas*. Here, by a tour de force as amazing as it is profound, Blanchot exhibits the artist projecting art in our presence. We actually see the narrative evolving as a debate, dialectical in form, between the narrator and his estranged self. The narrator tries to overcome the distance between them or to draw from it a third and impersonal person, the unselfconscious unity of both. But we soon learn that neither the self nor its need for an opposing self can be surpassed: that art remains an impossible project, aiming at the "concrete universal," aiming at true unselfconsciousness, yet always preventing its own success.

4. See *Phenomenology of Mind,* trans. J. B. Baillie, 2nd ed. (1949), pp. 241 ff., 507 ff.

How does Blanchot proceed? He enlists, first of all, the support of the greatest apostle against Hegel, Sören Kierkegaard. The unexplicit motive power behind the narrator, as behind all of Blanchot's characters, is *despair* in Kierkgaard's definition: the uncertainty, increasing with every increase of consciousness, that one has a true self. "The despairing man," says Kierkegaard (in *The Sickness unto Death),* "cannot die; no more than 'the dagger can slay thoughts' can despair consume the eternal thing, the self, which is the ground of despair, whose worm dieth not, and whose fire is not quenched." Blanchot's people are unable to die for this reason. And for the same reason they are unable to be born or reborn into life; they suffer an endless purgatorial state, a death-in-life identifiable with the alienated consciousness. Their quest for a true self must go through self-estrangement, and this increases their uncertainty in an inviolable self. Hegel's Philosopher is anathema to Kierkegaard and a stumbling block to Blanchot because he is inviolably self-assured. If, as Blanchot says, "the void is never void enough" *(Le dernier homme* [1957], p. 164), who can plumb self-estrangement deeply enough to arrive either at pure reality or pure self? The Philosopher, were he possible, would be the last man.[5]

In *Celui* the desired self becomes, specifically, the self of the Writer. The latter does not wish to die, only to write. To be a writer—to be that self—is the impossibility he seeks to realize by means of the *récit.* Adopting, perhaps, another idea of Kierkegaard's—that to break an enchantment (here of words) one has to retrace one's path exactly and at every error begin again—Blanchot undoes the spell of language in order to be able to write. With shuddering naïveté, with an eternal *ressassement,* he tries to step backward from words to the reality of the word. But desiring to

5. See *Le dernier homme* (1957). The "last man" is Hegel's Philosopher. Blanchot conceives of him as having no existence, i.e., no Being-for-others, which makes him, paradoxically, the central enigma for the other two characters of the novel—the writer or narrator and a young woman. The latter moves from the sphere of the narrator toward the last man, perhaps because her naïve realism, her desire to die intact at the strongest point, sorts better with the Philosopher (who seems to link the realms of death and life) than with the Artist (who tries to remain outside both). Cf. G. Bataille, *L'Expérience intérieure* (Paris, 1943), pp. 48 ff.

write, he is already writing, and falls under the spell he would escape from.

The *récit* begins with the narrator turning toward an unnamed "other." He complains, saying that he is at the end of his tether, that he wants to write and is afraid to write, that through writing he becomes so interested in the Other that he stands in danger of losing himself. In short, he wants to resolve a situation in which he is neither himself nor not himself. But the Other, whom he wants to appeal to directly and who is very clearly a redeemer-figure, created to make word or thought flesh, obliges the narrator to linger in uncertainty, to stay in the equivocal space of fiction and be (like his own characters) neither quite living nor quite dead.

Therefore, in one sense, art becomes the enemy of the artist and denies him the realization he desires. The Other, or Persona, is only negatively transcendent ("celui qui *ne* m'accompagnait *pas"*). Though the writer wants to be led into an absolute, this other self shows a curious interest in real things, asking no more of the writer than to stay in his room and describe it. But he feels this is impossible (he does not want to make the real Words but the Word real?), becomes curiously forgetful, moves nervously about (as in the earlier novels of mistaken rooms and identities, false entries, strange corridors), and also keeps glimpsing someone in the room or just behind the window. This new ghostly Other is probably the fictional double on the point of passing from a state of negative to that of real transcendence, as the writer is tempted to pass from the first person *(Je)* to the third person *(Il)* and thus into full self-estrangement ("l'alibi du Il indifférent" [*Le Livre à venir,* p. 199]). This, of course, is a necessary movement, if he is to find that original impersonal Word he seeks. Yet, by various means, the double (the second person) prevents him from losing touch with himself and passing totally into a symbol. The tension of relationship, of what Martin Buber calls the I-Thou situation, is maintained. As the narrator is asked to describe the face of this third person, the very effort of visualization makes him aware how much the figure may still depend on him. He cannot, as a writer, attain Being, only being-for-another (himself); and this difficulty of visualizing a face which has no resemblance or a word which has no relation will haunt him even more in *Le dernier homme:* "Face of Nothingness, perhaps. That is why you [the Other?] must watch over this empty space to preserve it, as I must watch to alter it . . . " (p. 115).

The *récit,* or art itself, is simply keeping this space open. It is using the act of writing to invent forms and situations that maintain the writer in the negative despite the strongest contrary pressure. For the *récit* is, at the same time, the writer's movement toward the reality of the double, his desire to identify. And though the Other repeats, "I can't do anything for you," he does admit being linked to the writer through writing ("par les *écrits").* The essential, inherent temptation is to desert the labor of the negative by going over into one's symbols. The artist posits a transcendence (metamorphosis) of this kind, but his art exists in order to resist him.

Art, therefore, cannot succeed in making the mind real rather than more conscious. A tension in its very nature prevents this. But it discloses the strength of the desire for a reality beyond consciousness. And in Blanchot's other novels the possibility of really transcending consciousness is expressed as follows. There is generally one character (a woman) who manages to die, while all others are deprived of death. The woman, by an act of will, by a metaphysical *Liebestod,* aims at a live transcendence: she seeks to pass whole from life to death, and there is, Blanchot suggests, one chance, only one, of doing so. Perhaps the artist in the space of his art also approaches that one chance of transcendence. Perhaps he can truly realize his other self and draw his mind from Consciousness into Being. It is this hope, however slender, however mystical, which moves him to write. If he fails, like Orpheus, it is because he does not dwell patiently enough in the space of alienation and so cannot "convert the negative into Being."[6]

But most of Blanchot's characters, like Kierkegaard's despairing men, are sick unto death yet deprived of the ability to die. Their sickness is consciousness. They suffer an alienation from life within life, and the milieu in which they look for death or else suffer their death-in-life is related to various ancient and modern hells—to purgatory, the Waste Land, the T.B. Mountain, and the

6. *Phenomenology,* p. 93. For the inversion of the Orpheus myth, see esp. *L'Arrêt de mort,* pp. 40–60, and *Thomas l'obscur,* pp. 112 ff.: "Anne thought of crossing over to death alive."

House of the Dead. (The milieu of *Le dernier homme* is indubitably a sanatorium.) It is not surprising, therefore, that Blanchot's plots retain features of the prototype of the Quest, but how it begins and what it seeks are peculiar. The mind-errant, having sought life and found death-in-life, now desires an authentic death. The Faustian mind, also begins with a perception of death-in-life (in Hegelian terms, with self-consciousness or thought) and proceeds ironically by a wager against life, although this wager dialectically affirms the thing it denies. Among similar ancestors of Blanchot's characters are the many wandering Jews and Mariners of the nineteenth century, figures deathless (immortally mortal) like the Sybil of Cumae, Blanchot's earliest complete story, "L'Idylle," has as its central figure that *étranger* who is the modern equivalent of Mariner, Wanderer, or Faust—in short, a type of the alienated mind.[7]

Our study of Blanchot has led us to a concept of man and a concept of art. His novels evoke a curious middle world, or rather middle void. The noble assumption of the Renaissance, that man is a late creation standing between heaven and earth and sharing the attributes of both orders, is held to but modified. Man is not a mixed mode, though he has the seeds of all life in himself, but one who keeps the realms apart, who avoids the contamination of both earth and heaven. Art helps him to find a "between" and to preserve it as the sphere of his liberty. This is a new and hard concept of mediation, which defines man purely by the quality of the void in him, and the artist by a resistance to symbols, human or divine, that would fill this void. Standing in the midst of things, and specifically in the midst of the treachery of words, the artist bears the curse of mediacy.[8]

7. "L'Idylle" bears direct traces, in the names of some of its characters, of Dostoevski's *Memoirs from the House of the Dead*. On death and deathlessness, see also "L'Œuvre et l'espace de la mort" in *L'Espace littéraire,* esp. pp. 161 ff. Blanchot is fully acquainted with Rilke, Broch, Beckett, and others.

8. For a complete exposition of the idea, see the commentary on Hölderlin (in Blanchot, *L'Espace littéraire,* pp. 283–92) which is deeply indebted to Heidegger. The latter has coined the term *Zwischenbereich* (mesocosm rather than microcosm!) to indicate the "between" status of man. I borrow the phrase "the curse of mediacy" from Ernst Cassirer, who says that language "harbors the curse of mediacy and is bound to obscure what it seeks to reveal" (*Language and Myth* [1925; trans. 1946]).

Blanchot, moreover, relates art to the mind's need or capacity for self-estrangement. Art is not consciousness per se, but rather its antidote, evolved from within consciousness itself. And though this view has been gained by bringing to bear on Blanchot a particular philosophic tradition, the latter is only one of many having a common base in Romanticism. The nineteenth century yields a profusion of anti–self-consciousness theories. But none, I think, has been quite so influential or provided a better foundation for understanding art generically. In England the nearest approach to a similarly adequate theory is Yeats's concept of the mask, the persona theory of Pound, and the impersonality theory of Eliot. American criticism has added the idea of the poem as an ironic structure. These have some truth and belong to a distinctive branch of inquiry—call it problematics—which should be as important as thematics or the history of literary ideas and forms. To study the problematics of art would be to consider each work as standing in a dialectical relation to consciousness and a critical relation to the whole activity of art.[9]

Hegel's prophecy of the end of art, like Plato's older grouse, in no way originates these special relations. But it has made critic and artist more attentive to them, above all in France where Marxism gives Hegel a redoubled voice. French critics tend to be overly philosophical: they have to fight Marxism on its own ground, to preserve art by a philosophy of art. In the meantime, of course, the cure being worse than the disease, literature may itself succumb to the philosophical habit. But perhaps it will suffer no more in this case than it did, for example, from neoplatonism. Blanchot's own curious strength is that his *récits* are neither philosophy nor straight fiction but an autonomous middle form. In a very tentative way his work is like the organon Schiller called for, one that would mediate between philosophy

9. Charles Feidelson (*Symbolism and American Literature* [Chicago, 1953]) was, I believe, the first to point out the distinctively problematic ("not merely in the sense in which every literary symbol is indeterminate, but more specifically in the sense that its characteristic subject is its own equivocal method") nature of a nineteenth-century American tradition, comparable in this to the French Symbolists. Other relevant studies are Erich Heller's treatment of the "ontological mystery" in *The Disinherited Mind* (New York, 1957), and Paul de Man's questioning of the "incarnationist" assumption in modern English and American criticism: "Impasse de la critique formaliste," *Critique* 12 (1956): 483–500.

and art. He who knows fiction will be led by it to consider philosophy, and vice versa; and this suggests that there is a new genre, or even type of literature, in the making. Yet Blanchot, it must be admitted, is not uniformly successful as an artist; sometimes, in fact, I have a sinking feeling that a few verses from Rilke or from Valéry express all he has to say. But this feeling, in turn, may show that Blanchot has taught me to read more strongly and relevantly such lines as Rilke's description of poetry—"Ein Hauch um nichts. Ein Wehn im Gott. Ein Wind"—or Valéry's many beautiful renderings of the sense of self-estrangement— "Qui pleure là, sinon le vent simple, à cette heure/Seule avec diamants extrêmes? . . . Mais qui pleure,/Si proche de moi-même au moment de pleurer?" Blanchot's *récits,* and especially the latest ones, are sombre and bewitching works, not without tedium, but teasing us vigorously out of thought.

Milton's Counterplot

Milton's description of the building of Pandemonium ends with a reference to the architect, Mammon, also known to the ancient world as Mulciber:

> and how he fell
> From Heav'n, they fabl'd, thrown by angry *Jove*
> Sheer o'er the Crystal Battlements: from Morn
> To Noon he fell, from Noon to dewy Eve,
> A Summer's day; and with the setting Sun
> Dropt from the Zenith like a falling Star,
> On *Lemnos* th'Ægæan Isle.
>
> [*Paradise Lost* 1. 740–46]

These verses stand out from a brilliant text as still more brilliant or emerge from this text, which repeats on several levels the theme of quick or erring or mock activity, marked by a strange mood of calm, as if the narrative's burning wheel had suddenly disclosed a jeweled bearing. Their subject is a fall, and it has been suggested that Milton's imagination was caught by the anticipation in the Mulciber story of a myth which stands at the center of his epic. Why the "caught" imagination should respond with a pastoral image, evoking a fall gradual and cool like the dying of a summer's day and the sudden, no less aesthetically distant, dropping down of the star, is not explained. One recalls, without difficulty, similar moments of relief or distancing, especially in the cosmic fret of the first books: the comparison of angel forms lying entranced on the inflamed sea with autumnal leaves on Vallombrosa's shady brooks; or the simile of springtime bees and of the dreaming peasant at the end of Book 1; or the applause following Mammon's speech in Book 2, likened to lulling if hoarse cadence of winds after a storm; or even the appearance to Satan of the world, when he has crossed Chaos and arrives with torn tackle in full view of this golden-chained star of smallest magnitude.

113

The evident purpose of the Mulciber story is to help prick inflated Pandemonium and, together with the lines that follow, to emphasize that Mammon's building is as shaky as its architect. This fits in well with the plot of the first two books, a description of the satanic host's effort to build on hell. But the verses on Mulciber also disclose, through their almost decorative character, a second plot, simultaneously expressed with the first, which may be called the counterplot. Its hidden presence is responsible for the contrapuntal effects of the inserted fable.

The reader will not fail to recognize in Milton's account of the progress of Mulciber's fall the parody of a biblical rhythm: "And the evening and the morning were the (first) day." The thought of creation is present to Milton, somehow associated with this fall. Moreover, the picture of angry Jove blends with and gives way to that of *crystal* battlements and the imperturbability of the summer's day through which the angel drops:

> from Morn
> To Noon he fell, from Noon to dewy Eve,
> A Summer's day:

while in the last part of his descent an image of splendor and effortlessness outshines that of anger or ignominy:

> and with the setting Sun
> Dropt from the Zenith like a falling Star.

In context, of course, this depiction is condemned as mere fabling, and there is nothing splendid or aloof in the way Milton retells the story:

> thus they relate,
> Erring; for he with his rebellious rout
> Fell long before; nor aught avail'd him now
> To have built in Heav'n high Tow'rs; nor did he scape
> By all his Engines, but was headlong sent
> With his industrious crew to build in hell.

> [1.746–51]

Yet for a moment, while moving in the charmed land of pagan fable, away from the more literal truth in which he seeks supremacy over all fable, Milton reveals the overwhelming if not autonomous drive of his imagination. Mulciber draws to himself a rhythm reminiscent of the account of the world's creation, and his story suggests both God and the creation undisturbed (Crystal Battlements . . . dewy Eve) by a fall which is said to occur later than the creation yet actually preceded it. Here, surely, is a primary instance of Milton's automatically involving the idea of creation with that of the Fall. But further, and more fundamental, is the feeling of the text that God's anger is not anger at all but calm prescience, which sees that no fall will ultimately disturb the creation, whether Mulciber's fabled or Satan's real or Adam's universal fall.

Milton's feeling for this divine imperturbability, for God's omnipotent knowledge that the creation will outlive death and sin, when expressed in such an indirect manner, may be characterized as the counterplot. For it does not often work on the reader as an independent theme or subplot but lodges in the vital parts of the overt action, emerging from it like good from evil. The root feeling (if *feeling* is the proper word) for imperturbable providence radiates from many levels of the text. It has been given numerous interpretations in the history of criticism, the best perhaps, though impressionistic, by Coleridge: "Milton is the deity of prescience: he stands *ab extra* and drives a fiery chariot and four, making the horses feel the iron curb which holds them in." Satan's fixed mind and high disdain are perverted reflectors of this same cold passion, but doomed to perish in the restlessness of hell and its compulsive gospel of the community of damnation. So deep-working is this spirit of the "glassy, cool, translucent wave," already invoked in *Comus,* that other poets find it hard to resist it and, like Wordsworth, seek to attain similar virtuosity in expressing "central peace, subsisting at the heart/Of endless agitation." Milton's control is such that, even in the first dramatic account of Satan's expulsion, he makes the steady flame of God's act predominate over the theme of effort, anger, and vengefulness: in the following verses "Ethereal Sky" corresponds to the "Crystal Battlements" of Mulciber's fall, and the image of a projectile powerfully but steadily thrust forth (evoked in part by the immediate duplication of stress, letter and rhythmic patterns) recreates the imperturbability of that other, summer space:

115

> Him the Almighty Power
> Hurl'd headlong flaming from th'Ethereal Sky
> With hideous ruin and combustion down
> To bottomless perdition, there to dwell
> In Adamantine Chains and penal Fire...
>
> [1.44–48]

One of the major means of realizing the counterplot is the simile. Throughout *Paradise Lost,* and eminently in the first two books, Milton has to bring the terrible sublime home to the reader's imagination. It would appear that he can only do this by analogy. Yet Milton rarely uses straight analogy, in which the observer and observed remain, relative to each other, on the same plane. Indeed, his finest effects employ magnifying and diminishing similes. Satan's shield, for example, is described as hanging on his shoulder like the moon, viewed through Galileo's telescope from Fiesole or in Valdarno (1.284–91). The rich, elaborate pattern of such similes has often been noted and variously explained. Certain details, however, may be reconsidered.

The similes, first of all, not only magnify or diminish the doings in hell but invariably put them at a distance. Just as the Tuscan artist sees the moon through his telescope, so the artist of *Paradise Lost* shows hell at considerable remove, through a medium which, while it clarifies, also intervenes between reader and object. Milton varies points of view, shifting in space and time so skillfully that our sense of the reality of hell, of its power vis-à-vis man or God, never remains secure. Spirits, we know, can assume any shape they please; and Milton, like Spenser, uses this imaginative axiom to destroy the idea of the simple location of good and evil in the spiritual combat. But despite the insecurity, the abyss momentarily glimpsed under simple events, Milton's main effort in the first books is to make us believe in Satan as a real and terrible agent, yet never as an irresistible power. No doubt at all of Satan's influence: his success is writ large in religious history, which may also be one reason for the epic enumeration of demonic names and place names in Book 1. Nevertheless, even as we are closest to Satan, presented with the hottest view of hell's present and future appeal, all suggestion of irresistible influence must be expunged if Milton's two means of divine justification—

man's free will and God's foreknowledge of the creation's triumph —are to win consent.

These two dominant concepts, expressed through the counterplot, shed a calm and often cold radiance over all of *Paradise Lost,* issuing equally from the heart of faith and the center of self-determination. The similes must persuade us that man was and is "sufficient to have stood, though free to fall" (3.99): that his reason and will, however fiercely tempted and besieged, stand on a pinnacle as firm and precarious as that on which the Christ of *Paradise Regained* (4.541 ff) suffers his last, greatest, archetypal temptation. They must show the persistence, in the depth of danger, passion, or evil, of imperturbable reason, of a power working ab extra.

This the similes accomplish in several ways. They are, for example, marked by an emphasis on place names. It is the *Tuscan* artist who views the moon (Satan's shield) from the top of *Fiesole* or in *Valdarno* through his optic glass, while he searches for new Lands, Rivers, Mountains on the spotty globe. Do not the place names serve to anchor this observer and set him off from the vastness and vagueness of hell, its unnamed and restless geography, as well as from his attempt to leave the earth and rise by science above the lunar world? A recital of names is, of course, not reassuring of itself: no comfort accrues in hearing Moloch associated with *Rabba, Argob, Basan, Arnon,* or sinful Solomon with *Hinnom, Tophet, Gehenna* (1.397–405). The point is that these places were once neutral, innocent of bloody or holy associations; it is man who has made them what they are, made the proper name a fearful or a hopeful sign (cf. 11.836–39). Will *Valdarno* and *Fiesole* become such bywords as *Tophet* and *Gehenna?* At the moment they are still hieroglyphs, words whose ultimate meaning is in the balance. They suggest the inviolate shelter of the created world rather than the incursions of a demonic world. Yet we sense that, if Galileo uses the shelter and Ark of this world to dream of other worlds, paying optical rites to the moon, Fiesole, Valdarno, even Vallombrosa may yield to the tug of a demonic interpretation and soon become a part of hell's unprotected marl.

Though the figure of the observer ab extra is striking in Milton's evocation of Galileo, it becomes more subtly patent in a simile

117

a few lines further on which tells how the angel forms lay entranced on hell's inflamed sea

> Thick as Autumnal Leaves that strow the Brooks
> In *Vallombrosa,* where th'Etrurian shades
> High overarch't imbow'r; or scatter'd sedge
> Afloat, when with fierce winds *Orion* arm'd
> Hath vext the Red-Sea Coast, whose waves o'erthrew
> *Busiris* and his *Memphian* Chivalry,
> While with perfidious hatred they pursu'd
> The sojourners of *Goshen,* who beheld
> From the safe shore thir floating Carcasses
> And broken Chariot Wheels . . .

[1.302–11]

A finer modulation of aesthetic distance can hardly be found: we
start at the point of maximum contrast, with the angels prostrate
on the lake, in a region "vaulted with fire" (298), viewed as leaves
fallen seasonally on a sheltered brook vaulted by shade; go next
to the image of seaweed scattered by storm; and finally, without
break of focus, see the Israelites watching "from the safe shore"
the floating bodies and parts of their pursuers. And, as in music,
where one theme fades, another emerges to its place; while the
image of calm and natural death changes to that of violent and
supernatural destruction, the figure of the observer ab extra becomes explicit, substituting for the original glimpse of inviolable
peace.

Could the counterplot be clearer? A simile intended to sharpen
our view of the innumerable stunned host of hell, just before it
is roused by Satan, at the same time sharpens our sense of the
imperturbable order of the creation, of the coming storm, and of
the survival of man through providence and his safe-shored will.
Satan, standing clear of the rout, prepares to vex his legions to
new evil:

> on the Beach
> Of that inflamed Sea, he stood and call'd
> His Legions, Angel Forms, who lay intrans't
> Thick as Autumnal Leaves . . .

but the scenes the poet himself calls up mimic hell's defeat before
Satan's voice is fully heard, and whatever sought to destroy the
calm of autumnal leaves lies lifeless as scattered sedge. The con-

tinuity of the similes hinges on the middle image of Orion, which sketches both Satan's power to rouse the fallen host and God's power to scatter and destroy it. In this plot counterplot the hand of Satan is not ultimately distinguishable from the will of God.

A further instance, more complex still, is found at the end of Book 1. Milton compares the host gathered in the gates of Pandemonium to bees at springtime (1.768 ff). The wonder of this incongruity has been preserved by many explanations. It is clearly a simile which, like others we have adduced, diminishes hell while it magnifies creation. The bees are fruitful, and their existence in the teeth of Satan drowns out the sonorous hiss of hell. Their "straw-built Citadel" will survive "bossy" Pandemonium. As Dr. Johnson kicking the stone kicks all excessive idealism, so Milton's bees rub their balm against all excessive demonism. But the irony may not end there. Are the devils not those bees who bring food out of the eater, sweetness out of the strong (Judg. 14:5–14)?

It may also be more than a coincidence that the most famous in this genre of similes describes the bustle of the Carthaginians as seen by storm-exiled Aeneas *(Aeneid,* 1.430–40). Enveloped in a cloud by his divine mother, Aeneas looks down from the top of a hill onto a people busily building their city like a swarm of bees at summer's return and is forced to cry: "O fortunati, quorum iam moenia surgunt [Oh fortunate people, whose walls are already rising]!" Then Virgil, as if to dispel any impression of despair, adds: "mirabile dictu [a wonder]!" Aeneas walks among the Carthaginians made invisible by divine gift.

Here the counterplot thickens, and we behold one of Milton's amazing transpositions of classical texts. Aeneas strives to found Rome, which will outlast Carthage. The bees building in Virgil's text intimate a spirit of creativity seasonally renewed and independent of the particular civilization; the bees in Milton's text represent the same privilege and promise. Aeneas wrapped in the cloud is the observer ab extra, the person on the shore, and his impatient cry is of one who desires to build a civilization beyond decay, perhaps even beyond the wrath of the gods. An emergent, as yet invisible figure in Milton's text shares the hero's cry: he has seen Mammon and his troop build Pandemonium, Satan's band swarm triumphant about their citadel. Despite this, can the walls of creation outlive Satan as Rome the ancient world?

All this would be putative or extrinsic if based solely on the

119

simile of the bees. For this simile, like the middle image of Orion vexing the Red Sea, is indeterminate in its implications, a kind of visual pivot in a series of images which act in sequence and once more reveal the counterplot. Its indeterminacy is comparable to Milton's previously mentioned use of proper nouns and his overall stylistic use of the pivot, by means of which images and words are made to refer both backward and forward, giving the verse period unusual balance and flexibility. The series in question begins with the trooping to Pandemonium, and we now give the entire modulation which moves through several similes:

> all access was throng'd, the Gates
> And Porches wide, but chief the spacious Hall
> (Though like a cover'd field, where Champions bold
> Wont ride in arm'd, and at the Soldan's chair
> Defi'd the best of *Paynim* chivalry
> To mortal combat or career with Lance)
> Thick swarm'd, both on the ground and in the air,
> Brusht with the hiss of rustling wings. As Bees
> In spring time, when the Sun with *Taurus* rides,
> Pour forth thir populous youth about the Hive
> In clusters; they among fresh dews and flowers
> Fly to and fro, or on the smoothed Plank,
> The suburb of thir Straw-built Citadel,
> New rubb'd with Balm, expatiate and confer
> Thir State affairs. So thick the aery crowd
> Swarm'd and were strait'n'd; till the Signal giv'n,
> Behold a wonder! they but now who seem'd
> In bigness to surpass Earth's Giant Sons
> Now less than smallest Dwarfs, in narrow room
> Throng numberless, like that Pigmean Race
> Beyond the *Indian* Mount, or Faery Elves,
> Whose midnight Revels, by a Forest side
> Or Fountain some belated Peasant sees,
> Or dreams he sees, while over-head the Moon
> Sits Arbitress, and nearer to the Earth
> Wheels her pale course, they on thir mirth and dance
> Intent, with jocund Music charm his ear;
> At once with joy and fear his heart rebounds.
> [1.761–88]

The very images which marshall the legions of hell to our view reveal simultaneously that the issue of Satan's triumph or defeat, his real or mock power, is in the hand of a secret arbiter, whether God and divine prescience or man and free will. In the first simile the observer ab extra is the Soldan who, as a type of Satan, overshadows the outcome of the combat between pagan and Christian warriors in the "cover'd field." The second simile is indeterminate in tenor, except that it diminishes the satanic thousands, blending them and their warlike intents with a picture of natural, peaceful creativity, Sun and Taurus presiding in place of the Soldan. "Behold a wonder!" echoes the *mirabile dictu* of Virgil's story and prepares the coming of a divine observer. The mighty host is seen to shrink to the size of Pigmies (the third simile), and we know that these—the "small infantry," as Milton had called them with a pun reflecting the double perspective of the first books—can be overshadowed by Cranes (1.575–76). The verse period then carries us still further from the main action as the diminished devils are also compared to Faery Elves glimpsed at their midnight revels by some belated Peasant. From the presence and pomp of hell we have slowly slipped into a pastoral.

Yet does not this static moment hide an inner combat more real than that for which hell is preparing? It is midnight, the pivot between day and day, and in the Peasant's mind a similar point of balance seems to obtain. He is not fully certain of the significance or even reality of the Fairy ring. Like Aeneas in Hades, who glimpses the shade of Dido *(Aeneid,* 6.450–55), he "sees, Or dreams he sees" something barely distinguishable from the pallid dark, obscure as the new moon through clouds. What an intensity of calm is here, reflecting a mind balanced on the critical pivot, as a point of stillness is reached at greatest remove from the threats and reverberations of hell! But even as the man stands uncertain, the image of the moon overhead becomes intense: it has sat there all the time as arbiter, now wheels closer to the earth, and the Peasant's heart rebounds with a secret intuition bringing at once joy and fear.

The moon, clearly, is a last transformation of the image of the observer ab extra—Soldan, Sun and Taurus, Peasant. What was a type of Satan overshadowing the outcome of the real or spiritual combat is converted into a presentment of the individual's naïve and autonomous power of discrimination, his free reason, secretly

121

linked with a superior influence, as the moon overhead. The figure of the firmly placed observer culminates in that of the secret arbiter. Yet this moon is not an unambiguous symbol of the secret arbiter. A feeling of the moon's uncertain, changeable nature—incorruptible yet spotty, waxing and waning (1.284–91; 2.659–66; see also "mooned horns," 4.978, quoted below)—is subtly present. It reflects this series of images in which the poet constantly suggests, destroys and recreates the idea of an imperturbably transcendent discrimination. The moon that "Sits Arbitress" seems to complete the counterplot, but is only the imperfect sign of a figure not revealed till Book 4. Thus the whole cycle of to and fro, big and small, Pigmies or Elves, seeing or dreaming, far and near, joy and fear—this uneasy flux of couplets, alternatives, and reversals—is continued when we learn, in the final lines of Book 1, that far within Pandemonium, perhaps as far from consciousness as hell is from the thoughts of the Peasant or demonic power from the jocund if intent music of the fairy revelers, Satan and the greatest of his Lords sit in their own, unreduced dimensions.

We meet the Peasant once more in *Paradise Lost,* in a simile which seems to want to outdo the apparent incongruity of all others. At the end of Book 4, Gabriel and his files confront Satan apprehended squatting in Paradise, a toad at the ear of Eve. A heroically contemptuous exchange follows, and Satan's taunts finally so incense the Angel Squadron that they

> Turn'd fiery red, sharp'ning in mooned horns
> Thir Phalanx, and began to hem him round
> With ported Spears, as thick as when a field
> Of *Ceres* ripe for harvest waving bends
> Her bearded Grove of ears, which way the wind
> Sways them; the careful Plowman doubting stands
> Lest on the threshing floor his hopeful sheaves
> Prove chaff. On th'other side *Satan* alarm'd
> Collecting all his might dilated stood,
> Like *Teneriff* or *Atlas* unremov'd:
> His stature reacht the Sky, and on his Crest
> Sat horror Plum'd; nor wanted in his grasp
> What seem'd both Spear and Shield: now dreadful deeds
> Might have ensu'd, nor only Paradise
> In this commotion, but the Starry Cope

> Of Heav'n perhaps, or all the Elements
> At least had gone to rack, disturb'd and torn
> With violence of this conflict, had not soon
> Th'Eternal to prevent such horrid fray
> Hung forth in Heav'n his golden Scales, yet seen
> Betwixt *Astrea* and the *Scorpion* sign,
> Wherein all things created first he weigh'd,
> The pendulous round Earth with balanc'd Air
> In counterpoise, now ponders all events,
> Battles and Realms . . .

[4.978–1002]

The question of Satan's power does not appear to be academic, at least not at first. The simile which, on previous occasions, pretended to illustrate hell's greatness but actually diminished hell and magnified the creation, is used here just as effectively against heaven. Milton, by dilating Satan, and distancing the spears of the angel phalanx as ears ready for reaping, creates the impression of a balance of power between heaven and hell. Yet the image which remains in control is neither of Satan nor of the Angels but of the wheatfield, first as its bearded ears bend with the wind, then as contemplated by the Plowman. Here the counterplot achieves its most consummate form. *Paradise Lost* was written not for the sake of heaven or hell but for the sake of the creation. What is all the fuss about if not to preserve the "self-balanc't" earth? The center around which and to which all actions turn is whether man can stand though free to fall, whether man and the world can survive their autonomy. The issue may not therefore be determined on the supernatural level by the direct clash of heaven and hell but only by these two arbiters: man's free will and God's foreknowledge. The ripe grain sways in the wind; so does the mind which has tended it. Between ripeness and ripeness gathered falls the wind, the threshing floor, the labor of ancient *ears,* the question of the relation of God's will to man's will. The ears appear to be at the mercy of the wind; what about the thoughts, the "hopeful sheaves" of the Plowman? The fate of the world lies between Gabriel and Satan, but also between the wind and the ripe ears and between man and his thoughts. Finally God, supreme arbiter, overbalances the balance with the same pair of golden scales (suspended yet between Virgin and Scorpion) in which the balanced earth weighed at its first creation.

123

Adam on the Grass with Balsamum

Start with the sun. When Adam wakes out of the hands of God, his first perception is of the sun in relation to himself:

> As new wak't from soundest sleep
> Soft on the flow'ry herb I found me laid
> In Balmy Sweat, which with his Beams the Sun
> Soon dri'd, and on the reeking moisture fed.
>
> [8.253–56][1]

This is a curious first image. "Reeking" need not have the pejorative sense it bears today,[2] but the picture of the sun feeding on man's sweat is startling enough. If it is a conceit on evaporation[3] one wonders about the decorum of introducing it at a point which is the inaugural moment of human consciousness. If it stresses the

1. My text is the Odyssey Press edition of *Paradise Lost,* ed. Merritt Y. Hughes. Reference is to the first line of each passage.
2. *Reeking:* "that rises as a vapor" (Laura E. Lockwood, *Lexicon to the English Poetical Works of John Milton* [New York, 1907]). The *OED* gives, however, many examples in which the word is tinged by pejorative meanings, mainly associated with sacrifice. "His browes with sweat did reek and steam" (Spenser, *Faerie Queene,* 7. 7. 40); "The violence of action hath made you reek as a sacrifice" (Shakespeare, *Cymbeline* 1.3.2); "The reeking entrails on the Fire they threw" (Dryden, trans. of Ovid, *Metamorphoses,* 12. 211). This is the only instance of the word in Milton's poetry.
3. Cf. Marvell, "Damon the Mower," st. 6; Sylvester's description of evaporation as "oderiferous sweat," *The Complete Works of Joshua Sylvester,* ed. A. B. Grosart (Edinburgh, 1880), 1: 41b (henceforth, Grosart); Merritt Hughes's note in his edition of *Paradise Lost* (New York, 1940) which refers back to 5. 426; and Plato's conception in the *Timaeus* of the elements "passing into one another in an unbroken circle of birth." The materialism of Milton's imagination (which later attracted Victor Hugo) is explored as to possible ideological sources by Denis Saurat, *Milton et le Matérialisme Chrétien en Angleterre* (Paris, 1928), esp. the chapter on "L'Echelle des Etres et la Circulation de la Nourriture." See also note 10, below.

"place" of the sun, its subordination to man who is the "Heir of the World":

> And God made two great Lights, great for thir use
> To Man...
>
> [7:346–47]

> Everything is ours that serves us in its Place.
> The sun serves us as much as is Possible, and more
> than we could imagine,[4]

we may still wonder at the extreme way in which that theme is expressed.

My purpose in what follows is not, primarily, to establish the decorum of an image. The theory of criticism does not seem sufficiently advanced to solve problems even of this elementary kind, since two quite opposite types of justification could be entertained: one demonstrating that the image is in its place, and a link contributing to the poem's unity; the other that it is displaced, yet expressive of some extraordinary feature of Milton's poetry or mind. To rule the image out of order might suggest, of course, a new order accommodating it; but one feels that poetry, like religion, cannot be ruled this way, and that Milton's idiosyncrasy is of the essence. I raise these issues to recall the difficulty of genuine critical decision and to suggest that the most criticism can do is to turn the curious excess of Adam's image into a curious felicity. My own purpose lies elsewhere. It is to imitate a more adventurous hermeneutic tradition, even at the risk of deepening, provisionally, the difference between criticism and interpretation. The ardent attention older exegetes gave to scripture will here be applied to one place in Milton. Not being able, however, to claim the *mens divinior* of those ancient men, my imitation will be belated and pale; and I can only quote, in apology, some words of Thomas Gray in a similar situation: "Enough for me, if to some feeling breast / My lines a secret sympathy impart."

The sun is not always seen in this manner. Satan's first thoughts in Eden are addressed to it and could hardly differ more from Adam's:

4. Henry Vaughan, *Centuries* (c. 1670), 1: 14.

> O thou that with surpassing Glory crown'd,
> Look'st from thy sole Dominion like the God
> Of this new World; at whose sight all the Stars
> Hide thir diminisht heads. . . .
>
> [4.32–35]

The contrast is heightened by Adam's words that follow spontaneously on his first image:

> Thou Sun, said I, fair Light,
> And thou enlight'n'd Earth, so fresh and gay,
> Ye Hills and Dales, ye Rivers, Woods, and Plains
> And ye that live and move, fair Creatures, tell,
> Tell, if ye saw, how came I thus, how here?
>
> [8.273–77]

Again we start with the sun, but the speech movement is excursive and expands from "Light" to enlight'n'd," from "fair Light" to "fair Creatures" (also from "Earth" to that partitive naming of Hills, Dales, etc.), and so to the synoptic and interanimating metaphor of "Happy Light" (8.285). The same sun, shining to the same spot and seen as if for the first time, yields radically different responses.

That Satan curses the light while Adam blesses it reflects their opposite moods; but more important, because more instinctive, is the interpretation each has of the sun's place. Satan's view is somewhat like his view of himself: "Our puissance is our own" (5.864). There is more than a touch of solipsism here. Compare him in his solar chariot, arrayed for the War in Heaven:

> High in the midst exalted as a God
> Th' Apostate in his Sun-bright Chariot sat
> Idol of Majesty Divine, enclos'd
> With Flaming Cherubim, and golden Shields.
>
> [6.99–102]

Adam, however, wakes to a world in which the sun is a creature *(res creata)*. If it feeds, it is because "Whatever was created, needs / To be sustain'd and fed" (5.414); and if it feeds on man's sweat it is because Milton wished to emphasize the conjunction of highest and lowest, of an ethereal body and creaturely

126

functions. The meridian sun participates in creation like an animal tending its newborn. By poetic intensification, "creature" becomes "animal." There is no "lordship of the sun."[5]

Adam in this follows Raphael. The latter had made the point that the sun's "virtue" is barren unless its beams find their fruitfulness in the earth (8.95) and his person exemplifies a similar lesson. His angelic nature is "sociable," and he is called to duty when God sees Adam and Eve wedding barren elm and marriageable vine (5.215).[6] Talking to Adam the first time he is called "Angelic Virtue" (5.371), where "virtue" surely retains its connotation of fructifying principle.[7] His opening words to Eve (Havah=Life, a meaning alluded to in her nativity story, 4.481 ff.), are a prophetic variation on a famous theme of virgin fruitfulness (5.388). When Adam wonders whether the Angel will eat earthly food Raphael evokes a picture of the Scale of Nature which provides Adam's image of the sun with its cosmic rationale. The conjunction of ethereal nature and creaturely function holds even for those higher in the Scale of Being than the sun—"For Eternity is a Creature" (Christopher Smart).

"Thy soul was like a Star, and dwelt apart," Wordsworth said of Milton, " . . . yet thy heart / The lowliest duties on herself did lay." Obedience is no virtue unless understood in this fruitful way, linked to Milton's vision of a "sympathetic" cosmos and a cooperative hierarchy. Yet Raphael could have dispatched his mission more briefly were this well-known concept of order (even in its finer consequences) his only news. If the Angel dominates the better part of four books it is because he bears a vision as well as a message. His purpose is to bring Adam out of ignorant bliss to the full knowledge of his happiness.

"Ignorant bliss" may seem overstated, yet Adam and Eve are strangers in Paradise. It is to know his happiness that Adam

5. See the chapter of that title in W. C. Curry's *Milton's Ontology, Cosmogony and Physics* (Lexington, 1957); and cf. Saurat, *Milton et le Matérialisme*, on "Le Soleil Dieu" (pp. 28–33).

6. "Ulmis aduingere vites," *Georgics* 1. 2—Virgil's rubric for plant-cultivation, treated in his second book, the most influential on Milton's own garden poem. See also Peter Demetz, "The Elm and the Vine: Notes Toward the History of a Marriage Topos," in *PMLA* 73 (1958): 521–32.

7. For this use of "virtue" (a poetical crux throughout Milton's poetry), cf. 3. 606–12 and 9. 103 ff.

queries the sun and the other creatures (8.280), and Eve is given to him for the same reason. When Raphael comes, Adam and Eve are still haunted by the "enormous bliss" (5.297)—the excess of fruitfulness—in all things. The meridian sun, under which Raphael approaches, presides over that excess:

> Him through the spicy Forest onward come
> *Adam* discern'd, as in the door he sat
> Of his cool Bow'r, while now the mounted Sun
> Shot down direct his fervid Rays, to warm
> Earth's inmost womb, more warmth than *Adam* needs.
>
> [5.298–302]

Start with the sun. As the sun has more warmth than Adam needs, so heaven has a greater glory than Eve can understand (4.657). The possibility of infinite domain joined to the impossibility of a more than ignorant possession weigh down Adam's speech with pun and word play:

> Sole partner and sole part of all these joys,
> Dearer thyself than all; needs must the Power
> That made us, and for us this ample World
> Be infinitely good, and of his good
> As liberal and free as infinite. . . .
>
> [4.411–15]

On seeing Raphael, Adam's words rehearse his obsession with plenty. He bids Eve go with speed

> And what thy stores contain, bring forth and pour
> Abundance, fit to honour and receive
> Our Heav'nly stranger; well we may afford
> Our givers thir own gifts, and large bestow
> From large bestow'd . . .
>
> [5.314–18]

Behind this Biblical hospitality (Genesis 18) dwells a mind puzzling over its function in the face of such gifts. Eve's punning intensifies the issue:

> *Adam,* earth's hallow'd mould,
> Of God inspir'd, small store will serve, where store,

> All seasons, ripe for use hangs on the stalk;
> Save what by frugal storing firmness gains
>
> [5.321–24]

Adam and Eve know the good only by goodies. They live in a consumer's paradise. This results in a troubled conscience even if they cannot quite articulate their trouble: their words insidiously foreshadow the Protestant concern with labor and its precarious link to grace.[8] They are neither creative (like God) nor productive (like workers); even procreativeness is, for the time being, withheld. Are they destined for a purely contemplative life? But their noble ease is perplexed by the energy of the sun and the radiance of the stars. Adam's "Sole partner and sole part" betrays his need for a participatory knowledge and recalls the motive leading to Eve's creation:

> Thou [God] hast provided all things: but with mee
> I see not who partakes . . .
>
> [8.363–64]

That need remains, though Eve is Adam's "partaker" in an even more literal sense than the sun he wakes to.

> I now see
> Bone of my Bone, Flesh of my Flesh, my Self
> Before me . . .
>
> [8.494–96]

To bring a man from (relative) ignorance to knowledge is the oldest formula we have for dramatic action. There would be no drama in paradise without man's need to become a partner of the divine vision. Raphael acknowledges this by bearing a vision as well as a message; and Satan exploits it by arguing that the forbidden fruit is a means to fuller communion. "Participating god-like food" Eve will become godlike (9.717). Physical analogies of this kind (Milton's central symbol is that of eating of the tree of knowledge) are basic to the epic, and Adam wakes to the very image of desire for participation. Where the sun

8. See the mention of "merit" in Adam's earlier speech, 4.416–19; and cf. 1.98, 2.5, 3.309, and 6.43.

shows "appetite" Adam shows mind; but mind is appetitive, as the rest of his story illustrates.

Adam's first moments of conscious life are short. Newborn, he falls asleep after a few questing motions. During his sleep God dream-walks him to Eden; and his second waking, in Eden, repeats in finer tone a suggestion of the first:

> Each tree
> Load'n with fairest Fruit, that hung to the Eye
> Tempting, stirr'd in me sudden appetite
> To pluck and eat; whereat I wak'd, and found
> Before mine Eyes all real . . .
>
> [8.306–10]

Consuming and waking are once more subtly conjoined. Consciousness is teased, however, not slaked. Adam, despite the "all real," despite the fact that he is in paradise, would have continued his quest if God had not reappeared as his guide (8.311). Complimenting Raphael, Adam says explicitly:

> sweeter thy discourse is to my ear
> Than Fruits of Palm-tree pleasantest to thirst
> And hunger both, from labor, at the hour
> Of sweet repast; they satiate, and soon fill,
> Though pleasant, but thy words with Grace Divine
> Imbu'd, bring to thir sweetness no satiety.
>
> [8.211–16]

The sweetness of divine knowledge satisfies and wakes at the same time, causing an *insatiabilis satietas*.[9] All other knowledge surfeits or deceives. So, after a further tasting and sleep, Adam and Eve rise up

9. A topos of mystical speculation. Dante calls Divine Philosophy "pan degli angeli" at the opening of the *Convivio* (i.e., The Banquet). "Many authoritative texts, from Augustine to Peter Damiani and Richard of St. Victor, describe the beatitude of the blessed as an *insatiabilis satietas*, where the celestial manna is given *ad plenitudinem, sed numquam ad satietatem*" (Erich Auerbach, *Romance Philology* 7 [1954]: 275). See also Purgatorio, 31.128; Paradiso, 2.108; and cf. *Paradise Lost* 5.633.

> As from unrest, and each the other viewing,
> Soon found thir Eyes how op'n'd and thir minds
> How dark'n'd . . .
>
> [9.1052–54]

Between Adam's original and this awakening lies the deep sleep or *tardemah* (Genesis 2) which produced Eve. After it Adam also wakes at first to loss, driven by a dream-image:

> Shee disappear'd, and left me dark, I wak'd
> To find her . . .
>
> [8.478–79]

This expresses the void Eve's creation has left. To be man's partner Eve must be his part. Unlike the sun, which taking from Adam fulfils both creatures, Eve part-takes from him and leaves a scar. The price for communion with created bounty is, paradoxically, partial sacrifice of that bounty, a "wounding" of earth (9.782) which is consummated when Adam gives up "these wild woods forlorn" for Eve's sake. "I feel / The Link of Nature draw me: Flesh of Flesh, / Bone of my Bone thou art" (9.913–15). Adam here repeats his marriage cry on first seeing Eve, and she who was intended to bring him close to Nature now leads him to forsake it.

Adam's awakenings into knowledge began with an image of the feeding sun. It suggested an entirely unhurtful, sympathetic, even symbiotic relation: what one creature takes from another benefits both. The relation of innocent knowledge (of the happy consciousness) to reality is like this: a feeding on created things which is not a theft or a wounding. How unlike Sin's offspring devouring the bowels of their mother! Milton's picture of Sin and Death is the antitype of this relation, an exact travesty of *participation mystique*. The sun feeding on Adam fortifies him; Sin's progeny inflict an endless birth wound. Alter slightly the balance of Adam's first image, and "sympathy" turns cannibalistic.[10] The desire for knowledge is an appetite for participation and may become a "horrid sympathy" (10.540).

10. The darker connotations (purely virtual) of Adam's image are reinforced if we see the "reeking moisture" with twofold vision: as "grateful smell" from the altar of earth (9.192–97; cf. 11.38) and as the smell of

131

That mind can be participatory without demonic consequences is shown in the best nativity scene of them all: the multiple "birthday of heaven and earth" (Book 7) of which Adam's story is a delayed portion. This greatest vision in English of a sympathetic universe links knowledge to fruitfulness in a remarkable way. The (permitted) fruit of knowledge is here quite literally a result of the fruits of earth and the organic consequence of a respect for Nature Milton calls "obedience." For the natural excess perplexing Adam and Eve is shown to be not an end in itself but a protective shade produced by the return of each creature upon its origin. Without this return, this reflection, earth might still be naked and void. By an instinctive act of commemoration earth's progeny cast over their parent a deep and fruitful shade from the very excess of their life, a shade in which eyes and ears could ripen:

> He scarce had said, when the bare Earth, till then
> Desert and bare, unsightly, unadorn'd,
> Brought forth the tender Grass, whose verdure clad
> Her Universal Face with pleasant green,
> Then Herbs of every leaf, that sudden flow'r'd
> Op'ning thir various colors, and made gay
> Her bosom smelling sweet: and these scarce blown,
> Forth flourish'd thick the clust'ring Vine, forth crept
> The smelling Gourd, up stood the corny Reed
> Embattl'd in her field: and th' humble Shrub,

---

sacrifice (10.272–81; cf. the pejorative meaning of *reeking* cited in note 2 above). By insisting with great and literal power on his vision of a sympathetic cosmos—for its antiquity see K. Reinhardt, *Kosmos und Sympathie* (Munich, 1926)—Milton diverged significantly from the *Divine Weekes* of Du Bartas. Lines 108–37 of the Fourth Day of the First Week refute "such as have thought that the Stars were living creatures that did eat and drink." In Sylvester's translation (Grosart, 1:53a) the essential verses are:

> And therefore smile I at those Fable-Forges,
> Whose busie-idle stile so stiffly urges,
> The Heav'ns' bright Cressets to be living Creatures,
> Ranging for food, and hungry Fodder-eaters;
> Still sucking up (in their eternal motion)
> The Earth for meat, and for their drink, the Ocean.

The prevalence of the theme of nourishment is finely stressed by W. B. C. Watkins, *Anatomy of Milton's Verse* (Baton Rouge, 1955), pp. 16 ff.

And Bush with frizzl'd hair implicit: last
Rose as in Dance the stately Trees, and spread
Thir branches hung with copious Fruit: or gemm'd
Thir Blossoms: with high Woods the Hills were crown'd,
With tufts the valleys and each fountain side,
With borders long the Rivers.

[7.313–28]

In this rising scale every progression is reflexive: growth upward enriches the source and outward movement redounds.
Earth puts forth grass, the grass in turn covers earth's face with
green. Each creature covers its parents' nakedness.[11] The vine
and other plants shoot high or broad yet cluster and cling to
earth with "embattl'd" density; the trees dance freely, with
spread branches, yet are weighed down by fruit or heavy blossoms. Then the zeugma of the last lines ("With high Woods the
Hills were crown'd . . . With borders long the Rivers") provides
the coda. The crown is still in the form of a limit. Nature has
built a "Shade above shade, a woody Theatre / Of stateliest
view" (4.141) in whose shelter man can dress his thoughts to contemplation. "In contemplation of created things / By steps we may
ascend to God" (5.511).

Analyze the sun. Why is it presiding at Adam's birth? It is
commemorating Genesis. What is, correlatively, Satan's sin? He
denies the day of his creation. To justify his revolt he utters
mockingly the very words with which God rallies Job in the
Bible:

who saw
When this creation was? remember'st thou
Thy making, while the Maker gave thee being?
We know no time when we were not as now;
Know none before us, self-begot, self-rais'd
By our own quick'ning power

[5.856–61]

This denial of creatureliness, this forgetting of creation, is the
origin and type of all sin. Raphael's discourse of the First Things

11. In Hell, Death and its offspring continually uncover their parents'
nakedness.

impels Adam to recall the day of his birth. He repeats Satan's point, but humbly:

> For Man to tell how human Life began
> Is hard; for who himself beginning knew?
>
> [8.250–51]

There follows the image of the creaturely sun.

The sun is but a sign clarified by a series of awakenings. Emphasis falls on the interpreter, on the mediation of both natural light (consciousness) and supernatural lighting (dream-vision).[12] Adam's first sight is already an interpretive leap which transforms perception into vision and makes us intensely aware of the difference between truth in its ordinary and its transfigured form. The image falls apart into nature as we know it and a glorified superstructure. It shows that Adam is really natural man at heart or that Milton's visionariness is limited by what Blake denounced as "Natural Religion."

In Adam's image, therefore, despite the cooperation of nature and imagination, sign becomes symbol so proleptically, imagination so imposes on nature, that an intrinsic discontinuity appears. This remains true even if we take the image as a learned conceit. The possibility of its being a conceit (on evaporation or the alimentary Chain of Nature) affirms, in fact, the difference between perception and vision by offering a middle term which proves to be as far out as the end term. The imaginative distance between nature and vision is so great that halving it is like halving infinity. The continuity between them is discontinuous enough to appear unbridgeable.

It is hard to say which problem is greater: that Adam is still at distance from vision, or that he is so close to it. Born visionary, can he become reflective? What kind of development is possible for a man born mature and with the sun at the meridian? Adam's progress can only be vision on top of vision, but it must also be

12. On Milton's use of the theological distinction between natural light (lumen naturale) and supernatural illumination, see my *Wordsworth's Poetry* (New Haven, 1954), pp. 51–53. A sensitive analysis of Adam's creation story is given by C. M. Coffin, "Creation and the Self in *P. L.*," *ELH* 29 (1962): 1–18.

self-emergence: a journeying from unorganized (unreflective) to organized (reflective) innocence. It is here that the labor of interpretation enters. What Adam *sees* remains to be *known:* it is, at first, only an emblem or dumb show of the truth.

Adam, feeling happier than he knows, at once sets out to "know" his happiness. "Splendour in the grass" (Wordsworth, *Intimations Ode*) leads to pensiveness "on a green shady Bank" (8.286).[13] So the young sun god in Keats's *Hyperion* is no sooner risen than he feels the burden of the mystery. He is haunted by his ignorance and by his fallow energies. Barely emerged he is already overcome by his desire for knowledge and then by knowledge itself. The problem of knowledge becomes that of preparing the individual to grasp consciously what is his —and what he is.

Start with the sun god. Or with a younger order of gods transcending an older one. Adam, too, is linked to the old gods in that his creation counterbalances their fall. He is the inheritor on whom more depends than it is good to know: there is a knowledge dangerous to him, a knowledge of good and evil, of "creations and destroyings" *(Hyperion,* 3.116). Like Apollo, moreover, he goes in foreshortened time from indolent vision to a sublime and terrible insight. Yet between him and Apollo there is a significant difference: the drama of his emergence is more graduated. If the divinity appearing to him overwhelms, it remains gentle and preparatory and continues to be so in "repetitions" Keats admired. To develop human consciousness and to prevent it foundering under the weight of self-consciousness—under the sense of its own powers—God relies on the ancient principle of *accommodation.*

It is this principle, however, which Keats and the Romantics rejected, at least in one crucial aspect. When Raphael, divine interpreter, likens spiritual to corporeal forms, he is following the principle of accommodation. It includes two different, even

13. Wordsworth starts at the same point, with visionary naturalism, and contemplates the passage from it to a more pensive fidelity to nature. Milton echoes Virgil's *Georgics,* 2.485: "Too happy, if they knew their happiness" (8.282). He alludes several times to this place, most poignantly in his exceptional apostrophe to Adam and Eve: "Sleep on, / Blest pair; and O yet happiest if ye seek / No happier state, and know to know no more" (4.773–75).

contrary ideas. Raphael brings truth down to earth (5.571–74) but in this way could gradually raise an earthly mind to heaven (5.574–76). The first aspect of accommodation is authoritarian and condescending; the second initiatory. It is the first aspect which the Romantics opposed. The burden of the mystery was to be borne by the individual directly: "If thou canst not ascend / These steps, die on that marble where thou art" *(Fall of Hyperion,* 1.107–08). The steps may lead into darkness rather than out of it, and man's capability is the "negative" one of being able to endure the mystery, to bear life's "weary, unintelligible weight" without cursing what light there is.

Blake, that great subverter of received ideas, knew exactly the concept involved. The concluding verses of his *Auguries of Innocence* go back, via Swedenborg, to Gregory of Nyssa:

> God Appears & God is Light
> To those poor Souls who dwell in Night,
> But does a Human Form Display
> To those who Dwell in Realms of day.

Gregory, perplexed by the darkening or self-shrouding nature of God (Exod. 20:21), explained it as an illusion experienced by the soul in its progress from innocence (God as light) to experience (God as "bright darkness"). "The Logos is first seen as light, but as one ascends, it becomes dark because one realizes that it surpasses ordinary knowledge and is separated from mortal comprehension by the *tenebrae*."[14] This idea, of an initiation into the divine light via a divine darkness, is the mystical obverse of the principle of accommodation which has God darken his bright because of the weakness of human eyes.

If Keats discovers a new version of the ascent into darkness,[15] Blake savagely parodies it as an imperfect critique of accommo-

14. I rely heavily here on D. C. Allen, "Milton and the Descent to Light," *Journal of English and Germanic Philology* 60 (1961): 614–30, from which the quotation comes. "Bright darkness" is Gregory's oxymoron. Allen points out that the Pseudo-Dionysius (with his tenth-century vogue) and Bonaventura, Ficino, and the Florentine Academy all shared this current of speculation.

15. Wordsworth's ascent to Mount Snowdon *(Prelude,* 14) is perhaps the most remarkable instance of what is both an ascent to darkness and a "descent to light." Cf. F. A. Pottle, "Wordsworth and Freud, or The

dation. He rejects the religious power of blackness as he rejects the orthodox power of light. For Blake, the light which is darkness, or shines in the dark, is a priestly lure imposed on the "glad day" of imagination. God has no need to "appear" this way, to fly in the night, except where the idea of accommodation is perverted and institutionalized—where it has become the cornerstone of a church that, like a covering cherub, keeps us from truth. If man rather than God is responsible for our fall into the body of this death, it is only because man's imaginings of what God is have trapped him into a sacrifice of imagination. "Man has closed himself up."[16] Change his idea of God, and you change man. The opposite of accommodation is needed: conflagration, a burning up of restrictive mystery, an opening up of man, a cleansing of the doors of perception. " 'What,' it will be Question'd, 'When the Sun rises, do you not see a round disk of fire somewhat like a Guinea?' O no, no,I see an Innumerable company of the Heavenly host crying, 'Holy, Holy, Holy, is the Lord God Almighty.' "[17] Start with apocalypse.

Raphael associated the authoritarian and initiatory aspects of accommodation in easy, speculative fashion, but Adam and Eve—born Romantics—do not fully see the connection. Adam seems to understand, yet clearly he pursues initiation (participatory knowledge) rather than education. So does Eve, and with fatal results. For her the forbidden fruit is like a drug, a hallucinogen that holds out the promise of jumping several rungs in the scale of nature, even of transcending from human to divine. Eve in the Sky with Diamonds (5.44 ff.). There is a small margin between vision and ecstasy, which is the educable margin; and Eve fails to respect it. She tries to go straight up, and falls.

Thus the only education possible for Adam and Eve is a tem-

Theology of the Unconscious," *Bulletin of the General Theological Seminary* 34 (1958): 18–27; and Northrop Frye's attempt to delineate the Romantic world-picture in "New Directions from Old," reprinted in *Fables of Identity* (New York, 1963).

16. See esp. *The Marriage of Heaven and Hell* (1793). Blake's early acquaintance with the idea of accommodation is shown by "The Little Black Boy" in *Songs of Innocence* and by "Principle 5th" of *All Religions Are One* (1788).

17. Letter to the Rev. Dr. Trusler, August 23, 1799.

pering of their minds toward divinity. "The imagination," Keats said, "is like Adam's dream: he awoke and found it truth." God prepares Adam for the truth of imagination by a series of visionary events. He does more than preceptorially warn him: He arranges an exemplary propaedeutics, these trials of Adam by vision. Adam is not born in paradise proper but dream-led to it; and this *staging* (important everywhere in Milton) expresses the gradual attuning of man to the consciousness of what he is, his entering the vision by degree. There is a stairway even to paradise.

Raphael's discourse is part of this propaedeutics, but so is Michael's prophecy after the Fall, which gives Adam his first sights of death. If man must abide the time—must suffer "history"—it is to ascend (more painfully now) the stairway of vision. The principle of accommodation, albeit in a form at once more condescending and participatory (the form of the Incarnation) is writ large in the movement of history "from shadowy types to truth."[18] Accommodation becomes typology: the progress of mankind from romance to reality is governed by the same principle as led Adam from dreams of paradise to the palpable garden. It is appropriate, therefore, that the very shape in which Raphael descends to Adam should mime this shift from prefigure to incarnate truth and express a poetics of accommodation.

"Why that shape, good Master Editor?" Dr. Bentley's question concerning Raphael's descent in the form—or seeming form —of a phoenix (5.270) has not been answered. "Among so many real Birds of grand magnitude and fine Feather, could none content you but a Phoenix, a fictitious Nothing, that has not Being but in Tale and Fable?"[19]

18. Cf. W. G. Madsen, *From Shadowy Types to Truth* (New Haven, 1968); C. A. Patrides, *"Paradise Lost* and the Theory of Accommodation," *Texas Studies in Language and Literature* 5 (1963): 58–63; and Allen, "Milton and the Descent to Light." Madsen differs from Allen by sharply distinguishing Christian from Neoplatonic theories of accommodation. On the role of light in Milton's use of "rising-to-fall and falling-to-rise" (patterns also discussed by J. I. Cope, *The Metaphoric Structure of Paradise Lost* [Baltimore, 1962]; and I. MacCaffrey, *Paradise Lost as "Myth"* [Cambridge, Mass., 1959]), see Madsen, *Shadowy Types,* pp. 122 ff.

19. *Milton's Paradise Lost, A New Edition,* ed. Richard Bentley (London, 1732), p. 157. Thomas Newton's answer, "He was not really a Phoenix, the birds only fancied him one" (*Paradise Lost, A New Edition* [London, 1947], 1:332–33), is not adequate, as Bentley's further remark

Two comparisons make Raphael's advent vivid. While still in the air, near towering eagles,

> to all the Fowls he seems
> A *Phoenix,* gaz'd by all, as that sole Bird
> When to enshrine his reliques in the Sun's
> Bright Temple, to *Egyptian Thebes* he flies.
>
> [5.271–74]

But in paradise Raphael resumes seraph form, his splendor mantled by six wings:

> Like *Maia's* son he stood,
> And shook his Plumes, that Heav'nly fragrance fill'd
> The circuit wide.
>
> [5.285–87]

Raphael's change, which marks the transition from air to earth, evokes two different conceptions of divinity. The phoenix is portrayed as an object of adoration, associated with pagan sun worship and engaged in a mysterious cycle of self-immolation and rebirth. The Angel's proper shape, however, emphasizes shade rather than sun and outgoing, serviceable energy rather than self-enshrinement. Greatness is at first a phoenix, self-begot, self-centered, and self-renewed; then, like Maia's son, delegated, partitive, and evangelical.

It has been thought that there is no genuine link between Raphael's seeming shape as phoenix and his proper shape as Archangel, but they are parts of a single propaedeutic event in which the later manifestation typologically transforms or fulfills the former.[20] Raphael's paradigmatic descent encompasses,

---

(5.276) shows. If Raphael was not really a phoenix, why does Milton say he returned to his proper shape? Cf. Thomas Greene, *The Descent from Heaven* (New Haven, 1963): "Why introduce a Phoenix here at all, figurative or real?" (p. 387).

20. See Erich Auerbach, "Figura" (1944), trans. in *Scenes from the Drama of European Literature* (New York, 1959); and, for Milton specifically, Helga Spevack-Husmann, *The Mighty Pan* (Muenster, 1963), pp. 30 ff. Greene's interesting discussion of Raphael's advent in *Descent from Heaven,* chap. 12, sets forth many of the parallels between the Angel's proper shape and phoenix legend, but he remains unsure whether they can be fitted into a single, coherent interpretation.

time as well as space and ends in the form it started with. The two-stage Angel enacts the fulfillment rather than abrogation of the phoenix image familiar to Milton through classical and medieval sources.

Three main traits were traditionally ascribed to the phoenix: (1) it was a "sole" bird in that only one of its kind lived at any time, each new bird springing from its father's dead body; (2) it was famed for brilliant colors, a mixed array of red, gold, and "cerulean"; (3) associated with the sun and the mystery of regeneration, it was placed in a region of myrrh and exotic perfumes. Milton's *Epitaphium Damonis* (ll. 185 ff.) compounds for the phoenix a dwelling made of "the waves of the Red Sea, the perfume-bearing Spring, the far-stretching shore of Arabia, and groves sweating (sudantes) balsam."[21]

In Raphael's seeming shape the idea of rebirth is present, but that of fruitfulness (spring, perfume, spices) is absent. Rebirth is a closed cycle, the eternal return of the same. The figure recalls Satan's view of the sun and a recurrent theological archetype which depicts God as absolutely self-contained. When Raphael touches ground, though he no longer seems to be a phoenix, his restored heavenly form (cf. Ezek. 1 and Isa. 6) develops implicitly the two omitted characteristics of the mythical bird. This transformation of Raphael from pagan into heavenly phoenix[22] needs all the details of his return to seraph form, not the Hermes simile alone:

> on th' Eastern cliff of Paradise
> He lights, and to his proper shape returns
> A Seraph wing'd; six wings he wore, to shade

21. Milton's three evocations of the phoenix (*Samson Agonistes,* 1699–1707 is the third) have been thoroughly studied as to classical and medieval influence. For details and bibliography, see Greene, *Descent from Heaven,* pp. 397 ff. While all of Milton's details have antecedents in tradition, no text has been found linking Raphael directly to the phoenix. Both, of course, are divine messengers, and the phoenix had been underwritten by Clement of Rome as a Christ symbol (Allen, "Milton and the Descent to Light"). In "Noon-Midnight and the Temporal Structure of *Paradise Lost,*" *ELH* 29 (1962), A. R. Cirillo suggests a "Christ-Phoenix-noon relationship" (pp. 388–90).

22. A suggestion may have been planted by Sylvester's "The Heav'nly Phoenix first began to frame / The Earthly Phoenix." See the Fifth day of the First Week, ll. 598 f.

His lineaments Divine; the pair that clad
Each shoulder broad, came mantling o'er his breast
With regal Ornament; the middle pair
Girt like a Starry Zone his waist, and round
Skirted his loins and thighs with downy Gold
And colors dipt in Heav'n; the third his feet
Shadow'd from either heel with feather'd mail
Sky-tinctur'd grain. Like *Maia's* son he stood,
And shook his Plumes, that Heav'nly fragrance fill'd
The circuit wide.

[5.275–287]

Into Raphael's plumage Milton has woven the colors and perfume of the phoenix. Instead of variegated (red, gold, cerulean) wings, those of the Angel show "colors dipt in Heav'n," "Sky-tinctur'd grain." The iridescent tints become a single attribute, fused as one shade or source of all color. Yet the original tints continue to glimmer through: "downy Gold" is there explicitly, "dipt in Heav'n" infers cerulean, and "grain" may carry an echo of red to complete the spectrum.[23] Then, with the allusion to Hermes, the theme of fragrance reemerges. It is not by chance that Milton's imagination riots with Myrrh, flowering Odors, Cassia, Nard, and Balm as Raphael passes through the "blissful" field to where Adam is (5.292 ff.). Blissful field is cognate with "Araby the blest," the phoenix's traditional haunt to which paradise is compared in 4.159 ff. Now that the Angel has arrived on earth, Milton gives him the phoenix's halo of perfume.[24]

What of the phoenix's link to the sun? Does it enter the completed figure? While the pagan phoenix is strongly identified with

23. G. W. Whiting remarks that "Even when Raphael resumes his proper shape of a winged seraph, his wings of 'downie Gold and colours dipt in Heav'n' and 'Skie-tinctur'd grain' resemble the brilliant golden plumage and the azure of the phoenix" *(Milton's Literary Milieu* [Chapel Hill, 1939], p. 85).

24. Whiting, Greene, and others sense the continuity. "Neither the Virgilian nor the Shakespearian Mercury shook his plumes and scattered heavenly fragrance. . . . The fragrance suggests that Milton still has the phoenix in mind, a suspicion that is confirmed by the lines following which describe the blissful field" (Douglas Bush, *Mythology and the Renaissance Tradition in English Poetry* [Minnesota, 1932], pp. 280 f.). The nearest verbal parallel is Sylvester, who shows the phoenix building its funeral nest "With Incense, Cassia, Spikenard, Myrrh, and Balm."

the sun (the sun's temple draws him, and he the gaze of all birds), Raphael transmutes this blaze of power. Light becomes shadow light, even a garment.[25] Wings of "downy Gold" gird the Angel like a "starry Zone," while the twofold sense of "mantling"[26] and phrases like "feather'd mail" produce a balance between ideas of containment and expansion, solid and ethereal substance. This is no jealous, covering cherub, however: the wings that veil Raphael also generate fragrance, a shadowy yet most expansive charm.

The self-veiling nature of divine light is, of course, related to the idea of accommodation and the possibility of converse between heaven and earth. While the phoenix's worship of the sun cannot be distinguished from self-worship,[27] Raphael, from the time that he accepts God's charge "Veil'd with his gorgeous wings" (5.250) to when in the same form he stands before Adam, is the very spirit of that winged obedience which mediates between human and divine and which could make Adam himself ascend winged (5.498). By restoring the Angel to his heavenly shape Milton suggests that Eden is a kind of heaven, more fruitful than speculative "worlds and worlds" (5.268). His folded, self-shadowing wings are a truer emblem of power than any phoenix-like display. The "bright darkness" of his accommodation belongs to the "shade above shade" of Eden (4.141): it is the light drawn from the light to overshadow it.[28] Raphael, transfigured bird of the sun, interprets the sun.

Adam's eyes complete Raphael's message. Start with the sun, but "in the beginning was the Word." If sight moves instinctively into voice (8.270), like breath into praise (9.192; Ps. 150:6), it is because of that inner word. It was a voice that created the

25. See Ps. 104: 2; *Paradise Lost,* 3.11–12; and the beautiful elaboration of the idea in 4.606–09. For a two-volume treatment of the archetype, see Robert Eisler, *Weltenmantel und Himmelszelt* (Munich, 1910).

26. (1) to envelop like a mantle; (2) to spread back and forth with the wing motion of a swan (7.438).

27. It is possible to find in the phoenix a suggestion of fidelity or piety, for he brings his father's remains to the temple of the sun and so returns upon his origin. But he remains a limited symbol, or prefiguration, of that virtue.

28. The "shade above shade" of Eden corresponds to the "Light above Light" (9.105) of Heaven.

light, itself created "before the Sun, / Before the Heavens" (3.8–9). Sight and light are mediated by the word, even as Milton's poem is basically words about the Word: an inspired commentary on scripture.

If we detach what Adam sees from the charm (8.2) of Raphael's voice, we still come on this mediation of the word. Adam's first image is less an image than an emblem. It resembles, in its visual quality, a Renaissance mode that translated words into pictures and gave moral, scientific, or scripture commonplaces an exotic resonance. In emblem books the text or motto is provided together with the illustration: the word within is written out. But in purely literary media the interior word may act like a genetic code and project a "speaking picture"—speaking to those able to solve the charade. To properly interpret these literary emblems we must hear images speak: Milton's text being based on a picture that is itself based on a text.[29]

Since Adam's image contains an especially subtle instance of this, it is better to begin with straightforward examples. First, Milton's simile of the careful Plowman (4.980–85), a georgic in little, which made even Richardson (that defender of Milton's similes) admit that the author may have "wandered into irrelevancies." Perhaps he did; but it is clear what led or misled him. The Plowman with his "hopeful sheaves" comes from emblem vignettes with the motto *Agricolas spes alit*.[30] Why Milton introduced the emblem at this point is a separate question. But he wants us to hear that image and to become, like the Plowman himself, pensive about the relation of labor to grace.

Our second example, also marked by amplification, has escaped general notice. The angels seduced by Satan are said to be

29. Marvell at one point calls this central feature of emblematic method "lending ears to eyes" ("insinuare sonos oculis" and "oculis impertire aurem"). See my discussion in "Marvell, St. Paul, and the Body of Hope," pp. 151–72. For emblems which seem to skirt, pictorially, Milton's conception here, see the refence of Denis Saurat *(Milton et le Matérialisme,* pp. 37–38) to Robert Fludd. The man-sun, or god-sun, also appears on the title page of Fludd's *Philosophia Moysaica* (Goudae, 1638) and on the title page of its *Sectio Secunda* (fol. 66).

30. See, inter alia, H. Peacham, *Minerva Britanna* (London, 1612), emblem 32; George Wither, *A Collection of Emblemes, Ancient and Modern* (London, 1635), Bk. 2, emblem 44.

> Innumerable as the Stars of Night,
> Or Stars of Morning, Dew-drops, which the Sun
> Impearls on every leaf and every flower.
>
> [5.745–47][31]

Two easy steps take us from darkness in heaven to a dawn linking heaven and earth. The stepping-stone for this happy descent is "Stars of Morning," a pivotal image referring back to "Stars of Night" in their association with Satan and forward to the starry dew-drops of an earthly dawn. Satan's power (the simile's overt purpose is to illustrate the size of his host) fades into the morning light of Creation.

The turn from Stars of Night to Stars of Morning, and so to dew drops, is an imagistic leap strongly mediated by tradition, specifically by scripture tradition, and in scripture by the associations of one word. It is all a rebus or visual pun on *Lucifer(s)*.[32] The lightbringers bring on the light. Unconscious instruments of good—for their fall will be counterbalanced by the Creation— Satan's followers, the lucifers, are already falling into the brightness of a natural dawn. The unusual plural, "Stars of Morning," followed by the image of that morning calm and fresh as on the first day, recalls a famous picture of the birthday of Creation:

> When the morning stars sang together
> And all the Sons of God shouted for joy.
>
> (Job 38: 7)

Thus Milton's simile ironically "completes the figure."[33] The form of its movement is comparable to the form of Raphael's descent, which foreshadowed the typological structure of history.

The rebus is an extreme case of emblem-making in that picture

31. Newton says (in *Paradise Lost, A New Edition*): "Innumerable as the stars, is an old simile; but this of the stars of morning, dew-drops, seems to me as new as it is beautiful." The "Innumerable as the stars" is as old as Gen. 15:5. William Empson, in *Some Versions of Pastoral* (London, 1950), esp. pp. 181–84, comments on the simile.

32. "How art thou fallen from heaven, O Lucifer, son of the morning" (Isa. 14:12). Cf. *Paradise Lost*, 5.708 f., 5.716, 10.425; and st. 12 of "On the Morning of Christ's Nativity."

33. James Whaler calls the movement of Milton's similes "proleptic" in his well-known essays "The Miltonic Simile," *PMLA* 46 (1931): 1034– 74, and "The Animal Simile in *P. L.*," *PMLA* 47 (1932): esp. 550–53.

is totally generated by motto: the image is the name. Yet Milton's simile is only a proximate rebus: not a tour de force but a tacit and highly characteristic use of associations to make an image resonate. Indeed, to create that image is to reverse the usual priority of sight over sound. This is what Macaulay had sensed in his famous remarks on the aural character of Milton's poetry and "the extreme remoteness of the associations by means of which it acts on the reader." Something of this kind happens, of course, in all interpretable verse—interpretation recovers hidden associations and evaluates them. But we see here exactly what is involved: the precise nature of those hidden terms or tacit associations.

In Milton, generally speaking, they "voice" the image. Mythos is shown to be based on logos, *numen* on *nomen*. Even parts of sound seem virtually to coalesce as morphemes or mythemes.[34] It is possible that Puritan hermeneutics encouraged this voicing of the image—"Faith cometh by hearing" (Rom. 10:17); "True acquaintance with God is made more by the ears than by the eyes" (Calvin).[35]

The middle terms, moreover, belong less to the plain sense than to the romance of scripture: to apocrypha, homiletic tradition, and curious learning. They often mingle with classical or pagan themes—as is, historically, quite natural, and because Milton is interested in the devious figure which takes us from error to intimations of a purer truth. His transition, for example, from "Stars of Morning" to "Dew-drops" is probably supported by harmonizing Job 38:28 with the myth that dew fell from heaven.[36]

34. Cf. W. K. Wimsatt, Jr., *The Verbal Icon* (1954), p. 210 on Milton's partial homophones and extenuated puns.

35. See U. Milo Kaufmann, *The Pilgrim's Progress and Traditions in Puritan Meditation* (New Haven, 1966), esp. chaps. 2 ("Puritan Hermeneutics") and 10 ("The Interior Voice"). Yet, as Arnold Stein has said, "In poetry . . . we see only through hearing." His important remarks on sound-symbols, in *Answerable Style* (Minneapolis, 1953), esp. pp. 150–53, transcend the specifically cultural context of Milton's verse.

36. God speaking out of the whirlwind, taunts Job with that picture of the morning stars and asks him (inter alia): "Hath the rain a father? Or who hath begotten the drops of dew?" The change of "Stars of Morning" into "Dew-drops" may be a subtle visionary comment on Satan's denial that he is begotten. On dew from heaven see Marvell's "On a drop of Dew," and Will Richter, ed. *Georgica* (Munich, 1957), p. 329.

This does not mean it is caused by those allusions (the flower-star combination has a mythopoeic vigor with special appeal to creation stories); rather, it is thematically integrated and justified by "proof-texts" like these. The poetry of such figures does not reside in the attractive errors of myth any more than their truth is locatable in doctrine: the poetry is *in* this wandering movement which subsumes and transmutes, which rejects by "impearling."[37]

Adam's image, though a highly condensed rather than amplified figure, makes essentially the same use of tacit middle terms. But this time we do not have to pass via an image to a motto, because a key phrase in the image tends already to absorb the latter and reveal how words become mythopoeic.

The key phrase is "Balmy Sweat." It stands out because of a semantic contrast between adjective and noun emphasized by the conventional pairings (general noun and more specific adjective) of "soundest sleep," "Flowery herb," "reeking moisture," and because "Beams the Sun" refers back through the B (m) S alliteration. This focus on "Balmy Sweat," reinforced by a second semantic ambivalence in "reeking," leaves us suspended between a simple and a complex reading of the phrase.

There are as many forces working to neutralize the contrasts as to sustain them. If "Sweat" is explained as an intensifying metaphor which substitutes a special term for a generic ("sweat" for "wetness"), there is no pejorative overtone, and the phrase means "pleasant, profuse wetness." Also, the B (m) S sequence of "Balmy Sweat . . . Beams the Sun" may weaken the contrast between adjective and noun if taken as decorative rather than semantic—as sound rather than sense, drawn out. But should an alliance form between the pejorative overtones of "reeking" and "sweat," and attention be returned to potential semantic contrasts, the B (m) S pattern helps to appose adjective and noun, so that "Balmy" stands against "Sweat" with nominative force. The phrase then moves toward its strongest internal contrast and becomes an oxymoron.

"Balmy Sweat" may therefore be read as "pleasant, profuse wetness," or as "sweet sweat"—an oxymoron that brings lan-

37. Stanley E. Fish, in *Surprised by Sin* (New York, 1967), a most forceful study of Milton's use of attractive error, errs, it seems to me, by relying solely on the condescending aspect of the principle of accommodation.

guage close to a limit of expression. The same phonemic space (the difference is but the modulation of a vowel) is competed for by opposite meanings.[38] This semantic labor, stylized and cool as it is, may coincide with a somatic labor which Adam's nativity circumscribes. Does not "Balmy Sweat," in this context of a birth scene, mingle proleptically the balm of fruitfulness and the sweat of the curse, the labor to come and the regeneration to come from that? "In sorrow thou shalt bring forth. . . . In the sweat of thy face shalt thou eat bread" (Gen. 3:16). Sweat is a balm because birth is not yet this wounding of man and of earth, or because the birth wound to come will prove to be a happy wound.[39]

A disclaimer is necessary at this point. To see so much meaning in the text is not to overcharge it, because such meaning remains virtual and because we are dealing not with an extraordinary stylistic phenomenon but with ordinary, if poetical, modes of implication. "Balmy Sweat" is hardly a daring coinage: it is close to being a stock figure of the kind which the next century (influenced by Milton) developed into poetic diction. As if grammar were fossilized myth, such figures waver between grammatical and mythic status.[40] To attack Milton one need only neglect

38. On Milton's larger use of oxymoron, see J. Peter, *A Critique of Paradise Lost* (New York, 1960), p. 39. "Sweet sweat" (cf. notes 43 and 44, below) seems to point to what de Saussure named the diacritical basis of signification, and it recalls Freud's remarks on the antithetical meaning of root words.

39. Lynn Thorndyke, in *A History of Magic and Experimental Science* (New York, 1923), 1: xvi, quotes examples from the Christian Apocrypha in which healing power is ascribed to perspiration and other secretions. One story tells of a balsam sprung up on the road to Egypt from the sweat which had run from Christ's body. For Paracelsus "Balm" is the element assuring the coherency and preservation of all things, an effluvium at once starry and earthy. Cf. Donne's "The generall balme th'hydroptic earth hath drunk," and W. A. Murray, "Donne and Paracelsus," *Review of English Studies* 25 (1949): 117–20.

40. Consider the figurative grammar in "On his Crest / Sat horror Plum'd" (4.989). Horror is personified by being sandwiched between a verb and an adjective that carry the animating metaphor. A noun, as it were, as well as a quality or effect, is being personified. The noun feeling remains and produces (without making the figure less efficient) that wavering between grammar and myth. J. I. Cope, in *The Metaphoric Structure of Paradise Lost,* speculates on Milton's word consciousness, but mainly on his tendency to spatialize and objectify (certainly a factor in poetic diction).

this in-between quality and take his phrases as epic boom—as inflating sound into substance, into the empty substantiality of mythic personification. But Milton's mind inhabits the region *between* logos and mythos: perhaps the region of language itself, that smithy of sense. It is a region of shadowy meanings, fleeting images, but also of surprising interchanges between sound and sense. Let us admit, then, that "Balmy Sweat" expands, by alliteration, into "Beams the Sun," and it begins to absorb the image. Let us "voice" this image and amplify the B (m) S alliteration till it approaches semantic or mythic power.[41]

"Balmy Sweat" paraphrases "sudantes balsama (silvae)," which refers in Milton's *Epitaphium Damonis* (l. 186) to the Balm trees where the phoenix makes his abode. Adam, like the phoenix, is a kind of sunbirth: an aurelian who emerges with surprising alacrity from the larval state. Is it possible that "Balmy Sweat" carries with it the idea of a phoenix birth? Could Adam's first image fuse the idea of generation with that of regeneration through the suggestive power of this "spermatic" phrase?[42]

It is not enough, of course, to show an association in Milton between balm, the phoenix, and sun birth. "Balmy Sweat" must be linked, at the same time, to the theme of labor in its relation to grace. If the same matrix has two sets of associations, one could then argue for their convergence in Adam's image.

Now "sudantes balsama (silvae)" is a veiled borrowing from Virgil's *Georgics* (2.118).[43] Virgil mentions the "odorato . . . sudantia ligno balsama" as a remarkable result of tillage in spe-

41. Here one approaches, of course, kabbalistic or magical techniques of personifying the letter—of ascribing generative power to certain vocables. That there is a link between mystical semantics and scientific semeiotics is suggested by some unpublished notes of De Saussure. They consider the idea that grammatical systems may be patterned on the "declining" of a divine name and that phonetic systems may be related to its covert distribution as an anagram. See J. Starobinski, "Les Anagrammes de Ferdinand de Saussure," *Mercure de France* (Février, 1964).

42. Seen in this perspective, a whole complex of ideas concerning the creation of man out of a material element (fire, water, earth) is evoked.

43. "That fragrant wood, from whence / Sweet Balsam sweats" *(Virgil's Georgicks,* Englished by Tho. May [London, 1622]). Cf. Crashaw's "Balsam-sweating bough," st. 12 of "The Weeper." Douglas Bush, pp. 271–86 of his *Mythology,* studies instances of "this veiled kind of borrowing . . . perhaps the most interesting of all."

cial, perhaps legendary soil. Through plants like these Virgil celebrates the efficacy of human labor. Yet he does not forget here or elsewhere the *praesentia numina* (1.10), the cooperative or disturbing presence of divine agency. Every harvest, in Virgil, is precarious: the field stands ripe for reaping, a sudden storm comes on, and the astonished farmer sees his "hopeful sheaves" fly about like chaff (*Georgics* 1.). Such moments acknowledge, in a poem glorifying human toil and science, the uncertainty of man's labor without grace; and they are among the strongest reasons for the poem's influence on Spenser and Milton.

Dryden translates the lines on the Balsam as

> Balm slowly trickles through the bleeding Veins
> Of happy Shrubs in Idumaean Plains.

Though there is nothing about "bleeding Veins" in the original, the translator draws on well-known literary sources. The "happy," equally gratuitous, stems from a related group of commonplaces. The shrubs are happy because they grow in the fortunate fields, in "Araby the blest." But the adjective's intrinsic function is to point up the contrast of "Balm . . . bleeding," which suggests a happy wound.[44] It is not far from this fortunate shrubbery to its inhabitant the phoenix, who might be said to suffer a happy death. As the wound of the incense tree is the sign of its fruitfulness, so the death of the phoenix prepares his renewal. This has no direct connections with Virgil but expresses the erotic mind exploiting pagan myths or the Christian mind seeking prefigurations.[45] "Balmy Sweat" and "bloody sweat," generative moisture and regenerative labor, merge easily enough. *O foenix culprit!*

James Joyce's genial garble also voices an image. "There are

44. Cf. "The myrrh sweete bleeding in the bitter wounde" (Spenser, *Faerie Queene* 1.1.9). Myrrh and Balsam, exotic Arabian plants, are often associated. "There growes (th'*Hesperian* Plant) the precious Reed / Whence *Sugar* sirrops in abundance bleed; / There weeps the Balm, and famous Trees from whence / Th'*Arabians* fetch perfuming Frankinsence" (Grosart, 1: 45a; cf. the sweet-sweat combination of 1: 43a). Gesenius glosses the Hebrew BeSaMim (myrrh, spices) as related to Balsam. As in Spenser, where the Myrrh is part of Error's wood, this image of the weeping or wounded tree is rarely without ambivalence.

45. As in Donne ("The Canonization") or Shakespeare ("The Phoenix and the Turtle").

times," it has been said of Milton, when "he anticipates Joyce's consciously exploited capacity of writing simultaneously as if in a new dimension of language on several levels."[46] *Finnegans Wake* depends on received emblems, now forcibly "collideor-scoped," systematically wounded. Whether it is a happy wound that Joyce inflicts on language remains moot. It may lead to that same "frustration of narrative interest" or "modification of the horizontal movement of human history" in favor of the "vertical motion of the spiritual life"[47] one finds in *Paradise Lost*. Narrative conduct, in Milton, is subordinated to hermeneutic structure: inner light, the divining rod of the interpreter, sounds scripture out. Narration becomes, in fact, a kind of concordance: a "harmonious vision" of places in scripture, of myth and scripture, or of the wanderings of the spirit through history. Milton's poem makes us more into interpreters than readers.

For Joyce, however, history is a palimpsest rather than a typological prophecy; it has adulteration, not accommodation, as its moving principle. His "abnihilisation of the etym" even tampers with the atom of the word. It produces an etymopoeic riot that questions the idea of virgin texts and sacred words. Concordance moves closer to contamination, in the sense of conflation (the generative principle of so many romances) as well as impurity. "In the beginning was the Word, and the Word was contaminated" —the artist's freedom and the critic's mission arise, perhaps, from the same trauma.

46. Watkins, *Anatomy of Milton's Verse,* p. 16. See also his mention of "O foenix culprit," p. 41 n. For experiments in multiple writing, see H. H. Hudson, *The Epigram in the English Renaissance* (Princeton, 1947), pp. 159–62; and Louis Martz, *The Paradise Within* (New Haven, 1964), pp. 5–18, on Vaughan.

47. The first quotation is from Donald Davie, *The Living Milton,* ed. F. Kermode (1960), p. 80; the last two from Allen, "Milton and the Descent to Light." The thesis that Milton's difficulties in *Paradise Lost* stemmed from an inherited and intractable plot line is A. J. A. Waldock's in *Paradise Lost and its Critics* (London, 1947).

Marvell, St. Paul, and the Body of Hope

Stanzas 5 and 6 of "The Garden" have become the cruxes of many contemporary interpretations of the poem. Starting with an analysis of their difficulties, I would like to come to a more adequate reading of both "The Garden" and the mower poems. My first section will be a purely contextual study of 5 and 6, but I shall seek help, after that, from the relations of seventeenth-century poetry to religious thought and to emblem techniques.

The poet in stanza 1 of "The Garden" ironically supposes man to run after the part (Palm, Oak, and Bays) instead of the whole (the repose of all flowers and all trees), where the whole does not even need running after. He himself retreats from the world and enters a garden (st. 2ff.) where he finds what he desires: repose, innocent love, solitude. But stanza 5 shows his quiet love for nature reciprocated with alarming intensity:

> What wond'rous Life in this I lead!
> Ripe Apples drop about my head;
> The Luscious Clusters of the Vine
> Upon my Mouth do crush their Wine;
> The Nectaren, and curious Peach,
> Into my hands themselves do reach;
> Stumbling on Melons, as I pass
> Insnar'd with Flow'rs, I fall on Grass.[1]

This is too solicitous a solitude, and the poet's mind returns to itself (st. 6):

> Mean while the Mind, from pleasure less,
> Withdraws into its happiness:
> The Mind, that Ocean where each kind

1. All quotations are from the Muses Library text of *The Poems of Andrew Marvell,* ed. Hugh MacDonald (London, 1952).

151

Does streight its own resemblance find:
Yet it creates, transcending these,
Far other Worlds, and other Seas;
Annihilating all that's made
To a green Thought in a green Shade.

The mind's new creation links repose to a vision of a world
beyond this world, to which the garden is no more than a porch.
Perhaps *perch* is the better word, since in the next stanza (7) the
poet slips his body off, and his soul flies up, not beyond the garden
but into the boughs. Thus the soul still ends in a tree (cf. ll. 27–28),
and the final stanzas emphasize its "garden-state," rather than its
anticipation of ultimate flight and metamorphosis. We are left
with the image of an artful, this-worldly garden, a mimesis of
Eden, in which the soul's labor of waiting is rewarded by what it
sought in the first stanza, the transforming of time into "all Flow'rs
and all Trees."

Three major queries attend the central stanzas. How do we
interpret the curiously erotic fruits of stanza 5? How is the mind's
withdrawal, described in stanza 6, related to their ardor? And
what precisely is the meaning of 6, with its suggestion of a two-
rung Platonic ladder, which seems to reach far beyond the Garden,
yet also ends in something "green"?

Whether or not these fruits are sexual, they effectively lessen
the poet in some way and so stand again his emphasis on the
garden's holistic nature ("All Flow'rs . . ." "Two Paradises . . . in
one" "holesome Hours"). Again, if the poet withdraws into the
mind, it is to pursue that for which he originally entered the
garden, having withdrawn from a too busy world: wholeness and
repose. But the mind does not immediately satisfy this desire,
being also crowded—with the ideal correlatives of natural things.
It may, however, imagine worlds transcending the consciousness
of ideal "kinds" (i.e., species or sexes),[2] worlds entirely beyond
duality.[3] The final lines of the stanza suggest an intuition that

2. "A class (of human beings or animals) of the same sex; a sex (in
collective sense)" *(OED* s. v. 7, but especially s. v. 10c). This usage is
common as late as Dryden and Pope.

3. "Resemblance" (l. 44), is probably colored by Christian Platonism
and could bear both an ontological and an amatory meaning. The former
is commonplace—Spenser uses it in the "Hymn in Honor of Beauty," ll.
120–21 ("faire soules, which have / The most resemblaunce of that
heavenly light")—but the *OED* does not quote, and I could not find a pure

fuses the real and the mental garden into one whole and reposeful entity.

The paradox, however, remains: that to know this imaginary body of things the mind must annihilate or make into nothing "all that's made" (perhaps the "ea quae facta" of Rom. 1:20). The paradox is strengthened by a doubling of "green" which suggests that the things which are not made are conceived within the context of a thing which is made, the garden. The succeeding stanzas enforce this impression of an inescapable relation between the garden and the poet. His mind may annihilate it, his soul be ever on wing to leave it, but the garden still stands between him and his greatest hope, his desire for wholeness. To understand this "between"—both obstacle and mediation—we call on a source familiar to Marvell.

I have anticipated it by a reference to Romans 1:20. This is one of two exceptional passages in Saint Paul dealing with nature's eschatological aspect. The other is Romans 8:19 ff. Both were commonplaces, proof texts giving nature an essential place in the scheme of salvation. Augustine remembers them in one of the

---

example of the word used metonymously for "the (ideally) resembling person or sex." Empson takes this meaning for granted when he writes: "the *kinds* look for their *resemblance* . . . out of a desire for creation" *(Some Versions of Pastoral* [London, 1950]). It is true, on the other hand, that a Platonist like Ficino, who remains untranslated in the 17th century, uses the Latin *similitudo* (and sometimes *simulacrum*) in the double meaning here attributed to "resemblance"; see Raymond Marcel, *Marsile Ficin Sur le Banquet de Platon ou de l'Amour* (Paris, 1956), pp. 206, 251, 252. The potential richness of "similitudo-resemblance" comes from its being used by two different yet constantly merging philosophical traditions: the essentially Christian of the "speculum" of creatures, and the Platonic of "Amorem procreat similitudo" (Ficino), of the lover drawn via the beloved to the "most resemblance" with God. See Wallerstein, "The Various Light," *Seventeenth-Century Poetic* (Madison, 1950); and cf. "God made the Universe and all the Creatures contained therein as so many Glasses wherein he might reflect his own Glory . . . *Remotiores Similitudines Creaturae ad Deum dicuntur Vestigium; propinquiores vero Imago* . . . Good Men . . . find every Creature pointing out to that Being whose image and superscription it bears, and climb up from those darker resemblances of the Divine Wisdom and Goodness . . . till they sweetly repose themselves in the bosom of the Divinity. . . ." (John Smith, *Select Discourses* [London, 1660], pp. 430–31).

most moving episodes of his *Confessions*.[4] Romans 1:20, associated with Platonic discipline raising the mind from visible to invisible things,[5] says that God, though invisible, is clearly revealed in nature: "Ever since the creation of the world his invisible nature, namely his eternal power and deity, has been clearly understood in the things that have been made."

The second passage from Romans justified yet more strongly a Christian, or even mystical, consideration of nature.[6] It reads:

> For the creation [creature] waits with eager longing [earnest expectation] for the revealing of the Sons of God; for the creation was subject to futility [vanity], not of its own will but by the will of him who subjected it in hope; because the creation itself will be set free from the bondage to decay and obtain the glorious liberty of the children of God. We know that the whole creation has been groaning together until now; and not only the creation, but we ourselves, who have the first fruits of the Spirit, groan inwardly as we wait for adoption as sons, the redemption of our bodies. [Revised Standard Version, Rom. 8:19–23; King James Version in brackets.]

4. 9.24–25. Cf. 10.9–10. Both recall an *ascensus mentis* from the "things that are made" to an intuition of the Wisdom "per quam fiunt omnia ista." (Wisdom, or Sapientia, has its own theological history; cf. Milton's "Omnific Word," *Paradise Lost,* 7.217.) When Crashaw wishes to hymn "The Name above every Name, the Name of Jesus," he calls on Nature and Art, "All Things that Are / Or, what's the same, / Are Musical." The Hermetic τὰ ὄντα may be implicated.

5. *Confessions,* the all-important Bk. 7, in particular 23–26. See also W. R. Inge, *Christian Mysticism* (London, 1899) whose two chapters on nature-mysticism carry Rom. 1:20 and 8:19 as epigraphs. Ruth Wallerstein, after quoting Tertullian, who relies on Rom. 1:20, observes: "Symbolic thought is thus rooted for the Christian tradition in the epistles of Paul. It will be noted that Plato stands beside Paul" (*Seventeenth-Century Poetic,* p. 31).

6. See Henry Vaughan, "And do they so? have they a Sense / Of ought but Influence? / Can they their heads lift, and expect, / And groan too?" The poem is prefaced by Rom. 8:19, quoted as "Etenim res Creatae exerto Capite observantes expectant revelationem Filiorum Dei" (*The Works of Henry Vaughan,* ed. L. C. Martin [Oxford, 1914] 2: 432). G. M. Hopkins's poem to the Ribblesdale landscape, "Earth, sweet Earth . . ." is prefaced by the same text (*Poems of G. M. Hopkins,* ed. R. Bridges [New York, 1948], p. 240).

Paul says that nature fell because of man, not of its own fault, and will be redeemed with man, not of its own power. Hence it looks to man with eager longing and groans, and man also groans, because he too is waiting, like nature, for redemption, though he has the first fruits of the Spirit—i.e., the knowledge, through Christ, of the redemption of the body (cf. 1 Cor. 15:20).

I propose to read stanzas 5 and 6 in the light of these *loci classici* on nature. The first statement becomes, in theology, one of the major proof-texts for the concept of *lumen naturale,* or the "light of nature," developed by Thomas Aquinas from beginnings in Augustine.[7] The Romans, says Paul, are inexcusable in not accepting the new faith, because like nature itself they have a purely natural capacity for recognizing what is divine. They must be blinding themselves to Christ. In later developments the polemical context of the passage becomes often less important than the idea in it that both man and nature possess an inherent source of illumination. If St. Paul could be in the mind of a poet dealing

7. Fuller documentation of the historical development may be found in Rudolf Eisler, *Wörterbuch der philosophischen Begriffe,* 4th ed. (Berlin, 1929), 2: 67–69. Rom. 1: 20 is introduced by Milton at exactly the right point in *Paradise Lost,* when Adam and Eve hymn the works of God at dawn (5.154–59). It enters again at 8.273–79, when Adam by the light of nature deduces the great Maker from his creation. The quotation from John Smith (note 4 above) refers implicitly to Rom. 1:20 and goes on to make the allusion explicit: ". . . they sweetly repose themselves in the bosom of the Divinity: and while they are thus conversing with this lower World and are viewing *the invisible things of God in the things that are made* . . . they find God many times secretly flowing into their Souls. . . ." In Dante the concept plays an exceedingly important role as Charles Singleton has pointed out in his lucid "The Three Lights," *Dante Studies* 2 (Cambridge, Mass., 1954); and the idea of the "light of nature" is, in my opinion, one of the important links between Medieval, Renaissance, and Romantic views of nature: it does not designate simply reason, or the inner light, but generally reason kindled by a contact with creatures. The most eloquent seventeenth-century formulation I know is Donne's Sermon preached on Easter Day 1628, *The Sermons of John Donne,* ed. E. M. Simpson and G. R. Potter (Berkeley and Los Angeles, 1953–62), 7 (1956), 219–36. Grotius, at Rom. 1:21 ("for although they [i.e., the Romans] knew God"), remarks: "Naturali iure, non familiari"; and goes on to quote the Church Fathers on the two "notitiae gradus," *Annotationes in Novum Testamentum* (Paris, 1646), 2: 178–79. Andrew Willet, in his *Hexapla . . . (Cambridge,* 1611), says at 1:19: "They had the knowledge of God by the light of nature, and by the light of the creatures."

seriously with nature (and especially this passage which played an important role in the Platonic-Christian synthesis), then the simple and well-known idea of the "light of nature" may aid significantly in interpreting "The Garden" and similar poems.

In stanza 5, for example, nature seems more knowing and intense than the poet in his strange naïvete ("What wondrous life in this I lead!"). Exactly what nature "knows" as if by its own light Paul's second statement will explain. Paul sees nature and man joined in their hope of attaining the same glorious end, a "redemption of the body," and it is the creature which looks earnestly to man for its liberation (either because man will be the cause of it or, more probably, because he is the dial and chronometer of its hope).[8] Stanza 5 might therefore be read as a witty emblem of man hunted by nature into one body with it. Nature is, in a sense, the wrong body, as we shall point out later on. But the gods of stanza 4 also pursue their prey *in order that* it metamorphose and become Tree, Laurel, Reed. They chase Ovid's women with (at least in point of syntax)[9] an eschatological purpose. The aggressive fruits of stanza 5, which show an analogue of that eager longing mentioned by Paul, also seem to wish to hasten redemption, to mingle their life with the poet's because his and theirs is ultimately intertwined. At the end of the stanza ("Insnar'd with flow'rs, I fall on Grass") the poet is near to being transformed, like the women of 4, into a green body.[10]

From a purely literary standpoint, what Marvell does is to take a Pauline figure of speech literally. This taking literally is, as

8. Cf. Willet, *Hexapla,* pp. 367–69; and Grotius, *Annotationes,* pp. 259–60.

9. Remembering the ambivalence of the Latin *ut* construction, which may introduce either a purpose or a result clause, Marvell here effects a synecdochal substitution of the first for the second *("Apollo* hunted *Daphne* so / Only that she might Laurel grow").

10. Stanza 77 of "Appleton House," to which 5 of "The Garden" has occasionally been compared, also contains, in the image of the "courteous *Briars"* urged by Marvell to nail him through, a hint of the redemptive relation of poet and nature. Both stanzas, moreover, suggest an ambivalence in this relationship to which I refer later: the ensnared poet is man reduced to a divine steadfastness of imagination by overhasty or foreshortened means. The similarity of "Bermudas," ll. 21 ff., probably comes through a common tradition of 'ideal landscape' *(locus amoenus),* but it is the function which each picture has in its poem that is important.

we shall see, a common device in Marvell; it may extend here to yet another scriptural metaphor. Stanzas 4–6 all depict metamorphoses of something human into something green, and many readers have felt that the "I fall on Grass" of 5 may mockingly echo a Biblical proverb—"All flesh is grass" (e.g., Isa. 40.6). It has not been observed, however, that the fruits of 5, which are given the passions of flesh, suggest the converse of this thought, namely "All grass (viz. fruit) is flesh."

Stanzas 4 to 6 become, through this, a variation on one eschatalogical theme. All flesh is grass; but the "green" thought to which the poet sacrifices all things (ll. 47–48) may well be its redemptive converse, pictured in lines 33 ff. and hinted at by stanza 4: "All grass is flesh." It is his hope in a redeemed body, and a love in accord with it, for which he (imaginatively) destroys "all that's made."

Perhaps the reading here advanced is possible even without reference to St. Paul. It may be unnecessary to harmonize "All grass is flesh" with Romans if one is attentive to the quicknesses of Marvell's mind. Yet the Christian source may actually suggest one reason why this poetry is not more overtly Christian. However complex the thought through which he passes, Marvell, wearing the pastoral mask, realizes it by "the light of nature."[11] The hope in redemption so wittily expressed is also literally a green thought, as if nature itself possessed it or brought it forth. The question why Marvell should wish to put on the pastoral mask cannot be answered at this point: he has, we suggest later, a religious reason related to his knowledge of the precipitous nature of hope and his desire to chasten hope into diffidence.

11. There is no need to bring in the iconographic tradition to help with the significance of "green." But at least nothing in it contradicts Marvell's use of the color to denote (roughly) "a hope involving or expressed by nature." Alciati has hope dressed green in emblem 94; emblem 117 explains that "Nos sperare docet viridis"; Whitney's *Choice of Emblems* (1586) picks up the reference in the emblem "In Colores"; and Peacham's *Minerva Britanna* (1612) says of Repentance; "The cullar greene, she most delightes to weare, / Tells how her hope, shall overcome dispaire." Ripa's *Iconologia* also has hope dressed in green. Cf. D. C. Allen, "Symbolic Color in the Literature of the Renaissance," *Philological Quarterly* 15 (1936): 81–92, esp. 86; and Wallerstein, *Seventeenth-Century Poetic*, pp. 159 ff. and 321 ff.

One thing, however, is clear. The special theological basis of the light of nature may actually have helped to make Marvell's poem more than theological in mode. The modern reader is tempted to take it as entirely secular or humanistic. The poem is certainly a step toward the Neoclassical, which shuns the direct treatment of the mystery part of religion, and toward the Romantics, who revive the mystery as an integral part of the human, rather than divine or enthusiastic, imagination. What Paul calls Hope becomes in them Imagination; and its dialectic is, in the main, freed from theology. Yet if "The Garden," by its curiously literal use of the idea of the light of nature, points forward to later poems, its continuity and inner logic remain linked to Pauline thought. I would now like to show that "The Garden" is essentially about the precarious relation of man's hope to his hope in nature. Behind it lies the disparity between nature and grace, continually overcome, continually reasserted.

According to St. Paul, faith or hope are based on the evidence of things not seen (Heb. 11:1). The pasture of the religious soul is a world beyond this one, although the first fruits of that world may be tasted here. Marvell, however, at the beginning of his poem, seeks the garden to make his hope directly visible, as in "The Mower's Song," where the mower's mind

> in the greenness of the Grass
> Did see its Hopes as in a Glass.[12]

The poet who enters the garden sees his hope in its plants, sees its innocence and repose as a kind of heaven on earth:

> Your sacred Plants, if here below,
> Only among the Plants will grow.

The "if" is the only remnant of uncertainty. Yet while his imagination turns to the garden, he perceives that its imaginations is turned toward him! As lovers are star-crossed, so man and nature are hope-crossed. The garden that in stanzas 2–4 was likely to embody his hope, in stanza 5 projects its own hope—man—to the poet. In this way nature paradoxically reminds him that his hope

12. There is a commonplace reference here to 1 Cor. 13:12.

cannot be turned to nature, that he must renounce visibility and turn into himself.

Stanza 6 then shows the poet withdrawing into the mind, beginning to hope for what he cannot see. "Who hopes for what he sees? But if we hope for what we do not see, we wait for it in patience" (Rom. 8:24–25). The dialectic between sight and a hope always transcending sight is pushed to its last conclusions. The mind, that ocean mirror, contains the ideal image (the Narcissus) of every species. It is, nevertheless, unsatisfied and annihilates, supremely, all visibles, all quicksilver bodies.[13] Instead of continuing to mirror natural species, it creates "far other" worlds, purely imaginary.

The Pauline context illumines, finally, the action of the entire poem. As in the Horatian Ode and "Upon Appleton House," Marvell is deeply concerned with the question of the redemptive use of time. His concern touches, yet goes beyond, the classical debate between the active and the contemplative life. And it is, very directly, the time sense of the poem which first charms and then continues to hold the reader. Marvell's timing is best described by comparing it to Saint-Amant's—a poet whose influence has been noted but not interpreted.[14] The stanzas of Saint-Amant's "La Solitude" and "Le Contemplateur" are neat and leisurely units, whose continuity is almost peripatetic. The French poet provides a personable series of tableaux; he wants to intensify our sense for the mind's freedom vis-à-vis time and nature. Marvell's "Mean while," introducing stanza 6, avoids like Saint-Amant's "tântot" the impression of strict sequence; all his transitions, in fact, explicit or implicit, evoke a similar mood of casual rather than causal progression. But if Marvell imitates the libertine meanderings of his French source, it is to counterpoint an inner hastiness. His poem begins with the theme of haste, and he knows only too well that hope, whether political or spiritual, also contains haste, in the form of a deep hate of medial time.

13. Empson suggests, in *Some Versions of Pastoral,* that "streight" in l. 44 is not only or necessarily an adverb of time: one could read "Does find its own resemblance [to be] streight," i.e., too narrowly circumscribed. Either way of reading the word could harmonize with the present interpretation.

14. See Wallerstein, *Seventeenth-Century Poetic,* pp. 318–55.

While Saint-Amant makes free with time, the poet of "The Garden" is always on the point of an untimely vaulting over it.

It is this tendency, or temptation, which brings us back to the Pauline context. The deceptive movement of "The Garden" is from the haste mentioned in stanza 1 to repose, but even within the garden haste reappears because it is integral to hope. Though man's mind should be purified of haste, of the too-active urging of its object, the poet who retires into his *hortulus* finds that the quiet plants of stanza 2 become the precipitous wooers of stanza 5; and he himself continues to objectify his hope in visible terms, to seek the "divine body" of imagination (I borrow the term from Blake). Thus the spiritual combat never ends, because hope has in it a tragic or ironic flaw by which it defeats its own expectation by anticipation. I said previously that nature, in stanza 5, hunts man into one body with it, which perhaps is the wrong body. The rococo fall pictured there points to a foreshortening of the Pauline travail of patience. The fruits are given the passions of flesh, but only succeed in turning flesh (the poet stumbling) to grass. If Marvell expresses less a particular eschatology than the form of eschatological thinking as a whole, one could say that the poet in stanza 5 is in danger of being trapped by the illusion of an earthly paradise. Insnared, he may not get beyond the upper point of Dante's Purgatorio, or what Blake calls the lower paradise (Beulah), marked by innocence, sensuous passivity, and the acceptance of contraries.

The poet escapes this temptation, but only by (paradigmatically) skirting a second. I think Marvel, in stanza 6, portrays himself falling in a different way, this time upward. The temptation he suffers is that of pure hope, of an absolute transference of hope to a world beyond this world. Just as nature had sought to hasten redemption (st. 5), so he too seeks to hasten it by the obverse means. Stanza 6 retains a hint of haste, of the poet's undue mental violence in the opposite direction (against "all that's made"). Only in 7 is haste clearly put off, and a true image of Paul's "waiting in patience" is given. The picture of the soul in 7 stands over against its previous evocations. Instead of being insnared (as in 5), it here does its own snaring—waves a "various light" in its wings as if to transform time into wing power.[15] The soul will not leave the garden by a premature ecstasy, as in 6; it stays there to gather strength for its eventual flight, perhaps to turn the "various" into a constant light. The "garden-state" (8) is this stasis,[16] the roosting place of the resolved soul, resolved not so much against created pleasure as against false bodies of hope. Though still divided from its true body, nothing (no Eve) stands between it and the substance of things hoped for.

The last stanza then recalls the garden as a *res facta* and work of patience:

> How well the skilful Gardner drew
> Of flow'rs and herbes this Dial new. . . .

Marvell implies the relation of faith and works, for here the gardener cooperates with nature to anticipate redemption. This last picture of the garden is marked by an emphasis on time and labor, but a flower time and a flowering labor. The new-drawn dial is at once temporal and floral, so that the victor's wreath (st. 1) now becomes a circle of time against time, a living garland of plants. It records an unhasty growing of creation into its true body, the redemption of nature with man, of all in all. But it remains, nevertheless, a symbolic gesture, an artifice, and recalls that the best our poet (like the gardener) can do is to gather us up into the "artifice of eternity."

15. The image has been enriched by Wallerstein's chapter, "The Various Light," in *Seventeenth-Century Poetic*. Hyman suggests an allusion to Genesis 1:14 ("Marvell's *Garden*," *ELH* 25 [1958], 21) which enforces, if correct, the idea of the soul's action within or on time. The image seems to me a fit emblem for Paul's "waiting in patience." A striking parallel to both Marvell's thought and emblem is found in John Smith's *Select Discourses:* "And because all those scatter'd *Raies* of *Beauty* and Loveliness which we behold spread up and down all the World over, are onely the *Emanations* of that inexhausted *Light* which is above; therefore should we *love* them all in that, and climb up alwaies by those Sun-beames unto the Eternall Father of Lights: we should look upon him and take from him the pattern of our lives, and alwaies eying of him should . . . (as *Hierocles* speaks) polish and shape our Souls into the clearest resemblance of him" (pp. 156–57).

16. For other connotations of "Garden-state," see Bradbrook and Lloyd Thomas, *Andrew Marvell* (Cambridge, 1940), pp. 59–64.

My close use of Paul's text need not argue a similar procedure on Marvell's part. Hope's paradoxes were a commonplace; the Pauline texts their natural scaffolding. The poet could range among them as seriously and wittily as Crashaw and Cowley.[17] It is not important, moreover, to recognize Paul behind Marvell because it is *Paul:* there may be, as is usual in a writer of the Renaissance tradition, an implicit harmonizing of several sources. What is essential to recognize is the peculiarly *textual* quality and response of the poet's mind. The reader who sees Galatians 5:17 behind "A Dialogue between the Soul and the Body," or who catches Romans 8:19 and a play on Isaiah 40:6 in stanzas 4 and 5 of "The Garden," gains more than a religious commonplace, more even than a new link between letter and spirit. He sees that Marvell has wrought a device or emblem for the scriptural text.

The emblem was commonly defined as a mute poem, or one which speaks to the eye.[18] It was praised, above all, for its econ-

---

17. See Cowley's verses on "Hope" and Crashaw's answer "For Hope" in *Steps to the Temple* (1646) and *Carmen Deo Nostro* (1652). Cowley also has his own "For Hope." I should add that Hope, one of the three theological virtues, was generally distinguished from Faith with some clarity. Faith, based on assent, did not of itself satisfy man's desire for truth. He needed, in addition, Hope, that "taster of eternity" (Crashaw), which yielded a preview of heaven to sustain the believer in this life. "Even when we have faith, there still remains in the soul an impulse toward something else, namely, the perfect vision of the truth assented to on faith . . . stirrings of hope arise in the soul of the believer that by God's help he may gain possession of the goods he naturally desires, once he learns of them through faith" (Thomas Aquinas, *Compendium of Theology,* trans. C. Vollert, S.J. [St. Louis and London, 1947], p. 313). In the Renaissance emblem books Hope is generally represented with a cross-shaped anchor (cf. Spenser, *Faerie Queene,* 1.10.14) and sometimes with a spade. This conception has not, as far as I know, been discussed: it involves a linkage of patient labor and hope (cf. the last stanza of "The Garden"; also Ripa's comment on "Agricoltura" in the *Iconologia)* and may indicate that hope is the virtue keeping man faithful to the earth. The anchor cross expresses perhaps Christ's example and the expectation of a final journey but is derived textually from Heb. 6:19—see Picinelli, *Mundus Symbolicus,* trans. Aug. Erath (Cologne, 1687), Lib. 20, cap. 1.

18. "An emblem is but a silent parable," says Quarles in his *Emblemes* (1635). "Les Emblemes sont des discours muets, une Eloquence des yeux, une Morale en couleurs," maintains François Menestrier, *L'Art des Emblemes* (Lyons, 1662), also appropriating Horace's "Ut pictura poesis."

omy, for the very thing that commends metaphor and image to the modern poet: "Toutes les richesses de la Nature sont en petit: toute sa majesté, comme parle Pline, est reserrée et à l'étroit."[19] No emblem really lived up to this eulogistic description, which defines the ideal not the fact. Yet how apposite to Marvell, when transferred from visual to verbal! His verse seems a renewal of the spirit of the Greek Anthology, of its epigrams so closely connected to lapidary and pictorial inscriptions.[20] Verses used to accompany emblems as a dependent aid or as their soul. Marvell's poems, however, are autonomous emblems in verse, approaching the compactness of pictorial form and even implying, at times, a scripture text for motto.[21]

Emblems were not, of course, a truly pictorial mode, but strongly literary in conception, and employed (especially by Catholics) as illustrated primer morality. The idea behind the mode was, nevertheless, quite serious and often mystical and surpassed each individual attempt to realize it as the idea of the epic its various seventeenth-century embodiments (Milton excepted). For the influence of emblems on literature, see inter alia M. Praz, "Emblems and Devices in Literature," *Studies in Seventeenth-Century Imagery* (London, 1939), 1: 108–207; R. Freeman, *English Emblem Books* (London, 1948); and Elbert N. S. Thompson, *Literary Bypaths of the Renaissance* (New Haven, 1924), pp. 29–67.

19. Pere Le Moine, *De L'Art des Devices* (Paris, 1666), quoted by Praz, *Studies* 1: 52.

20. Praz remarks that of Alciati's emblems roughly 50 out of 220 are imitated or translated from the Greek epigrams of the *Planudean Anthology (Studies,* 1: 20 ff.). The epigrams were, in fact, superscriptions, or a derived genre, conceits illustrating objects or events. The exact relation of Marvell's poems, in point of genre and style, to the epigrammatic tradition has not been discussed. They seem to be an exceptional blending of the naïve and pointed epigram which James Hutton distinguishes so well in his *The Greek Anthology in France* (Ithaca, 1946). Only H. H. Hudson, as far as I know, discusses the question of how the seventeenth century lyric might have developed from the epigram in his unfinished *The Epigram in the English Renaissance* (Princeton, 1947).

21. Herbert and Quarles are, of course, Marvell's forerunners, but his specific difference is implicitly suggested by Miss Freeman's comments on them: "In Quarles' Emblems the poetry simply deduces ideas from a given image; it consequently requires the presence of an actual picture for the verse to analyze in detail and build its argument u,on. Herbert's poetry brings its pictures with it. It remains primarily visual, but the images presented have already been explored and when they enter the poem they enter it with their implications already worked out" *(English*

163

To prove an exact relationship is somewhat difficult. The poems having no explicit epigraphs like the emblems, we must keep, for the most part, to internal evidence. Austin Warren, in his study of Crashaw, has pointed to the ingenuity of the baroque emblem-makers, whose designs translate scriptural metaphors into exact visual terms: " 'I sleep, but my heart waketh' takes form in the recumbent figure of a virgin who, though the eyes of her body are closed, holds at arm's length a large heart centrally occupied by a large and wide-open eye. . . . An art of bizarre ingenuity, the sacred emblem does not hesitate to translate into visual form any metaphor offered, in poetry, to the ear."[22] Marvell, I suggest, performs a similar feat of wit. He also paints (but in words) little scenes which project literally certain scriptural metaphors. A text, or its central notion, is translated into a rebus, a special form of the emblem representing words by things. In Marvell's use of the rebus, the text is projected by the picture or action of the particular stanza.

An obvious analogue to the rebus in stanza 5 of "The Garden" is stanza 50 of "Upon Appleton House." Isaiah says "All flesh is grass," and Marvel gives body to the words in a micro-scene:

> With whistling Sithe, and Elbow strong
> These Massacre the Grass along:
> While one, unknowing, carves the *Rail,*
> Whose yet unfeather'd Quils her fail.
> The Edge all bloody from its Breast
> He draws, and does his stroke detest;
> Fearing the Flesh untimely mow'd
> To him a Fate as black forebode.

Emblem Books, pp. 154–55). Considering Marvell's poetry as the third step in this liberation of the poem from the picture emblem, we can say that the image of the Mower has not been explored previous to the poet: it is he who works out its implications within the poem, relying nevertheless on an understanding nourished by emblems. Ruth Wallerstein has seen the debt Marvell's poems owe to emblems *(Seventeenth-Century Poetic,* pp. 151–80), but she did not specify his difference within the tradition. See also Jean H. Hagstrum's analysis of English iconic poetry in *The Sister Arts* (Chicago, 1958), pp. 112–20.

22. *Richard Crashaw, A Study in Baroque Sensibility* (Ann Arbor, 1957), p. 73.

Does this not paint the words of scripture literally or, as Marvell himself puts it, "impart hearing to the eyes?"[23] But the stanza depicts, in addition to the scripture text, the movement of the mower's mind toward it. Here a further resemblance to "The Garden" appears. The mower discovers that all flesh is grass by moving through its converse, all grass is flesh. The converse is already implicit in the poet's metaphor of "massacring" the grass; a metaphor which becomes literal almost at once when the Rail is "carved"; and this word, by the way, which likens the cut of the scythe to that of a neat table knife, also becomes nearly literal in the next stanza, where Thestylis "forthwith means on it [the Rail] to sup." The proleptic use of metaphor (the unapparent movement from the metaphoric to the literal) and the use of the converse are among the defining traits of Marvell's poetry,[24] and to speculate on their ultimate role would require a further essay. But they are clearly signatures of an intensely eschatological mind. Marvel uses both to reverse relations—especially of man and nature or of figurative and literal—with a quasi-divine ease of manner. The world he creates is a precarious

23. "Insinuare sonos oculis," *The Poems of Andrew Marvell,* p. 67. Marvell's Latin epigram is a retranslation into Latin of a part of Georges de Brebeuf's translation of Lucan's *Pharsalia (La Pharsale de Lucain,* 1655; cf. H. M. Margoliouth, *The Poems and Letters of A. M.,* 1: 228). It is interesting to observe that Menestrier in his *L'Art des Emblemes,* pp. 15–16, cites the French verses which Marvell retranslates into Latin and praises them as an elegant definition of what happens in emblems. I hope to collect, in another essay, evidence of Marvell's playfulness with regard to the emblem tradition. Hagstrum *(The Sister Arts,* p. 95) has noted the link between Brebeuf and Menestrier, but not that between Marvell and Brebeuf. The theme of the transposition of eye and ear is characteristic of emblematic speculation and might be linked to what Hagstrum terms "the one element that was new, or at least that received greater emphasis in the century of the baroque than in the Renaissance . . . the notion that in the union of body and soul, picture and word, sense and intellect, there was some kind of interpenetration" *(The Sister Arts,* p. 97).

24. I use the term heuristically to indicate figures that could include inversion and reversal. The wittiest mottos of the emblem books were generally conversions in this sense—e.g., "Qui captat capitur"—and the form is beautifully used in many poems of the Greek Anthology, as in the following epigram (trans. Grotius): "Ex viva lapidem me Di facere. Sed ecce / Praxiteles vivam me facit ex lapide."

realm which mirrors the dialectic of hope, the drama of the believer's search for redemptive acts or evidences; yet he himself remains strangely uninvolved, a gay artificer. A glance at his most original creation, the Mower, should bear this out.

"The Mower's Song" depicts a midget catastrophe, which seemingly inverts the lesson of Romans 8:19, for it shows man involving hopeful nature in his fall instead of in his redemption. Here are the first four stanzas:

I

My Mind was once the true survey
Of all these Medows fresh and gay;
And in the greenness of the Grass
Did see its Hopes as in a Glass;
When *Juliana* came, and She
What I do to the Grass, does to my Thoughts and Me.

II

But these, while I with Sorrow pine,
Grew more luxuriant still and fine;
That not one Blade of Grass you spy'd,
But had a Flower on either side;
When *Juliana* came, and She
What I do to the Grass, does to my Thoughts and Me.

III

Unthankful Medows, could you so
A fellowship so true forego,
And in your gawdy May-games meet,
While I lay trodden under feet?
When *Juliana* came, and She
What I do to the Grass, does to my Thoughts and Me.

IV

But what you in Compassion ought,
Shall now by my Revenge be wrought:
And Flow'rs, and Grass, and I and all,
Will in one common Ruine fall.
For *Juliana* comes, and She
What I do to the Grass, does to my Thoughts and Me.

The poem's relation to stanza 5 of "The Garden" and stanza 50 of "Appleton House" is evident. The refrain again projects the thought that all flesh is grass. This combines with the idea of the "mower mown," which is the neatest example of the converse in Marvell's poetry, and basic to the whole series of mower poems.[25] It is the emblem of apocalypse, a figure of divine ironies, of unpredictable reversals. The mowers of "Appleton House" (sts. 49–53) also move in this lucid realm of perplexities. Passing, like the Israelites, through the sea (a sea of grass), they are clearly redemptive harvesters; yet their cutting down of the green may suddenly become a cutting off and turn this green sea red.

"The Mower's Song" is Marvell's nearest approach to a verse emblem.[26] Its refrain, which has been rightly said to recall the sweep of a scythe, links it to the class of figure poems, a well known but limited way of imitating emblems in verse. The re-

25. In the final line of "Damon the Mower" ("For Death thou art a Mower too"), death is a redemptive figure healing Damon's wound by a more ultimate wound. But he is redemptive only if what he does to Damon will be done to him (Death, the mower, will be mown: cf. 1 Cor. 15: 54–55). Quintillian's distinction between figures of speech and figures of thought is very hard to maintain in the case of Marvell. Image reversals, synecdochal substitution, conceptual metonymy (st. 1 of "The Garden"), and such witty transpositions as all flesh is grass—all grass is flesh, inform most of his poems.

26. Unless we chose "The Mower to the Glo-Worms." It is certain, in any case, that the Mower poems as a group (excluding, perhaps, the more discursive "The Mower against Gardens") are conceived in the spirit of emblems and stand midway between the more dependent emblem poem of Mildmay Fane or Herbert and the free mythmaking of modern poetry. The glowworm has an emblematic tradition clearer than that of the mower, who is almost completely Marvell's new emblem. May it suffice to point for the mower to George Wither's *"A Collection of Emblemes Ancient and Modern* (London, 1635), Bk. 1, illustration 21 (motto: "initium mors vitae") and Bk. 4, illustration 48 (motto: "omnis caro foenum"). These are pale though true foreshadowings of Marvell's conception, which is found more explicitly in Picinelli's *Mundus Symbolicus,* s. v. *Gramen* (Liber 10 cap. 21): "Gramen, ut laetius crescat, falce demetitur, et humo tenus considitur. Symbolo subscripsit Philotheus . . . LAETIUS UT SURGAT." As to the glowworm, it was inter alia an emblem for prudence, being associated with the proverbial ant, to which it gives light in Mildmay Fane's poem, "The Fallacy of the outward Man," *Otia Sacra* (1648). But prudence itself may be associated with the Light of Nature in the theological sense explained in note 7 above—which makes

167

frain, moreover, acts as an invariant motto (the "mower mown") and caps each stanza's tenor with the same mysteriously joyous highpoint. The poem is clearly a song of hope, yet the hope in it is ironically linked to this destructive sweep of the scythe, a conjunction also emphasized by the change from the past tense ("When *Juliana* came") to the present ("For *Juliana* comes"). This suggests that the havoc wrought by the lady is not final enough for the mower: he seems to hope for a Second Coming as strong as that of Death itself, the greatest mower of them all. "For now we see through a glass, darkly; but then face to face: now I am known in part; but then shall I know even as also I am known."

Such strange alliance of hope and death is also reflected by the mower's Orlando-fury. Is not this fury the "annihilating all that's made" magnified into a superb emblematic action? The mower's pique is, in any case, given a resonance and amplitude no less than cosmic. Marvell's aggrandizement of pastoral clichés reminds one of Donne's exploitation of Petrarchan conceits, except that the mower eclogues must maintain the mask of the naïve singer.[27] The mower's fury and the temptation of hope seem to me related: hope may deny too quickly this world for the world beyond; and despair, in Marvell, is really a greater form of hope.[28] Milton's Adam is taught that "in contemplation of

---

the emblem even more relevant to Marvell. See Picinelli, s. v. Cicindela, Lib. 8, cap. 7. Another tradition stresses the Plinyan, micro-character of the glowworm, which makes it a fit marvel for the poet's world of "unfathomable grass" (as in Saint-Amant, "Le Contemplateur" [1629], st. 23). For an especially exquisite use of the. glowworm emblems, see Thomas Stanley, *Poems* (1647 and 1651).

27. The term *mower eclogues* is my own. J. C. Scaliger recognizes "mower pastorals" in Bk. 3, chap. 99 of the *Poetices:* "Pastoralia continent . . . Bucolica, Arationes, Messes, Foenisecia, Lignatoria, Viatoria, Capraria, Ovilia, Holitoria: quibus magnus vir Sanazarus ex Theocrito etiam addidit piscatoria: nos etiam Villica." I have not been able to find a classical or Neolatin example of "Foenisecia" and, but for this passage in Scaliger, would have thought Marvell an inventor, like Sannazzaro. The absence of dialogue would not disqualify his mower poems as eclogues; Scaliger thinks the amorous monologue came before the dialogue forms of pastoral *(Poetices,* Bk. 1, chap. 4).

28. "The Definition of Love," sts. 1 and 2.

created things/ By steps we may ascend to God,"[29] but Marvell views this ladder (the "scale of nature") with a post-lapsarian eye. He evokes, in fact, less a ladder or a progress than a precarious dialectic which sets ultimate hope catastrophically against hope in nature. And this holds true of all the mower poems, in which the contradiction between nature and grace finds a deeply oblique, unsacrilegious form. Their theme is the labor of hope.

The mower recalls Virgil's "agricola," and in the emblem books this spiritual peasant always labors in hope: *agricolas spes alit*.[30] Marvell, however, shows hope in nature frustrated by love or by the very strength of hope. The mower's revenge is clearly an untimely harvesting, or hastening of the end: what he had cultivated in hope he now destroys in hope. Yet this might well be the anagogical ministry of love, for the annihilating again ends in something green. Revelation, the seeing of one's hope face to face, or redemption, the reunion of man and nature, is pushed, not without irony, into death:

> And thus, ye Medows, which have been
> Companions of my thoughts more green,
> Shall now the Heraldry become
> With which I shall adorn my Tomb;
> For *Juliana* comes, and She
> What I do to the Grass, does to my Thoughts and Me.

Here the device or emblem enters the poem formally, to express on the tomb the mower's hope, which remains with nature or the green body of ultimate rebirth. Love ("the greatest of these") shows its greatness in a mysterious way. To achieve man's redemption it works catastrophically against hope, which is premature, tinsel-winged. Only love causes such mowing madness unto death, an outmoding of childish hopes, a happy fall.

A few additional comments may forestall misunderstanding of what I have wanted to say in this essay. "The Garden," as I see it, is dialectical rather than merely progressive in structure. It is true, but not all the truth, that the poet progresses from the

29. *Paradise Lost,* 5. 511–12.

30. Peacham, *Minerva Britanna,* emblem 32, pp. 126–29; Wither, *A Collection of Emblemes,* Bk. 2, illustration 44.

vanities of the world to the pleasures of the garden, and finally to a garden within this garden—to the Eden which the soul is enabled to foresee in this, its earthly state. It is likewise true, but not all the truth, that the main contrast in the poem is between the worldly fruits (of fame and love) and the sensuous yet innocent fruits which the garden offers; between, in short, the contrasty red and white and the unified amorous green. To see a progression of thought that is dialectical rather than linear completes rather than denies these views of the poem, and it modifies them only insofar as the poet is shown to be respectful of certain inherent (Pauline) paradoxes. Not only does the garden stand against the world, but within the garden a new opposition arises, engendered by hope itself and turning the poet inward. He enters a mental garden, this again is surpassed in the light of greater hope, but this hope remains tinged by the color and conceived within the context of the earthly garden—it is a "green Thought in a green Shade." Both views, the dialectical-progressive and the linear-progressive, are relevant; but I feel that the first subsumes the second and follows more closely the inner turns and surprises of Marvell's poem.

I would also urge that, while Marvell thinks within a Pauline context, his poetry expresses less a particular eschatology than the form of eschatological thinking as a whole. His figure of the "mower mown" might well be compared to Milton's "gatherer gathered," and though a Protestant background may explain them in part, it does not wholly.[31] The strength of Blake's poetry is likewise in its unfolding of a highly abstract eschatological scheme, belonging less to one religion than (as Blake says) to all religions insofar as derived from the Poetic Genius. Blake and Milton, however, claim and clothe an ultimate illumination. They move us, with irony and caution, toward a precise image of the last things. The specific subject of "The Garden" is also related to one of the last things; the poem prospects the redemption of the body, or nature's paradise-body. Yet Marvell evokes no sustained image of Eden, only the tastings and testings of

31. F. R. Leavis notices the pattern in *Paradise Lost,* 4. 268 ff., in *Revaluations* (London, 1949), pp. 62–63. Is it not present in *Paradise Lost,* 9. 426 ff. also? The situation of little T. C. is similar, or perhaps of "the nipper nipped." Donne's "spyed Spie" (*Satyre* 4) also belongs here.

170

hope by the individual mind. A morphology of hope is given us in miniature.

This miniature quality is of great interest, and related to the sophisticated naïveté of Marvell's poems, which I have touched on *ambulando*. It may be fruitful to explore in how far Marvell's miniaturism of mood and mode represents emblem techniques fully adjusted to poetry. Perhaps Marvell is constructing a poetic kind of heraldry, not unrelated to the very personal symbol-making of the modern poets. If the miniature quality prevails more strongly in Marvell, it could be because, unlike modern poets, he scruples to avail himself of his full creative autonomy, or because he makes an at once literal and ironic use of the idea of man as a little world or microcosm. His Damon, a diminutive Adam, instead of redeeming the world whose image in sharp he is, alienates himself from it through the mystery of hope.[32]

My main thesis, that Marvell is concerned with the "body of hope," has been variously anticipated. The amorous or even androgynous vegetation of "The Garden" has been traced to a Kabbalistic myth concerning the unfallen Adam, though it could also be derived from Aristophanes' story in the *Symposium*—Renaissance Platonism had already associated the two myths.[33] What matters is, in any case, that both are speculations on the same subject—the form of man's true or redeemed body. Marvell's use of the concept of metamorphosis has also been interpreted in this fashion.[34] It is certainly true that the Garden, in

32. On the poet's alienation from nature, cf. J. H. Summers, "Marvell's 'Nature' " *ELH* 20 (1953): 121–35.

33. E.g., Leone Hebreo, in his *Dialoghi d'Amore,* published posthumously in 1541; see Richard Benz, *Der Mythus vom Urmenschen* (Munich, 1955), esp. 31–49. For the commonplaceness of the conjunction, cf. Henry More, *Conjectura Cabbalistica* (London, 1653), pp. 123, 157 f. (But More rightly considers Plato's version to be a parody of the myth.) The archetype recurs, perhaps via Böhme, in Blake's poetry, also fundamentally concerned with the redemption of Man's original body, and it has a strong emblematic revival in some of D. H. Lawrence's animal poems.

34. Bradbrook and Lloyd Thomas, "Marvell and the Concept of Metamorphosis," *Criterion* 18 (January 1939): 236–54. In particular: "The concept of Metamorphosis, the basis of the poem, fuses the modern psychological idea of sublimation and the modern [!] theological idea of transcendence into something more delicate" (p. 243).

its most general aspect, appears as a place of various metamorphoses or changes of body. All are redemptive; yet some less
than others. But none, not even those depicted in stanzas 4 and 5,
suggest that the body of hope is in the image of a nature which
reabsorbs man. What they prefigure is a body or a love that stands
beyond the division of nature and man, or of the sexes.

> Such was that happy Garden-state
> While Man there walk'd without a Mate.

The beautiful lines

> No white or red was ever seen
> So am'rous as this lovely green

suggest likewise not an expulsion of sexual love but rather its
absorbed perfection, the passion and the duality overcome. Yet
if, in Christian theology, the exact nature of the redeemed (resur-
rected) body is in dispute and not a matter of doctrine; if the
imagination remained, in this respect, relatively free, the poet
still knew himself in the presence of a mystery not to be profaned.[35] Marvell confronts the mystery obliquely, through the
mask of Platonic thought, the concepts of microcosm and metamorphosis, and other pastoral or classical guises. His oblique—
the oblique of poetry—is more sensuous than the direct could
ever be.

35. See "On Mr. Milton's Paradise Lost" for Marvell's scruples that
poetry might ruin "The sacred Truths to Fable and old Song."

"The Nymph Complaining for the Death of Her Faun": A Brief Allegory

The allegories so far proposed have crushed the lightness of nymph and fawn, the high poetic spirits of Marvell's poem. Why allegorize at all?[1] The only good reason is that the poem itself teases us into thinking that nymph and fawn are also something else. This teasing should be respected: either there is some allegory here, or the poem is deceptively suggestive. Is the nymph the human soul; the fawn a gift of grace, or some aspect of Christ or Church? Such thoughts are especially encouraged by images reminiscent of the Song of Songs.

The fawn is not unlike the young hart of the Song of Songs or its fawns that feed among the lilies, while the nymph's garden is a kind of *hortus conclusus* with which fawn and Shulammite are linked. Such allusions, it is true, freely used in the love poetry of the time, do not of themselves establish the presence of allegory. Yet when imagery from the Song of Songs is used in comparable contexts—either directly, as in Crashaw, to celebrated divine

1. The issue was first raised by E. S. LeComte in *Modern Philology* 50 (1952): 97–101. He there disputes the suggestion by M. C. Bradbrook and M. G. Lloyd Thomas that the "love of the girl for her fawn is taken to be a reflection of the love of the Church for Christ" (*Andrew Marvell* [Cambridge, 1940], pp. 47 ff.). In answer K. Williamson insisted on the prevalence and importance of the poem's "religious overtones," *Modern Philology* 51 (1954): 268–71. Since then interpreters have divided into three camps (Leo Spitzer has preceded me in a similar division): (1) the literalists, like LeComte, who think the poem at most a "semi-mythological" piece (the phrase is Cazamian's); (2) the allegorists, who think the religious allusions too strong to be merely overtones; and (3) a third group, which seeks to attach the problem of overtones to a study of Marvell's technique—his use, for instance, of "associative metaphor" (D. C. Allen). Ruth Nevo's "Marvell's 'Songs of Innocence and Experience,'" *Studies in English Literature,* 5 (1965): 1–21, begins to transcend these divisions.

love in passionate terms, or allusively, as in Vaughan, to illustrate the quest for evidences of election—it reposes on well-established allegorical tradition.[2] Marvell may have chosen this tradition for its very bivalence, but a reader cannot miss the sacramental and even christological note emerging first in lines 13–24 ("There is not such another in / The World, to offer for their Sin"[3]), crowding around the imagery from Song of Songs (ll. 71–93), and sustained to the end of the poem, whose coda is a series of conceits on weeping that remind us strongly of Crashaw—a Crashaw scaled down to sharp diminutives.

If a literal interpretation could account for these features, I would prefer it. Only one nonallegorical approach, however, has been at all successful. According to Leo Spitzer the poem describes a young girl's desire for an impossible purity. He thinks the poem is an oblique psychological portrait. "The description of her pet reflects on her own character by indirect characterization, the increasing idealization of the fawn allowing inferences about the maiden who so idealizes it."[4] It is certainly true that

2. A short summary of the history of this tradition is found in *The Songs of Songs,* ed. A. Harper (Cambridge, Mass., 1907), pp. xli–xlv. That the Song of Songs was, as Peacham said, a "continued Allegorie of the Mysticall love between Christ and his Church" is a Renaissance commonplace: Milton calls the Song "a divine *pastoral* drama" *(Critical Essays of the Seventeenth Century,* ed. Spingarn, 1: 118, 196). A number of Vaughan's poems in *Silex Scintillans* are explicitly based on the Song; cf. also *The Odes of Casimire,* trans. G. Hils (1646), Augustan Reprint Society Publication number 44 (1953), pp. 30–33, 41–42, 82–89. For the relation of Renaissance poetry to the Song of Songs, see Israel Baroway, *Journal of English and German Philology,* 33 (1934): 23–45 (restricted to Spenser); Ruth Wallerstein, *Studies in Seventeenth-Century Poetic* (Madison, 1950), pp. 206–13, 335–65; and Stanley Stewart, *The Enclosed Garden* (Madison, 1966). F. A. Yates has shown in "The Emblematic Conceit in Giordano Bruno's *De Gli Eroici Furori* and in the Elizabethan Sonnet Sequences" *(Journal of the Warburg and Courtauld Institutes,* 6 [1943]: 101–21) how the allegorized Song of Songs helped to create the emblem speech of Renaissance poetry.

3. My text throughout is the Muses Library text of *The Poems of Andrew Marvell,* ed. Hugh MacDonald (London, 1952).

4. "Marvell's 'The Nymph . . .': Sources versus Meaning," *Modern Language Quarterly* 19 (1958): 233. The sixth chapter of D. C. Allen's *Image and Meaning, Metaphoric Traditions in Renaissance Poetry* (Baltimore, 1960) states a similar view. I am not convinced, however, that the religious overtones are explained by Marvell's use of "associative meta-

there is something childlike, deliciously naïve, and deeply human in the nymph, which breaks through the mythological setting as later in Romantic and Victorian poetry. Yet beside the fact that it would be hard to find, at this time, a single prosopopeia or "complaint" which is primarily psychological portraiture, Spitzer's view is open to a fundamental objection. It substitutes psychological for mythological categories, assuming that the latter are the poet's means of implying the former. His literalism, therefore, does not take the letter of the poem seriously enough: it refuses to explore the possibility that the nymph is a nymph—not simply a young girl, but a mythic being in a privileged relation to the wood-world of the poem, the world of fawns and nature. Yet Marvell insists clearly enough on the presence of this mythical level. While his troopers and their violence come from a contemporary world, almost everything else is set in a world of myth. The impinging, quick but fatal, of one level on the other should not be obscured by a translation into the psychological.[5]

A second approach, which also claims to be literal, is allegorical despite itself. Romance and pastoral may show the beginnings of passion in an innocent mind, the obliquities of a young girl prey to her first love. The theme derives perhaps from Longus's *Daphnis and Chloe* and contains that special admixture of naïveté in the subjects and sophistication in the author which is to be found here as elsewhere in Marvell. A strong suspicion is raised that the fawn's wound is the girl's, that the poem describes a sexual or at least an initiatory wounding. Yet what the reader may interpret in sexual terms, the nymph's consciousness views in terms of creaturely calamity. By some naïve and natural balm of vision, of which allegory is the organized form, she keeps within the confines of a pastoral view of things. She is a nymph rather

phor" (the fawn, says Allen, is *like* Christ, but never *is* Christ, symbolically speaking). I could agree that such a device might produce the peculiar allusiveness of Marvell's poem, but as the technical rather than formal cause.

5. To identify the two realms as nature and civilization is also insufficient. It is at once too general and too eighteenth century a constrast for the poem. But see LeComte's article (refererd to in note 1) and an interesting study by Ruel E. Foster, *University of Kansas City Review* 22 (1955): 73–78.

than a girl precisely because her soul is not yet humanized, her love not yet divided into profane and sacred. The fawn mirrors that undifferentiated love which allows her to pass gradually, and without mystery, from man to beast, from Sylvio to the deer. Her extreme grief, moreover, is so gentle ("ungentle men!") that she still seems to live in the last rays of a world where no sharp distinctions between good and evil obtain. She is too whole for the rage of good against evil, or any understanding of the rage of evil itself. She does not, even now, fall into duality, but abandons the whole (this impossible world) for another whole (the world beyond). The threshold of mature consciousness is not reached—and cannot be reached without a dying of the nymph into a girl or woman.

This ontological interpretation of the poem is, I believe, new. To put it in its simplest form, it respects mythology's insistence that states of soul are correlated with states of being.[6] But it implies a disjunction between the points of view of innocence and of experience, of nymph on the one hand and reader or poet on the other. The poem's playful and artificial flavor, however, betrays a degree of conspiracy between nymph and poet. Naïveté of mood expressed in jeweled conceits is, after all, Marvell's most distinctive trait as author. Instead of arguing that the nymph sees one thing and the poet, who looks at the action from the point of view of experience, sees another, we must suppose a greater unity between the poet and his persona. But once we do this, the nymph begins to appear as a Muse in little, a figure created by the poet to mourn a lost power, perhaps that of poetry itself. The supposition gathers strength if we think of Marvell's poem not in the tradition of complaint or prosopopoeia but in the more comprehensive one of pastoral elegy. The use of pastoral to lament the death of poets was one of its strongest Renaissance developments, and although the lament is usually spoken by an author in *propria persona* and for an individual, Spenser makes the Muses mourn "their own mishaps"[7] It is Marvell's special characteristic to reduce every-

6. The possibility of metamorphosis (ll. 81 ff.) points most clearly to this basic axiom of mythologies.

7. See his *Epithalamion,* line 7. The reference is to *Tears of the Muses.* For the tradition of "lachrymae musarum" (a common elegiac title), cf. Ergasto's song in Sannazaro, *Arcadia,* 11th eclogue.

176

thing to a microcosmic or little-world scale and to view the nymph as a Muse in miniature.

Indeed, the nymph's tragedy, caught in amber, would have reminded a contemporary reader of another tradition cognate with pastoral elegy but now almost extinct. I suspect that the meaning of Marvell's poem became problematic as the tradition lost its natural or commonplace vigor. The medallion, gemlike, or miniature effects found in Marvell can be traced to the epigrams of the Greek Anthology, a considerable portion of which are either verses made for pictures or else little pictures themselves.[8] Those acquainted with the poetry of the Pléiade will remember the impact of the Anacreonta and the Greek Anthology (mediated by the Neo-Latin poets) on Ronsard, Du Bellay, and Belleau, who began to develop an alternate tradition to the high style of the great ode which had been their main object of imitation. Not odes but odelettes, not epics and large elegies but little descriptive domestic or rural poems called *Petites inventions, Bocages, Jeux Rustiques, Pierres Précieuses, Idylles,* now became the delectation of their Muse. A strange riot of diminutives and diminutive forms begins. The word *idyll,* in fact, was commonly etymologized as a diminutive of *eidos,* a little picture. The idyll, says Vauquelin de la Fresnaie in his *Foresteries* (1555), "ne signifie et ne represente que diverses petites images et graveures en la semblance de celles qu'on

8. James Hutton says in his introduction to *The Greek Anthology in France* (Ithaca, 1946) that the Greeks invented and perfected for the West "the small poetical idea." Collections of translations from or imitations of the Greek Anthology carry such titles as *Trifles, Gems, Medallions.* Marvell's acquaintance, mediated or direct, with the *Greek Anthology* cannot be argued here, but to question it is like questioning his knowledge of scripture. At issue is rather the quality of his knowledge. Ruth Wallerstein approaches an understanding of his mode when she suggests that he may have been influenced by Mildmay Fane, whose poetry she describes as "a tumbling alphabet of emblems in little, or *argutiae*" (*Seventeenth-Century Poetic,* p. 167). To understand Marvell's relation to the Anthology, it is useful to recall the Renaissance doctrine of *allusio,* a liberal imitation which "attracts the poet by challenging him to invent for himself the terms of the situation" (Hutton, *Greek Anthology in France,* p. 42). In the Anthology epitaphs are often spoken by the dead person who recounts his manner of life and death to the passer-by, and Marvell's poem wittily extends this genre of the speaking picture or statue: the nymph, by a kind of swan song, dies into the statue for which her lament might be the inscription.

177

grave aux lapis, aux gemmes et calcedoines pour servir quelques fois de cachet. Les miennes en la sorte, pleines d'amour enfantines, ne sont qu'imagetes et petites tabletes de fantaisies d'Amour.[9] The fortunes of this mode of the minor are difficult to follow; it is always merging with so much else—with emblem poetry for example, or with sonnets and their "little rooms," or with various kinds of pictorialism. Its range is so great, its value so variable, that we can go from Belleau's *petite invention* "Le Ver Luisant" (1552) to Marvell's "The Mower to the Glow-Worms" (about a century later), or from a whimsical epitaph on some faithful pet to Ben Jonson's great verses on Elizabeth L.H. ("Wouldst thou hear what man can say / In a little? Reader, stay . . . "), and again from these to Henry King's moving trifle "Upon a Braid of Hair in a Heart" ("In this small Character is sent / My Loves eternal Monument").[10] The very range of the tradition, however, may be a result of the fact that the recurrent and operative topos of much-in-little constitutes a poetics as well as a theme: it is a defense of

9. According to A. Hulubei, *L'Eglogue en France au XVI siècle* (Paris, 1938), chap. 1, Vauquelin's attempt to define the idyll as specifically different from eclogue or pastoral is unusual. Though she is right in this, there develops in the Renaissance a special kind of "ludic" or playful pastoral (the first signal example being the Neo-Latin *lusus*) which easily corresponds to Vauquelin's definition whether or not actually called an "idyll." Characterized by an artificial naïveté that delights in itself (in *Le Jardin des Muses* [2nd ed. Paris, 1648], we find poems by Ronsard, Du Bartas, and Pelletier entitled explicitly "Descriptions naïfves"), and related in theme and tone to the sweet or mellow epigram of the Greek Anthology. Idylls are the *putti* of lyric poetry. Cf. the title of the first translation of Theocritus into English: *Six Idillia, that is sixe small, or pretty poems, or aeglogues* . . . (Oxford, 1588). So also, a century later, the *Dictionnaire Françoise* of P. Richelet (Geneva, 1680): "*L'Idile* est un mot Grec qui signifie une petite image. C'est un poëme qui contient ordinairement quelque plainte ou quelque aventure amoreuse. Les idiles les plus courtes sont d'ordinaire les meilleures." This idea of the idyll, as well as its connection with Greek epigrams, survives in Ambrose Philips's definition of song as "a little image in enamel." Cf. K. Scoular, *Natural Magic* (Oxford, 1965), pp. 90 ff. on the "association which existed between small poems and small creatures."

10. A favorite theme of these baby poems is naturally enough the powerful babe or "dreadful imp," a theme nourished both by Anacreon (e.g., ode 3), the Alexandrian Cupids of the Anthology, and the mythos of the Christ-child. Cf. Mario Praz, *Studies in Seventeenth-Century Imagery* (London, 1939), 1: 80 ff.

poetry's *ignobile otium,* the trivial yet mystical or contemplative nature of art.

Now Marvell's poem is not only an idyll in this sense, but an idyll of idylls. It is a little picture of the spirit of the genre—an apotheosis of the diminutive powers of poetry. Not only is the fawn a spritely embodiment of much-in-little, not only does the whole poem end with a metamorphosis into art, a votive image of nymph and fawn, but, as if to sum up the genre in one monument to itself, "The Nymph's Complaint" brings together the major types of the Greek epigram: dedicatory, sepulchral, ecphrastic, and amatory. An inspired syncretism produces something very like a collage (although, as in reading Homer, one must be taught to recognize the individual bits or formulae), a collage with two important and successful aims. The first is to fuse semipagan forms of sentiment into a recognizably contemporary genre, that of Spenserian pastoral allegory. What Spenser has done is here done again, but in a much less liberal and inventive, a much more deliberate and self-conscious, way. It is an openly synthetic reconstruction, a reassembly of Spenser's already diminished freedoms. Marvell's poetry has something of the embalmer's art, and his diminutive form points to an ideal it would preserve from total dissolution. The poet's second and correlative aim is to translate these various forms of the idyll (pictorial, votive, sepulchral, amatory) into a situation which is the living content of his poem, as if nature and artifice were interchangeable—and this interchange is itself a generative topic of some of the Greek Anthology epigrams, as of the Renaissance "speaking pictures" inspired by them. Though art, in other words, accepts itself as a tour de force, becoming deliberately diminished and artifactual in its aims, it will not give up a magical ambition to rival or supplant nature. The diminished form simply purifies art's power and concentrates its resemblance to hieroglyph, icon, or charm.

In Marvell, therefore, as in every authentic artist, technique is ethos: the form he has chosen—a playful shadow of greater forms, an artful rivalry of naïver forms—is at once a lament and an acceptance of his situation as poet. To understand that situation in its historical context, the vast continued design of Spenserian allegory shrinking and becoming a brief allegory, will help to interpret this "furthest and most mysterious development of

179

English pastoral poetry."[11] The following interpretation can be
extended from its specific allegory to the general problem of the
status of Spenserian allegory in Marvell's age. A consideration,
therefore, of that brief epic "Appleton House" must also concern
itself with the problematic status of the epic in Marvell's age.[12]
To this double task of finding a specific allegory and of clarifying
the status of Spenserian allegory I now turn.

Those who have tried to discover a sustained allegory in "The
Nymph" have made a curious error. This error explains not only
the failure of their attempt but also why this kind of interpretation
is discredited. Instead of basing their allegories on the action, they
have immediately sought to decipher the individual agents: nymph,
fawn, Sylvio. But in Spenserian allegory it is the action which
identifies the agents rather than vice versa. This by no means
excludes more static devices: Spenser's figures can have suggestive
names, like Sylvio in Marvell, even if the meaning of a figure is disclosed mainly by an intricate pattern of relationships extended
(and even scattered like clues) through canto or book. This type
of structure was called by Spenser and others continued allegory,
and the mistake of applying to Marvell's poem methods of de-
coding more appropriate to noncontinued allegories comes from
the fact that we have so very few lyrical pieces in this mode:
Marvell is almost *sui generis* in his short-form use of the dark conceit. The short allegories of Herbert and Vaughan are not really
dark, but rather vivified emblems.

Let us begin, therefore, with a description of the action: of what
happens in "The Nymph." The nymph traces in retrospect her
subtly changing relationship to the fawn. The fawn is first a love
gift, then a consolation, and finally a creature loved for its own
sake and even gathering to itself the nymph's love for all creatures.
The fawn, indeed, becomes so important that, when it is killed,
no creaturely consolation seems possible, and the nymph hastens
to die.

11. *English Pastoral Poetry,* ed. Frank Kermode (London, 1952), p.
253. The term *brief allegory* is my own coinage, on the analogy of
Milton calling the Book of Job a "brief epic" and to suggest that Marvell
has, as it were, crossed Spenserian allegory with the Greek Anthology
type of epitaph which Hutton calls a "brief elegy."
12. See also John M. Wallace, *Destiny his Choice* (London, 1968).

So highly stylized an action evokes a specific idea of the progress of the soul. The direct object of love is replaced by an indirect one, a live token, which is in turn replaced by a still more indirect one, an icon (ll. 111 ff.). And while the token comforts, the icon comforts only, if at all, as a symbol of the impossibility of being comforted: "I shall weep though I be stone." A love that has turned from temporal fulfillment to temporal consolation becomes a disconsolateness which is love still, but removed from this world.

The pattern is general and human enough not to require a special historical locus. It has such a locus, however, in the Christian idea of the soul's progress and the part consolation plays in this. The Christian soul is weaned from worldliness by privations that contain a comfort.[13] That comfort is usually thought of in other-worldly terms, but Marvell's position is rather complex. Though there is an apotheosis of the fawn, analogous to the Assumption of Astrea or other stellar figures (as Crashaw says, "heav'n must go home"), the fawn might have substituted for Sylvio. As Sylvio's surrogate it entices the nymph with a love that remains this-worldly, though chaste or wider than sexual. The fawn's mode of being is, in fact, so peculiarly mixed with nature's that the possibility of a nature-involved consolation seems to die with its ascent out of this world.

The theme of consolation, which points our poem in the direction of allegory, can be traced back to a specific and authoritative analogue. This is the scriptural story of the Comforter in John 14: 16, 26, and 16: 7 ff. Christ promises the Comforter (Paraclete) to his disciples when they do not suspect or do not understand that he must leave them. For them Christ is part of the approaching and expected apocalypse. But Christ, in preparing them for his absence, for temporality, tells them of the Comforter, who is to be his surrogate and a spirit dwelling with them in his absence,

13. The proximity of this pattern to sublimation has caused more sensitive critics to see the action in a psychological rather than religious light. "This tragic story could be called in modern (Freudian) terms one of frustration overcome by sublimation" (Spitzer, "Sources versus Meaning" p. 242). "The fawn, which Sylvio gives the girl as a token of love becomes, when he abandons her, a *surrogatus amoris*. . . . The nymph has brooded so much over losing her lover that she has enlarged the token of love into a life symbol" (Allen, *Image and Meaning* pp. 93–94).

more intimately even than He. (The Paraclete, Donne comments in a sermon, as well as a mediator and advocate, is "in a more intire, and a more internall, and a more viscerall sense, A Comforter.")[14] It is almost expedient that Christ should depart, so that this closer companion, also named "Spirit of Truth" (viz. "troth") and "Holy Ghost," should come to abide with men.

Three kinds of congruence between this analogue and the poem may be considered: the propriety of showing the Comforter as a fawn, the similarities of theme, and similarities bearing on the action as a whole. Concerning the issue of propriety, I can only say that the third Person is traditionally a dove, and that the Church Fathers often associate the third Person with charity, or pure creature-feeling, rather than with power (the first Person) or wisdom (the second Person).[15] To the nymph the fawn is simply a creature that loves her, and she reciprocates its love. When she says, "I cannot be / Unkind, t'a Beast that loveth me," Marvell renders her attitude succinctly, that it would be "un-kind" (unnatural, uncreaturely) to be "unkind." To see the fawn as an allegorical emblem for the Comforter at least respects the fact that the poem deals with the possibility of consolation. The fawn might have been, for a Protestant, a playful yet not unfitting image of the humble Spirit that prefers "th' upright heart and pure." The change from dove to fawn could have been imposed by the very mode of allegory, since the dove is, strictly speaking, not an allegory but a symbol of the third Person. Marvell, moreover,

14. *The Sermons of John Donne,* ed. E. M. Simpson and G. R. Potter, 10 vols. (Berkeley, 1949–62), 7 (1954): 450. The sermon was preached on Whitsunday, a favourite time for sermons on the Comforter (see Acts 2: 1 ff.).

15. I rely on the *Catholic Encyclopedia* (New York, 1910), on various texts of Thomas Aquinas, and on Lancelot Andrewes's "Sermons of the Sending of the Holy Ghost" in *Ninety-Six Sermons* (Oxford, 1841), 3: 107–401. I quote from the last mentioned: "The Spirit a dove, and Christ 'a lamb'—like natured both: what the one in the kind of beasts, the other in the kind of fowls; that we may see the Holy Ghost lighted right. *Super quem?* 'Upon whom shall my Spirit rest?' saith God, in Esay; and He answers, *super humilem,* 'on the humble and the meek' " (p. 235). It is not my suggestion, of course, that Marvell has fashioned a theological allegory: he has absorbed the spirit of it and makes a special one of his own, just as, in the Mower poems, he has absorbed the spirit of emblemmaking and makes an emblem of his own.

as his poem "On Mr. Milton's Paradise Lost" shows, is wary of the direct treatment of religious subjects. The classical image of Lesbia mourning her sparrow, or the archetypal images of child with bird and virgin with unicorn, may also have served to bring the subject to its deeply veiled and affective form. The change from dove to fawn is, however, strong and unusual enough to compel explanation or put the allegory in doubt.

A second, still insufficient congruence is that of theme. Keeping the story of the Comforter in mind, we note that the fawn is a memento given at a time when the nymph suspects nothing, and with a hint (not understood by her) that it will take Sylvio's place:

> Unconstant *Sylvio,* when yet
> I had not found him counterfeit,
> One morning (I remember well)
> Ty'd in this silver Chain and Bell,
> Gave it to me: nay and I know
> What he said then; I'me sure I do.
> Said He, look how your Huntsman here
> Hath taught a Faun to hunt his *Dear.*
>
> [ll. 25–32]

Here the fawn is clearly identified as Sylvio's surrogate. One huntsman will be replaced by another. The fawn, moreover, is to Sylvio as the Comforter is to Christ, insofar as the latter appears "unconstant"[16] compared to this more faithful household spirit. Without her lover the soul must find a way to redeem the time (cf.

16. This adjective has been the undoing of potential allegorists. LeComte has the Ben Jonson reaction to the thought that Sylvio and the fawn might be aspects of Christ—this would be blasphemy, considering the "unconstant." E. H. Emerson, who pointed out the huntsman analogy and who identifies the fawn as Christ's gift of a Church now threatened by iconoclastic "troopers," is careful to deny that Marvell called Christ inconstant ("At this point, as with some other passages, to read the poem as pure allegory is clearly a mistake"), which does not avert the obvious reply that one cannot so blandly separate adjective and noun: see *Etudes Anglaises* 8 (1955): 107–10, and 111–12. My own reading is not meant to rationalize a single word (the problem of "counterfeit" would in that case remain) but to suggest that what must be justified is the form in which the action is cast, the overall persona and plot, without which no dark conceit, no allegory.

ll. 37 ff.), and it is helped to do so by a subtle comforter who gradually wins her heart.

But against the fawn's wooing—at once a respect of time and nature—is set the irruptive disrespect of the troopers. For these troopers we find no immediate clue in the scripture story, though they could be carried over from another part of scripture. It is also not obvious why Sylvio must be shown as huntsman as well as lover. Adding our previous query, why dove is changed to fawn, the divergencies yield a pattern. They point to the imaginative realm of the spiritual chase. The story of the Comforter is conflated with this most common of Christian and Romance motifs, whose imagery harmonizes with that of Song of Songs.[17] The conflation, which helps to engender a richly detailed allegory, expresses with extraordinary neatness a spiritual chase that kills the spirit—the spirit being the Comforter, the residual and restitutive providence working patiently through church or nature[18] until the Second Coming.

The theme of the chase enters the poem from the beginning. The troopers' pursuit of the fawn[19] is sharply if elliptically distinguished from the way the fawn hunts the nymph, an action which occupies by contrast the major part of the poem. The fawn is subtle: it both entices the nymph and teaches her the futility of

17. See note 20 for some details linking the Song of Songs to the motif of the spiritual chase. The most perfect linking I know is in St. John of the Cross, *Canciones entre el Alma y el Esposo.* For the motif see also Evelyn Underhill, *Mysticism,* chap. 6, and Allen on the legend of the sacred deer. I should add that by "conflation" I do not mean to suggest something mechanical: medieval legend shows many natural instances, and there is no need to suppose that what J. L. Lowes found to be true of Coleridge is true only of him. Marvell's poetry seems often to stand exactly midway between older and more recent types of mythopoeia.

18. The Nature which comforts is very concretely the garden world (and garden thoughts) Marvell evokes in his poems, not an abstract *natura rerum.*

19. The poem's opening suggests a wanton or gratuitous slaying in "riding by" rather than a pursuit. But in pastoral, the casual is often a veiled form of the highly purposed (cf. Spenser's use of "chance"). The very offhandedness of the catastrophe intensifies our sense of much-in-little: for the prophetic weight pastoral allegory may carry. On Marvell's use of the pastoral as a form able to "insinuate and glaunce at greater matters" (Puttenham), see a tactful chapter in E. W. Tayler's *Nature and Art in Renaissance Literature* (New York, 1964), esp. pp. 145 ff.

chase. It intimates that the Spirit must seek and woo the soul, rather than vice versa:

> Among the beds of Lillyes, I
> Have sought it oft, where it should lye;
> Yet could not, till it self would rise,
> Find it, although before mine Eyes.
>
> [ll. 77–80][20]

The "wanton" troopers, however—the adjective *wanton* recalling Shakespeare's "As flies to wanton boys, so are we to the gods"— engage on a willful, crude, and untimely act. Their activism[21] paradoxically forfeits what they perhaps wished to gain.

> Though they should wash their guilty hands
> In this warm life blood, which doth part
> From thine, and wound me to the Heart,
> Yet could they not be clean: their Stain
> Is dy'd in such a Purple Grain.
> There is not such another in
> The World, to offer for their Sin.
>
> [ll. 18–24]

The blood they shed, unlike Christ's, has not purifying virtue[22]

20. This *locus amoenus* combines Song of Songs 2:7, 6:2 (or similar verses), and such scriptural proverbs as the lilies that do not toil and the spirit that bloweth where it listeth. Cf. "It whispered; *where I please*" of Vaughan's "Regeneration"—Vaughan quotes Song of Songs, 4: 16, as his text—and also Crashaw, "True Hope's a glorious hunter and her chase, / The *God* of nature in the field of grace" ("For Hope"). The wind-likeness of the fawn needs no emphasis.

21. LeComte points to evidence from the *NED* that "troopers" may first have been used in connection with the convenanting revolutionary army of 1640. Emerson extends it to the iconoclastic army starting from London in 1642. The word is, in any case, very contemporary, with connotations of activism. Marvell's famous remark about the Civil War in the *Rehearsal Transprosed* 1 may be relevant here: "I think the cause was too good to have been fought for . . . men may spare their pains when nature is at work, and the world will not go the faster for our driving."

22. I have adopted the traditional reading of this passage and made "this warm life blood" refer to the fawn. Spitzer ("Sources versus Meaning," p. 234) makes it refer to the nymph. I am not sure he is wrong, although his reasons for so interpreting may be disputed. His reading

because the fawn's migration to Elisium means the migration of the Comforter, our remaining source of *temporal* hope. The fawn's departure may be compared to the Ascension of the young girl's soul in Donne's *Anniversaries*. With it goes the world's "balm,"[23] the comfortable hope binding a soul to its station here below. The nymph's very haste to die reveals that she too has relinquished the hope of nature being allied to grace.

I would recall, at this point, that the theme of the spiritual chase and that of the Comforter are closely related. The idea of a Comforter enters the Gospels when Christ foresees a conflict between apocalyptic expectation and secular time. What attitude should his disciples take toward things temporal during his "desertion" and before the end of days? The end may be near, yet there remains a space of time not redeemed by the divine presence. One can hardly blame the expectant soul for showing impatience—it has waited sixteen centuries. Its dilemma, at once moral and political, a dilemma Protestantism sharpened, is whether to accept the temporizing character of the church. It is not difficult to see the troopers as the spirit of activism wishing to speed redemption or ruin—in short, to force the issue—by an act directed in a sense against time itself. The poem, of course, does not allow us to say more about their deed than that it is epochal, like the slaying of the albatross in "The Ancient Mariner." But to say this is enough: when their act is compared to the respect for time and nature shown by their victim, we are apprised of two opposite attitudes toward temporality.[24]

---

has the advantage of making the nymph suggest that the love between her and the fawn was so great that they had become as one person. The fawn's death means, therefore, a parting of the unified lifeblood. The point of the passage, in either reading, is that no temporal source of purification remains.

23. *The First Anniversary,* ll. 55 ff. An important Pàracelsian meaning is also present—see W. A. Murray, "Donne and Paracelsus," *Review of English Studies* 25 (1949): 117–20. (It is strange how the absence of Mary from the Protestant heaven calls up Mary substitutes.)

24. The theme of the chase is present in even subtler form in "The Garden," which starts with an ironic meditation on man's pursuit of worldly things, yet by st. 6 the irony bears on the chase that ensues on the poet's retreat from the world. His mind, though "annihilating all that's made," must still satisfy itself with patient hope (st. 7) and artifice (st. 9). On haste and temporality, cf. my "Marvell, St. Paul, and the Body of Hope," esp. pp. 159–60.

It is interesting that the chase after the spirit affects even the nymph. Though her wish to die has, like everything in the poem, a psychological justness, she too is *hastening the end*. The excess of love speeding her toward death:

> O do not run too fast: for I
> Will but bespeak they Grave, and dye
> > [ll. 109 f.]

perhaps resembles, on another plane, the haste of the troopers. It is not unusual in Marvell's world:

> Thus, though we cannot make our Sun
> Stand still, yet we will make him run.
> > ["To His Coy Mistress"]

> And Flow'rs, and Grass ,and I and all,
> Will in one common Ruine fall.
> > ["The Mower's Song"]

Such a chase out of or beyond nature stands directly against the fawn's example, its slow metamorphosis. The fawn prefigured a redemption with nature, not from it. The comfort it gave was that even the smallest thing in nature is worthy of love. Thus there are two similar violations depicted in Marvell's poem. Like wantonness, great spiritual love removes the soul from the sphere of redemptive patience.[25]

Marvell goes very far in depicting the fawn as an exemplar of the loving patience which effects the redemption of nature with man, of all in all. Because of the fawn, nymph and garden merge. With the strong images of Songs of Songs in the background ("I

25. Love, for Marvell, is generally a greater form of hope than hope itself, as in "The Definition of Love," st. 2, and "The Mower's Song." If Hope, in Spenser's House of Holiness (*Faerie Queene,* 1.10.14) and in the emblem books, is anchored to earth while her eyes are heavenward, love, one might say, draws heaven to earth. Its success, or failure, runs the risk of totality. The nymph's haste is the despair of love rather than of hope, and her changes of feeling toward the fawn might even be linked to the hierarchy of theological virtues. The fawn is at first a pledge of faith; next a keepsake, a token of hope; but "had it lived long" it would have been one with the garden, roses within, lilies without. This red and white (the familiar colors of love) may stand emblematically for *caritas:* the sensuous chastity of a soul bent on being redeemed with nature, whose inside is expectation and outside patience.

am the rose of Sharon, and the lily of the vallies"), the nymph comes close to being identified with the garden in which the fawn grazes; and when the fawn prints roses on her lips it suggests her metamorphosis, one parallel to its own. The pun in the strangely emphasized lines:

> Said He, look how your Huntsman here
> Hath taught a Faun to hunt his *Dear*
>
> [ll. 31–32]

marks this ultimate blending in a playfully prophetic way. The nymph, hunted by the fawn, approaches fawn nature. The distinction of kind is dissolved, and the statue the nymph imagines at the poem's end also draws her and the fawn into a single, if artificial, body—into an "artifice of eternity."

With this we have an allegory that respects the poem. The fawn, in its widest significance, wooing the soul to hope in a love redemption inclusive of nature, is a *Panunculus,* a little Pan; it foreshadows the reintegration or restitution of all things (see Rom. 8:32 and Acts 3:21). Thus the pastoral trappings (Sylvio, nymph, fawn) are not patina. The poet needs a world in which metamorphosis is possible—where a nymph is a nymph, able to assume both a human and an elemental shape, while her pet is equally amphibious.[26] This is the world of Pan, the reconciler of

26. Knowing Marvell's capacity for the subdued pun (time-thyme, "The Garden"), it is interesting to observe that his *fawn,* a young deer, and *faun,* a semi-deity part animal part human, are homophonous, and interchangeably spelled "fawn" or "faun" in the seventeenth century. The "faun," which is a nature-sprite, is originally little *Faunus*—Roman god of animals, crops, and prophesy, often identified with Pan. This double nature of the fawn may be thought too unusual yet is only a pun conceptually extended. Faunus, in turn, is often associated with Sylvanus, a wood-god (sylvae, Sylvio). The Faunus-Sylvanus-Pan relationship was topical knowledge: see Virgil, *Georgics,* 2. 493 ff.; *Paradise Lost,* 4. 707–08; and Herbert of Cherbury, *De Religion Gentilium* (1663; posthumously published), p. 155. Also Ruth Nevo, *Studies in English Literature* 5: 8–9. Faunus, I should add, appears twice in Spenser, and although he is represented as a wild-man figure, some motifs associated with him recur in Marvell: See *Faerie Queene* 2.2.9, with its (Ovidian) metamorphosis of the nymph into a weeping stone and the context of the ablution of guilt.

man and nature—in Marvell's conception, the reconciler of all things, even of Pagan and Christian. For in the poem hardly a sentiment or phrase must be taken as Christian.[27] The poet is himself a Pan who has created through the accepted magic of poetry a middle-world pointing to the ultimate reconciliation of Pagan and Christian. His consciousness, like the nymph's love, stands ideally beyond the division into sacred and profane.

Ideally, for there remains the opening and crucial event, the blood fact which thrusts us into the midst of, and itself on, this happy world. I want to comment finally, on its brevity. It stands against everything the pastoral stands for by a brutal shorthand.[28] As such it threatens not only the realm of the nymph but also that of *musing* generally. The event is the intrusion of a historical into a pastoral world. Perhaps even more: is not history here set fatally against poetry? The problematic situation of the poet begins to emerge.

Before Marvell, the opposition between history and poetry is more conciliable. A poet, following Virgil's example, begins with pastoral or "oaten reeds" and graduates to epic or "trumpets sterne." Not that pastoral is completely aloof from history, from politics in the largest sense. The pressure of the greater world is there for those who can recognize it. Virgil always sings of "arms and the man," even in his pastoral world which is no less precarious or competitive than the world of the *Georgics* or of the *Aeneid*. There are things, crucial things, to be gained or lost in all the worlds. But with Spenser the realm of the pastoral expands so much that we never reach epic as such. *The Faerie Queene* is pastoral which has swallowed both epic and romance. Whatever the reason for this, it is clear from the shape of Spenser's career —which begins with a translation of those strange emblem sonnets in Van der Noot's *Theater for Worldings*—that the opposition now is less between pastoral and epic than between pastoral

27. Lines 17–24 are possibly an exception to this. To a Christian reader, at least, their sentiment is overt. It is interesting that they were omitted in the first anthologizing of the poem in 1727 (Tonson's edition of Dryden's *Miscellany*).

28. Not brutal, of course, to the nymph's consciousness, which remains pastoral. The noticeably regular rhythm of the first two lines, a rhythm gradually more pathetic and modulated, acts both to subdue shock and to express a *fait accompli*.

and apocalypse. Van der Noot's *Theater,* a kind of visionary peep show, sets up a pastoral image (a stately ship, a fair hind, a pure spring of water) only to show its destruction—the ship sunk, the hind hunted to death, the spring defiled. This medieval, or now Calvinistic, exercise can but lead to a passionate cry to be delivered from the body of this death, or to a justifying and compensatory revelation—we are duly given both. Although Spenser's part in the *Theater for Worldings* may have been marginal, his mature poetry develops as an attempt to overcome this crude kind of hiatus or vacillation between levels of truth. His allegories are a marvellous blend of pastoral, historical, and apocalyptic—an imaginative, fluid, and shifty continuum. *The Faerie Queene* is a maze that cannot be threaded except by a kind of relay technique: one interpretation being suspended in favor of another just as, on the level of plot, an action may be suspended in mid-career. Spenser pays a price, however, for this essentially humble emphasis on the depth and deviousness of the progress from pastoral innocence to ultimate truth. His poetry is patently a conceit, a magnanimous yet artificial construct. It suggests that only as *poesis* can poetry mediate between pastoral appearances, historical darkness, and apocalyptic revelation.

Poetry's mediating virtue is still, for Marvell, the great and necessary virtue, but no longer a sufficient one. The new, perhaps desperate faith of his age in the *sortes* of history—its desire for a clean break and a clear commencement of the kingdom of God on earth—militates against an ethic of compromise which poets had learned from their long endeavor to reconcile classical forms and Christian sentiments. The opening of Marvell's "Horatian Ode,"

> The forward Youth that would appear
> Must now forsake his *Muses* dear[29]

---

29. There may be a simple yet appropriate pun in "Muses." Together with musing *(NED,* sv. muse, sb[2]) the youth is obliged to forsake poetry, the *Muses:* he lives in a time which considers poetry an *ignobile otium—* as Virgil said, thinking of that other strong-man divider and unifier of a nation, Caesar Octavianus. Yet in "Hortus" Marvell speaks of *otia sana,* and in "Appleton House" he refers to himself as an "easy Philosopher."

drives a wedge between acting and musing as clearly as "The Nymph's Complaint." It does so even as violently as that poem, because Cromwell,

> . . . like the three fork'd Lightning, first
> Breaking the Clouds where it was nurst,
> Did thorough his own Side
> His fiery way divide.

Cromwell's first act is that "bloody" stroke which in Marvell's poetry threatens so often the pastoral consciousness and expresses the necessity for civilization to proceed by and through schism. There is the stroke that separates church from church, and now sect from sect; the stroke that separates province from province; and the stroke that separates the head (the king) from the body. What can poetry do in this situation? It gathers to itself at the opposite pole the vision of lost and original unity, yet cannot be more (because separated by history from history) than a perennial monument of tears. Marvell's poem ends with an image of itself, an evocation of exquisitely fashioned grief.

The irremediable disjoining of—in particular—profane and sacred, or history and providence, is expressed most directly by the "Horatian Ode." Cromwell's rejection of the slowly grinding divine mills, his espousal of an actively urged salvation, violates, like the Troopers, a nature identified as providential time. A "bleeding Head" is once again and ironically the prerequisite for the body politic's wholeness. Marvell acknowledges this wound inflicted on the "great Work of Time." Yet he lives at the heart of the dilemma and refuses to hasten the end. He does not, like the nymph, forsake hope in temporal salvation because of a single unnatural act. There is no doubt, however, that Cromwell's mode of redemption is hazardous. The new order is forced to unify by the sword, by division, by a rape of time.

At this point the obvious classical analogue to Marvell's story of nymph and fawn becomes relevant. I refer to the slaying of Sylvia's stag in the seventh book of the *Aeneid*. Here also there is a wanton intrusion of history-bearers into a pastoral world. Marvell shares the Virgilian regret for a transcended world closer to nature's rhythm.[30] But that world is indistinguishable now from the state of mind that can evoke it, a state of mind which has no future and enshrines itself in idylls and precious relics. For despite Spenser's great example, the forsaking of the Muses has continued. Having ravaged many a blissful bower, the Renaissance hero will not spare the bower of poetry itself. In "The Nymph" Spenserian allegory laments itself in the pagan form of the brief elegy. The death of nymph and fawn denotes too deep a schism in human affairs for pastoral allegory to assuage.

30. Even here Marvell leads us finally to an archetype rather than to a prototype, to the general structure of the "interrupted pastoral" rather than to Virgil. Orlando lays waste the groves that sheltered him, Cromwell's force breaks "the Clouds where it was nurst," the Priest ("Appleton House," st. 93) must "cut the sacred Bud," and the nymph's garden world may have to be transcended.

Earl Miner's recent "The Death of Innocence in Marvell's Nymph Complaining for the Death of Her Faun" *(Modern Philology* 65 [1967]: 9–16) stresses the Virgilian prototype so strongly that Renaissance analogues tend to be discounted. He fully honors the link between the fawn and Sylvia's stag and is the first to relate both to the theme of the death of an older order. But he does not capture the specifically literary ideology of Marvell, the way the order of history seems to be set against that of poetry. The topical meaning which his essay helps to recover should include poetry as well as politics: the movement of history seems to doom the "ancient Rights" of poetry as well as those of a time-honored regime.

Blake and the Progress of Poesy

Blake's poems on the seasons, in *Poetical Sketches,* have not lacked recent commentators. The forceful inquiry that has made his other lyrics both richer and more problematic is now being devoted to them.[1] I would like to propose a point of view which would ground these earliest poems in Blake's sense of poetical vocation.

We feel at once their intensely vocative nature—that the prophetic or speaking out and the invocational or calling upon are more important than the conventional subject. Their mood is never purely descriptive but always optative or imperative: what description enters is ritual in character. It evokes an epiphany so strongly as to carry the poet toward it. "The hills tell each other, and the list'ning / Vallies hear; all our longing eyes are turned / Up to thy bright pavillions" paraphrases Psalm 19 with its feeling for "open vision," or prophecy in Blake's sense.

To grant the primacy of invocation, of thou-saying, of the prophetic impulse, is less to interpret than to raise the question on which interpretation should turn: What is being invoked? What presence or epiphany? If voice as voice has an exceptional place, it should still be brought together with a person and a situation. Who is calling, to whom, for what?

Now each of the lyrics is a formal ode that contains a clearly stated petition. A season is invoked and asked to visit, or stay in,

1. See esp. Harold Bloom, *Blake's Apocalypse* (Garden City, N.Y., Doubleday, Anchor Books, 1963), pp. 3–8; and Robert Gleckner, "Blake's Seasons," *Studies in English Literature* 5 (Summer 1965): 533–51. Gleckner refines M. Lowery's *Windows of the Morning* (New Haven, 1940) and approaches the complexity of Blake's season poems mainly through "his deliberate warping, reshaping, or inverting of poetic traditions . . . a technique which became more and more characteristic of him." His remarks on the parodistic element in "To Winter" (pp. 547–51) anticipate my own.

the speaker's land; in "To Winter" it is asked to stay away. On the literal level, therefore, it is the "voice of the bard" which adjures the seasons. This answer, however, makes little sense outside the charmed realm of convention. A natural force is asked to do what comes naturally; or it is asked not to do it and does it anyway ("To Winter"). In this light Blake's cycle is no more than a brilliant, condensed imitation of Thomson's *Seasons* with its pseudoritual invitations.

Blake's relation to Thomson will be discussed later. The comparison cannot be direct because Blake's are not long poems, like *The Seasons,* nor are they of a descriptive-didactic nature. These differences of genre put the emphasis back on Blake's condensed lyricism. Everything within this lyric space is food for a style of invocation. If calling the seasons is a gratuitous or ritual act, this but helps to move into the foreground the lyric pathos, the *ore rotundo,* of their style. Here voice calls upon itself, calls up images of its previous power. Blake indulges in a continuous reminiscence of that power by offering us a splendid pastiche of echoes and themes from the Bible, the classics, and even the high odic tradition of the eighteenth century. It is all poetic diction, but poetic diction in search of its truth—which is the identity, now lost, of the poetical and the prophetic spirit.

Even the measure of the poems is a reminiscence of a larger conception of poetry. Their blank verse is unusual, not only for its personality (the free enjambments, the energetic beat) but also for its very presence in short poems. Not until the 1790's will Southey, Coleridge, and Wordsworth experiment with *lyrics* in blank verse. With certain important exceptions, unrhymed lyrics before Blake were obvious imitations of the classics[2] or paraphrases of the Psalms, so that Blake's choice of verse may signify an "ancient liberty recover'd" and evoke the prophetic portions of both traditions.[3]

2. In Akenside's "Inscriptions," apparently the only series of blank verse lyrics before Blake, the measure clearly points to the classical source. Thomson's blank verse is not especially unconventional, *The Seasons* being a didactic *(Georgics*-inspired) poem.

3. See Milton's note on "The Verse" prefacing *Paradise Lost.* In a prefatory note to *Jerusalem* concerning the measure in which the poem is written, Blake rejects even blank verse as not unfettered enough. But this is some twenty-five years later.

The thought that Blake's season poems are about poetry—that they recall poetry's higher destiny, its link to energy, liberty, and the prophetic spirit—is encouraged by a simple progression within the first three odes. The progression moves the theme of poetry into the center. "To Spring" can be viewed as invoking a new energy or springtide of verse, anticipated by its exotic style. But what is on the level of style in "To Spring" appears in the last stanza of "To Summer" as theme, then carries the greater part of "To Autumn" as song, as a poem within a poem. Our unifying hypothesis remains, however, unsatisfactory on certain points—the relation of the apparent subject (the seasons) to the real subject (poetry); what to do with "To Winter"; and whether a modernist interpretation, that the poems are about poetry, respects the situation of a young poet writing in the England of the 1770s.

I propose not to deal with these problems one at a time but to reformulate the thesis in historical terms and then to apply it to the entire cycle. To say they are poems about poetry does not mean Blake is primarily concerned with poetry as artifact or with the poet as specialist: he is concerned with the *poetical spirit* (Gray's "Poetic Genius," Collins's "Poetical Character")—with its future in England and the West, with the relation of poetry to the spirit of the age and human destiny. One of the few genuinely visionary themes of the eighteenth century was that of the "Progress of Poesy," and it is in relation to this theme that Blake writes poems about poetry. His cycle is a visionary anticipation of the progress, or migration, of the poetical spirit to England, "our western isle." The primacy of the invocational-prophetic mode suggests that this progress is linked to the very energy of anticipation, to a poetry that can envision what it calls for.

The reader may recall the reverse epiphany concluding Pope's *Dunciad,* or Shelley's description of the "Triumph" of life. These are among the great examples (both ironical) of the Progress theme in an era desperately believing in progress. The Progress is always envisioned as a procession, apparently a triumphal one; yet the triumph can be heavily qualified. The Progress of Poesy, in particular, is represented less as a melioration than as a migration: like Astraea, poetry is forced into exile, though it remains on earth wandering from one civilization to another. Blake's little poem "To the Muses" alludes to this exile of the poetical genius, to the

195

Muses who may be wandering about on earth, in heaven, under the sea—they are somewhere, but they are clearly not in eighteenth-century England.

The vision of a Progress of Poesy expresses an epoch with a self-conscious interest in literary history and offers us a specific myth about that history. Blake could have found this myth in Thomson, Gray, Collins, or Thomas Warton. These men see a displacement of the poetical genius from East to West or South to North: from *Morgenland* to *Abendland*. This Westering of the Spirit is often explained by a supposed connection between liberty and letters: as liberty dies out in Greece (or prophecy in the Holy Land), poetry and learning depart and arrive finally in their new home, the "western isle." So Thomson in "Rule Britannia" (1740): "The Muses still with freedom found / Shall to thy happy coast repair."[4]

Yet only here and there is the conception of this Progress purely optimistic and a simple aggrandizement of national ambitions in the realm of letters. The hope was fading, by the middle of the century, that the greatness of English poetry might be sustained. Dryden and Pope had kept alive a spark of the hope kindled by. the Renaissance; but Warton's *History of English Poetry* (1774–81), published while Blake was composing *Poetical Sketches,* qualifies it significantly. Warton doubts that the poetical spirit, at least in its original fervor and true Oriental splendor, can make its permanent home in the West. Even the Nordic imagination (revealed, primarily, through Mallet's *Northern Antiquities*) is supposed to owe its vigor to an Oriental source via the migrations of Odin. For Warton, the Elizabethan was the golden age of English poetry because the Eastern influence had not yet receded before the light of Western civilization. "Reason suffered a few demons still to linger, which she chose to retain . . . under the guidance of poetry,"[5] as he said elegantly. Not superstition but enlightenment

4. For these remarks on the Progress poem and on the Progress of Poesy, cf. René Wellek, *The Rise of English Literary History* (Chapel Hill, N.C., 1941); and R. H. Griffith, "The Progress Pieces of the Eighteenth Century," *Texas Review* 5 (1920): 218–29. A second Progress theory, discussed below, emphasized a North-South movement. See also Northrop Frye, *Fearful Symmetry* (Princeton, 1947), pp. 179–82.

5. Wellek, *English Literary History,* p. 193.

dooms the poetical genius. In his curiously honest scheme the growth of reason and the decline of imagination are linked.

We possess only one influential Progress of Poesy poem, that of Gray. Its pessimistic ending is well known. But the theme is everywhere and can be the implicit background to an entire body of writings. Collins, for example, touches on the theme explicitly in the *Verses to Sir Thomas Hanmer* (and fleetingly in the preface to *Persian Eclogues*), and it is the hopeful or melancholy inspiration of almost every one of his odes. Thus, in the "Ode to Fear," he regrets his distance from the wilder and more terrible genius of Shakespeare and tries to recover something of the archaic force of personification; in the "Ode on the Poetical Character," he withdraws from his pursuit of Spenser and Milton, but not before leaving in the epode a proof of the mythopoeic power still in him; and in the posthumously published "On the Superstitions of the Highlands," seeking a more genial country for the imagination, he turns to the northernmost part of England. And though the balance in Collins is toward defeat, toward a necessary sacrifice of the poetical spirit to the spirit of his age, one poem remains exceptionally hopeful. In the "Ode to Evening" he invokes directly the Westering of the Spirit, and anticipates a new *Hesperidean* poetry —not only in hope but also in fact, for his ode is an unusual blend of archaic and sophisticated elements, of ancient superstition and modern sentiment.

Blake's "To Spring" also heralds a Westering of the Spirit. Its salient difference from the "Ode to Evening," that it is a dawn and not a dusk poem, should not obscure the fact that it draws on the same mythology of history. The emphasis falls on *our* (western) isle, *our* clime, *our* land. Blake's England awaits a dawning or second birth of that fervid—Oriental, biblical, Miltonic— imagination which his luxurious style once more evokes. There is no need to dwell on echoes from the Bible or on the great Oriental themes of coronation and sacred marriage. But a subtler echo, from Milton, should be mentioned, because it reveals how Blake already modifies the elder poet. He invites the poetical spirit to England in words that echo Milton's address, in *Lycidas,* to his "Genius of the shore." Is not Blake's "turn / Thine angel eyes upon our western isle" his version of "Look homeward, Angel, now"?[6]

In *Lycidas* Milton is also concerned with the destiny of the poetical spirit, its relation to the classics and the Bible, and with the role of an English poet in that destiny. It is he who linked the themes of liberty and poetry; and it is also he, in *Lycidas* as elsewhere, who associated poetry and the spirit of prophecy. His career, inspired by the desire to have poetry look homeward as well as toward the Ancients, anticipates that of Blake at every turn.

Yet Milton, perhaps, did not look homeward sufficiently. Blake repeats Milton's invocation as if everything were to be done again. Though his point of departure is the same, the poetry he foresees is different. Blake separates from Milton, as from Collins, on the matter of the role of the classics in the Progress of the poetical spirit. The aim of *Lycidas* is a native poetry of prophetic scope, yet the possibility of an English or Western poetry was not conceivable for Milton without Virgil's guidance. Virgil was the great literary mediator who showed (together with Horace) that poetry could be written even at a distance from the source: at a distance from the archaic, the naïve, the directly prophetic. Virgil, in fact, introduced the theme of evening into poetry.[7] He was often considered the first significant way station in the Westering of the Poetical Spirit: it might almost be said that through him the idea of a Progress of Poesy became possible. For his hero is an émigré, and his idea of nationality is visionary enough to encompass the local gods of both Greece and Latium. What poets imitate, therefore, is not Virgil's style as such but a method of mediation,

6. For "western isle," cf. Collins, "Ode to Peace," st. 4. It is significant that Hölderlin, who inherited the same mythology of history (see, e.g., his description of the flight of the eagle in "Germania," which is a Progress of Poesy from East to West), will also become involved, as prophetic poet, in a so-called *abendländische Wendung* which exactly parallels the turn ("Look homeward") attempted by Milton and then by Blake. The remarks made throughout this essay on the problem of mediation can provide a link between German and English Romanticism that is relatively comprehensive. That Hölderlin considered Homer rather than Virgil the first literary mediator is a significant but slight difference in the context of this larger unity of concern.

7. Erwin Panofsky, "Et in Arcadia Ego," *Meaning in the Visual Arts* (New York, 1955), pp. 300 ff. It was Dante, of course, who already understood, and transformed, this mediating function of Virgil's.

the self-conscious acceptance of a secondary, "translating" function. The "come hither" motif, the ritual invitation so important
in Milton and Collins, stylizes this concept of poetry as translation.
When Milton asks the Sicilian Muse to "call the Vales, and bid
them hither cast / Their Bells and Flowrets of a thousand hues"
—where "hither" is English poetry as well as the resting place of
Lycidas—he adapts the opening passages of Books 1 and 2 of
the *Georgics:*

> Et vos, agrestum praesentia numina, Fauni
> Ferte simul Faunique pedem Dryadesque puellae:
> munera vestra cano.
>
> [1.10–13]
>
> huc, pater o Lenaee, veni nudataque musto
> tinge novo mecum dereptis crura coturnis.
>
> [2.7–8]

It is precisely a Progress of Poesy based on cultural translation
which Blake refuses to acknowledge. His parody of the second
quotation, Virgil's address to Bacchus, is quite overt.[8] He insists
on immediacy, on a directness to the source which Virgil's example
and the body of classical tradition impede. Theirs is an insufficient,
even perverted, "reception of the Poetic Genius." Not that Blake,
in *Poetical Sketches,* rejects classical style: on the contrary, he
tries to restore its pristine vigor by bringing it closer to the poetical
parts of the Bible. It is a lapsed Orientalism, whose sparks have
to be fanned into a new and open flame.[9] We said that Blake's
"To Spring" heralds a Westering of the Spirit: we should have
said a new "Eastering." His are dawn and not evening poems—so
much so that "To the Evening Star," which competes with Collins
on classical ground, becomes almost a poem about dawn. It depicts
the evening star as another sun, a dawn risen upon evening:

8. Blake's Summer is asked to sit "beside our springs," to "throw
thy / Silk draperies off" and "rush into the stream"; while Autumn,
"stained / With the blood of the grape," is invited to "pass not, but sit /
Beneath my shady roof." By *parody* I mean a translation of the translation motif that subverts its original meaning: the motif is made to remind
us of the free, or "bacchic," nature of the poetical spirit.

9. "To Morning" *(Poetical Sketches)* is an especially strong mingling
of classical and Hebraic, in favor of the latter.

199

> Thou fair-hair'd angel of the evening,
> Now, whilst the sun rests on the mountains, light
> Thy bright torch of love; thy radiant crown
> Put on . . .[10]

The imperious vocatives, as in "To Spring," are no Collinsian, ritual supplications but seek to "awake the dawn" (Ps. 57:8) of which they speak.

It is not sufficient to conclude from this that Blake chooses the Asiatic over the Attic mode. He is not a formalist deciding between stylistic options. What is attacked is the very basis of Atticism, the ideological source of its power over the Augustans and even Milton. Blake rejects the idea of a consciously Hesperidean Muse, a muzzled Orientalism, an accommodated prophetic vision. He rejects Virgil's exemplary mediation, the conception of style as a compromise, and the position of classical literature as an important station in the Westering of the Poetical Spirit. There is no Westering; there is only an Eastering, an immediacy to the source renewed by each great poet. If, in *Poetical Sketches,* the style is aggressively Oriental, this is not because Blake believed in the East as the exclusive source of poetical inspiration but because Hebrew poetry, in its unmediated, prophetic vigor, is the right orientation. "Look homeward, Angel, now": Blake is not, like Virgil, the poet of a migration, of a man having to resettle his gods, his goods, his destiny, in a foreign land; he is the prophet of a spiritual homecoming, of a miraculous inner turn and restoration. In Blake the restoration is that of the poetical genius to England. The East is wherever poetry is.

It is time to look from "To Spring" to the entire cycle. The first three poems are clearly in the context of a Progress of Poesy. The come hither motif entices the seasons to England with one main suggestion: it is, or could be, the poetical country. If in the first poem the style itself must carry that suggestion, in the second the theme is explicitly stated:

> Our bards are fam'd who strike the silver wire:
> Our youths are bolder than the southern swains;

10. This also has traditional support in the conception of Hesperus as evening and morning star and Venus.

> Our maidens fairer in the sprightly dance:
> We lack not songs, nor instruments of joy

and in the third we actually hear a song, sung by Autumn to the poet's pipe, which recapitulates the three seasons and evokes a momentary impression of the perfection of all in all—of poetry as part of the harvest, as a song that seasons the season. Autumn's round does not flow, like Thomson's recapitulative *Hymn* of 1730, into a transcendent theme; it transcends only the previous invocations, or the spiritual state they reflect. The land is no longer lovesick, unmated, desiring ardently its regeneration; nor is it aggressively admiring, countervirile, as in the presence of Summer. It is the poetic land, a fulfilled and human landscape.

"To Winter" is, of course, on the horizon; but this temporary climax of the cycle in "To Autumn" suggests the equal if not higher dignity of the Western Muse. Here Blake is English Blake; yet to ascribe to him a nationalistic or even hemispheric conception is a partial truth at best. He is not Wordsworth, for whom being an English poet is achieved through being a nature poet. Though "To Autumn" does anticipate both Wordsworth and Keats, the progress Blake has in mind is not linked, ultimately, to a geopolitical march of the spirit. That conception survives as a frame of the whole because Blake is engaged in transforming a nationalistic mythology of history into a universal topography of the imagination. He understands the Progress of Poesy as a spiritual rather than place-conditioned fact: there is progress whenever mankind recognizes that the human, the divine, and the poetical genius are one and the same. Hence the double, and perhaps confusing, scheme of Blake's cycle: in borrowing the historical frame of the Westering of the Spirit and culminating in "To Autumn," the scheme is recognizably English; yet the progression is also universal because each poem expresses a different station in the resurgence of the poetical spirit anywhere. In this drama of three acts, the spirit of prophecy so conspicuous in the first poem and the spirit of liberty in the second advance toward their ripest epiphany as the poetical spirit of the third, its "golden load" of song.

Yet what of "To Winter"? It stands out from the sequence for several reasons. It reverses the come hither motif; it also reverses a second formula, for the stanza beginning "He hears me not, but o'er the yawning deep / Rides heavy" portrays an epiphany based on the god's not hearing, on his overriding the formal petition. It reverses, indeed, the entire direction of the cycle, since Winter is obviously a force which man cannot humanize. The poet assumes a Jobean humility ("I dare not lift mine eyes") and imagines a mariner figure, homeless in this demonic landscape.

Through the addition of "To Winter" Blake's quarrel with the traditional Progress is, if anything, put into clearer perspective. He seems to say to Winter "Thou hast thy music too," meaning there exists a genuine poetry of the North.[11] The poetical spirit is now seen to blow from all corners of the globe: from East ("To Spring"), South ("To Summer"), West ("To Autumn"), and North ("To Winter"). Blake will not localize the poetic genius; indeed, he considers the attempt to restrict it to one class or nation a major cause for the dying out of prophecy and the birth of Priestly Religion. Whatever Holy Land the poetical spirit seems to come from, "The true Man is the source, he being the Poetic Genius."

"To Winter" is, moreover, a perfect second climax to the cycle. As always in Blake, strength dies into strength: in "To Autumn" there was no dying music until the very end. Keats's Autumn ode contains within its final stanza an Ode to Evening, but only the slightest hint of autumn as fall. The processional image of Winter riding heavy in its "iron car" over the "yawning deep" rivals that of Summer's "fervid car" riding "o'er the deep of heaven." Winter really winters, even at the price of a retreat from the humanism of "To Autumn."

We can now face the delayed question of Thomson's influence. *The Seasons* is by origin a poem of the Scottish border and began naturally enough with a *Winter*. Thomson gives the Northern imagination full scope: not in the form of locodescriptive detail (there is little) but in the form of a poetry expressing the genius loci of an entire sphere. Part of his subject is the Genius of the

11. I.e., Ossian, the Eddas, "Northern Antiquities." The contents of *Poetical Sketches* are pretty evenly divided between homage to the Elizabethans (particularly Shakespeare) and to the North in the form of ballads and Ossianic paraphrases.

North, perhaps because it was constantly put in question.[12] There were two sharply conflicting opinions about the frozen North, and both were linked to rival Progress theories. One exalted Eastern (classical or biblical) origins, postulated a Westering of the Spirit, and viewed the North as a region intrinsically passive and barbarous. But in Thomson's age an opposite theory was in the ascendant, one which postulated a movement from North to South and exalted Celts, Goths, and Germani (not always discriminated) as the womb of nations and home of the spirit of freedom. This alternate Progress practically reversed the assumptions of the first. The North is now what the East was: the cradle of liberty and of imagination.[13]

In "To Winter" Blake seems to change to a Progress moving along a North-South axis. Is this a confused, if high-spirited, play with *topoi*? A youthful confusion cannot be ruled out. In the 1770s Blake was at the center of intersecting visions of historical progress. Mallet's *Northern Antiquities,* translated in 1770 by Percy, also showed uncertainty about what was Eastern or Northern in origin. The trouble is that Blake's confusion, if it exists, is permanent rather than youthful: the later Blake also indulges in it. Like Rudbeck the Elder, who identified Scandinavia with Plato's Atlantis, he identifies Albion with Jerusalem. A more likely interpretation of "To Winter" is that Blake, by shifting from one historical scheme to another, puts in doubt the historicity of either Progress and so reinforces his thought that poetry is coterminous with man and not with a region. It is only the Genius in the genius loci that interests him.

If the confusion is purposeful, foreshadowing the dialectical Blake, then we understand better his decision to represent the poetical spirit as a season. He corrects Thomson, as he will later seek to correct Milton. Blake's seasons are comparable to Thomsonian genii which determine, or represent synoptically, the domi-

12. Thomson is by no means a pure apologist for the North. See Alan D. McKillop's account of his treatment, throughout *The Seasons,* of the conflict between primitivism and progress: *The Background of Thomson's Seasons* (Minneapolis, 1942), pp. 106 ff. The theme of progress is a major concern of the poem.

13. See Thor J. Beck, *Northern Antiquities in French Learning and Literature* (New York, 1934); and McKillop, *Thomson's Seasons,* pp. 109 ff.

nant character of a region. Yet they are also quite different. The concept of genii loci helped Thomson to a peculiar kind of visionary history, which set man totally in the frame of nature, in the frame of migrations that are a Newtonian blend of spiritual force and cosmic determinism. *The Seasons* is a visionary history without a hero—the hero being Providence working through the forces of Nature. For Blake, however, the hero of any visionary history is the power of vision itself, the human and poetical genius, and Thomson's pseudoregional identification of this genius with a genius loci only narrowed it down, in his eyes, to druidism, deism, and nationalism. Blake is certainly right with respect to Thomson: *The Seasons,* which has a genuine visionary flair, was followed by *Liberty,* which has the right theme but little else.

The aim of Blake vis-à-vis Thomson is to view Genius as the only genius loci, the only true guardian of one's country. An England that has lost the poetical spirit has lost its identity. That is why Albion must call Jerusalem back and why the land in this cycle invokes something that is really an inalienable part of itself. Genius calls to Genius.

The exception is, again, "To Winter," where the poet is a mere figure in the landscape who vainly seeks to hold back, instead of inviting, the Genius of the North. Even if the latter is identified as the spirit of liberty moving relentlessly toward the South, it is a tyrannous power as well. Try as we may, "To Winter" will not settle down to any one interpretation. It comes at the end of the cycle like a satyr play calling all sacred themes into question. It is a confusing poem, perhaps a confused one; yet a strong impression of reversal remains. The poem even ends with an absurd plot reversal that is an inspired period cliché ("till heaven smiles," that is, Spring appears, and Winter, for all his bombast, turns tail). Thus "To Winter" moves close to absolute parody, and if we do not finally take it as such, it is because the other odes are not sufficiently different in style, and because the thought of young Blake experimenting comes to mind.

Granted, of course, that it is precarious to base too much on near-juvenilia, yet granted also that any thesis gains its strength from an understanding of Blake's total spiritual form, we must ask whether this early penchant for parody (to the point of self-parody) does not foretell Blake's later and radical illusionism.[14] The great show to come—the apocalyptic opera of the Prophetic Books—serves only to expand us back to ourselves, to the knowledge that "all deities reside in the human breast." The contrast in Blake's poetry between divine magic and apodictic humanism is such that one is tempted to see him as a Prospero and this pageant of the seasons as his earliest revel. A sense of masquerade hovers over it, with the Orientalism of "To Spring" as much a mask as the Northern sublimity of "To Winter."

I would like to end with a view of Blake as *homo ludens.* Are not his maskings a gay science, an applied humanistic magic, part of those "enjoyments of Genius" which to the Angels look like "torment and insanity" *(Marriage of Heaven and Hell)?* To the Angels still among us, Blake's competitiveness with the prophets must indeed appear wanton, if not mad. Yet the poetical spirit, to return to itself, to its former and natural greatness, had to put on the prophetic style once more. In Blake it is religion that is unmasked, but poetry gaily puts on the mask. For religion without its mask, religion demystified, is the Poetic Genius; and in that knowledge Blake moves poetry toward a happier consciousness of itself.

14. Another striking instance of parody in *Poetical Sketches,* which directly involves the Progress of Liberty from Troy to England, is the Minstrel's song at the end of "King Edward the Third." See David V. Erdman's interpretation in *Blake: Prophet Against Empire* (Princeton, 1954), pp. 69–70.

Wordsworth, Inscriptions, and Romantic Nature Poetry

The earliest genuinely lyrical poem of Wordsworth bears an elaborate title: "Lines left upon a Seat in a Yew-Tree, which stands near the Lake of Esthwaite, on a desolate part of the shore, yet commanding a beautiful prospect." The poem reached its final form between 1795 and 1797 and appears as the first of Wordsworth's productions in the *Lyrical Ballads* of 1798. Its structure is simple: an apostrophe to the passing traveler commends a solitary spot in nature; this is followed by a moral and biographical epitome of the recluse who so loved this spot and its view that he built the seat ("his only monument") mentioned in the title; the conclusion admonishes once more the passer-by, asking him to heed the story just told and the moral now drawn from it. The poem is in the mature blank verse of Wordsworth's meditative poetry, and it reflects his strong eye for nature and his general moral sensitivity.

It may seem irrelevant to ask what kind of lyric this is. Coleridge, in the verses that follow it in *Lyrical Ballads,* invents a genre of his own, calling "The Nightingale" a "conversational poem"; and Wordsworth's lyric challenges the same apparent freedom of designation. Its value, to us at least, does not seem to depend in any way on the recognition of the species to which it may belong. This is true, of course, of many of the best Romantic lyrics: consider "Tintern Abbey" or "Old Man Travelling," to stay only with *Lyrical Ballads.* There is a pleasure in not knowing, or not being able to discern, the traditional form; the lack becomes a positive virtue, and we begin to seek, not quite earnestly, for the proper formal description. Are the "Lines left upon a seat in a Yew-Tree" a fragment of meditative-didactic verse, a chunk freed from some longer topographical poem, a disguised anecdote, an extended epitaph? To the naïve yet careful reader the form may appear, above all, as an effective way to sweeten a moral by human interest and immediacy of situation.

It is certain, however, that Wordsworth's first characteristic lyric belongs to a special genre. Charles Lamb recognized it instinctively. He heard the poem while visiting Coleridge at Nether Stowey in July 1797—the famous visit during which "dear Sara" accidentally emptied a skillet of boiling milk on her poet-husband's foot and set the stage for another of his great conversational poems: "This Lime-Tree Bower my Prison." During this visit, Wordsworth read the "Lines left upon a seat in a Yew-Tree," and Lamb could not get them out of his mind. Shortly after returning home he wrote Coleridge about the poem. "You would make me very happy, if you think W. has no objection, by transcribing for me that inscription of his." And later in the same letter, "But above all, *that Inscription!*"[1]

The term Lamb uses twice, and the second time in a generic sense, identifies a lyrical mode that has not attracted attention, perhaps because it is such a normal, accepted, even archaic feature of the eighteenth-century literary scene. The inscription, as Lamb calls it, was more genus than species, being the primitive form of the epigram, and was connected therefore with most of the briefer forms of lyric in the eighteenth century. It was in theory, and often in fact, a dependent form of poetry, in the same sense in which the statues of churches are dependent on their architectural setting or partly conceived in function of it. The inscription was anything conscious of the place on which it was written, and this could be tree, rock, statue, gravestone, sand, window, album, sundial, dog's collar, back of fan, back of painting. It ranged in scope and seriousness from Pope's inscription on the collar of the Prince of Wales' dog: "I am his Highness' dog at Kew/Pray tell me sir, whose dog are you?" to Thomas Warton's "Verses on Sir Joshua's

---

1. *The Letters of Charles Lamb*, ed. E. V. Lucas, 2 vols. (London, 1935), 1: 112. It is pleasing to speculate that Wordsworth's verses (together with the boiling milk) may have been partially responsible for "This Lime-Tree Bower." The central emblem in both poems is a retreat, a tree prison; and Coleridge's mind, though meditating in solitude, follows a path contrary to that of the recluse by attaching love of nature to the development of the social sense.

Painted Window at New College."[2] This general form of the inscription was accompanied by a special form which we shall call the *nature-inscription,* whose popularity seems to have been proportional to that of eighteenth-century gardens. In Shenstone's *ferme ornée,* The Leasowes, one of the famous show gardens of the time, beautiful prospects were discreetly marked for the tourist by benches with inscriptions from Virgil or specially contrived poems.[3] It was this kind of inscription that provided a pattern for Wordsworth's "Lines left upon a seat"; though pattern is, perhaps, too strong a term. Wordsworth was able to liberate the genre from its dependent status of tourist guide and antiquarian signpost: he made the nature-inscription into a free-standing poem, able to commemorate any feeling for nature or the spot that had aroused this feeling.

A direct glance at the "Lines left upon a seat" yields many of the characteristics both of the inscription in general and of nature-inscriptions in particular. The swollen title, beside telling us where the poem is supposedly found, reflects the link between inscription and epigram. Since the epigram, especially in the later Renaissance, tended to be as brief and pointed as possible, the particular circumstances which had given rise to it were often placed in the title. There are epigrams with titles longer than the epigrams themselves. The relation between title (lemma)[4] and epigram was quite complex and varied, like the cognate relation

2. Though the "on" in Warton's title is only vestigially locative, and the poem could be placed among such different genres of the eighteenth century as effusion, impromptu, and even ode, the poet's situation (his sense of locality and spirit of place, and the fact that he responds to a work of art) relates his poem genuinely to the inscription. The term *inscription,* of course, simply translates *epigram.* Warton wrote an explicitly titled "Inscription in a Hermitage at Ansley-Hall, in Warwickshire" (composed 1758; published 1777) and published in 1753 an inscription for a Grotto translated from the Greek Anthology. For other inscriptions, see the section under that title (and also under "Epigrammata") in Richard Mant's edition of *The Poetical Works of Thomas Warton* (Oxford, 1802).

3. See R. Dodsley, "A Description of The Leasowes" (1764), affixed to the second volume of Shenstone's *Works in Verse and Prose.*

4. The lemma seems to have been an explanatory comment added to the epigram during the process of editing but which Renaissance fashion elaborated into a title. For the fashion, see H. H. Hudson, *The Epigram in the English Renaissance* (Princeton, 1947), pp. 11–13.

208

between motto and picture in the emblem; and I need hardly add that none of this complexity is found in Wordsworth. But his elaborated title does reflect the tradition of the epigram and may even reproduce, typographically, the effect of an inscription.[5] Most of the concrete detail, however, is included in the poem itself, which is far too lengthy to have been inscribed and resembles the Greek rather than Greco-Roman form of the epigram.[6]

The second feature to be noted is still common to both general and special forms of inscription. I can best suggest it by quoting from Lessing's treatise on the epigram—systematic theorizing about genre was his forte, and in England we find little or no sustained consideration of the epigram-inscription as such. Noting that the modern form of the epigram was derived, primitively, from actual inscriptions, Lessing comments: "The true inscription is not to be thought of apart from that whereon it stands, or might stand. Both together make the whole from which arises the impression which, speaking generally, we ascribe to the inscription alone. First, some object of sense which arouses our curiosity; and then the account of this same object, which satisfies that curiosity."[7]

The relevance of this structure to Wordsworth's poem is obvious. By the title—the admonition "Nay, Traveller! rest"—and indeed by the whole opening (to line 12), it presents an object that should arouse curiosity. It then goes on to satisfy that curiosity by its story

5. The "left on" in Wordsworth's title, though generally equivalent to "written on," links his poem also to the votive epigram which might be left under a picture, on a hearse, etc.—I have found no study of the titling of poems. Lengthiness of title as well as the emerging significance of place and date might also have been influenced by the journalistic broadside ballad which tended toward concrete and elaborate titles. One of them is parodied in Sir Walter Scott's *The Antiquary:* "Strange and Wonderful News from Chipping-Norton, in the County of Oxon, of certain dreadful apparitions which were seen in the air on the 26th of July, 1610, at half an hour after nine o'clock at noon . . ." Cf. "Verses found under a Yew-Tree at Penshurst, July 18, 1791. By a Country Blacksmith" (from *Gentleman's Magazine)* or "Written Sept. 1791, during a remarkable thunder storm, in which the moon was perfectly clear, while the tempest gathered in various directions near the earth" (Charlotte Smith, *Elegiac Sonnets,* no. 59).

6. On this distinction, see n. 21 below.

7. *Zerstreute Anmerkungen über das Epigramm,* first published in *Vermischte Schriften* (Berlin, 1771). I use the translation in Hudson, *Epigram,* pp. 9–10.

of the recluse, except that our attention, far from being dissolved, is steadily deepened. The Yew with its ingrown seat is explained, but not explained away. Our eyes are opened to a truth latent in the simplest feature of the landscape. Wordsworth moves psychology closer to archeology by resuscitating the story of the recluse from a trace strongly merged with nature.

The third feature of the inscription, and perhaps the most intriguing, is related to this sense for a life (in nature) so hidden, retired, or anonymous that it is perceived only with difficulty. This sense of hidden life is peculiar to the nature-inscription and betrays itself also in formalistic ways. There is first the context of anonymity which the poem partially dispels. The lines are "left" upon the seat, and they describe a person who has (1) lived unknown, in retirement, and (2) lived an unknown life. He resembles one of the "unhonour'd Dead" whose "artless tale" Gray begins to reveal in his *Elegy*. The anonymity of nature and the anonymity of the common man join to produce an elegiac tenor of feeling.

There is, moreover, a general convergence of elegiac and nature poetry in the eighteenth century. Poems about place (locodescriptive) merge with meditations on death so that landscape becomes dramatic in a quietly startling way. From it there emanate "admonitions and heart-stirring remembrances, like a refreshing breeze that comes without warning, or the taste of waters from an unexpected fountain."[8] Not only is the graveyard a major locus for the expression of nature sentiment, but Nature is herself a larger graveyard inscribed deeply with evidences of past life. This convergence of graveyard and nature, or of epitaph and locodescriptive poetry, is consecrated by the success of Gray's *Elegy* (1751), in which the division between countryside and cemetery is hardly felt. We move with insidiously gradual steps from the one to the other, and Gray enters so strongly into the spirit of his poem that he imagines himself as one of the unhonored dead rescued from anonymity only by his epitaph graved under a thorn. His poem ends, therefore, with an archaic image of itself—an actual

8. Wordsworth, "Upon Epitaphs" (first essay). See *The Prose Works of William Wordsworth,* ed. A. B. Grosart, 3 vols. (London, 1876), 2:32. E. Bernhardt-Kabisch in "Wordsworth: The Monumental Poet" has discerned how profoundly epitaphs influenced Wordsworth's sensibility and poetry *(Philological Quarterly* 44 (1965): 503–18).

inscription for which the whole elegy provides the setting, and this is nature in its most regular, ancient, and oblivious form.

Perhaps the clearest sign of the merging of epitaph and nature poetry is the address to the Traveler with which the Yew-tree poem begins. The "Nay, Traveller! rest" is the traditional *Siste Viator* of the epitaph. We are made to hear the admonitory voice of the deceased or of the living who speak for the deceased. Yet Wordsworth commemorates a strange spot in nature rather than a grave, since the seat in the Yew-Tree is not literally a tombstone. It is solely the poet's imagination which sees that pile of stones as a funeral pile.[9] The rudely constructed seat was merely the haunt of the recluse, yet because he used it as an escape, burying himself in "visionary views," and not allowing nature to take him out of his gloomy self, Wordsworth rightly treats it as his tomb. The "Lines in a Yew-Tree" exorcize the spot and rededicate the seat to its proper purpose of marking a beautiful view.

The call from a monument in the landscape or from the landscape itself, which deepens the consciousness of the poet and makes him feel he is on significant ground, is also encouraged by a sister-tradition to the epitaph. Most nature-inscriptions are related to the votive or commemorative epigram, which plays an important role in the Greek Anthology and comes into vernacular literature chiefly from that source.[10] The votive epigram took many forms: it was a simple statement identifying the donor, giving a brief yet lucid picture of the place and object dedicated, and saying to whom they are offered; it was, as in inscriptions of this kind which survive from Theocritus, a poem celebrating a votive painting (statue), or rather animating it; and it could be a short proso-

9. This is not altered by the fact that a fashion for funeral urns and commemorative benches prevailed in the second half of the century: see Dodsley, "A Description of The Leasowes," and J. Delille's *Les Jardins* (1780), chant 4.

10. For general information about the Greek Anthology, I am mainly indebted to J. W. Mackail, *Select Epigrams from the Greek Anthology,* (New York, 1906), and the two invaluable books of James Hutton: *The Greek Anthology in Italy to the Year 1800* (Ithaca, N.Y., 1935) and *The Greek Anthology in France . . . to the Year 1800* (Ithaca, N.Y., 1946). Though the Anthology has individual parts devoted to epitaphs and dedications respectively, it will become clear that, as Mackail observes in his introduction, "the earlier epigram [i.e., the Greek as distinguished from the Greco-Roman] falls almost entirely under these two heads."

popeia, the voice of the god or genius of the place (genius loci) who warns us that we are near sacred ground. The first kind is strangely and uncertainly naïve; and only Marvell uses it in an original way in his mower poems, where he sharpens its naïveté deliciously:

> I am the Mower *Damon,* known
> Through all the Meadows I have mown.

It does not play an important role, after Marvell, in the writing of nature poetry.[11]

The second kind does, for it is part of the tradition of iconic verse. Some of the most interesting descriptive poetry of the eighteenth century enters through such iconic and animating gestures as Behold, See, Mark, or through a rather special and limited genre—the Lines on (first) seeing a picture (artifact), which Anna Seward sometimes converts into "Inscription on the back of a Picture."[12] Since the pictures, at least in Anna Seward's case, are landscapes, a good amount of vigorous and picturesque description enters English poetry in this form.

I want to emphasize the third kind of votive epigram, in which the inscription calls to the passer by in the voice of the genius loci or spirit of the place. Like the epitaph it seems to derive from ritual formulae which admonished strangers not to disturb the remains of the dead. In the eighteenth century we find an extraordinary number of inscriptions for Bower, Grotto, Fountain, Seat, or similar Places of Retreat and Refreshment, which both

11. In English literature the naïvely paganizing strain is displaced by the hermit poem with its Christian simplicities, but Wordsworth's lyrics on Matthew here and there touch on the spirit of the older tradition. The sonnet, which was strongly related to the votive epigram and which allowed simple personal (and first-person) sentiment, is too large a subject to be broached here. See, however, a significant remark on Coleridge's introduction to his sonnets in the 2nd (1797) edition of *Poems on Various Subjects:* "Perhaps, if the Sonnet were comprized in less than fourteen lines, it would become a serious epigram. . . . The greater part of Warton's Sonnets are severe and masterly likenesses of the style of the Greek *epigrammata.*"

12. Jean Hagstrum in *The Sister Arts* (Chicago, 1958) covers—and recovers—this tradition as it extends from Dryden to Gray and clarifies its sources in earlier literature. I adopt his use of the term *iconic.* For Anna Seward's inscriptions, see *The Poetical Register and Repository of Fugitive Poetry for 1801,* pp. 177–80, 180–81.

invite and exhort the world-weary traveler. Pope's verses on his grotto at Twickenham are a familiar example. Such verses were directly encouraged by the interest in gardens and participated in the antiquarian fervor of the century. A disgruntled observer, looking in 1819 through Dodsley's collection, complains among other things about its "inscriptions in grottoes, and lines on fans innumerable."[13] But not many years before this complaint (so persistent is the fashion) we find in *Gentleman's Magazine* a competition for the best English rendering of Latin verses supposedly found on a supposed hermitage.[14]

Despite all misuses, the votive inscription is important for nature poetry in that it allows landscape to speak directly, without the intervention of allegorical devices. The voice of nature that calls us does not have to be formalized or pompously accoutered, although sometimes it is. The simplification in the form responds to a rural simplicity of feeling. We begin to hear and see a nature unobstructed by magnifying artifice. A waterfall may purge, momentarily, our selfish cares:

> Come, and where these runnels fall
> Listen to my madrigal!
> Far from all sounds of all the strife,
> That murmur through the walks of life;

13. Quoted by Victor Lange, *Die Lyrik und ihr Publikum im England des 18. Jahrhunderts* (Weimar, 1935), p. 60.

14. *Gentleman's Magazine* 78 (1808): 728, 924, 1020. T. Warton's "Inscription in a Hermitage" has been mentioned. Two more examples of interest are Mrs. West's "Inscription," *Gentleman's Magazine* 61 (1791): 68, and an anonymous "Ballad" in the *Poetical Register for 1802,* pp. 254–5. To the hermit poems, a devotional poetry in disguise, Wordsworth adds his "Inscriptions supposed to be found in and near a Hermit's Cell" (1818). They revert to the eighteenth-century quatrain style, though this is chastened, as the persona of the Hermit required, to hymnlike simplicity. Wordsworth practiced the conventional kind of inscription throughout his career: among his juvenilia are two versions of an inscription for a wayside bench which were never printed under his name, though one was published pseudonymously. His interest in Sir G. Beaumont's garden at Coleorton produces several further instances, and when he thinks he may have to leave Rydal Mount he composes an inscription to be placed in its grounds. The 1815 edition of his collected poems contains a section explicitly titled "Inscriptions." As late as 1830, remembering the old exhortation "Woodman, spare that tree," he writes some unusually playful verses on a stone saved from the builder's hand.

From grief, inquietude, and fears,
From scenes of riot, or of tears;
From passions, cankering day by day,
That wear the inmost heart away;

. . . .

Come, and where these runnels fall,
Listen to my madrigal![15]

Or the nymph of the grotto, still somewhat portentous, invites us:

Come, Traveller, this hollow Rock beneath,
While in the Leaves refreshing Breezes breath;
Retire, to calm the Rage of burning Thirst,
In these cool Streams that from the Caverns burst.[16]

Such moments are rarely deepened and even more rarely sustained.[17] Southey's inscriptions, of which eight were published in the first edition of his *Poems* (1797), often assume the bardic and officious voice of the interpreter instead of letting the genius loci speak directly to us. In this respect they do not differ from the odic or iconic modes of nature poetry in which the poet addresses the landscape in his own person, asking woods and valleys to mourn or rejoice or show their splendors or perform in one way or another. Yet the Hellenic originals, or intermediate models, chasten

15. W. L. Bowles, "Inscription," *The Poetical Works of William Lisle Bowles,* ed. Rev. G. Gilfillan, 2 vols. (Edinburgh, 1855), 1:155–56. The poem signs off: "Bremhill Garden, Sept. 1808." Bowles published a set of "Inscriptive Pieces" as early as 1801, distinguishing them from "Inscriptions" because of their more personal, impressionistic character; and his "Coombe Ellen," a blank-verse poem "written in Radnorshire, September, 1798," shows more patently than "Tintern Abbey" a formal indebtedness to inscriptive poetry. See Bowles, *Poems* (London and Bath, 1801), 2:15–27, 87 ff. On the influence of the early Bowles, see M. H. Abrams, "Structure and Style in the Greater Romantic Lyric," in *From Sensibility to Romanticism,* ed. F. W. Hilles and H. Bloom (New York, 1965), pp. 539–44.

16. "On a Cave. From the Greek of Anyta, a Lesbian Poetess," in Thomas Warton the Elder, *Poems on Several Occasions* (1748).

17. The middle of Bowles's poem, quoted above, reverts to the allegorizing which vitiates so many songs and descriptive pieces of the eighteenth and early nineteenth century. For a nondidactic allegorical song, see Shelley's "The Two Spirits: An Allegory" (1820). But the song, as a genre, has its own development and is not the subject of this essay.

Southey's verse into pictures of nature almost completely free of penseroro chimaeras and allegorical personifications:

> Enter this cavern, Stranger! the ascent
> Is long and steep and toilsome, here a while
> Thou may'st repose thee, from the noontide heat
> O'ercanopied by this arch'd rock that strikes
> A grateful coolness: clasping its rough arms
> Round the rude portal, the old ivy hangs
> Its dark green branches down, and the wild Bees,
> O'er its grey blossoms murmuring ceaseless, make
> Most pleasant melody. No common spot
> Receives thee, for the Power who prompts the song,
> Loves this secluded haunt. The tide below
> Scarce sends the sound of waters to thine ear;
> And this high-hanging forest to the wind
> Varies its many hues. Gaze, stranger, here!
> And let thy soften'd heart intensely feel
> How good, how lovely, Nature! When from hence
> Departing to the City's crowded streets,
> Thy sickening eye at every step revolts
> From scenes of vice and wretchedness; reflect
> That Man creates the evil he endures.[18]

One more instance of this increased directness is Coleridge's "Inscription for a Fountain on a Heath," first published in 1802 under the title of "Epigram." It is nothing more than a detailed and affectionate picture of a sycamore, musical with bees, to which a small spring adds its own melody. What differentiates his poem from Southey's is that he not only mutes that sententious moralizing, a relic of medieval Christian debates concerning the active and the contemplative life which is quite foreign to most Greek models, but also, though still speaking in his own person, lulls the reader into thinking that the place itself invites him, so calm and murmuring is his voice:

> Here Twilight is and Coolness: here is moss,
> A soft seat, and a deep and ample shade.

18. "For a Cavern that overlooks the River Avon" (written at Bristol, 1796). I have quoted the version in the *Poems* of 1797.

Thou may'st toil far and find no second tree.
Drink, Pilgrim, here; Here rest! and if thy heart
Be innocent, here too shalt thou refresh
Thy spirit, listening to some gentle sound,
Or passing gale or hum of murmuring bees![19]

We do not know with certainty how many of the poets were directly familiar with the Greek Anthology, or through what intermediaries its spirit came to them. Professor Hutton, who set out to write a history of the Greek Anthology in England, found himself obliged to write it first for Continental literature, since the Anthology came to England via the Continent. But the temptations of the way were so great that he did not end where he began, and we still have no report on England.[20] From my limited perspective, therefore, I can only say two things. The general change from Neoclassical to Romantic style parallels curiously the difference between the brief, witty, pointed epigram of the Latin tradition, influential on the development of the heroic couplet, and the simpler, more

19. *The Complete Poetical Works of S. T. Coleridge,* ed. E. H. Coleridge 2 vols. (Oxford, 1912), 1:381–82. The capitalization of Twilight and Coolness shows how close the allegorical habit is, and how finely subdued.

20. Hudson's *The Epigram in the English Renaissance* was left unfinished and covers but a small chronological area. Mr. Hutton was kind enough to communicate a list of authors indebted to the Greek Anthology, but the range, quality, and epoch of its possible influence would need a study as thorough as his own previous works. Much knowledge of Greek can be taken for granted (see the two books of M. L. Clarke: *Classical Education in Britain,* and *Greek Studies in England 1700–1830);* the Greek influence, moreover, was mediated by the best Latin writers in such poems as Horace's *Odes*—3.13 (to the Blandusian fountain) and 3.18 (address to Faunus), both of which spring from the votive epigram— and in Virgil's *Eclogues,* through which the blend of elegiac and pastoral poetry first reached England. It is interesting that one book of English versions of the Anthology (only three small volumes of translation have come to my hand in the period under discussion, but this might be explained by the custom of rendering the Greek into Latin rather than English) was published in 1791 for the use of Winchester School of which Joseph Warton was headmaster, and that his brother Thomas was the first to publish in England an edition of selections from the Palatine ms. *(Anthologiæ Graecæ a C. Cephala Conditæ* [1766]). See also, for an example of the use of inscriptions in a popular novel, *Paul and Virginia,* tr. from B. de Saint-Pierre's French by H. M. Williams (1st ed. 1795), p. 86.

descriptive, anecdotal epigram which is a staple of the Greek Anthology.[21] A conscious attempt to recall the virtues of the simpler model is made early by Thomas Warton the Elder, who translates three epigrams from the Greek with the advertisement that they can serve as "a Pattern of the Simplicity so much admir'd in the *Grecian* Writings, so foreign to the present prevailing Taste, to the Love of Modern Witticism, and *Italian* Conceit."[22] His first example is an inscription on a cave (see above, p. 214); his second a votive epigram from Theocritus; and the third, also from Theocritus, a little picture or anecdote. Warton's versions are not particularly felicitous—the Grecian simplicity is exaggerated into a muscular coyness and the couplet form still thrusts that simplicity into a Procrustean bed—but the very attempt is important. It is something of a shock to realize that the Grecian simplicity admired by Warton may have been achieved by Wordsworth in a poem like "Old Man Travelling." This piece could easily be taken as an epigram à la grecque—as an anecdote in plain language and with

21. On the difference between the Alexandrian (and earlier) epigram and the Augustan type, see Hudson, *Epigram,* pp. 6–9; Mackail, *Select Epigrams,* pp. 4–5; Hutton, *Greek Anthology in Italy,* pp. 55–56; and [R. Bland and J. H. Merivale,] *Translations chiefly from the Greek Anthology* (London, 1806), p. vii. Hutton states that "we preferably think of the Greek epigram as . . . the brief elegy, written before and during the Alexandrian age"; and Bland and Merivale say that "the small poems which claim the greatest attention, are those which are written as memorials of the dead, as tokens of regard for living beauty or virtue, or as passing observations and brief sketches of human life." Charles Batteux, interestingly enough, thinks the distinction between the two types of epigrams is one between the (earlier) *inscription* and the (later) *epigram:* "Plus on remonte vers l'antiquité, plus on trouve de simplicité dans les Epigrammes. . . . dans les commencemens . . . l'Epigramme se confondait avec l'Inscription qui est simple par essence. Il suffisoit alors que l'Epigramme fût courte, d'un sens clair & juste. Peu-à-peu on y a mis plus d'art & de finesse, & on a songé à en aiguiser la pointe" ("Traité de l'Epigramme et de l'Inscription," *Principes de la littérature* [Paris, 1774]). T. Warton's *Inscriptionum Romanorum Metricarum Delectus* (1758) tried to single out the simplest Roman inscriptions—so much so, in fact, that Shenstone writes they are too simple even for his taste. See *The Letters of William Shenstone,* ed. M. Williams (Oxford, 1939), p. 496.

22. *Poems on Several Occasions* (1748). The exact date of the translations is unknown: the *Poems* are published posthumously by Joseph Warton.

a muted point. The speech of the Old Man, its strangely quiet character, replaces here the ingenious final turn of the witty epigram.

My second remark concerning the possible influence of the Greek Anthology on nature-inscriptions and the Romantic style is that there seems to have been at least one important intermediary: Mark Akenside. As far as I know Akenside was the first, except for Shenstone, to formally print a group of poems under the collective title "Inscriptions": six poems appear under that heading in Dodsley's Collection of 1758, and two are added in the 1772 posthumous edition of his poetry.[23] Southey acknowledges that his own earliest inscriptions were inspired by Akenside, and it is also interesting that one of Coleridge's first publications is an "Elegy imitated from one of Akenside's Blank-verse inscriptions."[24]

This title, in fact, gives us one clue to Akenside's importance. His inscriptions created a new short form of poetry for blank verse. Prior to Akenside, blank verse was almost purely a dramatic, epic, or didactic measure;[25] lyric indeed, was invariably in rhymed

23. Three Shenstone poems under the title "Rural Inscriptions" were included in Dodsley's Collection of 1755. They are antique and simple only vis-à-vis the French-Italian tradition and cannot compare with Akenside's, which are genuine distillations of the mood and various types of the Greek votive epigram. Akenside seems almost to have written them against or in rivalry with Shenstone. All of the latter's inscriptions are given in Dodsley in his "A Description of The Leasowes."

24. Southey acknowledges Akenside as follows in a prefatory note to *Poems* (1797): "The Inscriptions will be found to differ from the Greek simplicity of Akenside's in the point that generally concludes them." (But what Southey calls "point," Chaucer would have called "sentence.") In the 1837 edition of his poems Southey also mentions the later influence of Chiabrera, whose epitaphs had made a vivid impression on Wordsworth and Coleridge (see Wordsworth's "Essays upon Epitaphs" and his translations from Chiabrera). The Italian poet may himself be strongly indebted to the Greek Anthology. Coleridge's early imitation of Akenside was published, according to his editor, in the *Morning Chronicle* for September 3, 1794 *(Poetical Works* 1:69–70) and has nothing Akensidean about it. The theme is treated in rhyme and with the sentimentality of the contemporary pastoral ballad.

25. I assert this with more conviction than I feel. There are, however, very few blank-verse lyrics wich are not (1) translations or close imitations of the classics, (2) paraphrases of the Scriptures, or (3) borderline cases in which didactic and lyrical blend as in Thomson's influential

form, and rime tended to emphasize point. But Akenside, by his inscriptions, suggested the possibility of a short form free of the obligation of closing the sense with couplet or quatrain, though maintaining some epigrammatic firmness by a subtly latinate syntax. The inscriptions previously cited from Wordsworth, Southey, and Coleridge also break the mold of the *Sinngedicht* (as Lessing called it) in which point is all and the sense is closed at short intervals. From a historical perspective, therefore, the lyrical lyric of the Romantics is a liberated epigram; and H. H. Hudson has said astutely that "the moment an epigram becomes very good—if it is not too funny or too obviously ingenious—it is now in danger of being classed as a lyric."[26]

When, to this relative freedom from point, we add a freedom from obtrusive personification, the way is cleared for a direct and sustained nature poetry. There are no persons in Akenside's inscriptions except the spirit of the place (or its interpreter) and the offstage traveler. If this traveler, moreover, is significantly identified as the poet himself, a still closer relation is established between nature and the poet. This is what happens in Akenside's first and last inscriptions, which take the genre a good step toward the Romantic blank-verse meditation. Akenside, in the last inscription, also reverses the pattern in which the genius loci calls to the stranger, for now it is he, the poet, who in his lonely anxiety for inspiration invokes the absent Muses of the bards of Greece:

> From what loved haunt
> Shall I expect you? Let me once more feel
> Your influence, O ye kind inspiring powers:
> And I will guard it well; nor shall a thought
> Rise in my mind, nor shall a passion move
> Across my bosom unobserved, unstored
> By faithful memory. And then at some

---

didactic-descriptive *Seasons*. (Though not a short poem, it can easily be divided into short episodes.) Cf. the relevant chapters in the second volume of G. Saintsbury's *History of English Prosody* (New York, 1961); H. A. Beers, *A History of English Romanticism in the Eighteenth Century* (New York, 1899), chap. 4; and H. G. de Maar, *A History of Modern English Romanticism* (Oxford, 1924), vol. 1, chap. 8.

26. Hudson, *Epigram*, p. 9.

More active moment, will I call them forth
Anew; and join them in majestic forms,
And give them utterance in harmonious strains;
That all mankind shall wonder at your sway.

Yet Akenside's sense of alienation is nothing as sharp as that of the Romantics. I suspect, in fact, that his inscriptions exerted a twofold charm: that of mixing naïve feelings for nature with melancholy and self-conscious ones, and that of clearly subordinating the latter to the former. We may recall that Wordsworth's Yew-Tree poem (like Coleridge's "Nightingale" which follows it) is intended to combat the melancholy use of nature, and that for Wordsworth this melancholy is symptomatic of a morbidly self-centered mind. Nature should aid us to go out of ourselves, to broaden our feelings by meditation, and to recover original joy. Akenside's inscriptions, like the best Greek epigrams, subdue sentiment—and sentimentality—to votive calmness of mind.

Through a reuniting, therefore, of elegiac and locodescriptive poetry, and through the strengthening influence of the radically Greek element in the Greek Anthology,[27] a new lyrical kind emerges: the nature-inscription. It is nearest in spirit, form, and potential to the Romantic lyric. I would not go so far as to call it the missing link, but it certainly is a vital intermediary between the conventional lyrical forms of the eighteenth century and the Romantic poem. The reason why it is rarely singled out as a distinctive literary kind is that as a special form of the inscription it was naturally classed among inscriptions in general, and inscriptions themselves were not always distinguished from epigrams. Wordsworth, in 1815, lumps together epitaph, inscription, sonnet, the personal verse epistle, and all locodescriptive poetry under the general category of idyllium.[28] This is not sheer muddlehead-

27. The two factors are probably related, since the Greek epitaph was the primitive form through which nature poetry developed but I keep them distinct to suggest the peculiar English interest in local poetry. Topographical antiquarian articles in, for example, *Gentleman's Magazine,* as well as numerous guidebooks, blend the interest in locality with interest in inscriptions and make the traveler a familiar figure of English landscape.

28. *Poetical Works of William Wordsworth,* ed. E. de Selincourt, 5 vols. (Oxford, 1940–49), 2, 2nd ed. (1952): 433. *Idyllium* was a conventional term for the kind of poetry represented by the idylls of Theocritus.

edness but a practical grouping that reflected the state of poetry in his time. The nature-inscription was an unstable genre, almost a chance product of the multiplication of inscriptions of all kinds in the seventeenth and eighteenth centuries. Anyone who has worked his way through anthologies of that time knows the inordinate variety of mediocre inscriptions they offer in the form of social verse, iconic verse, elegiac and commemorative verse, jeux d'esprits, and emblems. From these, in their combinations, and by a process at least as mysterious as natural selection, the prototype of the Romantic nature poem arose and was partially stabilized by Akenside's inscriptions in blank verse.

It was demonstrated some years ago that Wordsworth's *Lyrical Ballads* were not original in subject or sentiment, or even in many elements of form. Robert Mayo's article on their contemporaneity destroyed the clichés of literary historians who had held that this poetry was too bold for its time.[29] But the question of Wordsworth's greatness, or in what his poems really differed from their contemporary analogues, was left unanswered. To this question I would now like to address myself by using Wordsworth's relation to inscriptions as the point of departure.

What Wordsworth did is clear: he transformed the inscription into an independent nature poem, and in so doing created a principal form of the Romantic and modern lyric. One step in this transformation has already been described. When fugitive feelings are taken seriously, when every sight and sound calls to the passing poet—"Nay, Traveller! rest"; "Stay, Passenger, why goest thou by soe fast?"—then the Romantic nature lyric is born.

A second step in the transformation bears directly on the form of the poem. The inscription, before Wordsworth, is strangely void of natural detail though full of nature feeling, for the reason that the genre still depends on the site it supposedly inscribes. Rather than evoking, it points to the landscape. If it has an ex-

Wordsworth esteemed Theocritus as a poet faithful to spirit of place and the simple, permanent manners (ethos) of his time. See his letter of February 7, 1799 to Coleridge, *Early Letters of William and Dorothy Wordsworth,* ed. E. de Selincourt (Oxford, 1935), pp. 221–22.

29. "The Contemporaneity of the *Lyrical Ballads,*" *PMLA* 69 (1954): 486–522.

pressive function vis-à-vis the feeling of the poet, it has a merely indicative function vis-à-vis its setting. To develop as a free-standing form, the nature lyric had to draw the landscape evocatively into the poetry itself. The poetry, as in Shakespeare, becomes full-bodied when it incorporates or even creates the setting.[30]

Yet much depends on the way the setting is incorporated. The criterion of concreteness has only a limited relevance for the nature lyric. There is more descriptive vigor—more observations and pictures from nature—in an ordinary topographical poem like Wordsworth's own *Evening Walk* or *Descriptive Sketches* than in all of *Lyrical Ballads* together. In "Lines left upon a seat in a Yew-Tree" the natural setting is drawn into the poetry not so much as a thing of beauty that should startle the traveler but because it mingled with a human life and still mingles presently with the poet's imagination. We are made to see the vital, if perverse, relationship of the solitary to his favorite spot, and to hear the poet's *viva voce* meditation on this: he writes the epitaph before our eyes.

What is truly distinctive, therefore, is Wordsworth's enlarged understanding of the setting to be incorporated. This is never landscape alone. He frees the inscription from its dependence, he gives it weight and power of its own, by incorporating in addition to a particular scene the very process of inscribing or interpreting it. The setting is understood to contain the writer in the act of writing: the poet in the grip of what he feels and sees, primitively inspired to carve it in the living rock.[31]

30. One sign of the change from indication to evocation in nature poetry is that consciousness of place and of the moment of composition are stronger than before, but before Wordsworth this shows itself mainly in the titles, which remain, as they must, an indicative device. It is significant that a late commentator claims that Warton's "Inscription in a Hermitage at Ansley-Hall, in Warwickshire" was composed "upon the spot, with all the objects around him, and on the spur of the moment." See *Gentleman's Magazine* 85 (1815): 387–88.

31. Cf. Northrop Frye, "Toward Defining an Age of Sensibility," in *Fables of Identity* (New York, 1963). Frye overstates the degree to which, with the 1800 *Lyrical Ballads,* recollection in tranquillity took over from the Age of Sensibility's "concentration on the primitive process of writing" and "oracular process of composition." But his thesis is basically very sound and exciting. The 1800 *Lyrical Ballads* contain overtly identifiable inscriptions and also the "Poems on the Naming of Places" in which naming is a joyfully spontaneous act that almost escapes elegiac implications. About Wordsworth's primitivism compared to that of the poets of the Age of Sensibility, see below, esp. note 36.

But the very intensity of the desire for perpetuation produces (or reacts to) a kind of death feeling which Shelley described directly. The writer, in composition, is but a fading coal, and his poem dead leaves. A secondary consciousness of death and change associates itself with the very act of writing. Thus, in Wordsworth, the lapidary inscription, though replaced by the meditative mind, returns as part of the landscape being meditated. The poet *reads* landscape as if it were a monument or grave: this position is common to "Lines left upon a seat in a Yew-Tree"; "The Thorn" 's letter-like distinctness of pond, hill of moss, and stunted tree; "Harp Leap Well" 's three pillars set, like cairn or cromlech, in a desolate place; and "Michael" 's straggling heap of stones.[32]

The setting Wordsworth recovers is therefore of the most elemental kind. Yet he recovers it neither as pseudo-primitive nor as antiquarian but always as a man dealing with what is permanent in man. Inscribing, naming, and writing are types of a commemorative and inherently elegiac act. Despite this, his poems move from past to present, from death to life, from stone to the spontaneity of living speech. The "Lines left upon a seat" attempt to be an inscription written in the language of nature: a monument that comes to life and makes nature come alive. His verse, says Wordsworth, using one of the oldest *topoi,* is a "speaking monument."[33] This is also true of such greater poems as "Michael" and "Tintern Abbey."

"Michael" bears an obvious structural resemblance to the Yew-Tree poem. Its two basic parts are again a presentation of the curious object and the story or epitomized biography[34] which that object entails. The object, moreover, is a monument almost merged with nature: to interpret the stones of the unfinished sheepfold is to interpret nature itself. We are made to see the naked mind confronting an anonymous landscape yet drawing

32. This fundamental attitude of reading the (epitaphic) characters of nature joins "The Ruined Cottage" (1797–98) to Bks. 5 ff. of *The Excursion,* composed more than ten years later, in which the village Pastor resuscitates his parishioners in a series of "living epitaphs."

33. From the third sonnet of Wordsworth's *The River Duddon* (1820).

34. "Epitomized biography" is Wordsworth's own phrase (Grosart, *Prose Works of Wordsworth,* 2:69.) "The excellence belonging to the Greek inscriptions in honor of the dead," we read in the preface to [Bland and Merivale,] *Translations chiefly from the Greek Anthology,* "consists in the happy introduction of their names and peculiar characters or occupations."

from it, or interpolating, the humane story of "Michael." The poem begins in an act of the living mind bent over a riddling inscription, perhaps an inscription of death.

But "Michael" also reveals a historical connection between primitive inscriptions and nature poetry. One of the earliest forms of that poetry actually arose as a modification of the epitaph. The opening paragraph of "Michael" which carefully guides the reader to his strange destination, should be compared to Theocritus' love poem in the form of a wayside inscription, and to the wayside inscription in general. This type of epigram, stemming from the practice of wayside interments, was also used to guide the stranger to suitable watering or resting places; it branched finally into an ideal species that allowed elaborate directions in the form of pictures of nature. The Greek Anthology records many examples of the ideal type. I quote one from Leonidas of Tarentum:

> Not here, O thirsty traveller, stoop to drink,
> The Sun has warm'd, and flocks disturb the brink;
> But climb yon upland where the heifers play,
> Where that tall pine excludes the sultry day;
> There will you see a bubbling rill that flows
> Down the smooth rock more cold than Thracian snows.[35]

Wordsworth gives us stones instead of water, but as he tells his story it is clear what refreshment can flow from them. Robert Frost's "Directive" is a latter-day echo of the genre.

"Michael" leads us unexpectedly to a Greek prototype. To recognize this is to become more aware of Wordsworth's greatness in recovering elemental situations. Yet it is no part of that greatness to oblige us to recognize the specific prototype or genre. On the contrary, because Wordsworth recovers the generic factor, we no longer need to recognize the genre which specialized it. Wordsworth's form appears to be self-generated rather than prompted by tradition; and the greater the poem, the clearer this effect.

This is strikingly illustrated by the "Lines written a few miles

35. [Bland and Merivale,] *Translations chiefly from the Greek Anthology,* p. 30. I have slightly modified this still frigid version: cf. Mackail, *Select Epigrams,* p. 203. For Theocritus' wayside inscription, see *The Greek Bucolic Poets,* trans. J. M. Edmonds (London and New York, 1928), p. 367.

above Tintern Abbey, On revisiting the Banks of the Wye during a Tour, July 13, 1798." Of the nature-inscription in which they originate, only the subtlest vestiges remain. The prospect with its monument or ruin is still nearby; the long specific title still indicates the epitaphic origin of the mode, as does the elegiac tenor; and the poem still claims to mark the very place in which it was inspired. But there is no actual corpse in the vicinity, and the historical significance of the spot is hardly felt. Wordsworth again restores the universal and deeply ordinary context: the corpse is in the poet himself, his consciousness of inner decay; and the history he meditates is of nature's relation to his mind. We recognize the archaic setting purified of hortative tombstone. The power to make him remember his end or his beginning springs simply and directly from a consciousness involved with nature.

Yet though it is Wordsworth's supreme gift to purge the factitious and restore the elemental situation—in his poetry every convention, figure, or device is either eliminated, simplified, or grounded in humanity—a distinction should be made between two types of the elemental: on the one hand archaic; on the other archetypal or generic. Without this distinction we can still discriminate between Wordsworth's poems and their contemporary analogues, but we cannot properly separate greater and lesser in his own corpus. It is important to recognize that the Yew-Tree poem is more archaic in its use of particular conventions than "Tintern Abbey," even if the Romantics were occasionally forced to return to the archaic in order to reach a truly universal conception.[36]

The proposed distinction can center on Wordsworth's refinement of the belief in spirit of place—the archaic belief recovered in the Yew-Tree poem. The real sin of the recluse is against the genius loci: that beautiful prospect should have renewed his heart and attuned him to find pleasure in nature. But Wordsworth's belief in spirit of place determines more than the poem's doctrine.

36. The return to the archaic is found in most poets of the Age of Sensibility, and in Wordsworth's own "Vale of Esthwaite." We may have to decide that there are two, interrelated kinds of greatness: one represented primarily by Wordsworth (the directest "poet of the human heart"): the other by the tradition going from Collins to Blake and which Coleridge elected for his "Ancient Mariner."

It determines, in addition, the form of the poem, and perhaps the very possibility of Wordsworth's kind of poetry. Formally, it is the genius loci who exhorts reader or passerby; and the same spirit moves the poet to be its interpreter—which can only happen if, "nurs'd by genius," he respects nature's impulses and gives them voice in a reciprocating and basically poetic act.

Even a song as bare as "Tintern Abbey" is based on the superstition of spirit of place. The poet reads nature or his own feelings as if there were an ominous, admonitory relationship between this spot and himself. At the end of the poem, moreover, when Wordsworth foresees his death and urges Dorothy to perpetuate his trust in nature, he speaks as if he were one of the dead who exhort the living in the guise of the genius loci. But the archaic formulae are now generated out of the natural soil of the meditation. We feel that a superstition of the tribe has been genuinely recovered and purified. There is nothing patently archaic or poetically archaizing in Wordsworth's use of a belief which he grounds so deeply in the human passion for continuity, for binding together the wisdom of the dead and the energy of the living.

It is in the Lucy poems that the notion of spirit of place, and particularly English spirit of place, reaches its purest form. (I am not sure that all of the lyrics originated in the same impulse, and the cycle may have a life of its own which took over from Wordsworth's intentions.) Lucy, living, is clearly a guardian spirit, not of one place but of all English places—you might meet her ("a Spirit, yet a Woman too"[37]) by any English fireside or any cherished grove—while Lucy, dead, has all nature for her monument. The series is a deeply humanized version of the death of Pan, a lament on the decay of English nature feeling. Wordsworth fears that the very spirit presiding over his poetry is ephemeral, and I think he refuses to distinguish between its death in him and its historical decline. The Lucy poems, brief elegies[38] that purify both gothic

37. I adapt this to the Lucy poems from "She was a Phantom of delight." Lucy is a laric figure, if we admit that the fire she tends can burn in nature as well as in the home—that, in fact, nature and home are one to her. Compare Lucy as she appears in "I travelled among unknown men" with Louisa who "loves her fire, her cottage-home;/Yet o'er the moorland will she roam" ("Louisa" was also composed ca. 1801).

38. One can think of "A slumber did my spirit seal" (called "a sublime epitaph" by Coleridge) as an epigram or brief elegy (see Hutton,

ballad and mannered epigram, consecrate English spirit of place in suitable English. One could apply to Wordsworth a famous comment in praise of Theocritus: His muse is the muse of his native land.

The Matthew poems, which honor a village schoolmaster, can be our last example. Some of them try to restore the literal integrity of nature-inscription and pastoral elegy, but others almost completely abandon the archaizing mode. In the earlier and sometimes unpublished versions, the notion of spirit of place is used in a primitivistic manner: Wordsworth pretends, for example, that he is moved to write his inscriptions in the very places that had known Matthew best and where his spirit presumably lingers. One elegy is therefore "left in the schoolroom"; another is "written on a [commemorative] tablet" in Matthew's school. And in the most pagan and beautiful of the unpublished elegies, Wordsworth deplores that Matthew is not buried near his favorite tree, on which he proceeds to inscribe an epitaph:

> Could I the priest's consent have gained
> Or his who toll'd thy passing bell,
> Then, Matthew, had thy bones remain'd
> Beneath this tree we loved so well.
>
> Yet in our thorn will I suspend
> Thy gift this twisted oaken staff,
> And here where trunk and branches blend
> Will I engrave thy epitaph.[39]

But in "The Two April Mornings" this sense of a continuity between the noble dead and the noble living is conveyed in a natural rather than artificially naïve way, through a description of a picture (a true ex-voto) that rises in the poet's mind after his anecdote about Matthew:

Greek Anthology in Italy, p. 55). The sense of early and sudden death, the balance between personal lament and subdued hope in the living earth, and the casting of lament in the form of an epitomized action, are as if perfected from the Greek.

39. Selincourt, *Poetical Works of William Wordsworth,* 4: 451–54. See also the 1800 *Lyrical Ballads,* and *Poetical Works,* 4: 68–73.

Matthew is in his grave, yet now,
Methinks, I see him stand,
As at that moment, with a bough
Of wilding in his hand.

The living substance on which the memorial is graved is now the poet's mind itself, which moves, as in *The Prelude,* from past to present under the continuing influence of the past.

The modern lyric attempts the impossible: a monument to spontaneity, a poem that coincides with the act and passion of its utterance. It tries to overcome the secondary or elegiac aspect of language by making language coterminous with life. However paradoxical this project may be, it has redeemed the short poem from the bondage of the pointed or witty style. After the Romantics, of course, and partly in reaction to their fluidities, new restraints are imposed to concentrate the lyric's fire and to recover epigrammatic terseness. The neolapidary style of the Parnassians, the mystical essentialism of the *symbolistes,* the Imagists with a doctrine that helped trim Eliot's *The Waste Land* to fragments not unlike epigrams, and the still prevalent emphasis on verbal wit and metaphor—these are restrictive and reactionary rather than liberative and revolutionary measures. The real iconoclasts are found in the period 1750–1830, which saw the diverse and sometimes volcanic change of epigram into free-standing lyric.[40]

The means by which this change was effected differed from country to country, from writer to writer, and often from poem to poem. Blake, for example, could transform epigrams into proverbs in his Auguries of Innocence; he could also (going back to native or pseudoepigraphic sources) make primitive inscriptions of his own as in his pictured emblems and children's poetry; he was not above converting to his faith a Wesley-type hymn in "And did those feet in ancient times"; he recovered the mad songs of Shakespeare; he wrote his own Greek-style epitaph in "O Rose, thou

40. Rimbaud is probably the greatest exception to this general statement. French developments are especially complex: they begin with Chénier, whose favorite book was Brunck's edition of the Greek Anthology, and begin a second time with Lamartine and Hugo. But the older classicism was still so strong that a third insurrection, that of Rimbaud, was needed.

art sick"; and, in the blank-verse lyrics of *Poetical Sketches*, he paralleled Akenside's attempt to develop an unrhymed form for lyric poetry. Herder, in Germany, by expanding Bishop Percy's idea and recovering ballads and reliques from all nations (including epigrams from the Greek Anthology), helped to break the tyranny of the Frenchified song, a tyranny that cooperated with the pointed style. But for Herder, Heine's *Buch der Lieder*, which created a new blend of song and witty style, and such collections as *Des Knaben Wunderhorn* would not have been possible. About Hölderlin, Schiller, and Goethe it is hard to speak in a comprehensive and generalizing way; but the spirit of their effort—a radical classicism opposed to that of the French tradition—is indicated by the fact that Coleridge insisted on teaching Wordsworth (when both were in Germany) the prosody of the German classical hexameter and sent him an illustrative sample of verses:

> William, my head and my heart! dear Poet that
> feelest and thinkest!
> Dorothy, eager of soul, my most affectionate sister!
> Many a mile, O! many a wearisome mile are ye
> distant,
> Long, long, comfortless roads, with no one eye
> that doth know us.

Wordsworth, understandably, is not at all moved by their meter, only by their sentiment. He has already found a style: his letter of reply contains two of the Lucy poems as well as blank-verse episodes later incorporated in *The Prelude*.[41]

Though Romantic poetry transcends its formal origin in epigram and inscription and creates the modern lyric, it still falls short of the latter in one respect. The Romantic poets do not purge themselves of a certain moralizing strain. This is especially true, in England, of the first generation of Romantics. The urbane didacticism of the school of Pope is replaced by an oracular didacticism which the inscription, with its palpable design on the passerby, allowed. The overt interpreter is rarely absent from Wordsworth's poems: a purely lyrical or descriptive moment is

41. See *Collected Letters of Samuel Taylor Coleridge*, ed. E. L. Griggs, 2 vols. (Oxford, 1956), 1: 450–53, and Selincourt, *The Early Letters of William and Dorothy Wordsworth*, pp. 203–11.

invariably followed by self-conscious explication. In "The Old Cumberland Beggar," after passages of description subtly colored by his feelings, Wordsworth turns to the statesmen of the world in a sudden moralizing apostrophe longer than these passages. The poem, as a result, falls strangely into two parts, each having its own life: the first part descriptive and quiet, the second oracular.[42]

Byron deplored the Lake poets' lack of urbanity, while Shelley and Keats tried to purify the Wordsworthian mode of didactic intrusions. "A poem should not mean but be" is a modern dictum which reflects the fact that, after Wordsworth, the only obstacle to the autonomous lyric was its self-justifying dependence on preachment. The cold, lapidary finger of the original inscriptions had turned into the oracular apostrophe pointing to humble truth. The attempt to absorb truth into the texture of the lyric has its own history. It tells of poets in search of a modern equivalent to that fusion of reality and idea which haunted artists and theoreticians from Winckelmann on and which seemed to them the very secret of Greek art. It tells of Parnassians and Pre-Raphaelites endowing poetry with something of the mute eloquence or unravishable meaning of the other arts, of Mallarmé wishing to overcome even this dependence and to specialize the qualities distinguishing poetic speech from pictorial and musical, and of Yeats generating his lyrics by means of an invisible didactic framework which is the grinning skeleton behind their casual beauties. A critique of these developments is still needed: I can mention as a symbol of their limited success Keats's one mature inscription, the "Ode on a Grecian Urn," which turns from being to meaning in the final exhortation spoken by the art object itself: "Beauty is Truth, Truth Beauty." This brief oracle has caused an extended debate that ignored until recently[43] a genre essential to the rise of the modern lyric. But Keats uses the genre once more to teach what art can teach.

42. Wordsworth's split structure is curiously akin to the inscription's *ecphrasis,* in which the mute object, or its interpreter, addresses us. (The Begger is such a mute object.)

43. The proper literary context was first pointed out by Leo Spitzer in *Comparative Literature* 7 (1955): 203–25, and was also noted by Hagstrum, *Sister Arts,* pp. 22–23. Both Spitzer and Hagstrum refer to a wealth of secondary literature showing the prevalence of art epigrams and their closeness to sepulchral epigrams.

Hopkins Revisited

When Yeats said that Hopkins's style was merely "the last development of poetic diction,"[1] he spoke like a contrary old man,
but he spoke shrewdly. The mannerist element in Hopkins,
whether nurtured by traditional rhetoric or by the force of the
vernacular, is the dragon that lies in the gates of his verse.
Hopkins's small and idiosyncratic production, much of it fragments, must have seemed to Yeats a threat to what had already
been achieved without it. Yeats's desire was not for singularity
but for a new and modern species of universal poetry, and·Hopkins
was judged to contribute an interesting but dead mutation to this
evolving species. It was ironical, therefore, that he should have
become a test case in the struggle for the recognition of modern
poetry which achieved a certain intensity at Cambridge around
1930. I. A. Richards, William Empson, and F. R. Leavis cham-
pioned Hopkins as the classic example of the modern poet. They
agreed that his strength was bound up with the immediacy of his
relation to words: he seemed to fulfill the dream that poetry was
language speaking about itself, language uttering complex words
that were meanings *as* words.. Yeats challenged their estimate:
he suggested that Hopkins was to be counted among the decadents
rather than the innovators, that in a curious way his strong new
style was the sweet old style brought to a terminal contortion. This
is not unlike the feeling of Bridges, who first published the poems
of Hopkins in 1918 with strictures on their "luxurious experiments."

Yeats's minority opinion has been refined by Giorgio Melchiori,
but it has not been cast out. After almost fifty years of close reading and superb editing, Hopkins's verse remains something of a
scandal. For we continue to be uncertain as to whether Hopkins,
like Spenser, "writ no language," or whether he coins a radically

1. *The Oxford Book of Modern Verse* (Oxford, 1936), pp. xxxix f.

new idiom. The basic questions about his greatness, direction, and even plain sense are not yet answered. Almost every one of his poems has cruxes (like "Buckle" in "The Windhover") that defeat exegetical activity. There is a strange absence, among so many books and articles, of any that can be called definitive—definitive on some aspects of interpretation.

The one thing that has been clarified is that we must rethink the whole matter of Hopkins's diction. Austin Warren's scrupulous account of its lineage and John Wain's essay on its relation (or absence of relation) to Victorian literature are complemented by Sigurd Burkhardt's reflections on the changing status of words in the consciousness of poets from Herrick to Wallace Stevens. Hillis Miller has shown what Hopkins learned about language from Parmenides; and we know modern philosophy and poetry are both implicated in a verbal thinking about words. Still missing is a consideration of how Hopkins relates to the Romantic poets on the matter of diction; the remarks of Yvor Winters on his "Romantic" eccentricities do not speak to this point but to the loss of logical or analogical poetic structure. Yet F. O. Mathiessen noted in passing Hopkins's relation to Whitman and the Romantic revolt against "poetic diction."[2]

The Romantic revolt was, on one level, a reaction in the name of life, passion, or imagination against everything dead: dead language as well as dead emotions and the deadening intellect. But the maturer intent of that revolt was to make our powers, hopes, and even sufferings more ours. Whatever stood between man and life was thought to be spurious, and language too was suspected of being a false mediation. Poetry, moreover, instead of purifying language, seemed to have fallen into the hands of a literary caste that claimed to deal in universals externalized as poetic diction. Poetry had to be cleansed of these often inauthentic universals by becoming more concrete in form and thought. The end of Romantic poetry, then, is not concreteness or particularity for its own sake; rather it is the discovery from within nature or felt experience of truly universal universals—concepts and words that could spread, like joy, "in widest commonality." Wordsworth in his greatness encouraged a new Vulgate for the imagination: poetry

2. The essays here referred to are brought together in my *Hopkins: A Collection of Critical Essays* (Englewood Cliffs, N.J., 1966).

written in the strongest and simplest language, "words that speak of nothing more than what we are."

Yeats's remark on Hopkins and poetic diction reflects this Wordsworthian ideal of a difficult simplicity which Yeats himself rarely attained before his last decade. Hopkins also could not ignore the ancient truth revived by Wordsworth that the poet writes in a tongue that is like the things it describes, issuing from their very heart; yet he remembered another truth, equally ancient, that the poet is peculiarly learned and respectful of tradition. His religious beliefs, moreover, strengthened this latter, esoteric conception of poetry. Catholicism, compared to Protestantism, is a mystery religion, and the ambience in which Hopkins reached intellectual maturity—the Oxford of the 1860s—found the Church of England divided by a reform movement that had insisted on mystery, ritual, and the authority of tradition. Thus Hopkins relived at its source the double nature of the poet who is always both popular and learned, natural and artificial, holy and profane. The Protestantism into which he was born had come to regard poetry as the most viable and open aspect of religion, its vernacular as it were; while the Catholic faith to which he converted recalled him to the mystery, discipline, and tradition indispensable for a real presence of the spirit.

No wonder, then, that Hopkins's poetry is an uneasy blend of natural and learned elements and that its vivid surface leads on occasion not to clarity but to darkness. There is in many poems a residue of obscurity difficult to remove; Yvor Winters has blamed it on the convenient scapegoat of Romantic individualism. But it may equally well be blamed on something very different from Romanticism: Hopkins's desire for an impersonal and esoteric discipline. We know that his urge toward a sacrifice of intellect and a true religious anonymity was very strong; his letters to Dixon reveal an unremitting conflict between the priest and the poet as well as between the priest and the scholar. The Jesuit order seemed to demand a sacrifice of everything that might have led to fame and away from a daily *imitatio Christi;* and though we will never know how thoroughly Hopkins mortified himself before the "incredible condescension" of the incarnation—an ideal of service, unselfconsciousness, and sacrifice to the calling— he significantly refers to the burning of his early poems as a "slaughter of the innocents." One wonders how many slaughters there were, since we do not possess any of the works on Greek scansion which flushed him with an enthusiasm bordering on megalomania. Yet despite his own aspirations to anonymity, his service to the poetry of others was unstinting: his letters to Bridges, Patmore, and Dixon are full of exact and scrupulous remarks on art. He does not actively raise the question of a radical conflict between poetry and religion and indeed seems to hope that poetry can be justified. But what is a justified poem?

All poets lay restrictions on themselves, if only for the sake of poetry. In this spirit Valéry defined form as *difficulté vaincue*. A finished poem, impressive as a thing in itself, is more impressive for the threshold pressures apparently overcome. In Hopkins, precariousness is a religious quality that becomes a poetic quality. Sometimes, of course, we feel merely the pressures and the poet's failing spirit. But here too, in the kind of religious scruple he shows, Hopkins is modern. As a post-Romantic he identified poetry with "Selfyeast of spirit," and the question was whether poetry could authentically be anything more. Could one pass beyond the self to its other side? In an eloquently obscure passage of Trinitarian speculation, he tries to reconcile self, self-sacrifice, and creation. "It is," he writes, "as if the blissful agony or stress of selving in God had forced out drops of sweat or blood, which drops were the world." One is tempted to adapt the parable and say: "which drops were the poem." It was a matter of coming to terms, in poetry, with his own strength; of going out, by means of poetry, to the strength in nature; and of going through that to Christ. Each mortal thing "Selves—goes itself, *myself* it speaks and spells."

This procession is highly problematic, but the most hermetic poetry speaks and spells—opens on something. "Go forth," writes Bridges, in his envoi to the first edition of his friend's poetry, "amidst our chaffinch flock display/Thy plumage of far wonder and heavenly flight." If Hopkins has not quite "gone forth" even today, if he is still an exotic bird—a *rara avis*—it is because we think of his inner conflict as only a curious product of his orthodoxy. A similar conflict, however, between the religious (esoteric) and naturalistic (exoteric) conception of poetry is found in the

Symbolist movement on the Continent and continues to disturb the more candid speech of Yeats and Stevens. Despite obvious differences, Hopkins's seven year abnegation of poetry is comparable to Valéry's silence, and his hesitations may have an affinity with Mallarmé's "glacier" of stillborn flights. A religious or quasi-religious pressure of justification weighed on them all. To understand, in Hopkins's case, the form of that pressure clears even our secular judgment.

We begin with the well-known fact that Hopkins was familiar with Ignatian methods of meditation. The extent to which he was obliged to practice them, and the degree to which he exercised his obligation, are documented in his devotional writings. Yet the relevance of this kind of meditation, to all and not only Christian poetry, has not been fully understood. The meditational technique of Ignatius of Loyola, perhaps the most powerful spiritual technique invented by the West, adapts the mimetic principle to the life of Christ. Meditation is not primarily speculative, not thought or intellectual exploration moving from a relatively arbitrary point of departure to an adventurous conclusion. It is nearer to imitation in the older, religious meaning of the word. We say that art is imitation; and even in Aristotle, who modifies the sense of the word, the root notion of *imitatio,* or serious miming, persists. The aim of Ignatian meditation is to prepare a fuller *imitatio Christi* by bringing the mind as close as possible to the primal scene.

The first peculiarity, and justifying characteristic, of Hopkins's poetry is that it mimes what it represents. Not all miming is overtly religious: in "Hurrahing in Harvest," or "The Windhover," the first sighting of the subject is an exceptionally pure act of sense-prehension—deictic, vocative, evocative. Yet to enter so strongly into things—to speak, as it were, for or from nature—argues an exceptionally trained power of identification. If being divinely possessed means anything, it means speaking for or from the desired mode of being. This initial encounter, on its own terms, with nature or beauty is doubtless a lesser *imitatio,* a propaedeutic for the larger acting out to come. Thus the downing motion in the second part of "Hurrahing in Harvest" (a similar downing occurs in "The Windhover"):

I walk, I lift up, I lift up heart, eyes,
Down all that glory in the heavens to glean our Saviour,

is a mimic and optative gesture that recalls, together with the distance between heaven and earth, the spanning mystery of Incarnation. Having met nature, "barbarous in beauty," and having transcended or rather downed it in the name of a greater beauty, the poet at the end of his mime begins to "ascend wingèd." His transcendence we may feel to be a trick, but it acts out a Christian doctrine without intellectual sleight or theological complication. The justifying end of such poetry is for the poet to become Christ, to act Christ, who "plays in ten thousand places" of nature and man; and the justifying doctrine is that of the Incarnation harmonized with Romans 1:20 and 8:17 ff.

The impulse to imitation as miming is already central in "The Wreck of the Deutschland," which launched Hopkins's sacred poetry. It is felt in the style, in the ritual crying of thoughts, and in passages of unusual rhythmic mimicry. *Imitatio,* religious participation, is in fact the burden of the poem. Hopkins enters the scene he evokes, the nun enters by anticipation into glory, all things are said to go to Christ. The objective and subjective, narrative and lyrical, parts of the theme are interwoven, so that turns of the action become (after stanza 11) turns in the poet's mind, and narrator is transformed to celebrant. Thus the illumination which redeems the catastrophe is Hopkins's own illumination: it is he who delivers the meaning of the nun's call to Christ, and it is he who labors for it. The cry and its meaning are brought forth by an emphatic spiritual maieutics: "heart-throe, birth of brain, Word."

Though the meaning of that Word (specifically, the nun's cry) remains less clear than the impulse of the whole poem, it suggests the theme of participation once more. The nun calls for her bridegroom and the consummation of her mystical marriage. She does not do this, Hopkins is careful to say, for her own glory or from spiritual impatience. Her cry, rather, recalls that of Job: as in "Carrion Comfort," there is a wrestling with, if not a constraining of, God. "Her will was bent at God," Hopkins says of Margaret Clitheroe; and what he admires in the nun is the claim to which she rises. She seizes the occasion with a daring and energy already divine.[3] But this is the dangerous fruit of *imitatio,* its hardest, most ambiguous venture: to call up one's calling, to chose what one is chosen for. "It is as if a man said: That is Christ playing at me and me playing at Christ, only that it is no play but truth; That is Christ *being me* and me being Christ." Hopkins is always on this shadowy ground where personality, free will, and grace intertwine. It was merely a hint from his Superior which made him break a seven year silence and compose "The Wreck of the Deutschland." There must be a call, and the hint must have become that call: the paradox in Hopkins's early poem, "Elected silence sing to me / And beat upon my whorléd ear," is genuine.

Here appears a further characteristic closely allied to *imitatio* and justification. Hopkins's style is as vocative as possible. This holds for sound, grammar, figures of speech, and actual performance. Tell and toll become cognates. God, in that first vocative of "The Wreck of the Deutschland," is giver of *breath* and *bread* —two staples only a smallest voicing apart. We find cries within cries as in: "Not, / I'll not, / carrion comfort, / Despair, / not feast on thee." The poet's situation is essentially that of the "heart in hiding" which is called by the call of the nun, by the sighting of a falcon, by the rudeness of God. What is man, says Job, that Thou shouldst contend with him? Yet, as in Job, we feel the calling more than the being called—a voice constraining the void. The true contender is man, who cries for justice. So with Hopkins, who strains ears and eyes to transform the *not yet* into the *now:*

> like a lighted empty hall
> Where stands no host at door or hearth
> Vacant creation's lamps appall.

> ["Nondum"]

3. The formalized hesitations in stanza 28 of "The Wreck of the Deutschland" suggest the enormity of the thought the poet is about to express: that the nun, in extremity, turns from that aspect of the Imitation of Christ which Hopkins calls the root of all moral good, namely "the holding of himself back, and not snatching at the highest and truest good . . . his own being and self," to the claim (the snatching) she frankly makes. The poet's holding back issues in the exceptional not holding back and vision of Christ as glorious master rather than as servant: "Let him ride, her pride, in his triumph, despatch and have done with his doom there." In "The Windhover" the same notion of mastery stirs the heart in hiding

The more he packs his verse, the more we sense his Pascalian horror at that vacancy. "Verily thou art a God that hidest thyself."

In a stray comment Hopkins once urged what he names *"contentio,* or strain of address." No phrase can better describe his own strain of style. *Contentio* is a term from rhetoric designating an antithetical or pointed repetition of words. But in Hopkins's mind the term has somehow fused with the Jobean *contentio,* with a raising of the voice to God, with a like insistence of address. "You must not slovenly read it with the eyes but with your ears," he writes to Bridges about a poem, "as if the paper were itself declaiming it at you. . . . Stress is the life of it." And by such stress and strain of address, maintained until all parts of speech, all figures, seem to partake in the vocative, Hopkins revolutionized poetic style. He made forever questionable the neutral or high-objective mode of which Tennyson was the eminent nineteenth century practitioner. This style, called Parnassian by Hopkins, was a last try at the grand manner. It wished to combine the noble simplicity of Greek or Roman epic with the intensity of lyric and the modern interest in the picturesque. The result: a charming frigidity. "A horrible thing has happened to me," Hopkins writes in 1864, "I have begun to *doubt* Tennyson." And to illustrate the Parnassian mode he quotes from the latter's *Enoch Arden.* It is a passage worth reproducing:

> The mountain wooded to the peak, the lawns
> And winding glades high up like ways to Heaven,
> The slender coco's drooping crown of plumes,
> The lightning flash of insect and of bird,
> The lustre of the long convolvuluses
> That coil'd around the stately stems, and ran
> Ev'n to the limit of the land, the glows
> And glories of the broad belt of the world,
> All these he saw.

The destruction of the Parnassian style is accomplished by an extroversion of language that pushes verbal matter into the fore-

(cf. the "I was at rest" of stanza 24 of the "Deutschland") but the imitation of Christ-servant prevails. See also Phill. 2:5–11, and Fr. Devlin's introduction to *The Sermons and Devotional Writings* (London, 1959), pp. 107 ff.

ground. As color for the radical nineteenth century painters is no longer a ground (like the good earth) which does its carrying function quietly but is obtruded as part of the subject, so words come forward in Hopkins's poetry to reclaim what he calls their "inscape," their immediate power of address. They do not, for all that, exist in themselves or by some automatic virtue of revelation. On the contrary, they mimic, paint ("that is a lie, so to speak, of Lessing's, that pictures ought not to be painted in verse, a damned lie—so to speak"), and participate in argument. Language is shown to be *contentio* in essence—there is nothing disinterested or general about it; its end as its origin is to move, persuade, possess. Hopkins leads us back to an aural situation (or its simulacrum) where meaning and invocation coincide. Everything depends on the right pitch, or verbal cast.

But this is still an imperfect description of Hopkin's purpose. It fails to indicate the resistance met by the *ictus* of his voice. For it is no mean endeavor to make the voice "selve" or to attain what, by a characteristic metaphor, he calls "pitch of self." Resistance comes not only from the conventional sublimity of the Parnassian mode but also from the very nature of language. The substitution of "gash" for "gush" at the end of "The Windhover" (where embers "Fall, gall themselves, and gash gold-vermillion"), or semantic rhymes like "tread" and "trade" in "God's Grandeur," evoke the tendency of semantic distinctions to fall back into a phonemic ground of identity. There is, in other words, a linguistic indifference against which language contends, and contends successfully, by diacritical or differential means. It is no wonder, therefore, that Hopkins's mannerisms extrovert the diacritical basis of meaning and so appear to be linguistic rather than rhetorical in nature. Such favorite devices as tmesis[4] contain a virtuoso element (cf. the splitting of notes or words in music) and suggest the precarious emergence of the individualizing feature out of the ground of phonemic similarity. Hopkins's heavy line, and the heavy sonnet as a whole (his most distinctive contribution to genre), reenact this emergence and submergence pattern on a larger scale by the doggerel thickness of their phonemic material:

4. "Wind-lilylocks-laced"; "the O-seal-that-so feature"; "Forth Christ from the cupboard fetched." Words that (roughly) go together are separated by the interpolation of other words.

"Our tale, O our oracle! Let life, waned, ah let life wind / Off her once skeined stained veined variety. . . ."

Diacritical may need more explanation. It is best to offer this in the form of an example and to consider the following phrase in description of the coming of night: "her earliest stars, earl-stars, stars principal" ("Spelt from Sybil's Leaves"). A rhetorical analysis will not show more than an extended pun. A diacritical analysis, however, works on the basis of homophones to show how linguistic individuation occurs. The point about Hopkins's description is not the homophones or internal rhymes but the creatively tenuous process of disjunction. Hopkins separates "earl-stars" from "earliest stars" by natural elision or a modification of juncture and stress. Two syllables are elided: "her," which leans to "ear" of "earliest," and "est," which has already partially merged with "stars." Eliding all but the stressed syllables produces the clean shock of "earl stars," as if this phrase had been born of the first by a movement mimicking the "fire-featuring" procession of the actual stars. The elements that give meaning to the line are essentially vocalic: elision, juncture, stress.

Even a nontechnical reading can perceive the individuating stress and juncture progression of her/ear(l)iest/stars/earl-stars/ stars. The addition to this of "principal" is magically right: the word is itself an individuum, odd and learned, with a syllabic weight that compensates for sounds previously elided. Above all, it is a word independent of the preceding phonemic series, as if sprung loose or selved by it. Yet, like a joker or linguistic subplot, it repeats and justifies this series. Prince: principalis=earl:early.

The diacritical method might also be applied to the thorny problem of Hopkins's sprung rhythm. I cannot summarize here the controversy surrounding Hopkins's presumed innovation. But the essential feature of sprung rhythm, which he calls *counterpoint* and defines as "the super-inducing or mounting of a new rhythm upon the old," is structurally analogous to his linear mounting or juxtaposition of phonemically similar phrases differentiated by juncture or stress. This is seen by transcribing the end of "Spelt from Sybil's Leaves" so that its standard or ground rhythm contrasts visibly with its mounted rhythm:

> standard: thoúghts against thoúghts in groáns grínd
>
> mounted: thoúghts agaínst thoughts ín groans grínd

We will not always find so perfect a counterpoint, but the principle remains the same for imperfect cases. Stress is here revealed as a diaeresis on the level of rhythm, and the stress sign as a diacritical mark. A recessive part of the phrase is featured or selved. But this featuring, this counterpointing, may also have an important intralinear function. In trying to get from "against" to "in" to "grind," "thoughts" and "groans" obtrude strongly, not only because of standard stress but also because of an intralinear pull which assimilates the first "thoughts" to the second, and "groans" to "grind." The mounted rhythm, in other words, serves here to prevent intralinear mergings as well as discriminating cross-linear homophones ("thoúghts" in the standard line vis-à-vis "thoughts" in the mounted).

That sprung rhythm is only one form of the diacritical tendency is confirmed by such coinages as "black, white, right wrong" in the same poem. Here the reversal or counterpoint is not metrical in nature. Though patterned, probably, on the analogy of the reversed metrical foot, the phrase is a semantic chiasmus forcing the rhyme words too close together and so destroying rhyme by imbalance. A wobble rhythm is created comparable to the sensation that ensues on looking at a visual puzzle where now the white and now the dark squares stand out. Stress, pitch of self, the *principium individuationis* emerges from within a chiming of words that founds opposition of sense on identity of sound.

It almost seems as if transcendence for Hopkins came from a struggle of like with like. The end of the struggle being individuation, neutral elements of style, like unstressed elements in perception, disappear. The poem is justified as Jacob was justified, who wrestled with the angel, man to man, and attained his proper name (Gen. 32). The "like" or enemy-friend with whom Hopkins contends is language, nature, beauty, or even (as in "Carrion Comfort") God. Imitation begins with a direct grappling as the heart is caught by its like—say, the windhover. It grapples with the creature's drawing power. "Being draws-home to Being" is how Hopkins translates a passage from Parmenides: he is drawn to the falcon in the same way as the latter is itself "dapple-dawn-drawn." (Hyphens tend to be tension marks in Hopkins, similar to diacritical signs in that they prevent words or syllables from collapsing into one another.) Hopkins's verse, with its verbal runs, lives by such attraction to being, or to what he, anticipating the method of ordinary language philosophy, calls "the flush and foredrawn" (fore-drawn=predicate). Thus "being" is opposed to "individuation." But as anything completely one with itself and manifest, it is also the very ground of individuation.

Duns Scotus helps Hopkins to solve this paradox, but we do not really need him any more than we do Parmenides. The structure of Hopkins's transcendence is sufficiently defined in his poems. There is what we have named the lesser *imitatio,* a constraining of like by like, or nature drawing the heart of man in order to be realized and worded (see Rom. 8:18, and "Ribblesdale"). Man receives nature's beauty, or wrestles to equal her patience, by what Gaston Bachelard has called the imagination of matter. But Christ, or the greater *imitatio,* puts a stress on man's imagination that transcends any "instress" of nature's. This is because divine stress again demands likeness: whatever disparity there is between human and divine, man can become Christ just as God in Christ became man. The possibility of likeness (a dangerous ideal, since it must either utterly exalt or annihilate selfhood) is the agony: "O which one, is it each one?"

Hopkins's pattern of transcendence is not uniform: his passage from the lesser to the greater *imitatio* can be variously achieved. In "The Windhover" we find an abrupt montage of one on the other, the example of Christ usurping, counterpointing, and even figurally completing that of the kestrel. But in "That Nature is a Heraclitean Fire and of the Comfort of the Resurrection" the transition is discursive and doctrinal. Christian doctrine, however, is itself uncertain as to what is carried over from one state to the other. That is probably why the sonnet has two codas: the first suggests a radical discontinuity based on St. Paul's "We shall be utterly changed," but this is a hard comfort; the second reminds us that man "puts on" Christ by means of purification rather than by utter change. Of the properties enumerated by Hopkins in the penultimate line, a single one remains in the risen body—but one that was originally there:

> In a flash, at a trumpet crash,
> I am all at once what Christ is, since he was what I am, and
> This Jack, joke, poor potsherd, patch, matchwood, immortal
> diamond
> > Is immortal diamond.

Hopkins's singling out and reweighting of "immortal diamond" suggests the coincidence of individuation and purification. He is neither a poet of total immanence nor of radical transcendence. Imitation of Christ is the means whereby the principle of self is purified and the body redeemed. We return to the faith exemplified by the nun in "The Wreck of the Deutschland": man is great enough for God to condescend to, and there will be a redemption in the flesh. This is Christian hubris, but the amount of service it enjoins is incalculable. "As if his true vocation . . . were endless imitation."

Hopkins is limited by the fact that, though his concept of vocation is as deep as Browning's, he could not fully associate it with poetry. "Felix Randall," where the obituary and reflective mood is continually broken by "strain of address," shows what may be achieved when the vocations of poet and priest unite. But "Henry Purcell," despite virtuoso flashes of diction and thought inspired by the subject, remains an abstract admiration piece beset by religious scruple. It was no Romantic who said that "to follow Poetry as one ought, one must forget father and mother, and cleave to it alone" (Alexander Pope). Hopkins's defects are often traceable to his scrupling view of the poet's vocation. The parochialism, the punctilio in matters of craft, the unresolved experimentation, the mixing of linguistic orders and effects, the hypostatizing of and indulging in beauty (perhaps Pateresque, but suggesting a man who thinks he is secure enough to indulge mentally before turning away)—these betray a genius that will not risk itself beyond clearly marked virtuoso effects. Hopkins is certainly a great virtuoso in the tradition of Crashaw, and if he has not left us a "Music's Duell" we do have "The Leaden Echo and the Golden Echo." (Even as virtuoso he must still be compared to Swinburne.) Yet while nature and art are rivals in his poetry, between art and religion there cannot be an authentic challenge, only an uncertain progress from lesser to greater *imitatio*.

To judge is to compare, and it is useful to pursue the comparison with Crashaw and Browning. In one respect Hopkins surpasses both: his imagination is more directly and substantially engaged with air, earth, water, fire. He is our pre-Socratic among poets. It is also more directly engaged with the materiality of language as a fifth element. He not only loads every rift with ore but discovers unsuspected rifts to fill. Language, through him, is again part of the body of things, if not its very quintessence.

In a further respect he is at least their equal. Crashaw's style, with its audacities of wit, paradox, and point, was involved in a religious purpose and supported the Counter-Reformation against the developing plain style of Protestant England. Hopkins's poetry revives the pointed style in the lyric. Bridges complained of his *Marianism* where he could equally well have complained of his *Marinism*. But the great difference between the two Catholic poets is first of all historical, in that one had to revive what the other had merely to exploit (the pointed style); and secondly, that Hopkins is consciously English where Crashaw is catholic or universal and, if he must be typed nationally, Italian. Despite rhetoric, despite artifices of stress, Hopkins insists on the colloquial element. "I can't help being a little amused," Coventry Patmore writes to him, "by your claiming for your style the extreme of popular character." Patmore is right in being amused, or bemused: where Hopkins is the most colloquial, he is often the most hermetic. He does not always escape a cultic attitude toward language.

Browning, too, sought a more rugged lyricism, which Hopkins interprets in snobbish if acute terms. "He has got a great deal of what came in with Kingsley and the Broad Church school, a way of talking (and making people talk) with the air and spirit of a man bouncing up from table with his mouth full of bread and cheese and saying that he meant to stand no blasted nonsense." Whether or not the religious cause is fundamental, each poet introduces a new density of diction and structure into the lyric. Browning does it primarily by the dramatic method, by speaking through characters caught in a moment which is the equivalent of the fruitful or characteristic moment prescribed for the visual arts. Like Hopkins, therefore, he destroys the picturesque by cramming it, by forcing its fulfillment. The Parnassian style, as we saw, was related to the picturesque, and Hopkins seems to develop his lyric structures out of the Pre-Raphaelite dream vision. In his early "A Vision of the Mermaids" and "St. Dorothea" he may be struggling with such poems as Christina Rossetti's "The Convent Threshold" and Dante Gabriel Rossetti's "The Blessed Damozel," poems in which the poet stands at a lower level than the vision, or is irrevocably, pathetically, distanced. Yet Hopkins, perhaps inspired by Pindar, evolves a more participating and less picturesque stance, one that allows a precarious communion. In both Hopkins and Browning the lyric moves away from simple reflection or reminiscence. The dreamer is lifted into the dream; the past into the present. Imitation is project more than retrospect.

With one thing more, but that essential, Hopkins might have surpassed Browning, the modern Protestant, and Crashaw, the militant Catholic. Through Pindar he approached a truly athletic conception of poetry. Yet he again stopped short at the critical point: admiring what Pindar achieved in diction and structure, he dissociated these accomplishments from Pindar's remarkable consciousness of himself and of poetic vocation. Poetry, for Pindar, is as divine as the feat he celebrates yet is distinguished from other divine gifts by its human function. The athletic games are sublimated war games, but the game of poetry, equally skilled, may civilize the gods. Hopkins's view of poetic art is, in comparison, at once too serious and too light: too serious because the game is not played out as a game, and too light because the poet's imitation is always subordinated to the priest's *imitatio*. We can see a similar difference between Hopkins and Crashaw: Crashaw alone has the courage of a *jongleur* or court jester before God. The license of his art is truly extraordinary, while Hopkins shrinks from every audacity other than prosodic or lexical. There is no need to document the latter's prudishness: Patmore, who shared Hopkins's faith in the final redemption of the senses, is the truer follower of Crashaw:

> In season due, on His sweet-fearful bed,
> Rock'd by an earthquake, curtain'd by eclipse,
> Thou shar'd'st the spousal rapture of the sharp spear's head
> And thy bliss pale
> Wrought for our boon what Eve's did for our bale.
>
> [*The Unknown Eros*]

One can imagine Hopkins's own pallor at this. "That's telling secrets," as he once said to Patmore.

Even Browning, his tedious optimism and roughhousing aside, understands that poetry is a sacred game and that the game alone can justify the poet. Contentious and self-justifying, Browning's people direct their will at a hidden God. The poet is their advocate, caught in the same condition, and he refuses to give the game away. He demands yet does not preempt judgment. His poetry builds up a sacrifice for which the consecrating fire must come from us or from above. Hopkins, though the purer talent, often appears narrow and idiosyncratic when placed beside him. We never forget, in Hopkins's poetry, that it is a priest speaking, and one more Roman than the Romans in his scruples as to what his religious order might allow. He does not even dare to follow where Ignatian meditation leads. Overcome by a "course of loathing and hopelessness which I have so often felt before, which made me fear madness, and led me to give up the practice of meditation," he can do no more (he says) than repeat: *Justus es, Domine, et rectum judicium tuum.* However authentic a suffering speaks in this, it is a passive suffering. Here is where vision or prophecy or scandal might have begun: where within his vocation a new vocation might have been born. Hopkins's acceptance of the rule was so absolute that it did not permit him to be more than a pawn or servant in the sacred game he intuited. "Sheer plod makes plough down sillion shine." That shining remains his justification when, in his poetry, he is challenged by an image of divine mastery akin to brute beauty and when, so challenged, he becomes for a moment *magister ludi.*

The Poet's Politics

It is autumn of 1831, and a young writer goes to the big city to interest publishers in his work. We hear about his luck in a letter written by John Stuart Mill. "Carlyle," reports Mill, "intends staying in London all the winter . . . his object was to treat with booksellers about a work which he wishes to publish, but he has given this up for the present, finding that no bookseller will publish anything but a political pamphlet in the present state of excitement. In fact, literature is suspended; men neither read nor write." Six months later, and shortly after the passage of the Reform Bill of 1832, Mill writes to the same correspondent:

> One unspeakable blessing I now believe that we shall owe to the events of the last ten days; to whatever consummation the spirit which is now in the ascendent may conduct us, there is . . . a probability that we shall accomplish it through other means than anarchy and civil war. The irresistible strength of a unanimous people has been put forth, and has triumphed without bloodshed; it having been proved once for all that the people can carry their point by pacific means.

I start with the assumption that ours is a political age and even, as Napoleon said, that politics is destiny. What good, then, is poetry in this age? What claim does it have on our attention? It could be argued, of course, that all ages are political, that the crisis Mill records is a recurrent one. Indeed, as we look across literature, guided by present concerns, the idea of politics broadens itself. Every epic we know has a political, or cosmopolitical, subject. Men are drawn into a quarrel between clans of gods. Or a nation, as in the Bible, has to establish and then preserve its identity. Even in pastoral there are things to be gained and things to be lost: the pressures of the greater world are there for those who can recognize them. Those shepherds are highly competitive

247

in their silly play, and Huizinga's *Homo Ludens* has taught us to recognize how play is related to mature conventions. One can make no special claim for poetry that startles us with its subject rather than with itself and confronts us by shouting: admire me, I am relevant! dote upon me, I am topical! Of the poems chosen for discussion, those of Wordsworth and Wallace Stevens seem at first completely apolitical. I have included them to suggest how much depends on our own consciousness, on contemporary experience pressing against poetry and precipitating its meaning.

In the unrest of the 1930s (there was unrest in the 1930s) an attempt was made to find criteria that would separate radically poetry from propaganda—that is to say, from the doctrines of religious sects or the ideologies of parties. Against militant critics who insisted that only a committed art was relevant, Cleanth Brooks and others wrote a defense of poetry, saying that art, however passionate or ideological its subject matter, had to be sophisticated enough to bear an ironical contemplation. The famous dictum "A poem should not mean, but be" means cool it, play it cool, the poem is a play, a drama of attitudes testing the belief advanced. Much in this theory is important and right and still with us: the Beatles have learned a great deal from Mr. Brooks. But in the contemporary unrest, a defense of poetry is needed that will stress once more Shelley's intuition that poets are unacknowledged legislators—unacknowledged, probably, because they talk imperatively to the whole of the human condition, not to a special element in it. So I begin with my real topic: the politics of poetry.

Purely ideological poetry lives and dies with the emotion, or social condition, that produced it. No one remembers now Don West's "Southern Lullaby," a protest ballad of the 1930s:

> Eat little baby, eat well,
> A Bolshevik you'll be
> And hate this bosses' hell
> Sucking it in from me.
> Hate, little baby, hate deep.[1]

We can make up our own 1960s "Northern Lullaby": "Burn,

1. Quoted in Cleanth Brooks, *Modern Poetry and the Tradition* (Chapel Hill, N.C., 1939), p. 51.

baby, burn, / A militant you'll be," etc. This has nothing to do with great art, and yet great art has something to do with it. A first step toward understanding the relation of poetry and politics is to understand the interdependence of great art and popular art. I am reminded of a bad witticism in an experimental movie, where one character says to another: "Go to Art, and tell him Pop sent you." The consciousness that even highbrow art has a pop or folk basis arises strongly with the Romantics. Keats felt a double allegiance which marks all the greater poets of his period: "Let us have the old poets, AND Robin Hood." It's like saying today, let us have Eliot, Yeats, Stevens, AND Joan Baez. Wordsworth felt that Bishop Percy's *Reliques of Ancient English Poetry,* two small volumes of popular ballads and songs mainly from the sixteenth and seventeenth centuries, had "absolutely redeemed the course of English poetry." In Wordsworth's day, popular tales, political satire, and versified scandal about contemporary events still circulated in the form of broadsides hawked about on London streets. The streets themselves were a political cabaret. The older poets, too, the poets of the English Renaissance, were obviously in touch with popular sources—with legends, superstitions, romances. Chaucer is the first and clearest example; Shakespeare comes next. Even in Spenser and Milton popular elements remain: they are trying for a new type of sublimity, but it remains a vernacular sublime.

Yeats is concerned with the popular sources of art from the beginning of his career. He was an Irishman who used Celtic legend as a kind of public dream world. He did not want to be "alone amid the obscure impressions of the senses" but sought a "symbolic language reaching far into the past and associated with familiar names and conspicuous hills." Chaucer, he once said, saved his imagination from abstraction. And in a late poem he counts himself among the Romantics because of this respect for traditions, learned or popular:

> We were the last romantics—chose for theme
> Traditional sanctity and loveliness;
> Whatever's written in what poets name
> The book of the people.

["Coole and Ballylee"]

"The book of the people"—yet Yeats's poetry is far from plebeian. Though he uses simple forms and the ballad refrain as much as possible, his view of O'Leary and other Irish militants is not that of pure admiration. "September 1913" is a ballad that begins by exalting O'Leary and questioning, now that he's dead, the ability of the present generation to achieve his greatness of soul. But since poetry, as Yeats once said, comes out of a quarrel with oneself, as the ballad goes on it questions, almost despite its author, the noble dead. "What, God help us, could they save?" (st. 2), "that *delirium* of the brave" (st. 3, my italics). And the last verses suggest that it was delirium indeed, not a magnanimous passion for *rem publicam* but a carelessness for their own lives growing out of frustrated love: "Some woman's yellow hair/ Has maddened every mother's son." In Romantic Ireland, private and public passions interacted. Personal frustrations became political ambitions. Yeats questions the motive of these Irish heroes, but not what the refrain insists on: "Romantic Ireland's dead and gone."

In "Easter 1916" the eight line stanza with refrain becomes a more reflective sixteen- or twenty-four-line stanza. Yeats's questioning is now intense and complicated and almost purely a self-questioning—in "September 1913" it had been a questioning of others. What has changed in the poet? He now acknowledges that Romantic Ireland is not dead, indeed that a new and terrible Romanticism is born. Terrible not only because associated with rebellion, violence, and death, but because Yeats fears to acknowledge it as an exemplary ethos, as a way of conducting one's life. His attitude had been that politics narrow the soul; politics are not magnanimous and magnanimity is all. He recurs to that thought anxiously in each succeeding stanza: this woman's voice grew shrill, that man was merely vainglorious, and all these "Hearts with one purpose alone . . . Enchanted to a stone" sinned, by the obsessiveness of their purpose, against nature. Hatred, after love, fixed their heart. But if one passion, one idea, was like a stone in their heart, their example is now a stone in the poet's heart. His mind seems to have less room, in the way it turns around, in the way it worries and subtly repeats itself, than in the eight-line stanza of the previous ballad. Even though the upshot of the failed rebellion was simply to make us "know their dream," it is a dream that weighs on us and cannot be shaken off. "In dreams begin responsibilities," as he once said.

Around this time Yeats's whole attitude toward his own imagination changes. He elicits from it "daemonic images" and tries to read them. This is clear in poems like "The Second Coming" and "Leda and the Swan." He accepts, in others words, the romantic belief that the individual mind is in prophetic touch with the movement of history. The dream that sparked the Easter rebellion cannot be dismissed by criticizing its aim or the mixed motives of those who participated in it: the "terrible beauty" born of the dream announces a new era which he tries to face in "A Prayer for my Daughter" (1919). In this poem there are intimations of the "blood-dimmed tide" that will drown the "ceremony of innocence" he evokes at the end. A storm comes, like an omen of the future, out of the "murderous innocence" of the sea —where "murderous innocence" suggests both the impersonality of fate, of historical evolution, and the "terrible beauty" of historical revolution, its Dionysian element, the purging of private emotions in the suffering, communion and greatness of collective action. Yet in a new type of eight-line stanza which will inform some of his best poems, Yeats reasserts his older ideal of magnanimity, which excludes intellectual hatred and soul-narrowing politics. He prays in a sense against his own imagination, and what he prays for is that his daughter should be out of phase with history and able to preserve an older order. Her birth and the natural hopes it arouses are set movingly and precariously against that other, revolutionary, birth of terrible beauty:

> How but in custom and in ceremony
> Are innocence and beauty born?
> Ceremony's a name for the rich horn,
> And custom for the spreading laurel tree.

Thus Yeats is gradually forced to contrast the book of his mind with the book of the people. The masterful images of the latter no longer jibe with the demonic images of the former. The courteous romanticism of Spenser (that famous Irishman!) is not the terrible romanticism of MacDonagh, MacBride, Connolly, and Pearse, whom he formally names at the end of "Easter, 1916"— though their names, inserted in this way, remain proper nouns, casual and idiosyncratic, instead of permanent and symbolic through long association:

> I write it out in a verse—
> MacDonagh and MacBride
> And Connolly and Pearse
> Now and in time to be,
> Wherever green is worn,
> Are changed, changed utterly:
> A terrible beauty is born.

In Wordsworth there are no glittering emblems and only a few masterful images. The poet does not begin with a symbol— that is to say, an event or myth from the "book of the people"— but with an ordinary sight, a daily thing that seems to have no connection with the march of history or politics. This ordinary sight grows on the poet's consciousness until it attains an almost visionary intensity:

> The little hedgerow birds,
> That peck along the road, regard him not.
> He travels on, and in his face, his step,
> His gait, is one expression: every limb,
> His look and bending figure, all bespeak
> A man who does not move with pain, but moves
> With thought. —He is insensibly subdued
> To settled quiet: he is one by whom
> All effort seems forgotten; one to whom
> Long patience hath such mild composure given,
> That patience now doth seem a thing of which
> He hath no need. He is by nature led
> To peace so perfect that the young behold
> With envy, what the Old Man hardly feels.
> —I asked him whither he was bound, and what
> The object of his journey; he replied
> "Sir! I am going many miles to take
> A last leave of my son, a mariner,
> Who from a sea-fight has been brought to Falmouth,
> And there is dying in an hospital.—"
>
> ["Old Man Travelling"]

252

Though we are not given—as in Yeats—the poet's inner discourse, the poet in the act of questioning the strong image or event, we feel his mind turning around, puzzling, reflecting on the experience. The more intensely Wordsworth thinks, the more the Old Man grows on his imagination: thought increases, instead of resolving, a mystery. Is the strange patience of this man a sign of animal vigor or of religious faith? Does it express deeply working sources of life or mere feebleness and animal persistence in that feebleness? Here is someone moving his slow thighs toward a strange, if ordinary, destination.

In the first part of the poem (the first 14 lines) this destination seems to be nature—the Old Man is journeying back to the source. He moves so slowly, he is so much part of the landscape, that even the hedgerow birds regard him not. But the second part of the poem shows that his destination lies elsewhere. The patient, organic development suggested to us by his tranquility opens, with those four concluding lines of simple yet stately speech, into the opposite image of early and unnatural death, of a life cut off before maturation—one might almost say, naturation.

This quiet contrast, this inversion of the natural order of things (one could expect the young man to be traveling to the old man's death bed), is heightened to the point of visionary fear when we realize that all intermediate stages between the longevity of the old man and the premature death of his son have dropped out. A leap forward is suggested, as if Wordsworth's era, the era of the French Revolution and of the Napoleonic wars of which the son dying at Falmouth is a victim, were moving history along at so fast a pace it had become unnatural. We are again, as in Yeats, caught between two worlds, or standing at a fatal crossroads in the development of humanity: while the old order (essentially agrarian, slow-changing, in tune with nature) is dying, the new moves in so fast that nothing seems to be able to grow, to have the proper time for development. "A multitude of causes unknown to former times," writes Wordsworth in the preface to *Lyrical Ballads* (1800), "are now acting . . . to blunt the discriminating powers of the mind. . . . The most effective of these causes are the great national events which are daily taking place [war with France], and the increasing accumulation of men in cities [the Industrial Revolution], where the uniformity of their occupations produces a craving for extraordinary incident, which the rapid communication of intelligence [journalism] hourly gratifies." To counteract this "degrading thirst after outrageous stimulation," Wordsworth wrote his *lyrical* ballads. "Old Man Travelling" shows how a poet can penetrate the crisis of his time without bold symbols or violent poetic effects.

With Robert Lowell we are back not only in the realm of direct political poetry but also that of masterful images:

> The old South Boston Aquarium stands
> in a Sahara of snow now. Its broken windows are boarded.
> The bronze weathervane cod has lost half its scales.
> The airy tanks are dry.
>
> Once my nose crawled like a snail on the glass;
> my hand tingled
> to burst the bubbles
> drifting from the noses of the cowed, compliant fish.
>
> My hand draws back. I often sigh still
> for the dark downward and vegetating kingdom
> of the fish and reptile. One morning last March,
> I pressed against the new barbed and galvanized
>
> fence on the Boston Common. Behind their cage,
> yellow dinosaur steamshovels were grunting
> as they cropped up tons of mush and grass
> to gouge their underworld garage.
>
> ["For the Union Dead"]

There is something strange, however, as well as strong about these images. Like a dream we cannot quite follow, but in which every sight is overcharged, the continuity of Lowell's poem is casual to the point of discontinuity, as each stanza flashes an aggressive picture onto the screen of the mind. This forces us to question the character of the organizing consciousness: what kind of a mind must one have to see like this? While in Wordsworth we hardly feel contrasts, here they become crass juxtaposition: the "service" mentioned in the epigraph ("Relinquunt Omnia Servare Rem

Publicam") and the "servility" of the last stanza ("a savage ser-
vility/ slides by on grease"); the Boston Aquarium in a Sahara of
snow (st. 1); the fish in the air (st. 1); the air in the tanks (st. 1);
the bubbles rising from the fish (st. 2) and the drained faces of
negro children rising like balloons; bubbles and Colonel Shaw on
his bubble; the nose-snail of the child and the nose of the fish
(st. 2); the child pressing against the glass of the Boston Aquarium
(st. 2) and the man Lowell pressing against the fence of Boston
Common (sts. 3, 4). In a pun two meanings try to occupy one
word; in this poem all things press ominously to occupy the same
place. The personal past, the personal present, the historical past,
the historical present, space relations, and time relations—all
these come "nearer," mass like storm clouds on our sight. While
each stanza, practically, offers us a new emblem, nothing happens.
The last stanza, contrasted with the first, reveals merely another
complex apocalyptic emblem, suggesting that the men who think
they have mastered nature are really being mastered by it: the
waters of the Aquarium have flooded our world without our
noticing, and servile nature is secretly in control:

> The Aquarium is gone. Everywhere,
> giant finned cars nose forward like fish;
> a savage servility
> slides by on grease.

What kind of a mind, then, has constructed this curious machine of which all the parts are visionary, yet which moves so
elusively? We have called Lowell's images emblems, but they are
clearly infected by the crudity of pop art and are more like cartoons or topsy-turvy, promiscuous advertisements: the Mosler
Safe advertises the atom bomb (or vice versa); Colonel Shaw (in
the penultimate stanza) rides on his bubble, like Superman or
Colonel Glenn. The poet's mind cannot escape the infection of
the age, and perhaps that is the point. Lowell's poem intensifies
our sense of inverted values, disorder, and crisis. It expresses the
situated individual who confronts all this not only out there but
also in himself. This makes all the poets chosen here intensely
modern. Though Lowell is closest to Yeats in the way he elicits
yet draws back from ominous images, Wordsworth too is forced
to face the problem of the prophetic mind, of the darkness which

it senses, from which it draws back (like Lowell's hand in st. 3), yet which it must meet in some way. In this natural, daily facing of omens, the reflective mind can have no outside aid: no other force than mind defends the mind against itself.

It is a virtue of Stevens's "The Snowman" to catch consciousness in the act, to depict by one exemplary movement (which is the poem) this defense against overthink, against our relentless mental pollution of nature. I use the word *pollution* advisedly. What Lowell needs more than anything is the perspective of the snowman:

> One must have a mind of winter
> To regard the frost and the boughs
> Of the pinetrees crusted with snow;
>
> And have been cold a long time
> To behold the junipers shagged with ice,
> The spruces rough in the distant glitter
>
> Of the January sun; and not to think
> Of any misery in the sound of the wind,
> In the sound of a few leaves,
>
> Which is the sound of the land
> Full of the same wind
> That is blowing in the same bare place
>
> For the listener, who listens in the snow,
> And, nothing himself, beholds
> Nothing that is not there and the nothing that is.

The hygiene, the cleansing power of this wintery mind is clear, whether or not we understand the poem. Stevens's poetry is, in fact, so difficult to understand because our mind is not wintery enough. It tends to be too spiritual, or too fictional, or simply eager for thought. The surface and subject matter of "The Snowman" are so slippery that mind cannot take hold: the poem consists of one propositional sentence that, in fulfilling itself, also cancels itself out. Complete in line 7 (at the semicolon), the proposition ironically does not suffice the mind which proposed it and which now, running on, begins to defend itself against the very idea of ideas by a "structured and mounting negation" (Sigurd Burkhardt). This kind of poetry does not wish to become thought or afterthought. It is happy to be "the cry of its occasion," something heard, or at best something that cleanses the doors of the senses.

"The great poems of heaven and hell have been written," said Stevens, "the great poem of the earth remains to be written." His poetry, like Wordsworth's, is prelusive of that unwritten epic. The earth is all before him. He writes of ordinary evenings and dawns, of seasons and weathers, of sun and snow.

> How clean the sun when seen in its idea
> Washed in the remotest cleanliness of a heaven
> That has expelled us and our images.
> ["Notes toward a Supreme Fiction"]

To see winter, one must have a mind of winter; to see the sun one must have a sunny mind. But if we pollute our environment by "meanings," by pathetic fictions, we see merely ourselves in nature when our real desire is to see nature. Stevens asks us, therefore, to reverse ourselves and become what we see instead of seeing what we are. Since we have remade nature in our image—and behold, it is not good—now the link between us and the earth should no longer be balanced in our favor, even imaginatively. Unless we stop occupying nature with our ideas and anxieties we shall be in the dilemma recently expressed by Theodor Adorno. "I cannot look at nature," said Adorno, "I cannot look at the shadow of trees without the shadow of Buchenwald interposing." The woods of Arcady are dead indeed. What man has made of man and what man has made of nature are intimately joined, yet through the politics of poetry we may still open a chink in this claustrophobic mind and see "Nothing that is not there and the nothing that is." To quote Stevens a last time:

> You must become an ignorant man again
> And see the sun again with an ignorant eye
> And see it clearly in the idea of it.
> ["Notes toward a Supreme Fiction"]

257

The Maze of Modernism: Reflections on Louis MacNeice, Robert Graves, A. D. Hope, Robert Lowell, and Others

By the time Louis MacNeice began to publish—his first collection, *Blind Fireworks,* appeared in 1929, a year before Auden's debut, and his second, more significant *Poems* in 1935—a revolution had taken place. After the rigors of Pound, Eliot, and Hart Crane, the poetry of the 1930s initiated a period of consolidation and leveling. What one feels strongly in reviewing the career made visible by *Collected Poems* is the poet's tolerance for all kinds of verse, his wish to return to surface simplicities, and his desire to remove from contemporary poetry the stigmas of aestheticism and obscurity. Poetry, MacNeice once said, is the way we return to normalcy. The world may be a problem, but words, on the whole, are not: art is communication, its only asceticism is that of craft, and the poet like any man is a blend of flesh and spirit. These modest proposals were formulated, of course, with an eye to more than the dangers of art for art's sake. They also reflect an opposite pressure on writers of the 1930s: that of a commitment to political verse. To walk this tightrope between pure and impure poetry was MacNeice's doom, and it results in a subdued rejection of all absolutes:

> One place is as good as another. Go back
>   where your instincts call
> And listen to the crying of the town-cats and the
>   taxis again,
> Or wind your grammaphone and eavesdrop on great men.[1]

His poetry is indeed this shifting from place to place. Verses, some very wonderful and humane, appear on every subject:

1. All Louis MacNeice quotations are from his *Collected Poems* (New York, Oxford University Press, 1967).

258

Ireland, Iceland, England, Spain, America. . . . And what he writes is always true in sentiment and honest in words. Too honest perhaps. For how strange that he is never extreme in words or extreme in sentiment. As one of our first academic poets, he did not escape the modern curse of reflectiveness, though he constantly wrote against it. His poetry is primarily the cultured journalism of a specialist in empathy: thoughts, opinions, feelings for, chatter, observations. It domesticates with the heart, as Coleridge would have said; and it can repose, of course, on the example of the Horatian "sermon" and the verse letter. But the commitment seems finally to be to poems rather than to poetry. Except for occasional flirtation:

> Coral azalea and scarlet rhododendron
> Syringa and pin-horse chestnut and laburnum
> Solid as temples, niched with the sound of birds,
> Widen the eye and nostrils, demand homage of words.
> And we have to turn from them, fit out an ethic.

The result of so deliberate a turning away is a wry and modest poetry. It refuses to let us admire either its technique or the thoughts expressed by that technique.

MacNeice's methodical halfwayness has the reason already assigned—that he wished to steer a middle course between formalistic and utilitarian verse—but it may also have had to do with his basic attitude toward words. Though moved by human degradation, he is rarely moved by the degradation of words. His attitude toward words is still determined, of course, by his situation. Surrounded by poets whom he considered to be greater, by Auden and Spender as well as Eliot and Yeats, he made himself an identity of what they left or what they lacked. In his eyes their greatest weakness was a residual hankering after the prophetic or high style, and so he chose to become totally what he is only in part: the poet of "waifs and wraiths of image/ And half-blind questions." He writes an "Homage to Clichés" and the famous "Wolves," in which daily talk and laughter drown out "howling" prophets like Yeats:

> The tide comes in and goes out again, I do not want
> To be always stressing either its flux or its permanence,

259

> I do not want to be a tragic or philosophic chorus
> But to keep my eye only on the nearer future
> And after that let the sea flow over us.

He continues to admire the technical deceits and poses of Yeats, but he refuses them for himself. His figures of speech remain reflective and conversational, and it is only by lifting them from a perpetual stream of conversation that we give them a Poundian absoluteness:

> how can hungry
> Love be a proper analyst?
> For suddenly I hate her and would murder
> Her memory if I could
> And then of a sudden I see her sleeping gently
> Inaccessible in a sleeping wood
> But thorns and thorns around her
> And the cries of night

Yeats, Pound, Eliot, and Auden are led to great compromises by their nostalgia for high style—a nostalgia which allows them to render so poignantly the degradation of words and which hovers, for example, over *The Waste Land*. Yet MacNeice is so suspicious of strange fire that he begins to be suspicious of any strong image. When he does come on a powerful figure he fritters it away in a stream of sophisticated comment:

> The bloody frontier
> Converges on our beds
> Like jungle beaters closing in on their destined
> Trophy of pelts and heads.
> And at this hour of the day it is no good saying
> 'Take away this cup,'
> Having helped to fill it ourselves it is only logic
> That now we should drink it up.

He should have found a way to allow that first image, compressed like the narrowing situation it describes, to stand alone.

In one area MacNeice was a pioneer: with Auden, he sought to revive the long conversational poem. A journey to Iceland in 1936 strengthened the poets' attraction to oral tradition. Could they find modern forms similar to those of ancient formulaic verse? Was there not something built into speech itself, Kantian forms which made communication possible and might provide the modern formulary? Auden wrote his "Letter to Lord Byron," adapting the stanza of that master of gossip, and MacNeice followed with *Autumn Journal* (1938) and the radio poem *Autumn Sequel* (1953). Both poems canvass the return of a vigorous yet contemporary oral tradition. They directly oppose Pound's *Cantos* by rejecting the complex and subduing the striking image. I still find *Autumn Journal* a moving documentary of the conscience of the intellectual in the late thirties. One can easily criticize it on technical grounds: by reverting, in parts, to a natural prose, the whole would surely have gained in honesty and effect. But each time I return to it I am astonished at its clarity, its volatility, its completeness. It is a brave attempt to keep in touch with everything. If it becomes a purgatory of words which does not purge, a sea which does not ablute, that too is part of its honesty.

In MacNeice's poetry of the 1950s a new capability is added: a purged intensity of speech, a firmer acceptance of the authority of form. There is a return of the repressed, of the purely aesthetic elements, which is also a return to the beginning, for he was always basically a poet in love with the classics, seeking to modernize yet not too much. "Didymus," one of his neatest poems, classical in inspiration yet modern in implication, remains therefore his best epitaph. It reaffirms the secular *askesis* of the modernist—not to fall in love with God, with Abstraction, with Romance:

> Refusing to fall in love with God, he gave
> Himself to the love of created things,
> Accepting only what he could see, a river
> Full of the shadows of swallows' wings
>
> That dipped and skimmed the water; he would not
> Ask where the water ran or why.
> When he died a swallow seemed to plunge
> Into the reflected, the wrong sky.

Robert Graves does not share MacNeice's wariness toward art. He knows a poet must be saved from realism as well as from

261

abstraction: that realism often is the abstraction. Yet though he goes with ease from the "makeshift present" to "full leaf of insight and bloom of image," his verse remains reserved and surprisingly classical in temper. Unlike his prose, it is never a temple prostitute. His *New Poems,* for example, move in a time of their own, and at least three or four will survive because of their perfect reticence: a modicum of words, a hinted substance, and a religious simplification of knowledge. Their subject is, as it has ever been, the mystery of the relationship between man, woman, and muse. But they are also about every traditional theme: passion, purity, time, words, sympathetic magic. Elemental situations are expressed in elemental symbols:

> Alone, together,
> Recalling little, prophesying less,
> We watch the serpent, crushed by your bare heel,
> Rainbow his scales in a deathward agony.[2]

But elemental and commonplace lie very close together. A perfect sense of pitch is often needed to distinguish them and to appreciate these poems. Graves is the most classical of the modern Romantics and his muse the daughter of memory as well as of inspiration. The individual talent is subordinated to tradition—but to tradition of a special kind. Graves's classicism goes back to the strict oral discipline of Celt or Greek: an esoteric craft, needing not only long apprenticeship but also the right cultic attitude toward inspiration. Almost every poem in this book is about and addressed implicitly to the white goddess. She is not named, of course; nor does she appear separate from the women or sentiments she inspires; but she is, as it were, the open mystery on which this poetry is based.

Graves's strength is that he considers poetry a matter of troth rather than truth. He is committed solely to the art of the great poets and the muse they served. It is as simple as that—there is no further imperative, no direct concern with truth to self or to society. This is quite remarkable, since art today is too often either an impossible sincerity or a rhetorical calculation of some nicety. Yet Graves does not succumb to an art-for-art's-sake posi-

2. All Robert Graves quotations are from his *New Poems* (Garden City, N.Y., Doubleday, 1963).

tion. His conception of art is analogous to the scientist's view of science or the novice's attitude toward religion. Granted that the call is there, these vocations demand a long and devoted apprenticeship. It is the paradox of all disciplines that one must master them before mastering experience through them. Self-expression, therefore, takes a very secondary place: by studying the "rich darkness" of his compeer poets, Graves achieves something greater than a personal cypher, technique, or strategy. He achieves an absolute discretion, as in the following poem on innocence and experience, which goes back to a Greek epigram:

> Violence threatens you no longer:
> It was your innocent temerity
> Caused us to tremble: veterans discharged
> From the dirty wars of life.
>
> Forgive us this presumption: we are abashed—
> As when a child, straying on the cliff's edge,
> Turns about to ask her white-faced brothers:
> "Do you take me for a child?"

The increased simplicity of these poems, each of which is an icon, gives rise to a single untoward reflection. Graves's relations with the muse are strangely easy. True, he is the first poet, after many Romantic anticipations, to talk so humanly about them; this human simpleness, in fact, makes his poems mysterious, since every encounter with woman or muse is quietly *beatristic*. For the same reason, however, it is difficult to take some of his complaints or submissions as more than conventional. They recall many other delicious moans about the "cruel fair." That beauty has terror in it, that there are two women in every woman, and that the poet cannot possess that by which he is possessed are universal and inexhaustible themes; but the same poet, even though endowed with a lucid and masterful English, cannot forever renew them. There is something consoling in these reiterations, something like a spell repeated, which charms the mind even as it wakes it. But the greatest art, as Iris Murdoch has observed, "invigorates without consoling, and defeats our attempts to use it as magic."

Imagine a chariot with four wheels: one is the ferocity of Swift, one the energy of Blake, one the control of Pope, and one the "noble, candid speech" of Yeats. Yet it is instinct with a single motion, the spirit of an individual who is completely of his time though rarely subdued to a middle flight:

> Now the year walks among the signs of heaven,
> Swinging her large hips, smiling in all her motions,
> Crosses with dancing steps the Milky Valley.
> Round her the primal energies rejoice;
> All the twelve metaphysical creatures and the seven
> Swift spheres adore her vigour; the five oceans
>   Look up and hear her voice
> Ring through the ebony vault, where Ara Celi
> Flames, and the choiring stars at their devotions
>   With pure and jubilant noise
> Praise and proclaim four seasons in her belly.[3]

Hope's subject, revealed in this opening stanza from the "Soledades of the Sun and Moon," is love: a Venus seen in two-fold vision, at once uranian and earthly. The simplicity of this subject gives the poet a certain advantage. He accepts the fact that flesh and death, love and solitude, are connected by the strange justice of nature. They are a twin birth, like good and evil, yet lying beyond the moral judgment. Hope is not an original poet but, like Pope, one who adds to a traditional theme all the resources of energetic illustration, who single-mindedly concentrates and purifies a universal truth. Biblical as well as pagan mythology can serve him in this; in "Imperial Adam," for example, Eve's parturition is pictured with the clean and sacred horror that attends the turning-points of existence:

> The proud vicuña nuzzled her as she slept
> Lax on the grass; and Adam watching too
> Saw how her dumb breasts at their ripening wept,
> The great pod of her belly swelled and grew,
>
> And saw its waters break, and saw, in fear,
> Its quaking muscles in the act of birth,

3. All A. D. Hope quotations are from his *Poems* (New York, Viking Press, 1961).

> Between her legs a pigmy face appear,
> And the first murderer lay upon the earth.

To envy Hope's advantage is unfair. For though his poetry depends greatly on Yeats (it is also through Yeats, I suspect, that Swift and Blake enter), he has cast off system and metaphysics. He begins, therefore, where Yeats ends, with the morality inherent in such poems as "News for the Delphic Oracle." The power to respond to and suffer the condition of sexual love is the ever-recurring last judgment, the only truly martial test of man. Those like Plotinus or Plato who sought to avoid it are forced to return via the sea of generation to where "nymph and satyr/ Copulate in the foam." There is no such thing as sublimation, whether Platonic or Freudian. Psychoanalysis, for Hope, is only another form of Platonic error, an attempt to escape the body by looking for something deeper. Two savage poems emphasize this point of view. "The Return from the Freudian Islands" is a funny and macabre satire of depth-psychology's quest for "The Ultimate Visceral Reality." The other, greater poem, "The Damnation of Byron," goes beyond polemics to show the professional lover (who secretly escapes the commitment to love) as his own Don Juan in an underworld of pure eroticism:

> Held in his brain's deep lupanar they float,
> the tapering trunk, the pure vase of the hips,
> the breasts, the breasts to which the hands go out
> instinctive, the adoring fingertips.

Hope's destruction of the landscape of sublimation (which includes that of the pastoral) is thorough. His sensual flora and fauna make those of previous poets blush. It is remarkable that he seeks almost no aid from the Song of Songs; and he is probably right in refusing so spiritual a paganism. I have stressed his more dazzling poems, but there is also the quiet success of "Chorale" and "The Death of the Bird." The precision of the latter (an experiment, also, in alternating masculine and feminine rhyme) gives one that tingle of the spine by which Housman recognized the real poem. Hope's book, in all its parts, is one of the great tributes to the corporeal understanding, though not to the middle style which triumphs in the later Yeats and Auden, and becomes trivial in the standard lyric. He can use the middle style, as in "The Death of the Bird," but he is not afraid to heighten it in his neoclassical Epistles or his inversion of the theme of Donne's "To His Mistris Going to Bed." He can also fly beyond it and say: "Put on your figures of fable."

The early Robert Lowell, in curious rivalry with Hart Crane, took Eliot as a point of departure toward a complete reversal of direction. As thoroughly accusative as Eliot's poetry is evasive, *Lord Weary's Castle* raised the image to the power of a direct, admonitory emblem. The needles of a Christmas tree "nail us to the wall," "Time and the grindstone and the knife of God" assail us by their overt and cumulative presence, and verbal flushes learned from Hopkins obtrude ("The search-guns click and spit and split up timber/ And nick").

Approaching his fiftieth year, however, Lowell changed his style. The poetry in *For the Union Dead* is balanced in tone and elliptical in movement: its energy is more hidden; its exclamations are almost musical. There are freer rhythms, unexpectedly gentle contours, and a partial return to imagistic reticence. The best that can be done in evaluating this change of style is to balance the gain against the loss. To start with the loss: Lowell had recovered and mechanized an aspect of medieval style, the "definition poem." Now some of the definiteness is gone. The strange and splendid harshness, the pointed shards of images, the aggressive apostrophes—they have given way to a new and casual compactness. Lowell is also, perhaps, affected by a European or "international" style which seems to have reached American poetry in the sixties. The Hopkinsian, or over-energetic, use of language is being abandoned for a quieter, more naïve mode. Has Lowell succumbed to this *dolce stil nuovo* in such poems as "The Lesson"?

> No longer to lie reading *Tess of the d'Urbervilles,*
> while the high mysterious squirrels
> rain small green branches on our sleep![4]

4. All Robert Lowell quotations are from his *For the Union Dead* (New York, Farrar, Straus & Giroux, 19–65).

This, surely, is imitation, and to the point of parody. But Lowell's harsher stylistic appropriations are at least equally apparent, as in "Beyond the Alps," where a classical dawn comes with unclassical violence:

> the blear-eyed ego kicking in my berth
> lay still, and saw Apollo plant his heels
> on terra firma through the morning's thigh.

This is the Lowell one knows best, who associates birth with labor and violence. Things "bleed with dawn." And because this Lowell remains so essential in *For the Union Dead,* it is hard to consider the muted style very significant. If Lowell's poetry moves more haltingly between sentiments and stanzas, his images continue to be entries in a doomsday book: they come nearer and nearer to us, threatening our detachment, massing with prophetic intensity. Is the intermingling, then, of a subtler style, purely experimental, purely a technique? "Each drug that numbs," he says in "Soft Wood," "alerts another nerve to pain." Perhaps the new style is a drug of this kind.

It can be argued, however, that the style of *For the Union Dead* reveals a genuine spiritual change, a revision of thought on the deepest and most internal level. Let us begin with what remains constant in Lowell. The major concern of this book is, as ever, pain: pain and anguish at temporality. That "chilling sensation of here and now, of exact contemporaneity" which Elizabeth Bishop has praised is strongly present. Lowell's attitude toward time is paradoxical: time is the accuser, yet time is inauthentic. Time eyes us through objects that loom large, or through "unforgivable" landscapes, yet everything converges to no effect, like waves breaking harmlessly and sight blurring. Time and memory are the "backtrack of the screw"; yet their pressure—the pressure essentially of religious expectation—is unremitting. "Even new life is fuel," says Lowell ironically.

> No ease from the eye
> of the sharp-shinned hawk in the birdbook there,
> with reddish brown buffalo hair
> on its shanks, one ascetic talon

clasping the imperial sky.
It says:
an eye for an eye
a tooth for a tooth.

The *lex talionis* here referred to is an imperative laid by consciousness on itself, and it requires us to be perpetually on guard, open to every sight. Our verdict on temporal matters should be that they are "true and insignificant" ("Hawthorne"). Instead, because of an American or Puritan tension between trivia and magnalia, life becomes a restless search for evidence, a satanic going to and fro in the earth.

If time is inauthentic, can a poet do more than record or accuse this to and fro? What genuine visionariness is possible? The question has a bearing on Lowell's development and on his change of style. His earliest poetry strives for vision, but there is no vision except a methodical hastening of the end. In the poetry that precedes *Life Studies,* darkness calls to darkness: nature appears as a world of portents rising against the dominion of man, and the poet harshly welcomes the suggested reversal. His visionary method is a kind of *temporicide,* and his poetical method sets spiritual symbol against daily event. He is not a reconciling poet. The very grinding together of natural experience and supernatural emblem is part of a harshness directed against temporality.

But in *Life Studies,* and even more in *For the Union Dead,* Lowell resists methodical darkness. He is like Faustus at midnight, who cries "Lente, lente currite noctis equi." There is a first retreat from darkness and into life, when poetry becomes more confessional—a sharp-eyed census of the unreconcilable elements in life. The retreat, however, is very imperfect. For realism easily becomes expressionism, and Lowell's indicative mood tends to indite rather than describe. "The man is killing time," he writes in "The Drinker." Or, in the title poem of *For the Union Dead,* which turns on several apocalyptic emblems, "The ditch is nearer." This nearing, this investing of experience with doom, this dark gloating even, this aggressive parody of at-one-ment in the grim images and the massing of the very words ("The Duce's lynched, bare, booted skull still spoke") are the temptation as well as energy of his vision.

268

It is, however, the special distinction of *For the Union Dead* to retreat even further from darkness by taking this retreat for its subject. Here poetry itself, by virtue of a subtler style, holds back the darkening mind. A presumption of restraint is felt at every level. Lowell is more successful in avoiding the intrusive literary or apocalyptic symbol, though whales still rear their blubber and spiders march. A poem like "The Drinker," with its discreet, almost neutral ending, is utterly different from "The Drunken Fisherman" *(Lord Weary's Castle)* which outsped even Donne's imagination of ruin. The new portrait of "Jonathan Edwards" is unusually urbane in tone and meandering. Natural experience and supernatural emblem may even blend, as when Exodus 12 quietly supports the "red ear of Indian maize . . . splashed on the door" in "The Old Flame," a poem dealing with the old passing into the new. That Lowell should admit newness is itself new, though an ironic image of "the plow/ groaning up hill—/ a red light, then a blue . . ." flickers in memory and disturbs the idea of a definitive progress. "Water," another memory study, shows him in the very act of restraining a darkening yet consolatory movement of the mind:

> Remember? We sat on a slab of rock.
> From this distance in time
> it seems the color
> of iris, rotting and turning purpler,
>
> but it was only
> the usual gray rock
> turning the usual green
> when drenched by the sea.

The greatest of these memory studies, and the most difficult, is the title poem. Its precarious forward motion reflects the problem of the prophetic mind. There is a consistent drawing back from certain conclusions or imaginations, a vibrant imprisonment of apocalyptic themes. Lowell evokes great but repressed powers —powers waiting for "the blessèd break." Chief among these is the power of both Black and White to take the initiative in civil rights, though the rights struggle is in an eccentric rather than central position. The poem centers, if at all, on several themes (civil rights, Boston, urbanization, the slippage of time) and is held together by an elliptical biography and an ideal. The ideal finds its clearest expression in Lowell's inversion of a Christian paradox: service, leadership, is to "choose life and die"; and dying into life is what *Life Studies* already taught. The poem ends with a further inversion of a Christian theme and a parody of Revelation. Servility instead of service and the omen of a monstrous backlash flood the aquarium of memory:

> The Aquarium is gone. Everywhere,
> giant finned cars nose forward like fish;
> a savage servility
> slides by on grease.

This is still the poet of "The Quaker Graveyard," but quietly, consciously, in the eye of the storm.

Four poets, these, who consolidate rather than advance the modernist revolution (despite moments of audacity in Lowell). Writing anti-apocalyptic poetry in apocalyptic situations, they make us aware that even their immediate precursors—Pound, Eliot, Hart Crane, Yeats—were rebels within Romanticism. All remain conscious of the "giant forms" of tradition. They wish to save yet subdue the mighty abstractions of a craft with thirty centuries behind it. These abstractions are multiplying. The modern problem is not a lack of exemplary forms but a surfeit of outmoded forms refusing to die completely: they bounce back like defeated Titans. To displace or disconfirm them is just another way of acknowledging their presence.

Historical research, moreover, has so increased our knowledge of past forms that they become oppressive. For Northrop Frye it seems "as though the cemeteries were on the march, the entire past awakening to an aesthetic apocalypse" *(The Modern Century)*. This knowledge explosion returns us to an Eden in which we, like Milton's Adam and Eve, wonder what our employment might be. Is it to admire the monuments all around us and to prune the wild sweets of a fertility we cannot share? The secular resurrection of the past, which began in the Renaissance, when poets like Spenser begged the Muse to reveal the "ancient rolles" in her "everlasting scryne," sets the individual into a chaos of plenitude, to starve among impossible harvestings. It is, I suppose, a hopeful sign that recent scholars like Northrop Frye, W. J. Bate, and Harold Bloom have recognized the situation for what it is: resulting not only from an increase in subjectiveness, which pits the individual and finite will against infinite desire, but also from our intensified sense of the past as a shadow-world of forms.

That the burden of the past is often abstract—sensed rather than experienced—does not alleviate it. Modern poetry wants to get out from under, and it sees impositions where there are merely common obligations. Even literacy, to judge by the spread of idiolects and mixed media, is demoted from a necessity to a resource. The one thing, therefore, that divides most poets of today from the modernist tradition is their "conspicuous consumption" of historical forms. Words are so much *matériel,* and capacity (to use a favorite word of John Dewey's) is all. What in Joyce was methodical, even labored, is now an easy lack of reserve on both formal and emotional levels. The drive toward self-exposure merges with the exploitation of language. So Gregory goes to Greece and becomes Childe Corso among the Ruins, or to Italy and speaks to Saint Francis in the strange, spendthrift "altongue" he has made for himself:

> I praise you your love,
> Your benedictions of animals and men,
> When the night-horn blew,
> And the world's property was disproportioned,
> Where ere the winged children,
> The rabbit,
> The afterglow—
> Good human tree, birds come to rest.[5]

The syntax is dubious; when and where are mere rhythmic pointers; the images dissolve the barrier between feeling and world; and the thought is as simply utopian as can be. What saves the poem is the very inability of language to deaden a jubilee spirit. For language, like the church or the law, which solidify death— "Death is not man's property/ Yet man has raised a vast Hilton there"—becomes to an antinomian like Corso something

5. All Gregory Corso quotations are from his *Long Live Man* (Norfolk, Conn., New Directions, 1962).

external to man, a piece of real estate detached from (to adapt one of his phrases) the "goodly compassionate mouth." A utopian and oral poetry like his refuses to be an object and to be pointed at as I am now doing: it tries to be speech that does not know the negative, therefore adds instead of subtracts, and subsumes contraries in its affirmative sweep: "32 years old and four hard real funny sad bad wonderful books of poetry."

Yet Corso writes verses rather than poems: the situations are trivial and rarely sustained, and his high didactic style is recognized now as a debased version of what the Romantics stole from religious effusion, though then it was a Promethean act. It is difficult not to draw an analogy between our society's exploitation of natural resources and Corso's supposedly healthy expense of spirit. The only defense, perhaps, is to speculate that poetry is entering a new grass-roots era of growth, prepared for by this emancipation of the high style, this scattering of achieved forms. "The weed is joy."[6] But is it possible to esteem poems that do not feel liable—responsible to the great makers gone before? Leaves of weeds, with occasional wild flowers? Mediocrity is intolerable in art: here, if anywhere, what Carlyle called "heroarchy" seems justified.

Since Wordsworth's revolt against poetic diction—which Hazlitt identified as "levelling" or an extension of democratic principles into verse—a death-wish has shadowed poetry and the hierarchical idea of culture. In philosophy, too, that death-wish has taken hold. On the European scene, Nihilism is a productive (if aristocratic) impulse since Nietzsche. In Anglo-America, since Wittgenstein, philosophy has sought to do away with itself by becoming as ordinary as possible—by seeing the great issues as a kind of poetic diction, pseudo-problems arising from pressures put on language. The influence on literary study of sociological and anthropological perspectives has also been felt: the concept of literature is being replaced by that of *écriture,* and the idea of privileged artifacts meets with as much tolerance as that of sacred institutions. The leveling tendency is clear when we compare Emerson, a passable democrat, with Artaud. Emerson challenged the young to compete with former great men by native right: "We too must write Bibles." But Artaud's *mot d'ordre,* "No more

6. Allen Grossman, *A Harlot's Hire* (Cambridge, Mass., Boar's Head, 1961).

272

masterpieces," falls outside of humanism by envisaging a society without masters, or fathers.

Well, if Pan is dead, long live the Bunnies. If the Imago is dead, long live the Images. A "liberation of the images" is indeed taking place: Ginsberg, Corso, and others bring visionary language into the marketplace more effectively than Blake did. I saw Ginsberg fill the indoor stadium of a university, the only place large enough to hold his audience. He read via a public address system which inevitably broke down: a power-failure that led one to think about the magnitude of the means, both rhetorical and technological, needed to project his words. The old economy of *peu de moyens, beaucoup d'effet* no longer applied. The voice in that machine was limited to sentimental and sublime properties. The visionary deceptions of a Blake or the soft but relentless negations of a Wallace Stevens would never get through. Ginsberg that evening could not have turned off his audience had he wanted to: they kept listening patiently to the suddenly mute swirl of words issuing from his beard.

The public address system as fate—Ginsberg adjusts to it with detachment and humor. It helps him prophesy, in the old sense of speaking out. Did not the prophets themselves use symbols which were magnifications? But one cannot forget how liable they felt— how, like Jonah, they fled from before God, voice and feet stumbling. Will the school of Ginsberg have listeners as well as audiences, those for whom the outer voice becomes an inner voice, beating like another heart? Those who can live with the poem rather than the occasion? The man, the means, the medium, the fatal eloquence get in the way of a truly spiritual economy. There is, again, a profanation of the resources of language, a squandering of transmitted riches which—as the Hebrews said of the Greeks—yields flowers but no fruits.

The new pastoralists, with Pound or William Carlos Williams as influences, practice a different kind of relaxed style. They seek to bypass both the "morgue of convention" and the Romantic megaphone. Like Lowell's quieter mode, but less nervous, theirs is a style that brings imagism to a final, twilight phase:

> Over my head, I see the bronze butterfly,
> Asleep on the black trunk,
> Blowing like a leaf in green shadow.

Down the ravine behind the empty house
The cowbells follow one another
Into the distances of the afternoon.
To my right,
In a field of sunlight between two pines,
The droppings of last year's horses
Blaze up into golden stones.
I lean back, as the evening darkens and comes on.
A chicken hawk floats over, looking for home.
I have wasted my life.[7]

The last line is meant to be one impression among others: we have images and we have thoughts; here is a thought. James Wright does not subdue it to image because, unlike the imagists, he is relaxed in the presence of ideas and entertains them without stylistic repression. But when we put such poetry into the "realms of gold," difficulties of judgment arise. It cannot be compared with Keats's Autumn Ode or Heine's "Aus alten Märchen winkt es" or Thoreau's prose. As a healthy new development in contemporary American poetry, Wright's verse, along with Robert Bly's, has been gently purgative of what Salinger's Franny calls "syntax droppings." Yet the diction remains mannered, and the very distrust of rhetoric has left Wright open to the echoing of much rhetoric. In denying artifice he is exposed to rival traditions of denial. To make us read silences and disjunctions has always been a compelling virtue of poetry, yet how are we to determine the particular mode of silence?

My grandmother's face is a small maple leaf
Pressed in a secret box
Locusts are climbing down into the dark green
    crevices
Of my childhood. Latches click softly in the
    trees. Your hair is gray.

The arbors of the cities are withered.
Far off, the shopping centers empty and darken.

A red shadow of steel mills.

7. All James Wright quotations are from his *The Branch Will not Break* (Middletown, Conn., Wesleyan University Press, 1963).

Expressionistic montage, imagism, Zen, haiku discreteness—
perhaps something of everything. The theme of mutability seems
to extend into the very images used, which decay as if they had
only a half life. But as the distinction between memory and
prophecy disappears, the cutting edge of the present is dulled,
and we are left with an inauthentic tense that evades equally
burdens of memory and visionariness. This does not happen with
Lawrence, who also writes against the daytime consciousness. In
Lawrence we feel not only the "surgent, insurgent Now" but the
precise point at which traditional symbols join the poet's mind to
a larger mind:

> only under the moon, cool and unconcerned
> Calm with the calm of scimitars and brilliant reaping hooks
> Sweeping the curve of space and moving the silence
> We have peace.

["The Hostile Sun"]

Where can modernism go? Only toward itself. It will continue
to invent poems that circumvent prophecy and memory, sometimes literally so:

> Imagine a voice calling,
> "There is a voice now calling,"
> or maybe a blasting cry:
> "Walls are falling!"
> as it makes walls be falling.
> Then from the gradual grass,
> too serious to be only noise—
> whatever it is grass makes,
> making words, a voice:
>
> "Destruction is ending. . . ."[8]

Stafford's landscapes are infused by a subdued apocalyptic tenor.
Everything he encounters encounters him, like the dead, pregnant deer blocking his road in "Travelling through the Dark."
But he keeps us in the context of ordinary circumstances, and they
do not yield their moral easily. Sometimes, in fact, we feel nothing
but a visionary dreariness, a ghostly and unresolved situation.

8. All William Stafford quotations are from his *Travelling Through
The Dark* (New York, Harper and Row, 1962).

Over-schooled by the modern workshop, which has taught him to adjust a religious sensibility to irony and understatement, he pays out words too sparingly. But at least his violence against eloquence is linked to a venerable and poetic superstition: words are acts; they bring forth, they bring about. The apocalyptic sense, therefore, though integral to his poems, does not flower into magical or visionary machines. Nature's presence is set against the more terrifying possiblity of nature's absence. He grounds his superstitions in the elemental, exposed spaces of mid-America:

> At the end of their ragged field
> a new field began:
> miles told the sunset that Kansas
> would hardly ever end,
> and that beyond the Cimarron crossing
> and after the row-crop land
> a lake would surprise the country
> and sag with a million birds.
>
> You couldn't analyze those people—
> a no-pattern had happened to them:
> their field opened and opened,
>
> level, and more, then forever,
> never crossed. Their world went everywhere.

What if nature's power to ablute meanings, to purge us and our images, fails? If everything falls into a pattern, analyzable? Don't fence me in, says Nature in Stafford's claustrophobic verse, I am Virgin Land still. But for the mind that cannot fall back on nature, claustrophobia deepens. The space—a saving distance—between ordinary detail and telling symptom, or symptom and catastrophe, founders:

> He heard the engines screaming for more air.
> He pushed and drifted—waking smelled like steam.
> Below him were the blank and linked-up roofs
> Of suburbs—showers, crematoria . . .
> The john tiles where his father's soft eyes worked
> The crossword puzzle jackpots, poetry

> Of Jews, ten thousand dollars for first prize.
> Red bullets to the brain, the Seconal. . . .
> The world was turning into dawn, just as
> The jet plane's sixteen landing wheels set down.[9]

Though we can work out why "waking smelled like steam" and "scream" is echoed in "steam," the relation between thoughts remains both "blank" and "linked-up," like the roofs described by the airplane passenger. Not till we understand that the mind represented here is sick in a very ordinary way does the real dilemma emerge. The mind's disease is the analogue of aphasia in the realm of meaning: like the stutterer who wants to say something and can't, so the poet wants to mean something and can't. To complicate things, his eloquence is made possible by his semantic stutter. If his meaning were effable, it would be so terrifying or final that utterance might cease. "Showers, crematoria" must remain in this relation of disrelation. The collapse of both things into a single meaning is the nightmare.

With the past catching up and the future rushing toward us, poetry wishes to clear a space, a magic circle to ward off those psychic cannibals called meanings. "A poem should not mean/ But be"; it reinforces the buffer nature was. The poetry of A. R. Ammons continues a quest begun by Wordsworth to deliver us from palpable design. The poet goes to nature because it puts "circumference between" (Emily Dickinson). A purposiveness without purpose leads us on; or, as Ammons says:

> there's some intention
> behind the snow snow's too shallow
> to reckon with: I take in on myself.[10]

How hesitatingly language moves here across the landscape, as though it feared to stumble on what it desired, on some deep intention or fixating clarity. Ammons is, in his way, as wary of nature as any primitive: he approaches the center eccentrically, stalking a transcendental prey or following its numinous trace with misgiving. There is no grasping at symbols, no exaltation. On the contrary, outriders of language clear the way for, rather than precipitate, felt energies:

9. Frederick Seidel, *Final Solutions* (New York, Random House, 1963).
10. All A. R. Ammons quotations are from his *Uplands* (New York, Norton, 1970).

some quality in the air
of summit stones lying free and loose
out among the shrub trees: every

exigency seems prepared for that might
roll, bound, or give flight
to stone: that is, the stones are
prepared: they are round and ready.

No telos-ridden perception could tolerate this propriety and imminence, this gerundive mood. Alvin Feinman goes further in the same direction: he sees speech itself as a positive always to be purified. "An ignorance/ That stands as though it were a center" swerves from one lyric phrase to another and falsifies them all:

Vagrant, back, my scrutinies
The candid deformations as with use
A coat or trousers of one now dead
Or as habit smacks of certitude

Even cosmographies, broad orchards
The uncountable trees   Or a river
Seen along the green monotonies
Of its banks   And the talk

Of memorable ideals ending
In irrelevance   I would cite
Wind-twisted spaces, absence
Listing to a broken wall

And the cornered noons
Our lives played in, such things
As thwart beginnings, limit   Or
Juxtapose that longest vision

A bright bird winged to its idea
To the hand stripped
By a damaged resolution
Daily of its powers   *Archai*[11]

11. Alvin Feinman, *Preambles* (New York, Oxford University Press, 1964).

Thought thinks its ruin here without widening speculation. It finds what will not suffice. This labor of the negative (or "decreation," as Stevens would have said) is not unmotivated, of course: it seeks to get back to authentic starting points, *archai*. Yet Feinman's poetry performs so total an *epoché* on "discursions fated and inept" that only the stumble toward a preamble is left. For so rigorous a sensibility, writing verse must be like crossing a threshold guarded by demons: the ghosts of great thinkers as well as great poets. But the poet's respect for the past is in the bated breath, not in complaint or loose confession. And, occasionally, a beginning is found which is not muted, a voice that in giving birth to light clears away false lights:

> And the light, a wakened heyday of air
> Tuned low and clear and wide,
> A radiance now that would emblaze
> And veil the most golden horn
> Or any entering of a sudden clearing. . . .

If I understand Vico, we once saw nature apotropaically, and great myths sprang from that seeing. Today, that aspect of nature being dead, we see history apotropaically, as a *Kulturschuld* which oppresses the individual. Some pretend that history, too, is dead. They make it play dead in their poems; and we get that irreconcilable split between a Charles Olson and a David Jones, between a poet who views Curtius's vision of European culture as a "great shitting from the sky"—an abandonment of the present for messianic culture politics—and a poet who argues that to describe daffodils one must be able to evoke Persephone, Flora, or Blodeuedd. "The flowers for the muse's garland would be gathered from the ancestral burial-mound—always and inevitably fecund ground, yielding perennial and familiar blossoms, watered and, maybe, potted, perhaps 'improved,' by ourselves. It becomes more difficult . . . when where was this site and were these foci there is *terra informis*" (Jones, *Anathémata*). It is as if Ezra Pound had come apart.

I don't see how we can put that Humpty-Dumpty together again. But Olson and Jones represent different types of *virtù,* false only in dogmatic isolation: the courage to live on nothing and the courage to live on a great deal. The first type is actually more common, an asceticism renouncing the past or whatever is too much with us. Our development has reached the point where we could exist on little; it appears as if society alone forced an over-head—material or spiritual, living standard or superego—on us. Thoreau lurks in most men. Yet were all to live outside of social bonds, they would live in competition once more. The kind of courage that is harder, because more against nature, against the ability to survive outside of society, is that of relying on one's heritage and its entailed responsibilities. Culture is the most liberal part of the entail, but some there are that dream of freedom even from culture:

> Strong in defeat, in death rewarded,
> The head dreams what has destroyed it
> And is untouched by its destruction.[12]

In Jarrell's "The Bronze David of Donatello," David dancing on Goliath's head is the body dancing on its own head. The head that dreams, and which is fallen is the ego become the id, a reversal which may emancipate David from both. David's body has the chance of a new birth, free from the old warfare; and the poet's symbol recalls the myth of Athene springing virginal from Jove. Yet the vanquished head exerts a greater fascination on Jarrell than David's physical grace. He knows how close the desire for redemption is to the desire for death, and his subdued style knows it also:

> Upon this head
> As upon a spire, the boy David dances,
> Dances, and is exalted.
>   Blessed are those brought low,
> Blessed is defeat, sleep blessed, blessed death.

12. This and the following quotation are from Randall Jarrell, *The Woman at the Washington Zoo* (New York, Atheneum, 1960).

IV

False Themes and Gentle Minds

The writers of the Enlightenment want fiction and reason to kiss. They are inexhaustible on the subject. "Buskin'd bards henceforth shall wisely rage," Thomas Tickell announces, foreseeing a new Augustan age.[1] "The radiant æra dawns," writes Akenside, when the long separation of imagination and science shall be overcome, and wisdom shall once more "Imbrace the smiling family of arts."[2] The anonymous French author of *Poésies philosophiques* (1758) admonishes the new school of poets to invent "believable marvels": "Sans marcher appuyé du mensonge et des fables / Venez nous étaler des merveilles croïables." Another explains more curiously his desire for chaster fictions. "Women of today," he writes, "are so sated with fine phrases that there is no way of succeeding with them except to appeal to their reason."[3] The enthusiasm for reason—and reasoning—is so great that Crébillon fils, in *Le Sopha* (1740), a degraded and libertine version of the metamorphosis myth, puts his hero-narrator in jeopardy of having his head cut off should he be tempted to *reflect upon* rather than simply *tell* his story. "By my faith," says the Sultan, "I swear I shall kill the next man who dares to reflect in my presence." Even with this threat, the novel ends on a defeated note. How difficult it is to tell a good, rousing story in an Age of Reason. "Ah Grandmother," sighs the Sultan, thinking of Sheherezade, "that's not the way you used to tell stories!"

It does not prove easy to give up the sophisticated superstitions by which literature had always amused, shocked, or instructed. Writers become intensely conscious of the primitive nature of these beliefs but also ingenious in accommodating them to rationality. In William Collins's *Ode on the Popular Superstitions of the*

1. *On the Prospect of Peace* (1712, dated 1713).
2. *The Pleasures of Imagination,* 1st ed. (1741), Bk. 2.
3. A. Berquin, "Discours sur la Romance," in *Romances* (1776).

Highlands of Scotland,[4] the problem is honestly and movingly set forth. Collins feels that he must forbear those great local myths which now live only in the far north and which he encourages his friend Home to keep up:

Nor need'st thou blush, that such false themes engage
Thy gentle mind, of fairer stores possest;
For not alone they touch the village breast,
But fill'd in elder time th'historic page.
There SHAKESPEARE'S self, with ev'ry garland crown'd,
In musing hour, his wayward sisters found,
And with their terrors drest the magic scene.

This dichotomy of "gentle mind" and "false themes" (where "false themes" means the materials of romance, popular or classical in origin) remains the starting point of the great majority of writers between the late Renaissance and Romanticism.

The story I wish to tell is how that dichotomy is faced and perhaps overcome. Many, of course, accepted the alienation of the literary mind from the "exploded beings" (the phrase is Dr. Johnson's) of folklore or mythology. They knew too well that great literature was magic and that reason could only flee from it, as from an enchanter. But others dared to think that literature might become a rational enchantment. They toyed with forbidden fire (with the "Eastern Tale", the Gothic romance, the Sublime Ode) and called up the ghosts they wished to subdue. In this they followed the example of the great poets of the Renaissance, who had at once revived and purified romance tradition. I begin, therefore, with Milton, the last about whom Collins could have said, as of Tasso: his "undoubting mind / Believed the magic wonders which he sung."[5]

Milton is already belated; and it is his problematic rather than naïve relation to Romance which makes him significant. He somehow transcends the very dichotomy of "gentle mind" and "false theme" which appears early in his poetry. Thus he dismisses as a

4. Written in 1749; published in 1788 in the *Transactions* of the Royal Society of Edinburgh.
5. *Ode on the Popular Superstitions,* xii.

false surmise his vision of nature spirits lamenting for Lycidas without renouncing that machinery of spirits, that multiplication of persons and gods, which is the clearest feature of romantic art —romantic in the largest sense of the word. He accepts a principle of plenitude which belongs to the Romance imagination rather than to an epoch in Lovejoyean history and which sets all action within a conspiracy of spirits. The world is made new or strange by opening into another world: an overhead—or underground— of mediations, of direct, picturable relations between spirit-persons. In such a world the human actor is only one kind of being, and his mind—or whatever else makes him the king-piece—is the target of a host of contrary intelligences.

Keats, thinking about the Enlightenment (the "grand march of intellect"), said that in Milton's day Englishmen were only just emancipated from superstition. It is true: Milton's consciousness is always ambushed by pagan or Christian or poetical myths. He is important for Collins and the Romantics because he shows the enlightened mind still emerging, and even constructing itself, out of its involvement with Romance. He marks the beginning of modern Romanticism, of a romantic struggle with Romance; and it is as a stage in the growth of the English poetic mind that I now want to present his poetry's earliest magic, the *Allegro-Penseroso* sequence.

You know how each poem opens, with a ritual exordium banning the undesired mood. In the first poem melancholy is dismissed; the second poem, like a recantation, hails melancholy and banishes joy. Milton, it has been argued, wished merely to picture the right kind of joy and a purified melancholy. Yet the dramatic aspect of each poem is the stylistic breach as the speaker turns from anathema to invitation. It is like going from an older world creaking with morality plays and heavy emblems to a brave new world in which man is the master of his mood and his spirit machinery correspondingly fluent. The poet seems as interested in purifying an older style as in purging a humor. The poems are Milton's notes toward a gentler fiction.

If mythology old-style showed the mind at the mercy of humors or stars or heavy abstractions, these personifications of easy virtue, which constitute a mythology new-style, reflect a freer attitude of the mind toward the fictions it entertains. The change from

> Hence loathed Melancholy
> Of *Cerberus,* and blackest midnight born,
> In *Stygian* Cave forlorn
> 'Mongst horrid shapes, and shreiks, and sights unholy

to

> Come pensive Nun, devout and pure,
> Sober, stedfast, and demure

recapitulates the entire Renaissance movement toward a *dolce stil nuovo*. It recalls the great change in men's attitudes toward the ancient superstitions, which in the century preceding Milton allowed that freer use of Romance associated with (among others) Ariosto and Spenser.

In Milton's double feature it is not the character contrast of the two personae (melancholy and mirth) which is important, but this newer and emancipated kind of myth-making. Milton uses no less than three sorts of mythical persons: established divinities (Venus, Mab, Aurora); personified abstractions (Melancholy, Tragedy, Mirth); and spirits of place (the "Mountain Nymph, sweet Liberty"). He does not encourage us to discriminate these kindred spirits; in fact, by mixing them with a fine promiscuity, he produces the sense of a middle region in which everything is numinous or semidivine. This in no respect demythologizes his poetry but suggests that man lives in easy rather than fearful, and daily rather than extraordinary, intercourse with an ambient spiritworld. He walks in a feather-dense atmosphere among "the unseen Genius of the Wood," strange music, "dewey-feathered sleep," and the phantasms of his own imagination. It is an atmosphere that works against sharp moral or ontological distinctions; when the merry man is said to view

> Such sights as youthfull Poets dream
> On Summer eeves by haunted stream

there is delicate ambiguity, because the sights could be public performances ("mask, and antique Pageantry"), dream thoughts, or a real vision. And when Shakespeare is called "fancy's child," the cliché has power, in this context, to suggest once more an intermingling of gods and men—that numinous half-essence which bathes every feature of these landscapes.

286

What is the reason for this promiscuous and light-hearted divinization? Milton has created a new and sweeter style, but also one that is peculiarly English. Most of his early poetry moves programmatically beyond the erudite pastoralism of the Italians and toward the fresher pastures of an English lyricism. Yet in *L'Allegro* and *Il Penseroso* Milton does more than state his program. He seems to have found the right kind of spirit, or spirits, for English landscape. He has taken the exotic machinery of the classical gods and the ponderous abstractions of moral allegory and treated them all as, basically, local spirits. In Britain they must be temperate like the British, so that extremes of mirth and melancholy, and even of divinity itself, are exorcized. The genius loci suits the religio loci: Milton's romantic machinery is grounded in the reasonableness of a specific national temperament.

That this reasonableness, this pride in a via media, may be a national myth does not concern us: although it will concern Blake, who rejects Milton's compromise and engages on a radical confrontation of the poetic genius with the English genius. Milton himself takes the issue onto a higher level in *Paradise Lost,* where the old and sublimer mode of myth-making is reasserted. From that post-bellum height, *L'Allegro* and *Il Penseroso* appear like exercises in the minor mode of pastoral romance. Even as only that—as an accommodation of Romance to the English mind— they remain a significant attempt to have this kind of fiction survive an increasingly enlightened climate.

That *L'Allegro* and *Il Penseroso* are a special type of romance appears as soon as we go from the nature of the personifications to that of the persona or presiding consciousness. Who is the speaker here if not a magus, dismissing some spirits and invoking others? If we do not have an actual romance, at least we have a romancer: the poems are thoroughly ritualistic, with their exordium, invocation, and ceremonial tone. But the imperatives ("Tow'red Cities please us then," "There let *Hymen* oft appear") are really optatives, while the tone is lightened by Milton's easy, peripatetic rhythm. His style of address intimates a new power of self-determination vis-à-vis the spiritual environment in which we live and move and have our being. Though that environment remains demonic, the magus is clearly in control: the most formal sign of control is, in fact, the conceit governing his invitations, which

reverses the oldest religious formula known to us, the *do ut des*—
I give, so that you give. In *L'Allegro* and *Il Penseroso* the poet is
not petitioning but propositioning his goddess: you give me these
pleasures, and I will be yours. He lays down his conditions and
enjoys them in advance. It is his pleasure or option to do these
things, to be merry or melancholy—a pleasure of the human
imagination.

Thus psyche emerges from the spooky larvae of masques and
moralities like a free-ranging butterfly. Though still in contact
with a world of spirits, it is no longer coerced or compelled. The
spiritual drama is, as always in Milton, seduction rather than compulsion. The poet begins to invite his soul and opens the way to
an authentic nature poetry. A similar development takes place on
the Continent with Théophile de Viau and Saint-Amant, imitators
of the lighter Pléiade strain, and who may have influenced Marvell.
Their nature poems are little romances, adventures of the liberated
and—as the case may be—libertine spirit.

Our mention of psyche may be more than a figure of speech.
According to traditional speculation on genius or ingenium, each
person was accompanied by two genii, a good and a bad, a protec-
tor and a deceiver. These are important figures in many morality
plays and still appear in Marlowe's *Faustus*. Could Milton have
changed this feature of popular demonology into his humors or
states of mind, which are competing spiritual options? If so, he
has adjusted an axiom of demonic religion to a more temperate
zone and brought us an essential step closer to the modern idea
of genius. By tempering the genii's astral nature, he has made
them into attendants of the creative mind.[6]

With Milton the spirit of Romance begins to simplify itself. It
becomes the creative spirit and frees itself from the great mass of
medieval and post-medieval romances in the same way as the
Spirit of Protestantism frees itself from the formalism of temples.
L'Allegro and *Il Penseroso* are not romances but romantic mono-
logues. They show a mind moving from one position to another
and projecting an image of its freedom against a darker, demonic

6. E. Panofsky's study of Dürer's *Melencolia I* has pointed to one
source of the modern idea of Genius in the Renaissance concept of "generous melancholy." See Klibansky, Panofsky, and Saxl, *Saturn and Melancholy* (New York, 1964), chap. 2, and also pp. 228 ff. on *Il Penseroso*.

ground. Poetry, like religion, purifies that ground: it cannot leave it. The newborn allegoric persons retain, therefore, something of the character of demonic agents even while being transformed into pleasures of the imagination. Indeed, the poems' rigidly stylized form reminds us that the imaginative man must join some god's party: the either/or situation remains; he cannot but assume a persona. Personification is still derived from the persona instead of the latter being freely inferred, as it is in modern poetry, from the projection of living thoughts.

If Romance is an eternal rather than archaic portion of the human mind, and poetry its purification, then every poem will be an act of resistance, of negative creation—a flight from one enchantment into another. The farewell to the impure gods becomes part of a nativity ode welcoming the new god. New personifications are born from old in *L'Allegro* and *Il Penseroso;* and *Lycidas* purges the genii loci of Italian pastoral only to hail a new "genius of the shore." This romantic purification of Romance is endless; it is the true and unceasing spiritual combat. At the conclusion of the first book of *Paradise Lost,* Milton transforms the Satanic thousands into fairies of Albion. Their moony music charms the ear of a belated peasant. It is, surely, a similar conversion of the demons which helps to animate the landscapes of *L'Allegro* and *Il Penseroso.* The haunted ground of Romance is aestheticized; the gods become diminutive, picturesque, charming—in a word, neoclassical. But is this change perhaps a Mephistophelian deceit, a modern seduction? The gentle mind thinks it is free of demons, but they sit "far within / And in their own dimensions like themselves" *(Paradise Lost,* 1. 792–93).

It is as if Milton had foreseen the triumph and trivialization of the descriptive-allegorical style. *L'Allegro* and *Il Penseroso* become the pattern for eighteenth century topographical fancies with their personification mania. His nature-spirits are summoned at the will of every would-be magus. Romance loses its shadow, its genuine darkness: nothing remains of the drama of liberation whereby ingenium is born from genius, psyche from persona, and the spirit of poetry from the grave clothes of Romance. By the end of the eighteenth century poets must begin once more where Milton began, though fortified by his example. They must "in the romantic element immerse" and not be deceived by the neoclassical psyche flitting with faded innocence through gaudy landscapes. Keats's imitation of Milton leads from those superficial bowers to the face of Moneta, dark (like Melancholy's) with excessive bright, from pleasures of the imagination to the burdens of a prophetic spirit. This is the path inaugurated by Collins, who uses the formula of *L'Allegro* and *Il Penseroso* to invite a creative Fear—stronger even in Shakespeare than in Milton—back to his breast:

> O Thou whose Spirit most possest
> The sacred Seat of *Shakespear's* Breast!
>
> . . . .
>
> Teach me but once like Him to feel:
> His Cypress Wreath my Meed decree,
> And I, O *Fear,* will dwell with *Thee!*

The theories accompanying the revival of Romance in the second half of the eighteenth century have often been studied. Van Tieghem's chapter on "La Notion de la vraie poésie" in *Le Préromantisme* contains in suggestive outline what needs to be known. But a fine essay by Emil Staiger on that strange confectioner of supernatural ballads, the German poet Bürger, takes us beyond theory to the inner development of romantic poetry.[7]

Gottfried August Bürger was a witting cause of the ballad revival in Germany and an unwitting influence on Wordsworth and Coleridge. His ballads, first collected in 1778, sent shudders through the sophisticated literary circles of Europe. Their influence reached England in the 1790s: Scott became a ballad writer because of him, and Anna Seward describes how people petitioned her to read them Bürger's most famous work, the *Lenore:* "There was scarce a morning in which a knot of eight or ten did not flock to my apartments, to be poetically frightened: Mr. Erskine, Mr. Wilberforce—everything that was everything, and everything that was nothing, flocked to Leonora. . . . Its terrible graces grapple minds and tastes of every complexion."[8] Bürger is like the country

7. Emil Staiger, "Zu Bürgers 'Lenore,' vom literarischen Spiel zum Bekenntnis," *Stilwandel* (Zürich, 1963).

8. *Letters of Anna Seward, Written between the Years 1784 and 1807,* 6 vols. (Edinburgh, 1811), 4:231. The letter is from the year 1796, which saw five separate translations of *Lenore* published. See Alois Brandl, "Lenore in England" in Erich Schmidt, *Charakteristiken* (Berlin, 1902), pp. 235–38; also F. W. Stokoe, *German Influence in the English Romantic Period* (Cambridge, 1926).

boy in the fairly tale who finally taught the princess to have goose-pimples by putting a frog in her bed. Yet, like almost every poet of the period, his first treatment of supernatural themes was jocose. Staiger shows that what began as a literary flirtation led suddenly to genuine "terrific" ballads. The sorcerer's apprentice is over-powered by spirits he had playfully evoked.

What interests us here is Bürger's literary situation and its difference from that of the English poets. Collins and later writers of the Age of Sensibility were also making mouths at the invisible event. When Gray, Percy, Mallet, Mason, Macpherson, and Blake were not redoing old romances, they inflated the neoclassical "god-kins and goddesslings" as giant epiphanic forms—pop art addressing a spiritualistic society. They could risk this because they knew the Enlightenment had gone too far for the old superstitions really to come back. Collins's visionary cry

> Ah *Fear!* Ah frantic *Fear!*
> I see, I see Thee near

invokes an emotion which is truly frantic: it wants to get at the poet, who wishes to be got at, but a historical fatality—the gentle mind, polite society—keeps them apart.

Now Bürger's situation is both more hopeful and more difficult. German poetry had had no golden age, no Renaissance. Hence there was no one between the poet and Romance tradition—no one, like Milton, to guide his steps, but also no one to demonstrate the difficulty and belatedness of such an enterprise. Where are *our* Chaucer, Spenser, Shakespeare, and Milton, Herder asks in an essay of 1777, which commends Bürger.[9] English Renaissance poetry, according to Herder, was reared on the old songs and romances which originally belonged just as much to German poetry, because of a common Nordic heritage and because the spirit of Romance is everywhere the same: "In allen Länder Europas hat der Rittergeist nur ein Wörterbuch." But this heritage not having been mediated by poets like Shakespeare and Milton,

9. "Von Ähnlichkeit der Mittlern Englischen und Deutschen Dicht-kunst" (*Deutsches Museum*). How fast things were moving toward a recovery of the Romance heritage is evidenced by the fact that Goethe's *Urfaust* dates from 1775 and Wieland's *Oberon* ("the first long romantic poem of modern Europe," says W. W. Beyer in his *The Enchanted Forest*) was published in 1780.

the modern German writer has no living tradition of older poetry through which he might renew himself and grow as if on the very stem of national life. With us Germans, laments Herder, everything is supposed to grow a priori ("Bei uns wächst alles a priori").

Thus Bürger must somehow raise the Romance tradition by his own arts. What he knows of that tradition is limited: mainly popular songs and superstitions, copied (so he claims) from songs picked up in city or village streets at evening, in the awareness that the poems of Homer, Ariosto, Spenser, and Ossian were also once "ballads, romances, and folksongs."[10] He is like a Faust who does not need the devil because the *Erdgeist* has agreed to be his spirit.

Among the most famous of Bürger's ballads is *The Wild Huntsman (Der Wilde Jäger)*. It depicts the rising blood-lust of a Sunday morning's hunt, and its tempo is wild from the start:

> Der Wild- und Rheingraf stiess ins Horn:
> "Hallo, Hallo, zu Fuss und Ross!"
> Sein Hengst erhob sich wiehernd vorn;
> Laut rasselnd stürzt ihm nach der Tross;
> Laut klifft' und klafft' es, frei vom Koppel,
> Durch Korn und Dorn, durch Heid und Stoppel.

This breakneck pace augments: two horsemen enter to accompany the earl; the right-hand one counsels him to respect the sabbath and turn back, the left-hand one spurs him on. The hunter overrides every objection; the pack rampages on, over a poor farmer's property, over the very bodies of a cowherd and his cattle; finally the earl pursues the beast into a hermit's sanctuary, violating it and blaspheming God. All at once—the transition takes place within one stanza—the clamor of the chase is gone, everything is vanished except the earl, and a deathly silence reigns. He blows his horn, it makes no sound; he halloos, no sound; he cracks his whip, no sound. He spurs his courser: it is rooted in the ground, stock-still. The silence is that of the grave;

10. "Aus Daniel Wunderlichs Buch" (*Deutsches Museum,* 1776). Bürger probably knew something of Percy's *Reliques,* although he did not study them till 1777. See Staiger, *Stilwandel,* p. 90; and Erich Schmidt, *Charakteristiken,* pp. 93–94.

into it comes, from above, a voice of thunder condemning the hunter to be, until the Last Judgment, the prey of an eternal and hellish hunt.

The poem is totally steeped in myth and superstition: there is the motif of the blasphemy immediately answered (call the devil, etc.); that of the ride ending in the grave, perhaps indebted to the Nordic myth of Odin, who rides in the sky with his troop of dead souls; and, above all, the theme of the hunter lured by his prey beyond nature into visionary experience.[11] Bürger wants to pack as much Romance as possible into each poem, as if to make up for Germany's lost time. He even classifies the ballad as a lyric kind of epic, not so much to stress that it must tell a story as to emphasize its ambition. The ballad is an epic in brief, a romance in brief. It sums up a life, a destiny, a whole ancient culture.

Yet behind these ballads is a pressure not explained by this ambition, which shows itself in their precipitous, "Würfe und Sprünge," the speed of action ("gesagt, getan"), the heroes' reckless *amor fati,* and everything else that tends to minimize the reflective moment. Here there is no shadow between the conception and the act, or even between this life and afterlife. No sooner has the earl blasphemed than he reaps his blasphemy; and Lenore's bitter yet innocent deathwish is rewarded in the same gross way. The mind is not given enough natural time in which to reflect.

Indeed, time in Bürger is intrinsically demonic. Although the supernatural erupts only at the climax of the action, it is there from the outset. One cannot speak of development: the earl is a hunted man from the first lines, a fated part of horse and pack and spurring sound; and the fearful symmetry, whereby hunter and hunted are reversed in the second part, appears like a natural rather than supernatural consequence. The first open hint of the supernatural is, of course, the appearance of the right and left

11. The theme of the spectral horseman is most vivid, of course, in *Lenore*: on the folklore (popular) as distinct from the mythic (learned) basis, see Scott, *Ballads and Lyrical Pieces* (1806), introductory note to his translation of Bürger's poem. On the hunter lured into visionary experience cf. Malory's *Morte Darthur,* 1. 19–20; and D. C. Allen, *Image and Meaning* (Baltimore, 1960), pp. 99–101.

horsemen, whose intrusion is so easy because in a sense they have been there all along. They are clearly the good and evil genii; and we see how externally, even superficially, the theme of reflection is introduced. There is only token retardation: the action consists of incidents arranged in climactic order with time moving irreversibly to the point of retribution. Having reached that point, the nature of time does not change: the hunter has simply run into himself. After a moment of absolute silence, which is like entering the looking glass, the reversed image appears and time continues its avenging course. There is no reflection and no true temporality: only this eschatological self-encounter.

Thus Bürger's ballads are ghostly in the deepest sense. But are they romantic? Are they not gothic—or, if you will, gothic romances? They belong to the world of that *Totentanz* explicitly evoked in *Lenore* and not absent from the mad and macabre ride of the earl. Death marries the bride, Death leads the hunt. This is not the world of the romances, not chivalry, and not *Rittergeist*.[12] There is little of genial digressiveness, courtesy, or natural magic. Instead, the classical unities of action, time, and place become the strait and narrow road leading to a single, surreal, pietistic confrontation. The space for reflection is tighter than in Poe's *The Pit and the Pendulum* and more stingily inauthentic than in Kafka. Bürger did create a new visionary form, but at a certain cost. The false theme triumphs at the expense of falsifying the mind, which has become a mere reflector of compulsions and spectator of fatalities.

To turn from *The Wild Huntsman* to Wordsworth's *Hartleap Well* (1800) is to know the rights of the mind—the pleasures and pains of ordinary consciousness—fully restored. No ballad could be more parallel, and more opposed. The first lines strike the keynote of difference:

> The Knight had ridden down from Wensley Moor
> With the slow motion of a summer's cloud

We begin with the chase almost over; that dramatic accumula-

12. In Chaucer's *Pardoner's Tale*, where Death leads the hunt for Death, the Christian elements blend with, rather than overpower, such figures from Romance as the Old Man whose mode of being contrasts so movingly with the unreflecting action of the rioters.

tion of incident, so essential to Bürger's pace, is at once subordinated to what Wordsworth named "character," but which is more like a consistent weather of the mind.[13] His first image therefore describes a mood as well as a motion and places both into encompassing nature. The stanzas that follow explicitly defuse Bürger's climax by incorporating it in the features of a natural scene:

> But, though Sir Walter like a falcon flies,
> There is a doleful silence in the air
>
> But horse and man are vanished, one and all;
> Such race, I think, was never run before.
>
> Where is the throng, the tumult of the race?
> The bugles that so joyfully were blown?
> This chase it looks not like an earthly chase:
> Sir Walter and the Hart are left alone.

The silence means only that Sir Walter has outdistanced his helpers; there is nothing supernatural in it. Yet it does lead to an unearthly moment of solitude and reflection. There is something mysterious in the staying power of the stricken animal and in the knight's joy which overflows in a vow to commemorate the hunt. His joy, even so, may be consonant with a chivalric ethos, while the strength of dying creatures is proverbial. A naturalistic perspective is maintained. What hidden significance there may be must await the second part of the ballad, which is purely reflective.

This part introduces no new incidents. The poet, speaking in his own person and not as a naïve bard à la Bürger, reveals that the story just told was learned from a shepherd he met on the way from Hawes to Richmond while pondering in a desolate spot marked by ruins. The natural and the contemplative frame of the story come together as he and the shepherd exchange views in the very spot where Sir Walter was left alone with the Hart. If part one is action, part two is reflection; yet part one was already reflective in mood. Hunter, shepherd, poet: all are contemplatives.

13. Some remarks by Wordsworth on "character" versus "incidents" can be found in a letter to Coleridge on Bürger (Wordsworth read him in Germany during the winter of 1798–99). See *The Collected Letters of S. T. Coleridge,* ed. E. L. Griggs, 4 vols. (Oxford, 1956, 1959), 1 (1956): 565–66.

Their contemplations, however, are of a deeply primitive kind. They center on a feeling of epiphany, of revelation associated with a particular place: here a revelation of nature as a sentient and powerful being. Sir Walter erects his pleasure-house on a spot where a natural power verging on the supernatural was manifested. The peasant thinks the spot is cursed because nature sympathized with the agony of the beast. The poet also thinks its death was mourned by "sympathy divine," by "The Being, that is in the clouds and air, / That is in the green leaves among the groves," but he refuses to go beyond what nature itself suggests, beyond the simple, imaginative feeling of desolation. He rejects the idea that there is a blood curse. Thus the poem is really a little progress of the imagination, which leads from one type of animism to another: from the martial type of the knight, to the pastoral type of the shepherd, and finally to that of the poet. And in this progress from primitive to sophisticated kinds of visionariness, poetic reflection is the refining principle: it keeps nature within nature and resists supernatural fancies.

Wordsworth's animism, his consciousness of a consciousness in nature, is the last noble superstition of a demythologized mind. All nature-spirits are dissolved by him except the spirit of Nature. His poetry quietly revives the figure of *Natura plangens,* one of the great visionary personae of both pastoral and cosmological poetry.[14] This link of Wordsworth's Nature to the Goddess Natura makes the formal moral of *Hartleap Well* almost indistinguishable from that of Bürger's poem: the one turns on "the sorrow of the meanest thing that feels"; the other on "Das Ach und Weh der Kreatur."[15] But while Bürger's demoniacal horseman parodies the chivalric spirit (the *Rittergeist*), Wordsworth accepts chivalry as a false yet imaginative and redeemable way of life. In Wordsworth the new and milder morality grows organically from the old: there is no apocalyptic or revolutionary change, just due process of time and nature.

Now this kind of continuity is the very pattern, according to

14. E. R. Curtius, *European Literature and the Latin Middle Ages* (London, 1953), chap. 6, "The Goddess Natura."

15. Cf. also Coleridge's *Ancient Mariner,* with its obliquer use of the hunt theme, but overt moral: "He prayeth best who loveth best / All things both great and small."

Herder, of the English poetic mind, which builds on popular sources and so revitalizes them. By giving the ballad precedence over his more personal reflections and allowing the characters of knight and shepherd their own being, Wordsworth exemplifies a peculiarly English relation of new to old. The internal structure of his poem reflects a historical principle of canon formation. Even when, as in *The White Doe of Rylstone,* he begins with personal speculation rather than with an impersonally narrated ballad, the essential structure remains that of the reflective encirclement and progressive purification of symbols from Romance.

There are, in the Romantic period, many variations on this structure. The emergence of the gentle out of the haunted mind is not always so gradual and assured. Coleridge's *Ancient Mariner,* a "Dutch attempt at German sublimity" as Southey called it, follows the Bürgerian model. Yet it has, in addition, something of the meander of Romance and of that strange interplay of dream vision and actual vision found in Malory or Spenser. It is clear that Milton is not the only master for the English mind. But he is among those who assured the survival of Romance by the very quality of his resistance to it.

Romanticism and Anti-Self-Consciousness

The dejection afflicting John Stuart Mill in his twentieth year was alleviated by two important events. He read Wordsworth, and he discovered for himself a view of life resembling the "anti-self-consciousness theory" of Carlyle. Mill describes this strangely named theory in his *Autobiography:*

> Ask yourself whether you are happy, and you cease to be so. The only chance is to treat, not happiness, but some end external to it as the purpose of life. Let your self-consciousness, your scrutiny, your self-interrogation exhaust themselves on that.[1]

It is not surprising that Wordsworth's poetry should also have served to protect Mill from the morbidity of his intellect. Like many Romantics, Wordsworth had passed through a depression clearly linked to the ravage of self-consciousness and the "strong disease" of self-analysis.[2] Book 11 of the *Prelude,* chapter 5 of

1. *Autobiography* (1873), chap. 5. Mill says that he had not heard, at the time, Carlyle's theory. The first meeting between the writers took place in 1831; Mill's depression lasted, approximately, from autumn 1826 to autumn 1828. Mill called self-consciousness "that demon of the men of genius of our time from Wordsworth to Byron, from Goethe to Chateaubriand." See Wayne Shumaker, *English Autobiography* (Berkeley and Los Angeles, 1954), chap. 4.

2. Thought as a disease is an open as well as submerged metaphor among the Romantics. There are many hints in Novalis; Schelling pronounces naked reflection (analysis) to be a spiritual sickness of man (*Schellings Sämtliche Werke,* ed. K. F. Schelling [Stuttgart, 1856–61], 2: 13–14); the metaphor is explicit in Carlyle's *Characteristics* (1831) and commonplace by the time that E. S. Dallas in *The Gay Science* (1866) attributes the "modern disease" to "excessive civilization and overstrained consciousness." The *mal du siecle* is not unrelated to the malady we are describing. Goethe's *Die Leiden des Jungen Werthers* (1774) may be seen as its terminus a quo, and Kierkegaard's *Sickness unto Death* (1849) as its noonday point of clarity.

Mill's *Autobiography,* Carlyle's *Sartor Resartus,* and other great confessional works of the Romantic period show how crucial these maladies are for the adolescent mind. Endemic, perhaps, to every stage of life, they especially affect the transition from adolescence to maturity; and it is interesting to observe how man's attention has shifted from the fact of death and its rites of passage, to these trials in what Keats called "the Chamber of Maiden-Thought" and, more recently still, to the perils of childhood. We can say, taking a metaphor from Donne, that "streights, and none but streights" are ways to whatever changes the mind must undergo, and that it is the Romantics who first explored the dangerous passageways of maturation.

Two trials or perils of the soul deserve special mention. We learn that every increase in consciousness is accompanied by an increase in self-consciousness, and that analysis can easily become a passion that "murders to dissect."[3] These difficulties of thought in its strength question the ideal of absolute lucidity. The issue is raised of whether there exist what might be called *remedia intellectus:* remedies for the corrosive power of analysis and the fixated self-consciousness.

There is one remedy of great importance which is almost coterminous with art itself in the Romantic period. This remedy differs from certain traditional proposals linked to the religious control of the intellect—the wild, living intellect of man, as Newman

3. Wordsworth, "The Tables Turned" (1798). For the first peril, see Kierkegaard's *Sickness unto Death,* and Blake: "The Negation is the Spectre, the Reasoning Power in Man; / This is a false Body, an Incrustation over my Immortal / Spirit, a Selfhood which must be put off & annihilated alway" (*Milton,* Bk. 2). This last quotation, like Wordsworth's "A reasoning, self-sufficient thing, / An intellectual All-in-All" ("A Poet's Epitaph"), shows the closeness of the two perils. For the second, see also Coleridge: "All the products of the mere reflective faculty [viz. the "understanding" contradistinguished from what Coleridge will call the "reason"] partook of DEATH" (*Biographia Literaria,* chap. 9): Benjamin Constant's definition of one of the moral maladies of the age as "the fatigue, the lack of strength, the perpetual analysis that saps the spontaneity of every feeling" (draft preface to *Adolphe*); and Hegel's preface to *The Phenomenology of Mind* (1807). Hegel observes that ordinary analysis leads to a hardening of data, and he attributes this to a persistence of the ego, whereas his dialectic is thought to reveal the true fluency of concepts. Carlyle most apodictically said: "Had Adam remained in Paradise, there had been no Anatomy and no Metaphysics" (*Characteristics,* 1831).

calls it in his *Apologia*.[4] A particularly Romantic remedy, it is nonlimiting with respect to the mind. It seeks to draw the antidote to self-consciousness from consciousness itself. A way is to be found not to escape from or limit knowledge, but to convert it into an energy finer than intellectual. It is some such thought which makes Wordsworth in the preface to *Lyrical Ballads* describe poetry as the "breath and finer spirit of all knowledge," able to carry sensation into the midst of the most abstract or remotest objects of science. A more absolute figure for this cure, which is, strictly speaking, less a cure than a paradoxical faith, is given by Kleist: "Paradise is locked . . . yet to return to the state of innocence we must eat once more of the tree of knowledge." It is not by accident that Kleist is quoted by Adrian at a significant point in Mann's *Doktor Faustus,* which is *the* novel about self-consciousness and its relation to art.

This idea of a return, via knowledge, to naïveté—to a second naïveté—is a commonplace among the German Romantics. Yet its presence is perhaps more exciting, because suitably oblique, among the English and French Romantics. A. O. Lovejoy, of course, in his famous essay on the "Discrimination of Romanticisms" (1924), questions the possibility of unifying the various national movements. He rightly points out that the German Romantics insist on an art that rises from the plenitude of consciousness to absorb progressively the most sophisticated as well as the most naïve experience. But his claim that English Romanticism is marked by a more primitivistic "return to nature" is weakened by his use of second-rate poetry and isolated passages. One can show that the practice of the greater English Romantics is involved with a problematical self-consciousness similar to that of the Germans and that, in the main, no primitivism or "sacrifice of intellect" is found. I do not mean to deny the obvious, that there are primitivistic passages in Chateaubriand and even Wordsworth, but the primary tendency should be distinguished from errors and epiphenomena. The desire of the Romantics is perhaps for what Blake calls "organized innocence," but never for a mere return to

4. *Apologia Pro Vita Sua* (1864), chap. 5. In the same chapter Newman calls reason "that universal solvent." Concerning Victorian remedies for "this disease / My Self" (Marianne Moore), see also A. Dwight Culler, *The Imperial Intellect* (New Haven, 1955), pp. 234–37.

the state of nature. The German Romantics, however, for a reason mentioned later and because of the contemporaneous philosophical tradition which centered on the relations between consciousness and consciousness of self (Fichte, Schelling, Hegel), gained in some respects a clearer though not more fruitful understanding of the problem. I cannot consider in detail the case of French Romanticism. But Shelley's visionary despair, Keats's understanding of the poetical character, and Blake's doctrine of the contraries reveal that self-consciousness cannot be overcome; and the very desire to overcome it, which poetry and imagination encourage, is part of a vital, dialectical movement of soul-making.

The link between consciousness and self-consciousness, or knowledge and guilt, is already expressed in the story of the expulsion from Eden. Having tasted knowledge, man realizes his nakedness, his sheer separateness of self. I have quoted Kleist's reflection; and Hegel, in his interpretation of the Fall, argues that the way back to Eden is via contraries: the naïvely sensuous mind must pass through separation and selfhood to become spiritually perfect. It is the destiny of consciousness or, as the English Romantics would have said, of imagination, to separate from nature so that it can finally transcend not only nature but also its own lesser forms. Hegel in his *Logic* puts it as follows:

> The first reflection of awakened consciousness in men told them they were naked. . . . The hour that man leaves the path of mere natural being marks the difference between him, a self-conscious agent, and the natural world. The spiritual is distinguished from the natural . . . in that it does not continue a mere stream of tendency, but sunders itself to self-realization. But this position of severed life has in its turn to be overcome, and the spirit must, by its own act, achieve concord once more. . . . The principle of restoration is found in thought, and thought only: the hand that inflicts the wound is also the hand that heals it.[5]

The last sentence states unequivocally where the remedy lies.

5. *The Logic of Hegel,* trans. from the *Encyclopedia of the Sciences* by W. Wallace, 2nd ed. (Oxford, 1904), pp. 54–57. The first sentences given here come from passages in the original later than the remainder of the quotation.

Hegel, however, does not honor the fact that the meaning he derives from the Fall was originally in the form of myth. And the attempt to think mythically is itself part of a crucial defense against the self-conscious intellect. Bergson in *The Two Sources of Morality and Religion* sees both myth and religion as products of an intellectual instinct created by nature itself to oppose the analytic intellect, to preserve human spontaneities despite the hesitant and complicated mind.[6] Whether myth-making is still possible, whether the mind can find an unselfconscious medium for itself or maintain something of the interacting unity of self and life, is a central concern of the Romantic poets.

Romantic art as myth-making has been discussed convincingly in recent years, and Friedrich Schlegel's call in "Rede über die Mythologie" (1800) for a modern mythology is well known. The question of the renewal of myth is, nevertheless, a rather special response to the larger perplexities of reflective thought. "The poet," says Wallace Stevens in "Adagia," "represents the mind in the act of defending us against itself." Starting with the Romantics, this act is clearly focused, and poetry begins to be valued in contradistinction to directly analytic or purely conceptual modes of thought. The intelligence is seen as a perverse though necessary specialization of the whole soul of man, and art as a means to resist the intelligence intelligently.

It must be admitted, at the same time, that the Romantics themselves do not give (in their conceptual moments) an adequate definition of the function of art. Their criterion of pleasure or expressive emotion leads to some kind of art for art's sake formula, or to the sentimentalism which Mill still shared and which marks the shift in sensibility from Neoclassic to Romantic. That Mill wept over the memoirs of Marmontel and felt his selfhood lightened by this evidence of his ability to feel, or that Lamartine saw the life of the poet as "tears and love," suggests that the *larmoyant*

6. *Les Deux Sources de la Morale et de la Religion* (1933), chap. 2. Both religion and "la fonction fabulatrice" are "une reaction défensive de la nature contre le pouvoir dissolvant de l'intelligence." (Cf. Newman calling the intellect "that universal solvent.") As Romanticism shades into modernism, a third peril of over-consciousness comes strongly to the fore—that it leads to a Hamlet-like incapacity for action. Bergson, like Kierkegaard, tries to counter this aspect especially.

vein of the later eighteenth century persisted for some time but also helped, when tears or even joy were translated into theory, to falsify the Romantic achievement and make Irving Babbitt's criticism possible.

The art of the Romantics, on the other hand, is often in advance of even their best thoughts. Neither a mere increase in sensibility nor a mere widening of self-knowledge constitutes its purpose. The Romantic poets do not exalt consciousness per se. They have recognized it as a kind of death-in-life, as the product of a division in the self. The mind which acknowledges the existence or past existence of immediate life knows that its present strength is based on a separation from that life. A creative mind desires not mere increase of knowledge, but "knowledge not purchased by the loss of power" (*Prelude*, 5). Life, says Ruskin, is the only wealth; yet childhood, or certain irrevocable moments, confront the poet sharply and give him the sense of having purchased with death the life of the mind. Constructing what Yeats calls an anti-self, or recovering deeply buried experience, the poet seeks a return to "Unity of Being." Consciousness is only a middle term, the strait through which everything must pass; and the artist plots to have everything pass through whole, without sacrifice to abstraction.

One of the themes which best expresses this perilous nature of consciousness and which has haunted literature since the Romantic period is that of the Solitary, or Wandering Jew. He may appear as Cain, Ahasuerus, Ancient Mariner, and even Faust. He also resembles the later (and more static) figures of Tithonus, Gerontion, and *poète maudit*. These solitaries are separated from life in the midst of life, yet cannot die. They are doomed to live a middle or purgatorial existence which is neither life nor death, and as their knowledge increases so does their solitude.[7] It is,

7. "I lost the love of heaven above, / I spurned the lust of earth below" (John Clare, "A Vision"). By this double exile and their final madness, two poets as different as Clare and Hölderlin are joined. See Coleridge's intense realization of man's "between-ness," which increases rather than chastens the apocalyptic passion: "O Nature! I would rather not have been—let that which is to come so soon, come now—for what is all the intermediate space, but sense of utter worthlessness? . . . Man is truly and solely an immortal series of conscious mortalities and inherent Disappointments" (*Inquiring Spirit*, ed. K. Coburn [London, 1951], p. 142).

303

ultimately, consciousness that alienates them from life and imposes the burden of a self which religion or death or a return to the state of nature might dissolve. Yet their heroism, or else their doom, is not to obtain this release. Rebels against God, like Cain, and men of God, like Vigny's Moses, are equally denied "le sommeil de la terre" and are shown to suffer the same despair, namely, "the self . . . whose worm dieth not, and whose fire is not quenched" (Kierkegaard). And in Coleridge's Mariner, as in Conrad's Marlow, the figure of the wanderer approaches that of the poet. Both are storytellers who resubmit themselves to temporality and are compelled to repeat their experiences in the purgatorial form of words. Yeats, deeply affected by the theme of the Wandering Jew, records a marvelous comment of Mme. Blavatsky's: "I write, write, write, as the Wandering Jew walks, walks, walks."

The Solitary may also be said to create his own, peculiarly Romantic genre of poetry. In "Tintern Abbey," or "X" Revisited, the poet looks back at a transcended stage and comes to grips with the fact of self-alienation. The retrospective movement may be visionary, as often in Hölderlin; or antiquarian, as in Scott; or deeply oblique, as in lyrical ballad and monologue. In every case, however, there is some confrontation of person with shadow or self with self. The intense lyricism of the Romantics may well be related to this confrontation. For the Romantic "I" emerges nostalgically when certainty and simplicity of self are lost. In a lyric poem it is clearly not the first-person form that moves us (the poem need not be in the first person) but rather the I toward which that I reaches. The very confusion in modern literary theory concerning the fictive I, whether it represents the writer as person or only as persona, may reflect a dialectic inherent in poetry between the relatively self-conscious self and that self within the self which resembles Blake's "emanation" and Shelley's "epipsyche."

It is true, of course, that this dialectic is found in every age and not restricted to the Romantic. The notion of man (as of history) seems to presuppose that of self-consciousness, and art is not the

---

But to ask death instead of life of nature is still to ask for finality, for some metal quietus: it is the bitter obverse, also met at the beginning of Goethe's *Faust,* of the quest for absolute truth.

only major reaction to it. Mircea Eliade, following Nietzsche, has recently linked art to religion by interpreting the latter as originating in a periodic and ritually controlled abolition of the burden of self, or rather of this burden in the form of a nascent historical sense. It is not true, according to Eliade, that primitive man has no sense of history; on the contrary, his sense of it is too acute, he cannot tolerate the weight of responsibility accruing through memory and individuation, and only gradually does religious myth, and especially the Judaeo-Christian revelation, teach him to become a more conscious historical being. The question, therefore, is why the Romantic reaction to the problem of self-consciousness should be in the form of an aggrandizement of art, and why the entire issue should now achieve an urgency and explicitness previously lacking.

The answer requires a distinction between religion and art. This distinction can take a purely historical form. There clearly comes a time when art frees itself from its subordination to religion or religiously inspired myth and continues or even replaces them. This time seems to coincide with what is generally called the Romantic period: the latter, at least, is a good *terminus a quo*. Though every age may find its own means to convert self-consciousness into the larger energy of imagination, in the Romantic period it is primarily art on which this crucial function devolves. Thus, for Blake, all religion is a derivation of the Poetic Genius; and Matthew Arnold is already matter-of-fact rather than prophetic about a new age in which the religious passion is preserved chiefly by poetry. If Romantic poetry appears to the orthodox as misplaced religious feeling ("spilt religion"), to the Romantics themselves it redeems religion.[8]

8. I have omitted here the important role played by the French Revolution. The aggrandizement of art is due in no small measure to the fact that poets like Wordsworth and Blake cannot give up one hope raised by the Revolution—that a terrestrial paradise is possible—yet are eventually forced to give up a second hope—that it can be attained by direct political action. The shift from faith in the reformation of man through the prior reformation of society to that in the prior reformation of man through vision and art has often been noted. The failure of the French Revolution anchors the Romantic movement or is the consolidating rather than primary cause. It closes, perhaps until the advent of Communism, the possibility that politics rather than art should be invested with a passion previously subsumed by religion.

Yet as soon as poetry is separated from imposed religious or communal ends it becomes as problematic as the individual himself. The question of how art is possible, though post-Romantic in its explicitness, has its origin here, for the artist is caught up in a serious paradox. His art is linked to the autonomous and individual; yet that same art, in the absence of an authoritative myth, must bear the entire weight of having to transcend or ritually limit these tendencies. No wonder the problem of the subjective, the isolated, the individual, grows particularly acute. Subjectivity —even solipsism—becomes the subject of poems which qua poetry seek to transmute it.

This paradox seems to inhere in all the seminal works of the Romantic period. "Thus my days are passed / In contradiction," Wordsworth writes sadly at the beginning of *The Prelude*. He cannot decide whether he is fit to be a poet on an epic scale. The great longing is there; the great (objective) theme eludes him. Wordsworth cannot find his theme because he already has it: himself. Yet he knows self-consciousness to be at once necessary and opposed to poetry. It will take him the whole of *The Prelude* to be satisfied *in actu* that he is a poet. His poem, beginning in the vortex of self-consciousness, is carried to epic length in the desire to prove that his former imaginative powers are not dead.

I have already confessed to understanding the *Ancient Mariner* as a poem that depicts the soul after its birth to the sense of separate (and segregated) being. In one of the really magical poems in the language, which, generically, converts self-consciousness into imagination, Coleridge describes the travail of a soul passing from self-consciousness to imagination. The slaying of an innocent creature, the horror of stasis, the weight of conscience or of the vertical eye (the sun), the appearance of the theme of deathlessness, and the terrible repetitive process of penitence whereby the wanderer becomes aware through the spirits above and the creatures below of his focal solitude between both—these point with archetypal force to the burden of selfhood, the straits of solitude, and the compensating plenary imagination that grows inwardly. The poem opens by evoking that rite de passage we call a wedding and which leads to full human communion, but the Mariner's story interposes itself as a reminder of human separateness and of the intellectual love (in Spinoza's sense) made possible by it.

To explore the transition from self-consciousness to imagination and to achieve that transition while exploring it (and so to prove it still possible) is the Romantic purpose I find most crucial. The precariousness of that transition naturally evokes the idea of a journey; and in some later poets, like Rimbaud and Hart Crane, the motif of the journey has actually become a sustained metaphor for the experience of the artist during creation. This journey, of course, does not lead to what is generally called a truth: some final station for the mind. It remains as problematic a crossing as that from death to second life or from exile to redemption. These religious concepts, moreover, are often blended in and remind us that Romantic art has a function analogous to that of religion. The traditional scheme of Eden, Fall, and Redemption merges with the new triad of Nature, Self-Consciousness, and Imagination—the last term in both involving a kind of return to the first.

Yet everything depends on whether it is the right and fruitful return. For the journey beyond self-consciousness is shadowed by cyclicity, by paralysis before the endlessness of introspection, and by the lure of false ultimates. Blake's "Mental Traveller," Browning's "Childe Roland to The Dark Tower Came," and Emily Dickinson's "Our journey had advanced" show these dangers in some of their forms. Nature in its childhood or sensuous radiance (Blake's "Beulah") exerts an especially deceptive lure. The desire to gain truth, finality, or revelation generates a thousand such enchantments. Mind has its blissful islands as well as its mountains, its deeps, and its treacherous crossroads. Depicting these trials by horror and by enchantment, Romanticism is genuinely a rebirth of Romance.

In the years following World War I it became customary to see Classicism and Romanticism as two radically different philosophies of life and to place modernism on the side of the anti-romantic. André Malraux defined the classical element in modern art as a "lucid horror of seduction." Today it is clear that Romantic art shared that lucidity. Romanticism at its most profound reveals the depth of the enchantments in which we live.

We dream, we wake on the cold hillside, and our sole self pursues the dream once more. In the beginning was the dream, and the task of disenchantment never ends.

The nature poetry of the Romantics is a case in point. Far from being an indulgence in dewy moments, it is the exploration of enchanted ground. The Romantic poets, like the Impressionist painters, refuse to "simplify the ghost" of nature. They begin to look steadfastly at all sensuous experience, penetrating its veils and facing its seductions. Shelley's "Mont Blanc" is not an enthusiastic nature poem but a spirit-drama in which the poet's mind seeks to release itself from an overwhelming impression and to reaffirm its autonomy vis-à-vis nature. Keats also goes far in respecting illusions without being deluded. His starting-point is the dream of nature fostered by Romance; he agrees to this as consciously as we lie down to sleep. But he intends such dreaming "beyond self" to unfold its own progressions and to wake into truth. To this end he passes from a gentler to a severer dream-mode: from the romance of *Endymion* to the more austere *Hyperion*. Yet he is forced to give up the *Hyperion* because Saturn, Apollo, and others behave like quest heroes instead of gods. Having stepped beyond romance into a sublimer mode, Keats finds the quest for self-identity elated rather than effaced. It has merely raised itself to a divine level. He cannot reconcile Miltonic sublimity with the utterly human pathos that keeps breaking through. The "egotistical sublime" remains.

It was Wordsworth, of course, whose poetry Keats had tried to escape by adhering to a less self-centered kind of sublimity: "Let us have the old Poets, and Robin Hood." Wordsworth had subdued poetry to the theme of nature's role in the growth of the individual mind. The dream of nature, in Wordsworth, does not lead to formal Romance but is an early, developmental step in converting the solipsistic into the sympathetic imagination. It entices the brooding soul out of itself, toward nature first, then toward humanity. Wordsworth knew the weight of self-consciousness:

> It seemed the very garments that I wore
> Preyed on my strength, and stopped the quiet stream
> Of self-forgetfulness.
>
> [*Prelude* (1850), 5. 294 ff.]

The wound of self is healed, however, by "unconscious inter-course" with a nature "old as creation." Nature makes the "quiet stream" flow on. Wordsworth evokes a type of consciousness more integrated than ordinary consciousness, though deeply de-pendent on its early—and continuing—life in rural surroundings.[9]

The Romantic emphasis on unconsciousness and organic form is significant in this light. *Unconsciousness* remains an am-biguous term in the Romantic and Victorian periods, referring to a state distinctly other than consciousness or simply to unself-consciousness. The characteristic of right performance, says Carlyle in *Characteristics* (1831), is an unconsciousness—" 'the healthy know not of their health, but only the sick.' " The term clearly approaches here its alternate meaning of unselfconscious-ness, and it is to such statements that Mill must be indebted when he mentions the "anti-self-consciousness theory" of Carlyle. In America, Thoreau perpetuates the ambiguity. He also prescribes unconsciousness for his sophisticated age and uses the word as an equivalent of vision: "the absence of the speaker from his speech." It does seem to me that the personal and expressive theory of poetry, ascribed to the Romantics, and the impersonal theory of poetry, claimed in reaction by the moderns, answer to the same problem and are quietly linked by the ambiguity in *unconscious-ness*. Both theories value art as thought recreated into feeling or self-consciousness into a more communal power of vision. Yet can the modern poet, whom Schiller called "sentimental" (re-flective) and whom we would describe as alienated, achieve the immediacy of all great verse, whatever its personal or historical dilemma?

This is as crucial a matter today as when Wordsworth and Coleridge wrote *Lyrical Ballads* and Hölderlin pondered the fate of poetry in "Der Rhein." Is visionary poetry a thing of the past, or can it coexist with the modern temper? Is it an archaic revela-tion, or a universal mode springing from every real contact with

9. Mill, Hazlitt, and Arnold came to approximately the same estimate of Wordsworth's poetry. Comparing it to Byron's, they found that the latter had too much fever of self in it to be remedial; they did not want their image cast back at them magnified. Carlyle prefers to compare Goethe and Byron ("Close your Byron, open your Goethe"), yet his point is the same: Goethe retains a strong simplicity in a tormented and divided age, while Byron seems to him a "spasmodically bellowing self-worshipper."

nature? "To interest or benefit us," says a Victorian writer, "poetry must be reflective, sentimental, subjective; it must accord with the conscious, analytical spirit of present men."[10] The difficulties surrounding a modern poetry of vision vary with each national literature. In England the loss of "poesy" is attributed by most Romantics to a historical though not irreversible fact—to the preceding century's infidelity to the line of Chaucer, Spenser, Shakespeare, and Milton. "Let us have the old Poets, and Robin Hood," as Keats said. Yet for the German and the French there was no easy return to a tradition deriving its strength from both learned and popular sources. "How much further along we would be," Herder remarks, "if we had used popular beliefs and myths like the British, if our poetry had built upon them as wholeheartedly as Chaucer, Spenser and Shakespeare did."[11] In the absence of this English kind of literary mediation, the gap between medieval romance and the modern spirit seemed too great. Goethe's *Faust* tried to bridge it but, like *Wilhelm Meister,* anticipated a new type of literature which subsumed the philosophical character of the age and merged myth and irony into a "progressive" mode. The future belonged to the analytic spirit, to irony, to prose. The death of poetry had certainly occurred to the Romantics in idea, and Hegel's prediction of it was simply the overt expression of their own despair. Yet against this despair the greater Romantic poets staked their art and often their sanity.

10. R. M. Milnes, *Palm Leaves* (London, 1844).

11. *Von Ähnlichkeit der mittlern englischen und deutschen Dichtkunst* (1777). Cf. Louis Cazamian on French Romanticism: "Le romantisme n'a donc pas été pour la France, comme pour l'Angleterre, un retour facile et naturel à une tradition nationale, selon la pente du tempérament le plus profond" *Essais en Deux Langues* [Paris, 1938], p. 170).

Romantic Poetry and the Genius Loci

> Reason suffered a few demons still to linger, which she chose
> to retain under the guidance of poetry.
>
> —Thomas Warton

It is no longer necessary to protect the Romantic poets from the charge of neoprimitivism. But it may be timely to consider them as fulfilling, in addition to criticizing, the Enlightenment. Their concern with the darker graces of poetry, with the realities of myth and the relation of the poetic and the religious genius, did not mean an unscrutinized use of archaic beliefs. On the contrary, the struggle of the Romantic poets with romance is a moving, intense, and endless one. They knew that light must be fought with light and that the great intellectual movement which preceded them, and in which they continued to participate, could not be reversed. Between the time of Gray and that of Wordsworth—the epoch here considered—the fate of poetry seemed to depend on poetry's revaluation of its founding superstitions. I would like to study one of the most persistent of these, the belief in spirit of place, in a genius loci.[1]

1. For the most convenient summary of the belief, see Andrew Tooke, *The Pantheon of the Heathen Gods,* 1st ed. (1698), Pt. 5, chap. 2, "The Genii." Also, tendentious but important, see Blake's *The Marriage of Heaven and Hell* (1793): "The ancient Poets animated all sensible objects with Gods or Geniuses" and so on. A late but absolutely conventional statement, representing the most common form of the belief, is found in T. L. Peacock, *The Genius of the Thames* (1810), in his note on "the tutelary spirits, that formerly animated the scenes of nature." For the genius idea as it enters English literature, the following may be consulted: E. C. Knowlton, "The Genii of Spenser," *Studies in Philology* 25 (1928): 439–56; D. T. Starnes, "The Figure of Genius in the Renaissance," *Studies in the Renaissance* II (1964): 234–44; and C. S. Lewis, "Genius and Genius," in *Studies in Medieval and Renaissance Literature* (New York, 1966), pp. 169–74. The latter contains an exceptionally clear distinction between genius *sive Natura* and genius as alter ego. No study exists on the fortunes

Returning from Italy in 1741, Gray revisited the monastery of the Grande Chartreuse and inscribed in its album an Alcaic Ode composed in memory of his stay two years earlier. I quote from the opening invocation:

> O Tu severi Religio loci,
> Quocunque gaudes nomine (non leve
> Nativa nam certe fluenta
> Numen habet, veteresque sylvas;
> Praesentiorem et conspicimus Deum
> Per invias rupes. . . .)
> Salve vocanti rite, fesso et
> Da placidam juveni quietem.[2]

In length, subject, and tone, the poem is a genuine inscription.[3] It is addressed to the Spirit of the Place, except that the poet writes "Religio loci" for genius loci[4] to avoid the least hint of superstition and to suggest that the religion is not his but "of the place," although more universal than the particular name might suggest ("Quocunque gaudes nomine").[5] He who pays this ritual

---

of the belief beyond the Renaissance, but Maynard Mack has shown its purified yet amazing hold on Pope in "A Poet in His Landscape: Pope at Twickenham," *From Sensibility to Romanticism,* ed. Frederick W. Hilles and H. Bloom (Oxford, 1965), pp. 3–29, esp. 10–12, 19–21. For German thought and literature there is the splendid entry on "Genie" in *Deutsches Wörterbuch,* by Jakob and Wilhelm Grimm and others.

2. "O Thou, Religion of this stern place, or whatever name pleases Thee (for surely no negligible divinity rules these native streams and ancient forests; and surely we behold God more present amid pathless steeps . . .) hail to Thee! And if I invoke Thee correctly, grant to a weary youth quiet and repose." For a complete text and translation, see *The Complete Poems of Thomas Gray,* ed. H. W. Starr and J. R. Hendrickson (Oxford, 1966), p. 151.

3. On Inscriptions as a genre, cf. my "Wordsworth, Inscriptions, and Romantic Nature Poetry," pp. 206–30 above.

4. Eighteenth century translations of the ode bring this out. "O Thou, the Genius of this Wild Retreat" (Edmund Cartwright, *Poems* [London, 1786], p. 64); "Oh Genius of this hallow'd place" (*European Magazine* 19 (1791): 285.

5. A very old liturgical formula: see E. Norden, *Agnostos Theos* (Berlin, 1913), pp. 143 ff. Cf. Milton's varying of the place name for the seat of inspiration, *Paradise Lost,* 1.6–12. The formula, as Milton and Gray use it, modifies the idea of Christianity as a religio loci or local religion.

tribute ("Salve vocanti rite"), is a stranger yet one who respects the divinity of the region.

In this early poem Gray's attitude toward the genius loci is circumspect. Since it is also a Latin poem, where more liberty might be taken, the scruple is doubly remarkable. Gray seems to abandon such scruples, if we believe Dr. Johnson: *The Bard* incurs the latter's wrath for indulging in "the puerilities of obsolete mythology." Yet Gray remains the most careful of poets: in his devotional poetry and his few epitaphs there is no trace of what the Protestant Enlightenment called "Superstition"—mythological ideas associated with paganism or the Counter-Reformation. A neoclassic decorum makes them resemble, like the Alcaic ode, Universal Prayers. The pagan element, moreover, in such poems as *The Bard,* is clearly a virtuoso development of the personification style common to Gray's time.

Dr. Johnson has, nevertheless, a sure instinct for the problematic. The problem is not myth as such (pagan or Christian) but the bolder vision of poetry it implies. The presence of myth is a sign of poetry's higher destiny, of its link to inspiration and prophecy. Gray's early style avoids more than pagan fictions; it avoids the prophetic, the speaking out. He never spoke out, was Arnold's verdict on him. It is part of the decorum of the Alcaic ode that it mutes the epiphany of the genius loci. Only the odes reprehended by Dr. Johnson began to speak out and to acknowledge the connection of poetry and vision. According to Gray's Nordic and Pindaric odes, true poetry means heroic poetry, high deeds in high style, prophecies and dooms. *The Bard* is one long and ferocious speaking out.

Yet even in Gray's boldest poems there is a reluctance to rouse the English lyre from its torpor. If the *Progress of Poesy,* echoing the Psalms, starts with the opposite impulse—"Awake, Aeolian lyre, awake"[6]—and ends on a note heralding Blake—"O! Lyre divine, what daring Spirit/ Wakes thee now?"—the question reveals the doubt. Can England be the home of a strong-spirited poetry? It promised to be in the time of Shakespeare, Milton, and even Dryden. The Muses, having left Greece for Latium, follow the progress of liberty and seek Albion next (2.3). But the end of

6. Gray himself footnotes the echo to David's Psalms in the 1768 edition. But "Aeolian," as he adds in the note, comes from Pindar.

that epoch seems already at hand. Gray refuses to engage in a reversal of the destiny of poetry in the Enlightenment. In *The Descent of Odin* it is, characteristically, the prophetess' unwillingness to speak which dominates the visionary interview:

> Now my weary lips I close:
> Leave me, leave me to repose.

Now the existence of a genius loci (the "rising Genius" as he was sometimes called) is intrinsically related to vision and prophecy: to determining the destiny of an individual or a nation.[7] We continue to sense this in the Alcaic ode, which expresses a charged if transient moment of encounter, one that made Gray aware of "a road not taken." In comparison, however, with his letters ("Not a precipice, not a torrent, not a cliff, but is pregnant with religion and poetry") and the poetry of Wordsworth and Shelley which it anticipates, Gray's ode is but a formal tribute to the divine Presence working through nature ("Praesentiorem conspicimus Deum"). It will require Wordsworth to truly acknowledge the *visibilia* of the region and to undergo through their hold on his memory something like a conversion.[8] A second ode of Gray's,

7. See, inter alia, Virgil, *Aeneid*, 7.31 ff.; Spenser, *Faerie Queene*, 2.12. 47–48; Milton, *On the Morning of Christ's Nativity*, 19 ff. (where the "parting Genius" is linked to the cessation of the oracles); Thomson, *Liberty*, 4 (esp. the episode of the "Genius of the Deep"); Hölderlin, *Patmos* and *Hymne an den Genius Griechenlands;* Shelley, *The Daemon of the World;* Carlyle, *Sartor Resartus*, "It was his guiding Genius (Dämon) that inspired him; he must go forth and meet his Destiny" (Bk. 2, chap. 5). A genius, of course, is not inevitably "local": Socrates has his familiar *daimon*, comparable to a guardian angel, and the examples cited above from Spenser and Shelley show Genius as demiurge or god of nature. Yet the place associated with the appearance of such a genius is felt to be sacred; the genius is often held to be *ingenium*, or so closely associated with birth (a "natale comes qui temperat astrum," as Horace says) that time and place become charged with significance (fatal or fated births are what mythical stories elaborate); and calling Shakespeare "Sweet Swan of Avon" suggests that the birth of a genius (in the ordinary sense) consecrates the place of which he becomes the genius loci.

8. See *The Prelude*, Bk. 6. The lines referring specifically to the region of the Grande Chartreuse (see also note 11, below) celebrate the theophanic qualities of the place (the "imaginative impulse" from forests, cliffs, and floods that allow us "to look with bodily eyes, and be consoled") and are like a descant on the plainchant of Gray's ode. Shelley's *Mont Blanc* moves, spiritually, in another direction but is not unaware of the "Praesentiorem

On a Distant Prospect of Eton College, will confirm this muting of the figure and visionary implications of the "rising Genius."

In the Eton ode, with its evocation of overarching presences— "Ye distant spires, ye antique towers . . . Henry's holy Shade"— spirit of place again confronts the poet. As in Wordsworth, moreover, the idea of place blends with that of time: what confronts the poet's consciousness is best rendered by *prospect* in the modern sense of the word. Unlike Wordsworth, however, Gray withdraws from envisioning a future that restores a lost happiness. The past is a "distant prospect," and the future, at least the future within the proper realm of speculation, is not open. It is characterized for all men by the same fatality: manhood and the pains of manhood. Vision therefore is but the knowledge of suffering, and there is no point in disturbing those without it. "Why should they know their fate," the poet asks of the "little victims" that play in the shadow of Eton (their Eden).

The inutility of vision is curiously illustrated by the ode's one explicit instance of genius loci personification. Gray's address to the towers, hills, and fields culminates in an invocation to Father Thames, who is asked to identify this new generation of children at play:

> Say, Father THAMES, for thou hast seen
> Full many a sprightly race
> Disporting on thy margent green
> The paths of pleasure trace,
> Who foremost now delight to cleave
> With pliant arm thy glassy wave?

Dr. Johnson remarks tartly that "Father Thames has no better means of knowing than [Gray] himself." Yet Father Thames is presented as a guardian genius of the place and is also therefore its historian: like the Muse in epic poetry, he could tell, having seen the generations as they pass.[9] Homer, moreover, used the device to

conspicimus Deum" tradition or of the habit of entering inscriptions in the Albums of the neighborhood. Cf. Harold Bloom, *Shelley's Mythmaking* (New Haven, 1959), pp. 11 ff.

9. A genius is comonly employed for the historian's function: Francis Coventry in *Penshurst* (1750, see note 30, below) addresses the "Genius of Penshurst" for the same purpose, and Milton had introduced the "Genius of the Wood" into *Arcades* as a similar kind of authority.

number the warriors before Troy, and Gray expects us to understand his development of the topos, which brings into one picture
children at play and soldiers fated to die. But the ultimate pathos
is that as a guardian or father spirit the Thames should be able
to protect the children from the ambush in wait, those murderous
allegorical abstractions which replace the nature personification in
the poem's latter half:

> Lo, in the vale of years beneath
> A griesly troop are seen,
> The painful family of Death . . . .

Yet Father Thames is eloquently mute, there is no formal prosopopeia, and the invocation is purely rhetorical and does not expect an answer. An inauthentic figure of speech becomes an authentic figure of silence.

The muteness of the genius loci is even more significant in the
light of tradition. In his turn toward pathos and away from the
sublime or prophetic occasion, Gray extends (as is his wont) a
literary commonplace. Father Thames appears at the end of
Pope's *Windsor Forest* dressed like Virgil's Father Tiber and,
like him, a prophetic *deus ipse loci*.[10] When his prophecy threatens to overflow the decorum of a georgic poem, Pope intervenes
("Here cease thy Flight") and repeats Virgil's famous apology
("Enough for me, that to the listening Swains/ First in these Fields
I sung the Sylvan Strains"; cf. *Georgics* 4.563 ff.). This would be
sufficient to establish a precedent, but the formal tension be-
tween higher and lower styles had a greater English master than
Pope.

The conclusion of *Windsor Forest* recalls the "uncouth Swain"
of Milton's *Lycidas,* and in that poem also the prophetic threatens
to transgress the pastoral mode. Milton's progress of mourners
reaches a first climax with the appearance of Camus, the river god
and genius of Cambridge, who speaks but a single line: "Ah! Who
hath reft . . . my dearest pledge?" The real climax, the prophetic
admonition or "dread voice," is reserved for a Christian tutelary
spirit—St. Peter. His words, as if already heralding the Apocalypse, "shrink" the streams that murmur through Milton's Sicilian

10. *Aeneid* 7.31 ff., and note 7, above.

elegy. Yet Milton allows the pastoral mode to reestablish itself and keeps the incident of his friend's death from forcing him prematurely into the visionary's role.

Camus or St. Peter? Milton's "long chosing" ends on the side of the latter, with the Judeo-Christian rather than Greek tradition. The relative muteness of Camus (which may be compared with the real muteness of Gray's Father Thames) and the impotence of the invoked troop of nature spirits anticipate this choice. Yet Milton is a divided person. His lines in the Nativity ode on the "parting Genius" left their imprint on almost every major poet of the following century.[11] The idea of English poetry is associated for him with the idea of a nature poetry transformed from the classics, and at the highest level with Spenserian romance.[12] When, in *Lycidas,* he asks the Sicilian Muse to "call the Vales, and bid them hither cast/ Their Bells and Flowrets of a thousand hues," the "hither" is England—English poetry as well as the resting place of the dead poet whom he promotes to be the "Genius of the shore." He wants an English genius for an English place. "Remembrance oft shall haunt the shore" is Collins's extension of the classical conceit in his lament on "Druid" Thomson.

English tradition in the seventeenth and eighteenth centuries concentrates on how to create a native poetry which would express the special destiny of the nation. The poetical genius should reflect the genius loci, the spirit of England's religion, history, and countryside. From Milton through Thomson, Gray, Collins, and

11. "It is usually thought that by Pope's time the nymphs have departed, leaving no addresses; but this judgment is not altogether correct: the 'Genius' Milton sees 'parting,' Pope sees persisting as a 'Genius of the Place,' who continues to embody that intuition of a mysterious life in things which for another two hudred years his descendants will also embody, in a succession of changing forms, from ancient mariner and old leech-gatherer to scholar gypsy, Mr. Apollinax, and the cartoons of Charles Addams" (Maynard Mack, "Pope at Twickenham," p. 10). For direct allusions to the "parting Genius," see, e.g., Thomas Warton, Ode 7 ("Sent to a Friend on His Leaving a Favorite Village in Hampshire"); and James Beattie, *The Minstrel,* 2.48. When Wordsworth visits the Grande Chartreuse and fears that the French Revolution will dispossess this natural temple, he imagines voices of lament and admonition coming from nature: "are they by the parting Genius sent / Unheard till now and to be heard no more?" (*The Prelude,* ed. E. de Selincourt and H. Darbishire [Oxford, 1959], p. 556).

12. The marriage of the Thames and the Medway (*Faerie Queene,* 4.11) could have been a prototype for Milton's procession of rivers in *Lycidas.*

the Romantics, the idea of a Progress of Poetry from Greece or the Holy Land to Britain is essential:

> The Muses, still with freedom found,
> Shall to thy happy coast repair.[13]

Blake is "English Blake"; and Keats's *Hyperion,* like Wordsworth's *Prelude,* is still under the influence of this largest of Enlightenment clichés: the migration of the spirit of poetry and of liberty from East to West.[14]

The spiritual map of eighteenth century England is, of course, a complicated one and should not be simplified. It seems certain, however, that the Protestant Enlightenment—the powerful combination of an intellectual and a religious movement—incited a new and prophetic consciousness in the vocation it wished to demystify: the vocation of poetry. I do not mean, by this consciousness, certain enthusiasms peculiar to the Age of Reason—nationalistic georgics on English agriculture, commerce, science, and liberty. Your sage and serious poet was concerned with something different, which forced him into despair or prophetic hope.

13. Thomson, "Rule, Britannia!" *The Masque of Alfred* (1740).

14. For Blake, see Northrop Frye, *Fearful Symmetry,* pp. 172–77, and my "Blake and the Progress of Poesy," pp. 193–205 above. For Keats, E. B. Hungerford, *The Shores of Darkness* (1941), and R. H. Griffith, "The Progress Pieces of the Eighteenth Century," *Texas Review* 5 (1920): 218–29, esp. 227 f. The opening of *The Prelude,* where Wordsworth discusses the epic subjects he had considered, also reflects the link between the progress of poetry and liberty. For the earlier history of the concept, see Irwin Primer, "The Progress Piece in the English Literature of the Seventeenth and Eighteenth Centuries," Ph.D. diss., Yale University, 1960; A. L. Williams, *Pope's Dunciad* (Baton Rouge, 1955), pp. 42–48; J. Hagstrum, *The Sister Arts* (Chicago, 1958), pp. 301–06; and René Wellek, *The Rise of English Literary History* (1941 and 1965), chap. 3. Wellek shows that the idea is fundamental to the beginnings of English literary historiography but full of variations and contradictions. What remains constant is the growing importance of the idea of a genius of the age or genius of place, as of various climate theories; the close, but not unchallenged, association of liberty and letters; and the description of a "Genius of the East" from which, in the case of Warton's *History,* all strongly figurative and imaginative conceptions are supposed to be derived via an East-West movement. For a second Progress theory, on a North-South axis, see Thor J. Beck, *Northern Antiquities in French Learning and Literature* (New York, 1934).

Could poetry outlive the Enlightenment, when it was perfectly clear that the great works of the past had been based on "Superstition"? The thought that a new poetry might be founded, peculiarly English, both great and enlightened, enchanting and rational, inspires the hope that culminates in Romanticism.

The Elizabethan Age had already pointed to this synthesis of imagination and reason.[15] Between the time of Milton and Gray, however, a formula arose which anticipated the new poetry more completely. It suggested that the demonic, or more than rational, energy of imagination might be tempered by its settlement in Britain—its naturalization, as it were, on British soil. This conversion of the demon meant that the poetical genius would coincide with the genius loci of England; and this meant, in practice, a meditation on English landscape as alma mater—where landscape is storied England, its legends, history, and rural-reflective spirit. The poem becomes, in a sense, a seduction of the poetical genius by the genius loci: the latter invites—subtly compels—the former to live within via media charms.[16]

The formula is strongest in local poetry, which took the scheme of *Cooper's Hill* and added to it a Miltonic observer, melancholy or carefree or vacillating in mood. It is also seen in the pleasures of imagination poem, where a moody poet finds "what will suffice" (dark or joyful) in a nature he half creates. In many of these poems there is a tension between the high Miltonic mode and the vernacular, because the aim is to create a new middle or georgic style which would reflect this accommodation of the visionary temperament to an English milieu. Thomson's *Seasons* are therefore especially important: they attempt a direct cultural translation of the *Georgics*. The brilliant yet simple idea of changing Virgil's didactic fourfold into a seasonal fourfold allowed a varied if still cultic celebration of the English countryside. Season and weathers, not pagan gods, are now the presiding deities of the natural cycle. Thomson's popularization of these *dii minores* opened the way for some of the finest romantic odes from Collins to Keats.

15. Wellek, *English Literary History,* esp. pp. 192 ff.
16. P. S. Wood, in "Native Elements in English Neo-Classicism," *Modern Philology* 24 (1926): 201–08, describes the political aspects encouraging a similar ideal.

Looking back once more to the Eton ode—this subtlest of prospect poems—we see that the formula merges with an ultimate issue: who the genius or tutelary power of human progress may be. The ode is about the human condition, not only poetry; but it is also about poetry's role in aiding the human condition. Gray makes us aware of the exposed nature of man and questions whether any tuition can ultimately be of use. He puts in doubt the visionary hopes of both science (learning) and art. Though he evokes an English landscape shadowed by ancient and protective presences—at Eton, "grateful Science still adores/Her Henry's Holy Shade"—he suggests that these protectors, these genii loci, are powerless. There is, for instance, that "progress" of lazar-house spooks (ll. 61–90) compared to which that other "progress" of science is spectral. Poetry fares no better. Coleridge, in the Dejection ode, accepts his exclusion from joy by thinking of the joy of others, but Gray thinks of his absence of bliss as the portion of man and as something poetry cannot alter. This is made very clear by what happens to the ode's ritualism. Though Gray addresses the "shades" of Eton three times, the near anacoluthon of the first stanza and the fact that the opening invocations do not culminate in formal petition subvert the ritual structure and prepare for the muted question to Father Thames. Does not this impotence of the ritual form reflect on visionary poetry as a whole? The poet, like the other shades, seems a mere ghost in the landscape, a guardian genius unable to help:

> Alas, regardless of their doom
> The little victims play!

It is not that he has no vision (if hindsight is vision), but vision cannot avail and engenders at best pathos and dramatic irony.

If Gray, then, does not attempt to reverse the fate of poetry, it is not because he accepts the thesis that it is doomed by the Enlightenment or some other progress. His position may be termed religious: man is too radically exposed to find shelter anywhere but in "The bosom of his Father and his God." The advancement of learning does not ensure, and the recession of poetry does not prejudice, salvation. Yet Gray's attitude, though religious, is also historically self-conscious. That man is naked may be a religious and universal truth, but that science and poetry are of little avail is not equally true of all ages. Gray suggests, as is well known, that poetry played a more authentic role in the previous century. He declares that the fire that was holy in Shakespeare and Milton is now in eclipse or a questionable flame. So pronounced is his modesty toward himself and his age that he opposes greatness to goodness and leaves genius, including the poetical genius, in doubt of its justification.[17] It is no longer death to hide one's talent. This recessiveness, this almost theological self-incrimination, harmonizes easily with the neoclassical thesis we have been discussing: that the age demands something other than genius—in fact, an accommodation of genius to the genius loci. Collins will give the thesis a stormier, but also more hopeful, embodiment. We turn to him and initially to the *Ode to Evening*.

Mr. Wimsatt's essay on Romantic nature imagery discerned a problem of structure where many readers had tended simply to approve or condemn. In certain Romantic poems we find landscape playing a dual role: the poet represents it as animated both by its own and by a transcendent spirit. "We have a double personification conjured from one nature, one landscape, in a wedding that approximates fusion."[18] Collins's *Ode to Evening* provokes a similar question: "Is Evening a divine person who governs the scene or is she immanent in the scene itself?"[19]

The answer is that Evening has a double nature modeled on that of the genius loci. As spirit of place, she is both spirit and place. She is also, as the poem makes clear, a divine guide ("Now teach me," "Then lead me") and a wisdom figure who outlives temporal change (ll. 41 ff.). Collins's Evening is virtually the guide, guardian, and nurse of the poet's moral being. These functions belonged preeminently to the genius loci.

Yet, as Mr. Wimsatt points out, referring to Ruskin, the Greek gods of nature were depicted as distinct from their element ("This something, this great Water Spirit, I must not confuse with the

17. See the ending of *The Progress of Poesy,* and *Stanzas to Mr. Bentley*.
18. W. K. Wimsatt, Jr., "The Structure of Romantic Nature Imagery" (1949), republished in *The Verbal Icon* and elsewhere.
19. Martin Price, *To the Palace of Wisdom* (New York, 1964), pp. 375–76.

waves, which are only its body") and from the viewer's mind (that "curious web of hesitating sentiment, pathetic fallacy, and wandering fancy").[20] Milton's Camus and Pope's and Gray's Father Thames are such distinct persons, decorated sometimes with the symbols of their state, yet separate and confronting powers—in Gray less so than in Pope or Milton. And in Collins the "curious web" weaving together person and element is complete; the theme of weaving may even enter directly through the imagery and the poem's winding progress. If Collins is inspired by the ancient concept of the genius loci, he is differently inspired. The problem of understanding a new type of poetry remains, though we may have found what is common to both types, what is restructured.

The new poetry projects a sacred marriage: that of the poet's genius with the genius loci. To invoke the ghost in the landscape is only preparatory to a deeper, ceremonial merging of the poet's spirit and spirit of place—hence the new structure of fusion. Poetry is to be attuned with this place and this time. Teach me to sing to you with your own music, says Collins. Let mine be thine, and thine mine. The "musing slow," which almost deprives the main connectives ("now," "when," "then") of temporality and delays the formal petition, emphasizes a calm extension of poetical thought which suits the stealing stillness of the spirit invoked. The delicate Spenserian syntax and the weaving in and out of the measured verse evoke a dance like that of the Hours, a ritual as well as temporal progress which draws (like a marriage procession) a "gradual dusky veil" around the scene. The poem's probable source in conventional odes to an evening star, which guides lover to beloved in the dangerous dark,[21] may also help to induce this prothalamic effect.[22]

20. See "Of Classical Landscape," in *Modern Painters,* chapter 13. Ruskin's positive Hellenism on this point should be compared with Coleridge's attack, in the name of Hebrew poetry, on Greek "godkins" and "godesslings." Cf. M. H. Abrams, *The Mirror and the Lamp* (1953), 10.5.

21. *To the Evening Star* was a well-known "idyllium" attributed to Moschus. It was often translated and imitated in the eighteenth century, although the examples I know are later than Collins's ode. Cf. Spenser, *Epithalamion,* 11. 282 ff.

22. When Collins ends his first invocation with "I hail / Thy genial lov'd Return," the stock word *genial* may mean "congenial" or may refer us to its original derivation from the genius who guards and fructifies the marriage bed. Cf. Spenser, *Epithalamion,* 11. 398 ff.

A literalist might object that Evening is not a spirit of place. He would be wrong: Collins's Evening is distinctly Occidental in its gradual advent. Evening is a regent ("Thy Springs," "Thy darkening Vale"), and the region governed is less a specific country than the West, the *Abendland*. It is the Westering of the Spirit which is hailed and which in the *Ode to Peace* issues explicitly in a sacred marriage: "Come to grace thy western Isle. . . . With Him [British Honor] for ever wed!"

But the literalist is right insofar as Collins has conflated the genius loci notion with that of the spirit of the age. Collins is evoking, in the exact sense of calling forth, the possibility of a Hesperidean Muse—inspired by the archaic *numen* of nature poetry yet genuinely expressive of the ideals of polite society. In the coda (the obscurest part of an intricate poem), therefore, the four seasons may represent passions transformed into Fancy, Friendship, Science, and Peace by the civilizing influence of the Evening Muse.

That the *Ode to Evening* foresees a "holier reign" in which an Eastern genius is wedded to a Western region is also shown by subtle amalgams. Eastern, we should recall, can imply both Asiatic and Attic. Thus when we read, near the beginning of the ode, of the "bright-hair'd Sun" that "Sits in yon western Tent," we recognize an allusion to the biblical verse depicting the sun as a "bridegroom coming out of his chamber," but with a 180° westerly conversion of scene and mood.[23] When, similarly, toward the end of the opening strophes, we read of Evening's "Dewy Fingers," we recognize the Homeric "rosy finger'd dawn," again westernized. The capstone evidence, however, comes from a poem directly on the subject of poetry. In the *Ode on the Poetical Character,* the beautiful if extravagant image of Milton's "Ev'ning Ear" contrasts with that of the "rich-hair'd Youth of Morn" to suggest once more this Westering movement, but which by Collins's time is feared to have lost contact with the source. The final scene is upon us, an alienation of poetic power; the "gradual dusky veil" seems to have "curtain'd close . . . from ev'ry future View" Milton's and Spenser's visionary landscapes.

Thus an alliance of the poetical genius with a Western or English climate remains doubtful. The Elizabethans, and Milton as

23. Ps. 19:5–6; cf. Milton, *On the Morning of Christ's Nativity,* 26.

323

the last in that tradition, may have achieved it; and the *Ode to Evening* tries to summon the hope once more. Wordsworth still talks of Milton's "Union of Tenderness and Imagination," as Collins at one point praises Shakespeare's "beauteous Union" of *"Tuscan* Fancy, and *Athenian* Strength."[24] Yet in his first publication, the *Persian Eclogues* (1742), Collins admits that in Oriental poetry "there is an Elegancy and Wildness of Thought which recommends all their Composition; and our Geniuses are as much too cold for the Entertainment of such Sentiments, as our Climate is for their Fruits and Spices." His next publication, the *Verses to Sir Thomas Hanmer* (1743), expresses an admiration for Shakespeare somewhat in conflict with the Enlightenment scheme of the gradual improvement of the arts:

> Each rising Art by slow Gradation moves,
> Toil builds on Toil, and Age on Age improves.
> The Muse alone unequal dealt her Rage,
> And grac'd with noblest Pomp her earliest Stage.

The *Ode to Fear* explicitly recognizes poetic power as daimonic and addresses Fear as a genie in the primitive classical (and Oriental) sense:[25]

> Dark Pow'r, with shudd'ring meek submitted Thought
> Be mine, to read the Visions old,
> Which thy awak'ning Bards have told.

Even the *Ode to Evening,* that late prothalamion which celebrates "gentlest Influence" and delays by its intricate turns the decline into darkness, contains a moment where a glint of the demon appears:

24. See Lamb's report in *The Letters of Charles Lamb,* ed. E. V. Lucas (London, 1935), 1:246; and Collins's *Verses to Sir Thomas Hanmer,* 1. 60.

25. "In the *Odes* of William Collins the 'Thou' seems to me always a type of daemon, most obviously so in the *Ode to Fear"* (Angus Fletcher, *Allegory, The Theory of a Symbolic Mode* [Ithaca, 1964], p. 51, note 1). Fletcher's seminal book shows the demonic basis of allegory and personification. His first chapter, "The Daemonic Agent," is especially relevant to the present study. For the ritual sources of personification in Collins, cf. Kurt Schlüter, *Die Englische Ode* (Bonn, 1964), chap. 6; for the progress of "horror-personification" in the eighteenth century, see P. M. Spacks, *The Insistence of Horror* (Cambridge, Mass., 1962).

> Then let me rove some wild and heathy Scene,
> Or find some Ruin 'midst its dreary Dells,
>   Whose Walls more awful nod
>   By thy religious Gleams.[26]

Collins rarely breaks through to the new poetry. His personifications are divinities, principalities, Blake's later "giant forms," which seduce or compel our imagination. He returns to an archaizing mode, like so many of the poets succeeding him: Smart, Macpherson, Chatterton, Blake, even Coleridge. The genius of Poetry becomes a genie once more, a compelling psychic force that works its own salvation in a man, and often as an adversary to accepted values. The poetry now written believes in a formula it violates—the progressivist's formula, which envisages a domestication of the "daemon of poetry"[27] on British soil. The Ossianic songs, for example, are the genie idea gone wild, dead warriors or dead memories rising up everywhere from spots associated with them, compulsive myths in ghostly converse with the faltering identity of belated poets. A Macpherson spirit is a Collinstype demonic abstraction with a Gaelic habitation and name.

Yet the demon odes of Collins remain within the sophisticated tradition of the sublime ode. Caught in the middle, their personifications are "forcible *and* picturesque,"[28] the first term pointing to the demonic and the second to the sophisticating element. So in eighteenth century poetic theory there is a constant vacillation between the Longinian sublime, which emphasizes "ravish't ears" and "ravish't eyes," and the pathetic or picturesque, which is indebted to Milton's *L'Allegro* and *Il Penseroso,* poems that begin by dismissing the demonic machinery of the sublime style while raising from it (like a free-ranging butterfly out of its spooky cocoon) new and airy personifications.

Collins does teach us, however, that the generic subject of the sublime ode (as distinct from that of individual poems) is the

26. Collins later changes this stanza, perhaps to remove the darker suggestion.

27. "This man is the very Daemon of poetry, or he has lighted on a treasure hid for ages" (Gray on Macpherson, to T. Warton, July 1760).

28. My italics. Said by Collins of Cooper and cited by A. S. P. Woodhouse, "Collins and the Creative Imagination," *Studies in English by Members of the University College* (Toronto, 1931), p. 100, note 20.

poetical character: its fate in an Age of Reason. The odes are generally addressed to invited powers and, like the gothic novel, raise the ghosts they shudder at. Their histrionic, sometimes hysterical, character stems from the fact that they are indeed theatrical machines, evoking a power of vision they fear to use. Collins, like a sorcerer's apprentice, is close to being overpowered by the spirit he summons:

> Ah *Fear!* Ah frantic *Fear!*
> I see, I see Thee near.
> I know thy hurried Step, thy haggard Eye!
> Like Thee I start, like Thee disorder'd fly.

We easily recognize this as a displaced or heightened mode of ritual identification.[29] But that is the point: where there is ritual there should be a divinity and a votary, and Collins had the courage to invoke those "Divine Emotions" which art must raise but the Enlightenment wished to repress.

Toward the latter half of the eighteenth century the main options before the ambitious, nonsatirical poet were the sublime ode and local poetry. As in Gray's ode and even Collins's, or such poems as Thomas Warton's "On the Approach of Summer" (Ode 12), the two types could mingle. What helped lyric and narrative genres to combine was the formula of the poet guided by the genius loci. In many poems the mythological assumptions are felt only in the ritual syntax, that sublimated compulsion which aids the narrative line: lead me, teach me, guide my steps, let me be thine. A leading genius of this kind is never far away; the only question is its relation to the poet's mind, its benignant or demonic influence. Francis Coventry's *Penshurst,* a topographical poem from the middle of the century,[30] shows the formula in its explicit form.

The poet begins with an address to the genius loci:

29. Collins is not unwittily adapting Horace's "Si vis me flere." If you want me to be terrified, you yourself must show terror. His two odes on fear and pity treat of the "tragic" emotions, those closest to sacred or ritualistic drama and hence most closely concerned with participation.

30. First published, 1750. Also in Dodsley's *Collection,* 4.50 ff., from which I print my text.

> Genius of Penshurst old!
> Who saw'st the birth of each immortal oak,

begs permission to enter the sacred realm:

> O suffer me with sober tread
> To enter on thy holy shade;

recalls the spirit of liberty which is part of the spirit of the place:

> Here thoughtful-walking Liberty
> Remembers Britons once were free
>
> . . . .
>
> Ere yet their *Lares* they forsook,
> And lost the genuine British look,

recalls the spirit of poetry, Genius and Fancy merging in this poet-haunted domain:

> Come, friendly Genius! lead me round
> Thy sylvan haunts and magic ground;
> Point every spot of hill or dale,
> And tell me, as we tread the vale,
> "Here mighty Dudley once wou'd rove . . .
> . . . There looser Waller . . .
> . . . And Philip. . . . "

and reaches a rapturous climax as we approach the seat of inspiration, the Dodonian oak planted the day Sidney was born:

> Hark! I hear the echoes call,
> Hark! the rushing waters fall;
> Lead me to the green retreats,
> Guide me to the Muses' seats
>
> . . . .
>
> What Genius points to yonder oak?
> What rapture does my soul provoke?

Some two hundred verses later, having toured house and garden, Coventry ends with a last salute to the genial soil, mother of heroes and poets, which (we now learn) has been the place of his first poetic attempt, these very lines.

Wordsworth will also begin with a local poem—"The Vale of Esthwaite" (ca. 1787). It was encouraged, moreover, by a school exercise written at Hawkshead, which has some interest as a clear if commonplace expression of the Enlightenment theory of history. Thinking about the founding of his school, Wordsworth sees the "Power of EDUCATION" rising to eulogize the joint reign of Protestantism and Science:

> Science with joy saw Superstition fly
> Before the lustre of Religion's eye;
> With rapture she beheld Britannia smile,
> Clapp'd her strong wings, and sought the cheerful isle.[31]

Superstition will reappear, with other demon personifications, in "The Vale of Esthwaite." It is clear that Wordsworth wished to see Esthwaite as a home for the enlightened imagination. Yet apocalyptic and superstitious fancies lead him astray: he enters a ghostly "world of shades" influenced by the imagery of Collins's *Ode to Fear*. The spirit of the valley, its true genius loci, is undetermined; it vacillates between benign and demonic. The poet appears as a quester in search of a leading genius—his own identity. Which of the nature spirits haunting the valley is *his* guide? The early manuscripts of what was to be *The Prelude* reflect the same dilemma:

> Yes there are genii which when they would form
> [A favor'd spirit] open out the clouds
> As with the touch of lightning seeking him
> With gentle visitation. Others use
> [Less homely?] interference ministry
> Of grosser kind & of their school was I[32]

31. *The Poetical Works of William Wordsworth,* ed. E. de Selincourt, (Oxford, 1940), 1:260.
32. *The Prelude,* ed. de Selincourt and Darbishire, p. 638. Cf. Akenside's "Genii" in the opening of *The Pleasures of Imagination* (1744):

> Be present, all ye Genii, who conduct
> The wandering footsteps of the youthful bard,
> New to your springs and shades; who touch his ear
> With finer sounds; who heighten to his eye
> The bloom of Nature, and before him turn
> The gayest, happiest attitude of things.

[1.25–30]

But the identity crisis is perhaps that of poetry itself. Wordsworth would not be so centrally concerned with the character of his leading genius unless prompted by the hope that an enlightened poetry—the union of poetical genius with English spirit of place—was possible. This hope, this union, is the very "consummation" for which his poetry aims to be the "spousal verse." The metaphor of a holy marriage is explicit in the prospectus of his ambitions prefixed to the 1814 *Excursion* but which originally climaxed his greatest local poem, "Home at Grasmere." Wed the human mind to nature, and you will find paradise "A simple produce of the common day." The spirit is sufficed, the need for fictions dispelled, the burden of the mystery lifted. This is the *Wordsworthian* Enlightenment.

Thus Wordsworth refuses to renew archaic modes. An unghostly poetry is born, a true vernacular, "words that speak of nothing more than what we are." He never abandons the idea that England can provide a homecoming for the poetical spirit: his poems remain an encounter with English spirit of place. Yet the difference between Wordsworth and the archaizing poets is not as absolute as it seems. At the end of *Vala,* Blake describes the moment of apocalypse, when Mystery is finally consumed: "Where is the Spectre of Prophecy? where is the delusive Phantom?/Departed. . . . The dark Religions are departed & Sweet Science reigns." This is as triumphant a statement as the Enlightenment ever produced. Blake is ready to disenchant himself, like Prospero at the end of *The Tempest,* and even to suggest a parallel between all prophecy (his included) and the "parting Genius" exorcized by Milton. In Blake as in Wordsworth, vision plots the end of vision: it desires to be consummated by realities.

What difference is there, then, between the two poets? It is a

---

But Akenside's use of the word still echoes pictorial tradition, where "genii" are often the attendant or subordinate spirits (occasionally *putti*) surrounding the main figure. Thomson, in *Liberty* (1735), can use the word in its original sense of tutelary spirits ("earth, forsook/ By her best Genii, lay to Demons foul,/ And unchain'd Furies, an abandon'd prey") and in its extended, pictorial sense ("The native Genii, round her [Britain] radiant smiled"). When Lessing, in *Wie die Alten den Tod gebildet,* calls the winged boy holding a torch upside down a "Genius," he blends these senses. It is exceedingly hard, in eighteenth century poetry, and even at times in Shelley's poetry, to distinguish a picturesque from a mythopoeic conception.

329

difference in their response to a common problem: if poetry is Oriental in spirit, and the genius of the West is on the side of Enlightenment, how can poetry survive? Blake and Wordsworth agree on one thing: they reject the halfway house of neoclassical style, its temperate Orientalism, its endless delicate compromises between the demands of reason and imagination. But while Blake adopts and seeks to rationalize an aggressively Eastern style (his poetry is a veritable Battle of the Genii), Wordsworth creates a new and distinctly Hesperidean mode—deeply reflective, journeying constantly to the sources of consciousness. There are no ghosts, no giant forms, no genii in the mature Wordsworth. He is haunted by a "Presence which is not to be put by," but it is a ghost without a ghost's shape, not a specter but an intensely local and numinous self-awareness. The spirit of poetry survives in both Wordsworth and Blake, wherever "The very sunshine spread upon the dust/Is beautiful," or where "The Sky is an immortal Tent builded by the Sons of Los."

East and West (or South and North) are not necessarily points on a map. The Romantics, indeed, as distinct from the generation that goes from Gray and Collins to Blake, tend to consider the Westering of the Spirit less a geographical event than a development within the individual consciousness. Theirs is mainly a spiritual topography. Blake is a complex intermediate figure who transforms the previous generation's mythology of history into a systematic topography of the human imagination. "Albion" and "Jerusalem" are converging states of the soul. But the form of his complex machinery—of "Albion," "Jerusalem," and similar representations—is not clear without reference to the historical vision that inspired poets from Gray to Wordsworth: the union, as in the Renaissance but even more intense and conscious, of the prophetic East and the "western isle," of the Poetical Genius and England's genius loci.

The history of English literature since the Renaissance suggests a continuous process of demystification. Thomas Warton observed of the Reformation that "Truth propagates Truth, and the mantle of mystery was removed not only from religion but from literature."[33] This is a statement both Blake and Wordsworth could

33. *History of English Poetry* (1774–81), sec. 61.

support. There may be lapses or relapses, but they do not affect the "great stream of tendency."

Whether literature, to be demystified, must also be demythologized has never been resolved, however. And with respect to myth and personification, there have clearly been several Enlightenments: the first an era of "civilized superstition,"[34] which began with the Elizabethans but which the Augustans refined and Gray's scruples still attest to; and the Wordsworthian Enlightenment, which attempts an unghostly and entirely "Western" kind of visionariness. For Wordsworth personification may be trivial, but it is not innocent. Collins had restored the psychological and ritual link between it and the demonic persona.

A third kind of demystification is easy to mistake for mystification, because it works from within a revival of Romance and of the damonic Persona. Blake is its great exponent, but Coleridge takes its part in the original plan of *Lyrical Ballads* ("my endeavours should be directed to persons and characters supernatural, or at least romantic"),[35] while Shelley and Keats develop it mainly from Elizabethan sources. Its meaning is best approached through a short synopsis of the original concept of personification, which Collins helped to revive.

The Persona, in Roman times, was the mask worn by actors; but we know that similar masks were used in initiation ceremonies to represent gods or heroes or deified father spirits. There is evidence that divine masks of this kind were set in the fields as tutelary objects of worship; hence, perhaps, a link to pastoral poetry and the theme of the tomb in the fields. There existed, moreover, ancestral masks called *imagines,* which were kept in the home as a guardian influence and were used to impersonate ancestors at funeral rites. Thus personification is at least distantly related to the ritual assumption of god or ancestor via his mask.[36]

---

34. Ibid.

35. *Biographia Literaria* (1817), chap. 14.

36. C. Kerenyi in "Man and Mask" (*Spiritual Disciplines, Papers from the Eranos Yearbooks* 4 [1960]) brings evidence for masks worshipped in wood and field and describes the masks as "creating a relation between the living and the dead" and in many cases an "encounter" with a father archetype. "The human face—otherwise the vehicle of individual features of *personality,* as this unique entity is named by a shift in meaning of the Latin word for mask, *persona*—is here the form in which the universal and

How much weight the Persona has shed when we consider the current use of the term! Of the Enlightenments so far described, the first trivialized it by the extensive use of personification-allegory for picturesque ends, while the second, or Wordsworthian Enlightenment, sent it underground. For examples of the heavy persona we must return to the Renaissance. The revival of antiquity included a passion for masque, masquerade, pageant, emblem, and *imagines*.[37] Lyric poetry was not unaffected by this: it absorbed such operatic features as ritual exordiums, allegorical persons, processional structure, and pictorialism. Not until Romantic poetry, and then chiefly in Wordsworth, do the longer forms of lyric poetry overcome this operatic style. In other countries, France for example, it takes even longer to "purify the words of the tribe." We think of the rhetorical inflation of a Victor Hugo, the *classicisme noir* of a Baudelaire, and the influence of Wagner. When, in the most original poetry of the 1850s, Nerval's "Il Desdichado" begins:

> Je suis le Ténébreux, le Veuf, l'Inconsolé,
> Le Prince d'Acquitaine à la tour abolie

we still feel as if an actor had stepped forward and begun his aria. The person who speaks is in costume, with his heraldic lute that bears "le soleil noir de la mélancolie."

In Wordsworth, an exceedingly undramatic poet, the problem of Persona arises only surreptitiously. Demonic confrontations take place as usurpations, as waylayings—great moments which the poet records but which do not alter his purpose. One such waylaying is imagination "rising up" to halt the mental traveler of

---

collective are manifested." For the *imagines maiorum* and their role in funeral ceremonies, see Polybius, *History,* 6.35.5. (Scipio, in the famous dream recorded by Cicero and preserved via Macrobius' *Commentary,* recognizes his father Africanus by the latter's likeness to the *imago* in the house). Cf. F. M. Cornford, *From Religion to Philosophy* (1912), pp. 106–08, and Jane Harrison, *Themis* (1912), chap. 8, for the relation between father archetype and local demon.

37. Cf. Warton's description of the mythomania of the Elizabethan Age in sec. 61 of the *History*. For France, see Jean Rousset, *La Littérature de l'âge baroque en France* (Paris, 1954); and for Germany, "Allegorie und Trauerspiel," in Walter Benjamin, *Ursprung des deutschen Trauerspiels* (Berlin, 1928).

1804, the poet in the process of completing his autobiography *(Prelude* 6.525). Imagination here is exactly like genie or kelpie confusing the wanderer in some lonely place. A second self rises up, challenging the basis of his poem and the very project of his life.[38]

The marriage of genius and genius loci (of imagination and nature) remains, therefore, precarious. A demonic agent—bardic, prophetic, ancestral—is never far away. A central incident in "The Vale of Esthwaite" reveals this spectral figure, "on one branded arm he bore / What seem'd the poet's harp of yore," who leads the fledgling poet into "Helvellyn's inmost womb" where he is initiated.[39] *Tintern Abbey,* the perfect instance of a meditation on English landscape as alma mater, still shows Wordsworth's mind moving toward a ghostly figure, that of the Hermit. The most striking appearance of the Persona, however, is in *Resolution and Independence,* where that "oldest man . . . that ever wore gray hairs" materializes suddenly in the landscape. Here is another Father Thames, an ancestral figure, virtually prophetic, the genius of the place, and even associated with waters. "His voice to me was like a stream / Scarce heard." That Wordsworth seems to have drawn, consciously or not, on biblical rather than classical sources makes no difference. The situation is that of visionary encounter.[40]

What modern literary theory tends to call an epiphany involves a confrontation with a second self in the form of genius loci or Persona. There is a djinee in every well-wrought urn.[41] Ironically enough, these concepts of Genius and Persona have practically disappeared because of the very success of the Wordsworthian Enlightenment. We no longer require a Romance or Eastern mode to express visionary encounters. Wordsworth writes Westerns only. Compared to *Resolution and Independence,* Cole-

38. For an extended discussion of the incident, see my *Wordsworth's Poetry, 1787–1814* (New Haven, 1964), pp. 39–48.

39. *Poetical Works of William Wordsworth,* ed. de Selincourt, 1:277–78.

40. Cf. my *Wordsworth's Poetry,* pp. 202–03, 272–73. A remark of Kerenyi's is intriguing: "The Greeks had many legends concerning the father role of the river gods; in the marriage rite the river god preceded the bridegroom. Ultimately, the . . . mask became that of Father Oceanos himself, the Homeric 'source of all things' " (ibid.).

41. I borrow this phrase from the title of an essay by W. J. Ong (see *The Barbarian Within* [New York, 1962]).

ridge's *Ancient Mariner* is Eastern: an open vision of demonic agency centering imaginatively and morally on the genius loci. The Mariner in his ancientness is the admonitory persona; the world he describes is demonic; his drama is that of "Compulsion," of a journey in which the self is kidnapped by various genii and made to suffer a number of spectral confrontations; the crime is basically one against the genius loci;[42] and the punishment, a homeless voyaging, fits the crime. This account by no means exhausts even the grosser structure of the poem but does suggest its inner relation to the contrary poetics of *Resolution and Independence*.

Yet just as Wordsworth effects a rhetorical and spiritual purification, so the *Ancient Mariner* is a light and winged thing compared to Spenser's "Faerie," which already volatilized heavier medieval machines. A further essay on "The Discrimination of Enlightenments" would be needed to show the play (in Huizinga's sense) of allegorical Romance in the poetry of Shelley, Keats, and Blake.[43] Not, perhaps, until Wallace Stevens does the Wordsworthian tradition triumph over its rival mode. Even so, it may be doubted that poetry in the allegorical or mythological mode is a thing of the past. That would be making the mistake of the Age of Reason all over again. There is, for instance, a purely internal deepening of the spirit which forces poets to make contact with transcended forms. Keats's *Hyperion,* with its two generations of gods, heavier and lighter, seems to mimic directly the Progress of Poetry we have traced. Yet Apollo, the new god, moves with alarming speed from the dawn of indolent sensation to the overpowering second dawn of prophecy. The epoch of a new sensibility, in which the burden of the mystery is lifted, lasts no

42. Coleridge's gloss at the end of Part 5 identifies it as a wrong done to the Polar Spirit, who is a demon of the earth or middle air. Wordsworth apparently suggested the nature of the crime. "Suppose . . . you represent him as having killed one of these birds on entering the South Sea, and that the tutelary Spirits of those regions take upon them to avenge the crime" (*Poetical Works of William Wordsworth,* ed. de Selincourt, 1: 361).

43. One of the services rendered by Harold Bloom's *The Visionary Company* (New York, 1961) is to reaffirm this dialectical aspect of Romantic myth-making in England. In Germany, of course, Romantic irony is an explicit concept.

longer than the morning dew.[44] The poet wrestles once more with what Yeats will call the mask, the anti-self, the body of fate.

In fact, whenever the question of persona arises in a radical way, whenever self-choosing, self-identification, becomes a more than personal, indeed a prophetic, decision—which happens when the poet feels himself alien to the genius of country or age and destined to assume an adversary role—poetry renews itself by its contact with what may seem to be archaic forces. Such a turn of events is clear in the poetry of Blake, Shelley, and Byron. They could not, like Wordsworth, equate the England of their day with the spirit of liberty. That spirit, having migrated from East to West, must blow, if at all, from the West: the French Revolution, in its original form, was often thought to be an extension of British ideas of freedom.[45] "Be thou, Spirit fierce / My spirit" is Shelley's prayer to a West Wind that rouses both Mediterranean and Atlantic. Shelley in self-exile and Blake as an inner émigré were forced back on an ancient religious theme with revolutionary implications: the Oriental "heavy" allegory of a War in Heaven.

This is the very theme Milton revives and Wordsworth passes by "unalarmed"[46]—which he silences, in fact, by his bloodless purge of the gods. We need only compare *The Prelude* with Blake's *Milton* to see how differently they "redeem" England's great champion of liberty and prophetic poetry. For Wordsworth as for Keats, Milton is part of a "grand march of intellect" and contributes to that humanization of the mind (the true subject of the *Prelude*) which frees poetry from his kind of divine machinery. For Blake, however, Milton is limited not by the historical horizon of his age but, like every man, by his attitude toward the power in him. *Paradise Lost* and the Bible are the great Testaments of a human imagination afraid to be human: instead of expanding into the form of man, it shrinks back into the mystery of religion. Blake's War in Heaven is a human war—a war in the human breast to reunite Albion, the Genius of England,

44. *Hyperion,* 3.31 ff.

45. Cf. M. H. Abrams, "English Romanticism: The Spirit of the Age," in *Romanticism Reconsidered,* ed. N. Frye (New York, 1963).

46. Prospectus to the 1814 *Excursion, Poetical Works of William Wordsworth,* ed. de Selincourt, 5: 4–5.

with the Poetic Genius, the "eternal all-protecting Divine Humanity"[47] which a priestly religion had usurped. The prophetic spirit of Blake's poetry is therefore a measure of the extent to which his native country is already being recalled to itself:

> I will not cease from Mental Fight,
> Nor shall my Sword sleep in my hand:
> Till we have built Jerusalem,
> In England's green & pleasant Land.

47. *Milton* 1, pl. 14.

The Voice of the Shuttle: Language from the Point of View of Literature

Aristotle, in the *Poetics* (16.4), records a striking phrase from a play by Sophocles, since lost, on the theme of Tereus and Philomela. As you know, Tereus, having raped Philomela, cut out her tongue to prevent discovery. But she weaves a tell-tale account of her violation into a tapestry (or robe) which Sophocles calls "the voice of the shuttle." If metaphors as well as plots or myths could be archetypal, I would nominate Sophocles' voice of the shuttle for that distinction.

What gives these words power to speak to us even without the play? No doubt the story of Tereus and Philomela has a universally affecting element: the double violation, the alliance of craft (cunning) and craft (art), and what the metaphor specifically refers to: that truth will out, that human consciousness will triumph. The phrase would not be effective without the story, yet its focus is so sharp that a few words seem to yield not simply the structure of one story but that of all stories in so far as they are telltales. Aristotle, in fact, mentions Sophocles' kenning during his discussion of how recognition scenes are brought about; and it is interesting that other examples cited by him share the characteristic of seeming to exist prior to the plays that embody them, as if they were riddles or gnomic words imposed by tradition and challenging an adequate setting. Take, for example, "So I too must die at the altar like my sister" (Orestes); or "I came to find my son, and I lose my own life" (Tydeus); Or, again, "Here we are doomed to die, for here we were cast forth" (Phineidae, *Poetics* 16.6). These phrases, overheard, bring about a recognition. Like the voice of the shuttle they have little meaning without a story that sets them. Yet once a story is found, their suggestiveness is not absorbed but rather potentiated. And this, perhaps, is what *archetype* means: a part greater than the whole of which it is a part, a text that demands a context yet is not reducible to it.

Can a rhetorical analysis of this phrase clarify its power? "Voice" stands for the pictorial legend of the tapestry by a metonymic substitution of effect for cause. We say similarly, if less dramatically, that a book "speaks" to us. "Shuttle" stands for the weaver's instrument by the synecdochal substitution of part for whole, but it also contains a metonymy which names the productive cause instead of the product. Thus we have, in the first term (voice), a substitution of effect for cause, and in the second (shuttle), of cause for effect. By this double metonymy the distance between cause and effect in an ordinary chain of events is significantly increased, and the termini of this chain are over-specified at the expense of intermediate points (figure 1, p. 353). What this etiologic distancing means is not clear from the expression taken out of context. You and I, who know the story, appreciate the cause winning through, and Philomela's "voice" being restored; but by itself the phrase simply disturbs our sense of causality and guides us, if it guides us at all, to a hint of supernatural rather than human agency. (The inanimate speaks out, cf. blood crying from the earth in Genesis 4.)

A rhetorical analysis, therefore, brings us quickly to a limit. But we learn certain things from it. The power of the phrase lies in its elision of middle terms and overspecification of end terms. This could bear on two features every theory of poetic language seeks to explain: "aesthetic distance" which usually favors the cool, reflective, nonrepresentational virtues; and "iconicity" which usually abets the concrete, motor, representational ones. These features, however, are no more dissociable than are periphrasis and pointedness in Sophocles' figure. We find ourselves in the presence of an antinomy which is restated rather than solved by calling art a concrete universal. The tension of this figure from Sophocles is like the tension of poetics.

I make this large claim in purely heuristic spirit. There is something cross-eyed about the figure and something cross-eyed about every explanatory poetics. "It must be visible or invisible," says Wallace Stevens in *Notes toward a Supreme Fiction,* "Invisible or visible or both / . . . An abstraction blooded, as a man by thought." Now while Nature, according to an old saying, loves mixtures ("la nature aime les entrecroisements"), science does not. I must therefore steer an ambiguous course between nature and science and sketch for you a playful poetics: one that asserts nothing directly about logic, ontology, or linguistic science yet brings together the smallest literary patterns with the largest, the analysis of single metaphors or verses with the comprehensive kind of anatomy practiced by Aristotle in *The Poetics.* So far all we have learned is that figures of speech may be characterized by overspecified ends and indeterminate middles, that this structure may explain the shifting relations of concrete and abstract in poetics, and that (I add this now) the very elision or subsuming of middle terms allows, if it does not actually compel, interpretation. I mean that the strength of the end terms depends on our seeing the elided members of the chain (e.g., the full relation of Tereus and Philomela); the more clearly we see them, the stronger the metaphor which collapses that chain, makes a mental bang, and speeds the mind by freeing it from overelaboration and the toil of consecutiveness. A great verbal figure gives us the second wind of inspiration; it makes us sure, after all, of overtaking the tortoise.

I begin with a line from Milton: "Sonorous metal blowing martial sounds" *(Paradise Lost,* 1.540). A balanced line, with adjective-noun phrases flanking the pivotal verb. The syntactical sequence (1 2 1 2) is counterpointed, however, by a chiastic pattern of alliteration (1 2 2 1, s m m s). Milton, too, it seems, "aime les entrecroisements." Yet it is very hard to make something significant of such formal patterns, which are not unusual in Milton. Suppose, however, you take the line as complete or self-balanced: an inspired throw of the verbal dice. We may then look at it as generated from a redundant concept, "sonorous sounds," which we recover by collapsing the ends. The verse, from this perspective, is the separating out of "sonorous sounds"; a refusal, by inserting a verbal space between adjective and noun, to let them converge too soon. "Sonorous" is divided from "sounds" and assigned to "metal"; while "metal," as it were, gives up "martial" which is assigned to "sounds" by syntactical transfer. Here metaphor is as much a function of syntax as syntax of metaphor. While the chiastic alliteration, moreover, helps to

339

overcome the redundance of "sonorous sounds," the syntactical
parallelism lightens the secondary redundance of "martial metal."
These two features, previously mentioned, distribute and differentiate the sonic mass like God dividing elemental matter in order
to get the sixfold creation.

Compare now Sophocles' metaphor and Milton's line. In
Milton the middle terms need not be recovered by interpretation:
his line effects its own middle by separating the ends (fig. 2,
p. 353). What is created in both is a breach or space—an opening with the sense of freedom implicit in that word—but while in
Sophocles this space functions as etiologic distancing, as a suspension of normal causality, in Milton it allows the emergence
of words out of sheer sound and is linked to a distancing intrinsic
to language, one which differentiates sounds as meaning by a
"diacritical" (de Saussure) or "binary opposition" (Jakobson)
method.

The idea of space now introduced is not the same as aesthetic
distance, nor the tendency of the Miltonic or Sophoclean figure
to collapse into a strong redundancy or tighter than normal idea
of causation the same as iconicity. I doubt we can reach these
very general concepts except by approximation. But we already
glimpse what makes the "tension" of single figures or the literary
work as a whole. Take a second, and more ambitious, Miltonic
figure. In *Comus* music is heard "smoothing the Raven doune/
Of darkness till it smiled." Here "smoothing" and "smiled" converge slightly, but the real interest lies in the central metaphor,
the raven down of darkness. The most likely model of how it
originated is to posit a seed-phrase, "the raven of darkness," a
simple imaginative concept justified by Virgil's "bird of night"
(cf. *Aeneid,* 8.369), and with a tang of redundancy which can
be brought out by translating it as "the dark bird of darkness."
Some such overlap exists in any metaphor, in so far as it is
analogical; and Milton diminishes the redundance by the syntactical insertion of a second figure which distances "raven" from
"darkness." This figure, the "down of darkness," has nothing
conceptually redundant in it. A surprising trope, it is linked to
one terminus—"darkness"—by alliteration and to the other—

"raven"—by imagistic extension.[1] Thus the linear, syntactical insertion of this second metaphor works exactly like the "metal . . . martial" segment which was also linked by consonants. In Milton, syntax differentiates metaphor just as metaphor differentiates something more massive which it continues to express.

The "transformational" poetics here emerging can be clarified by polarization: going, on the other hand, to the microstructures of literature, entities studied by linguists, and on the other hand to the macrostructures studied by all of us. In a phrase like "le monocle de mon oncle" the redundancy of sounds is obvious, yet there is no semantic redundancy. Indeed, the wit of the phrase is that a slight difference in sound (between "monocle" and "mon oncle") releases such vast, if dubious, difference of meaning. It's like a man slipping on a banana peel—cause and effect are totally disproportionate. Technically defined the difference in sound is a slight distortion of quantity but primarily a matter of what linguists call "boundary" or "juncture"—here typographically indicated by "monocle" dividing into two words, "mon oncle."[2] What metonymy is to the "voice of the shuttle" or syntax to Milton, juncture is to this witty title from Wallace Stevens (fig. 2, p. 353).

Juncture is simply a space, a breathing space: phonetically it has zero value, like a caesura. But precisely because it is such a mini-phenomenon, it dramatizes the differential or, as de Saussure calls it, diacritical relation of sound to meaning. In any crucial arrangement of words, a small change goes a long way, as we learn through slightly mistranslated words in diplomatic messages. Split the atom of sound (and speech is fission) and you detonate an astonishing charge of meaning. With juncture we may have reached an analogue on the level of speech to aesthetic distance in art, especially as it remains linked to that explosive, if har-

1. The possibility that "down" puns on the adverb ("At every fall [of music] smoothing the Raven doune/ Of darkness") increases, if anything, its tmetic force.

2. I am not attempting an exact linguistic analysis: *juncture* is used only as the best available term, and I am aware that "oc" and "onc" contain a different phoneme. However, the impression occurs that as "mon" separates from "ocle" the latter compensates by expanding into "oncle." Elizabeth Sewell calls such impressions the "sound-look" of words.

341

nessed, *enargeia* (picture power) which we sometimes name iconicity.

The importance of zero values like juncture becomes more obvious when we turn to the smallest literary unit, the pun. Artemidorus records in his *Oneirocritica* that when Alexander of Macedon was besieging Tyre he dreamt he saw a satyr dancing on his shield. By dividing the word into sa-tyros, "Tyre is thine," this became a favorable omen for the siege. Freud, who cites the story and is fascinated by the immense role words play in dreams, gives many examples of what he calls "condensation." The image of the satyr, for example, is a visual condensation of a compound phrase (sa-tyre), but when the form of condensation remains verbal, we get punning or portmanteau phrases like Joyce's "mamafesta." Joyce extraverts the fact that language itself has its dream work which dreams seem only to imitate. This dream work shows itself, before Joyce, in naming rather than nouning, and especially in the resonant appeal of mythic names:

> Abhorred *Styx* the flood of deadly hate,
> Sad *Acheron* of sorrow, black and deep;
> *Cocytus,* nam'd of lamentation loud
> Heard on the rueful stream; fierce *Phlegeton*
> Whose waves of torrent fire in flame with rage
> > [*Paradise Lost,* 2.577 ff.]

Each of these lines is, at it were, a decontraction of the name.

This leads to the thought that nouns may be demythologized names. We are told that under the Hebrew word *TeHOM* in Genesis 1 (translated "the deep") the divine Babylonian monster *TIAMAT* may be couchant, reduced by the Bible from monster to mere noun. How are the mighty fallen, into syntax! What is true of nouns may be true of language in general. For Emerson language is fossilized metaphors; de Saussure thought that grammatical systems might have originated in anagrammatic distributions of a sacred name; and Shelley asserted "language itself is poetry. . . . Every original language near to its source is itself the chaos of a cyclic poem."

Whatever the truth of these speculations, they share a common feeling. Reading a poem is like walking on silence—on volcanic silence. We feel the historical ground; the buried life of words. Like fallen gods, like visions of the night, words are erectile. A poet can "speak silence" as simply as Chatterton did by opening up words through a mock-archaic spelling: "When joicie peres, and berries of blacke die,/ Doe daunce yn ayre, and call the eyne arounde. . . . " That "joicie" is Joycean. Joyce's more Freudian understanding of words simply brings literature abreast of language: he dramatizes the language jam in which we are stuck, the intrinsic duplicity, racial mix, and historically accreted character of living speech. "Mamafesta" not only mocks patriarchal imperatives but plays on the structural impurity of language, which mingles, like any doctrine or myth, opposing strains. There is the mother tongue (mama) and the learned, generally latinate layer (manifesto). English is especially prone to this happy impurity, not having suffered, like French or Italian, a decisive neoclassical sublimation of the vernacular. The division of language into sounding words or periphrases (e.g., "the deep backward and abysm of time," a Shakespearean blend of colloquial and learned) and its contraction into those resonant vocables from which, like dream interpreters of old, Milton draws new meanings, are part of one and the same rhythm. It compounds "the imagination's Latin with / The lingua franca et jocundissima" (Wallace Stevens).

It is a far cry, of course, from mystical semantics to modern semeiotics. Both, however, respect the function of silence, those zero values of juncture, elision, and decontraction which play so vast yet intangible a role in poetry. It is not mystical to call poetic language the voices of silence. Let us watch Milton creating meaning out of zero values in a famous pun: "O Eve in evil hour . . . " *(Paradise Lost,* 9.1067).

The pun again involves a name, though the latter does not release a new meaning by juncture. Instead, as is characteristic of Milton, it distributes itself in linear fashion by transfer or contamination. To go from "Eve" to "evil" is metaphor on the level of sound. But is the direction of the transfer from "Eve'" to "evil," or from "evil" to "Eve"? Milton, it could be argued, does not need the word "Eve" except to spell out a pun that is not particularly good. He adds reader insult to language injury. But the double "Eve-evil" gives us the sense of a third term or matrix, a common root from which both might have sprung. Thus juncture may be involved after all: whatever the matrix malorum is, it contains at this fateful hour both "Eve" and "evil."

This hypothetical matrix is like the redundant concept, "sonorous sounds," which generated a verse-line already studied. The present half-line is also curiously, beautifully redundant. The more we listen to it, the more it becomes one modulated crying diphthong—a breaking or ablauted Oh. . . . The end terms *O* and *hour* stand in the same intensified relation as the chiastic middle terms "Eve" and "evil." It is fanciful, yet true to the sound-shape of the line, to say that "evil" is "Eve" raised a phonetic rather than a grammatical degree, an impression reinforced by the fact that both "evil" and "hour" are quantities hovering between one syllable and two so that "evil" can be heard as a decontraction of "ill" (fig. 2, p. 353). The semantic energy and affective pitch of the line is again determined by properties that approach zero value (O . . . hour; Eve . . . evil).

From juncture, usually represented by a slash, it is only a step to the grammatical figure of tmesis, best represented by a dash. Tmesis, from the Greek "to divide" (cf. *atom,* "the undividable"), can be as simple as in Gerard Manley Hopkins's "Brim, in a flash, full." Two words conventionally joined, are disjoined to accommodate an intruded middle (fig. 2). The effect is that of interjection, of bursting in, but it gives extra value to the enclitic "full," which otherwise would have been slurred. The end terms are stressed ("in-stressed," Hopkins would say) by their being distanced, crowded away from each other. This is not unlike what happens through metonymy in the voice of the shuttle.

The continuity of juncture and tmesis is best shown by a graded series of examples. The enjambment in

> I have
> Immortal longings in me

is a hovering kind of juncture and depicts Shakespeare's Cleopatra on the point of crossing a fearful divide. She crosses it, wishfully, by a mere breathing or aspiration. Donne's running speech, his self-persuasive eloquence, tries to leap a similar divide, but the strain is more evident:

> thinke that I
> Am, by being dead, Immortal. . . .

At once nervous and peremptory, this "I Am Immortal" asserts itself in quick sequence against the line-end severance of subject and copula and a tmetic severance within the copula. Severance may seem too strong a word for pauses ("I/Am") or suspensions ("Am . . . Immortal") natural to spoken speech. Tmesis here is not a violent or artificial device but a more difficult enjambment, a heightened form of juncture which continues to individuate the basic words as they incline toward finality, carried by the proleptic verve of speech. Severance is the right term, however, when we look beyond speech to poetry. The qualified haste, the precarious finality of Donne's poetry is also that of religious hope. How to "cross-over"—or the dangers of passage —is the central theme:

> In what torn ship soever I embark
> That ship shall be my emblem of thy ark.

"Whatsoever" opens and swallows "torn ship" as the poet severs the grammatical bond to interject his fear. But "embark" also opens to let a saving rhyme, "emb(lem) . . . ark," emerge as the poet converts fear into hope by further prolepsis.

A more complicated form of tmesis distends the syntactical bond almost beyond repair. The normative adjectival space in "a lush-kept plush-capped sloe" is strained to the utmost; in fact, by the internal rhyming of the twofold compound adjective Hopkins reverses ends and middles, since rhyme is characteristic of line endings. Wishing to restore, in *The Wreck of the Deutschland,* our sense of the scriptural "In the beginning was the Word," which he opposes to the understated habit of English speech, Hopkins creates these hysteron-proteron formations (the Word, i.e., Christ as the Word, which is always confessed last, should be uttered first by us). We can see another result of this upbeat style in a line which describes the Windhover riding "The rolling underneath him steady air" (fig. 2, p. 353). The introversion of all these modifiers between the adjective ("rolling") and the noun ("air") parallels the trick of inversion in classical imitators or neoclassical rhymers. The middle of the line is so strong, compared to the conventional ends, that it almost jumps out like the word "Buckle" in the same poem, which, escaping its grammatical tie like a chemical its bond, becomes plosive:

> Brute beauty and valour and act, oh air, pride, plume, here
>   Buckle!

"Buckle" (the first word of the second line) is as true a rhyme word as "here" (the last word of the first line) because it at once condenses and detonates the sound pattern of the preceding words with their complex chiastic alliteration. The last becomes the first once more.[3]

It is strange that the ultimate form of a zero value like temsis should be a surplus value like rhyme. But tmesis, you will remember, splits a conventionally bonded phrase by means of an assertive middle term, creating stronger poles as well as intruding a strong middle. Now in rhymed verse the poles regress to a line-end position, becoming *bouts rimés,* while the rest of the verse is inserted between these rhymed ends. We see by this that Milton's rejection of rhyme is related to Hopkins's freeing rhyme from its fixed terminal position and making the last first (in soundshape, not merely line-place). The end terms of Milton's figures tend, in fact, to be redundant like perfect rhymes; and he uses syntactical tmesis to distance them, to insert phrases that remain bonded to the poles. A Miltonic middle, which separates, for example, "sonorous" and "sounds" or "raven" and "darkness," is a brilliant modification of redundancy, the distribution of an overly-rich mental or aural concept.

Thus rhyme is not an isolated phenomenon. Every birth of meaning has, like rhyme, a binary form, since meaning emerges through the opposition of similar-sounding entities. Consider "Humpty-Dumpty": it suggests, like "Eve . . . evil," a unitary word embracing the divided elements, yet nothing can put Humpty-Dumpty together again. Humpty-Dumpty is the portmanteau word that failed, but its fortunate failure reveals the

---

3. Compare the relation of "west" and "Waste" in:
    Her fond yellow hornlight wound to the west, her
        wild hollow hoarlight hung to the height
    Waste

["Spelt from Sibyl's Leaves"]

binary form. The hyphen joining Humpty and Dumpty is at once disjunctive and conjunctive; we may interpret it as the generalized tmetic sign which points to the middle between all *bouts rimés*. When a pun or portmanteau word sorts itself out, and similar sounds are put in line-end positions, we get rhyme. Rhyme is but another example of a figure with overspecified ends and an indeterminate middle. Is all poetical or figurative speech of this structure? Is it all a modified punning?

You can define a pun as two meanings competing for the same phonemic space or as one sound bringing forth semantic twins, but, however you look at it, it's a crowded situation. Either there is too much sound for the sense or too much sense for the sound. This aspect we have named the redundancy principle, and it makes poetry radically oblique in terms of sign function. Poetry either says too much—approaches the inexpressible—or too little —approaches the inexpressive. "The voice of the shuttle" could be an inflation of the proper term, an inane periphrasis for tapestry (cf. "fruit of the loom"). It could also be a miraculous condensation so packed with meaning that it skirts the oracular. Poetry will always live under a cloud of suspicion which it discharges by such lightnings.

We don't know, to be honest, what a perfect verbal system is like. But we do know language develops by what Coleridge calls desynonimization and the structuralists call binary opposition. A breathing space, a division within redundancy, appears and makes room for us, for our word. So Tiamat, its mythological fatness, is degraded from name to noun, and from monster to vague mystery. But the artist, like God, broods on the deep noun and makes it pregnant. A new meaning comes forth, a new word, a new world.

You probably feel as impatient with me, and all this talk about zero values, as Bishop Berkeley with Newton's infinitesimals. He called these entities, calculable only by Newton's theory of fluxions, the "ghosts of departed quantities." I now turn from minims to maxims, and to more tangible values.

No critic can refrain from having his say on the *Oedipus*. I am tempted to build on it not only a theory of life, like Freud, but a theory about what makes literature vital to life. Freud never brought his theory of "dream-work" together with his theory about Oedipus. Yet it is clear that what he calls "condensation" is crucial to a tragedy which compresses life to coincidence and a smallest possible freedom. For, talking now about plot, mythos, and such maxistructures, we can say that Oedipus, killing his father and marrying his mother, simply elides individual identity and is allowed no being properly his own. The oracle takes away, from the outset, any chance for self-development. Oedipus is redundant: he is his father, and as his father he is nothing, for he returns to the womb that bore him. His lifeline does not exist.

Except for the illusion that it exists, which the play relentlessly negates. This illusion is important, it is all Oedipus has to develop in. Achilles' career is also limited by a prophecy: short life and glory, or long life and none. But it is not "condensed" like a Greek epigram in which the marriage bed is also the deathbed. Oedipus converges on his fate like an epigram on its point or a tragedy on its recognition scene. The etiologic distancing collapses, the illusion bursts, the supernatural leaves the natural no space. The placenta of illusions has been eaten by the stichomythia.

Human life, like a poetical figure, is an indeterminate middle between overspecified poles always threatening to collapse it. The poles may be birth and death, father and mother, mother and wife, love and judgment, heaven and earth, first things and last things. Art narrates that middle region and charts it like a purgatory, for only if it exists can life exist; only if the imagination presses against the poles are error and life and illusion—all those things which Shelley called "generous superstitions"—possible. The excluded middle is a tragedy also for the imagination.

In human history there are periods of condensation (or concentration, as Matthew Arnold called them) where the religious spirit seems to push man up tight against the poles of existence. Middles become suspect; mediations almost impossible. Things move by polarizing or reversing (peripeteia) or collapsing. "The best lack all conviction, and the worst/ Are full of passionate intensity," as Yeats said, seeing the center breaking up. The Reformation was an era of this kind, and it produced, in its purity, a most awesome concentration of human consciousness on a few existentials. The space filled by boughten mercies and mediations is collapsed into a direct, unmediated confrontation of the individual and his God. What does art do in this situation? Does it—

can it—save the "ghost of departed mediations"? Is there any authentic way of inserting a middle strong enough to satisfy a now extremist imagination?

Emily Dickinson often begins with death, or a moment near it. Her poems are as laconic as tombstones that speak from the wayside. In the following poem she has come to a way station called Eternity. The poem "condenses" at that point:

> Our journey had advanced -
> Our feet were almost come
> To that odd Fork in Being's Road -
> Eternity - by Term -
>
> Our pace took sudden awe -
> Our feet - reluctant - lead -
> Before - were Cities - but Between -
> The Forest of the Dead -
>
> Retreat - was out of Hope -
> Behind - a Sealed Route -
> Eternity's White Flag - Before -
> And God - at every Gate -

These are strangely detached, inconclusive verses for all their exactitude. We are told that the soul must pass through death ("the forest of the dead") to the city of God. Yet though you cannot reach Eternity except through death, the poet opened by saying that she was near Eternity to start with, while in the last stanza Eternity precedes the soul with a safe-conduct. In this little quest-romance Eternity is always *before* you.

The difficulty may lie in the very idea of Eternity, which cannot be represented by space or time categories. This does not explain, however, why Emily Dickinson is haunted by a conception impossible to depict. The conception, obviously, is a motivating one in terms of the poem. The poet sees to see. Her mode is infinitive. Each stanza infers that one step which is not taken—into epiphany, or visibility. Nothing is at once more and less visible than white: "Eternity's white flag before." There is, to quote Wallace Stevens once more, a "seeing and unseeing in the eye." The God at every gate multiplies an opening through which we do not pass.

It is a poem, therefore, which three times brings us to a limit and three times displaces that limit. Our feet had "almost" come (st. 1); "The forest of the dead" intervenes (st. 2); the gate god as concrete as eternity's color (a "colorless all-color") is vague (st. 3). The limit is also, of course, a limen or threshold; yet the imagination that moves to cross it and see God does no more than see limits. Will God open or block the gate? And is not his very appearance, finally, as gate god, the block? Eternity becomes seeable only at that risk: the poet has advanced, if she has advanced at all, from Terminus to Janus. Her destiny—or is it her choice—seems to be to stay profane: *profanus,* on the threshold of vision.

The space Sophocles wrested from the gods was the very space of human life. That space is illusory, or doomed to collapse as the play focuses on the moment of truth which proves the oracle. In Emily Dickinson, predestination corresponds to the oracle. No wonder "Our pace took sudden awe." That next step, into death, is also, according to the faith of her fathers, a step into destination—into judgment and eternity. Protestantism has shrunk the breathing space between death, judgment, and apocalypse, so that the last things are one thing, and purgatory is no more. Like an oracle, in fact, judgment is already there at birth; death only justifies it or renders it visible. What is life, then, except death's threshold? Since the "ocular proof" comes with death, the life of the mind is centered on that moment, which is any moment. A man should live as if it were the moment preceding judgment. He is always, to quote the absolute opening of another poem, "The man—to die—tomorrow." We anticipate for whom the bell tolls; the time is always zero minus one.

Yet Emily Dickinson's tone is unhurried, as if there were time to puzzle "that odd fork in Being's road." Placing "Eternity" near "term" even shows, in the following line, a bookish wit. The mind remains slightly apart or off-center, like the rhymes; off-center also to the body. The impersonal constructions—"our journey," "our pace," "our feet"—elide the agony of self-consciousness and suggest a speaker positioned above the vehicular body. There is a distance between her and her feet compounded at once of awe and detachment. Her attitude is almost spectatorial.

Can we define that attitude exactly? It is clear that Emily Dickinson's art creates a space. It allows the threshold to exist; it extends the liminal moment. The poet's minutes are our days and hours. If rhymes are there, it is not because they condense, but because verse should be orderly, even in extreme situations. They decondense rather; especially the last and best of them: "god . . . gate." Here off-rhyme moves from line-ending into the midst of the verse. Some will hear in "god . . . gate" the echo of a closing door: she fears she may not be admitted. But it is better to leave it, like the rhyme itself, slightly ajar.

That her feet are "toward eternity" does not alter, radically, the poet's state of mind. She is carried off, perhaps, but she does not give herself. As the journey takes her along, her poem remains a bourgeois ledger, an extension of Christian watchfulness. To remain what she is steadfastly, unterrified, amounts to an election of self: she will not change utterly. Thus personality is not pushed beyond the human sphere as in Greek tragedy. Behind Philomela —the weaver—looms, like an oracular or archetypal shadow, the figure of fate. Fate too spins. On her shuttle she divides and spins the thread of human existence. But also, perhaps, a sound: is not Sophocles' "the voice of the shuttle" a symbol for oracular utterance? Fate alone could tell all, and Philomela, when her voice is restored through art, participates for a moment in divinity. She triumphs over a terrible doom, yet the recognition she brings about continues a tragic chain of events. Emily Dickinson does not "tell all"; there is no staring recognition in her poetry. Her fate is to stay profane, outside the gates, though in sight of "the promised end."

Interpretation is like a football game. You spot a hole and you go through. But first you may have to induce that opening. The Rabbis used the technical word *patach* ("he opened") for interpretation. Gershom Scholem has shown that the extravagance of the Kabbalah is linked to their opening Scripture to the suffering and concreteness of secular history. Deucalion's interpretation of the "bones of his mother" as the "stones of the earth" was an imaginative wager that saved a race.

We have art, said Nietzsche, so as not to die of the truth. A vital hermeneutics, it limits the sacred or makes room for life in life. Truth unmediated by art is deadly because it is too present, too specific. The truth-seeker is like the child who sees exactly "a hundred and three" sheep in a landscape; the artist like one who knows that what was seen is "about a hundred over there *and* three here." "103" is shown to be a hendyadis, or a poetic diction, which overspecifies the ends (cf. "finny tribe," "the voice of the shuttle") yet saves the sense of a middling.

Naming, like counting, is a strong mode of specification. It disambiguates the relation of sign to signified, making the proper term one end and the thing that is meant the other. Two terms complete the act; signification itself is elided, or treated as transparent (fig. 3, p. 353). Naming of this kind does not draw attention to itself. Literary speech does, however; and not by an occult quality (a secret third term), but rather by structures like periphrasis which under- and overspecify at the same time. Poetical figures habitually take away the proper term: "The sun must bear no name." Yet when Stevens adds "gold flourisher" he suggests how creative this decreation is, how his "abstraction" compounds under- and overspecification.[4]

The final hermeneutics art practices on itself. "It is written" or "everything has been said" is the somber oracle that denies the individual talent. In stories there is a period of error or quest, that wonder-wandering which makes them stories and evades an eternally fixed world. In this "wonder and woe" youth becomes "mündig"—is given its proper voice. Old names are cleansed; new tongues flicker. Creative error makes the blue darter hawk (it is blue and it darts) into a "blue dollar hawk," "the outmost sentinel of the wild, immortal camp." Tribal imperatives remain, however: individuality is wrested from the overwhelming presumption that we have a duty in common. Stories begin, therefore, with something that means too much: a corpse (as in *Hamlet* or the latest thriller), an oracle, an archetype, an overdeterminable symbol. Art does not add itself to the world of meanings: it makes room in meaning itself.

It is an axiom of contemporary poetics that a word is not simply a meaning: "A poem should not mean/ But be." Confusion sets in, however, as soon as we attempt to define how words are released from their bondage to meaning. The alternative to meaning must be within the aura of meaning, even part of

4. This holds true even when abstraction is attacked. The *New Republic,* wishing to restore the proper term, spells it like it is: $A + B + M =$ Lunacy. The scientific form loses its cool; it is made to collapse into the colloquial, like technical into ordinary language philosophy. An abstract ABC adds up to a Luna—C. One side of the mock equation, by overspecifying the "proper" term, reveals a deceptive underspecification in the other.

its structure: so Kant's "purposiveness without purpose" remains within the aura of teleology. Meaning is everywhere; the problem is that of fullness rather than emptiness, of redundancy and insignificant signification. Things come to us preinterpreted: Stevens asks the sun to shine in a heaven "that has expelled us and our images." Superfetation of meanings in our world is like the proliferation of gods and spirits in the ancient world. "And still the world pursues"—no wonder Mallarmé wished to evoke an "objet tu" by means of an "ombre exprès." There is always something that violates us, deprives our voice, and compells art toward an aesthetics of silence. "Les yeux seuls sont encore capable de pousser un cri," writes Char about his experiences in the second World War. And Nelly Sachs, alluding to the suffering of her people:

> Wailing Wall Night
> Carved in you are the psalms of silence.

FIGURE 1

(effect)	(cause)
voice	*shuttle*
(cause)	(synecdoche)
pictures	loom
(cause)	(effect)
tapestry	tapestry

FIGURE 2

sonorous		sounds
raven		darkness
mon		o(n)cle
sa		tyros
i	(eve)	ll
brim	(in a flash)	full
what	(torn ship)	soever
a		sloe
rolling		air
Humpty		Dumpty

FIGURE 3

sign	signified
	finny tribe
overconcrete ←	→ overabstract

353

BIBLIOGRAPHICAL NOTE

On "condensation," see Freud, *The Interpretation of Dreams* (Vienna, 1900). The satyros story is mentioned on p. 99 of the 1911 edition. On the glamor of grammar, see C. Brooke-Rose, *A Grammar of Metaphor* (New York, 1959); Morton W. Bloomfield, "The Syncategoremic in Poetry: From Semantics to Syntactics," in *To Honor Roman Jakobson* (The Hague, Janua Linguarum Series Major 31, 1967), 1: 309–17; and T. Todorov, "La grammaire du récit," *Langages* 12 (1968): 94–102. A. J. Greimas's remarks on the "syntactical distance" between defined and solving word in crossword puzzles may have implication for poetics through the intermediate notion of periphrasis *(To Honor Roman Jakobson,* 1: 799–815). W. K. Wimsatt, Jr., notes Milton's syntactical "dislocations" in "One Relation of Rhyme to Reason," *The Verbal Icon* (Lexington, Ky., 1954).

Owen Barfield in *Poetic Diction* (London, 1928), pp. 66 ff. and 116 ff., has genial remarks on the making of meaning through abridgment or etymological development. He utilizes Emerson's essay on "Language" and Shelley's "Defense of Poetry." De Saussure's notes on words within words and anagrammatic grammar are analyzed by J. Starobinski, *Mercure de France* (Février 1964); and in *To Honor Roman Jakobson,* 3: 1906–18. Kenneth Burke's "On Musicality in Verse," *The Philosophy of Literary Form* (Baton Rouge, 1941), studies concealed alliteration in Coleridge and approaches De Saussure. His "A Theory of Terminology," in *Interpretation: The Poetry of Meaning,* ed. R. Hopper and D. L. Miller (New York 1967) pp. 88 ff., summarizes much of his concern with tautology and graded series. For "Joyce as Philologist," see Richard M. Kain, *Mosaic* 2 (1969): 74–85, and the relevant works of David Hayman and J. S. Atherton. I have previously tried a structuralist analysis in *Hopkins: A Collection of Critical Essays* (Englewood Cliffs, N.J., 1966), pp. 8–9.

In Lewis Carroll's *Through the Looking Glass* Humpty-Dumpty defines a *portmanteau* phrase as "two meanings packed up into one word." See also Carroll's preface to the 1896 edition of that book. His story "Novelty and Romancement" is based on the misapprehension of "boundary." The ontological role of error in figurative speech is the subject of Walker Percy's "Metaphor as Mistake," *Sewanee Review* 67 (1958): 79–99. I take from him the example of the "Blue Darter Hawk." Sigurd Burkhardt's *Shakespearean Meanings* (Princeton, 1968), esp. chap. 2, discusses the "bondage of meaning" and how poetry breaks the "semantic identity" of words. Cf. Elizabeth Sewell, *The Structure of Poetry* (London, 1951), esp. p. 16. The modern "Aesthetics of Silence" is discussed by Susan Sontag in *Styles of Radical Will* (1969). Also, for the basically oblique relations between literary sign and signification, see Maurice Merleau-Ponty, "Le Langage indirect et les voix du silence," in *Signes* (Paris, 1961). On the possibility of a "science de la littérature" based on a linguistic model, see Roland Barthes, *Critique et vérité* (Paris, 1966), pp. 56–63. The Russian Formalists' distinction between the significant (phonemic) and nonsignificant (phonetic) relation of sound to meaning is summarized by V. Erlich, *Russian Formalism,* 2nd ed. (New York, 1965), pp. 218 ff.

Of the many areas omitted in this essay, the most important perhaps is that of the sociology of language, or rather "literacy." The work of Kenneth Burke, Roland Barthes, Michel Foucault, George Steiner, and others complements in this field philologists like Karl Vossler, Leo Spitzer, and Erich Auerbach. The notion of an "écart stylistique" is essential to them. Some studies of particular interest: A. Van Gennep, "Essai d'une théorie des langues spéciales," *Religion, moeurs et légendes* (Paris, 1909); J. Huizinga, *The Waning of the Middle Ages* (London, 1924); Ernest Jones, "A Linguistic Factor in English Characterology," *Essays in Applied Psycho-Analysis* (London, 1923); Wilhelm von Humboldt, *Schriften zur Sprachphilosophie* (Wissenschaftliche Buchgesellschaft, Darmstadt, 1963).

Toward Literary History

I am concerned with the idea of history by which men live; and especially with the idea of history by which poets have lived. No one has yet written a history from the point of view of the poets —from within their consciousness of the historical vocation of art. To write decent literary history is, of course, important in itself: we are all disenchanted with those picaresque adventures in pseudo-causality which go under the name of literary history, those handbooks with footnotes which claim to sing of the whole but load every rift with glue. Twenty years ago Wellek and Warren were forced to ask: "Is it *possible* to write literary history, that is, to write that which will be both literary [in subject] and a history?" Most histories of literature, the authors continued, "are either social histories, or histories of thought as illustrated in literature, or impressions and judgments on specific works arranged in more or less chronological order."[1]

The dissatisfaction with literary history is not limited to this country. In 1950 Werner Krauss, the distinguished East German scholar, published an essay entitled "Literary History as a Historical Duty" ("Literaturgeschichte als geschichtlicher Auftrag"); and Hans Robert Jauss recently delivered an inaugural lecture at Konstanz on "Literary History as Provocation."[2] American scholars have, in fact, been slower than their European colleagues in shaking off that distrust of speculative ideas which came in reaction to the giddy era of *Geistesgeschichte* and the equally dubious if more sober pomps of the history of ideas. This cautiousness has long degenerated into the positivist's medley of

1. *Theory of Literature* (1948), chap. 19.
2. Krauss, *Studien und Aufsätze* (Berlin, 1959), pp. 19–72; Jauss, *Literaturgeschichte als Provokation der Literaturwissenschaft* (Konstanz, 1966). See also Max Wehrli, "Sinn und Unsinn der Literaturgeschichte," *Neue Zürcher Zeitung* (February 26, 1967) no. 813.

fact and fashionable ideas or into a formalistic type of literary criticism only vaguely in touch with history writing.[3] Yet if I raise the question of literary history, it is not merely to urge its importance as an intellectual discipline or to deplore the absence of methodological thinking in that area. There are just too many areas in which one could be thinking more clearly and generously. My argument will be that literary history is necessary less for the sake of intellect than for the sake of literature—it is our historical duty because it alone can provide today a sorely needed defense of art.

Since Aristotle, the best defense of art has been to call it more philosophical than history. Despite recent advances in sociology, literature continues to escape historical research at some point. To demonstrate, as Lucien Goldmann has done, that the dramas of Racine participate in the public thought of his time—that there is nothing in his plays not illuminated by the conflict within church or state—is a significant authentification of the reality principle guiding even the most abstract or stylized art and a cogent reminder that literature is never as self-centered as it seems to be.[4] But the influence of Racine, the continuing resonance of his language and form, even for those who do not know of the topical historical issues, remains unclarified. There exists, in other words, a principle of authority in art which is purely authorial: which seems to derive from art alone, or from the author's genius rather than from the genius of his age. Werner Krauss, troubled by this characteristic autonomy of literature, by this "capacity of artforms to outlast the destined hour," admits that Marxist theory has not been able to understand the phenomenon. Whether or

3. There are honorable exceptions. American Studies, strongly in touch with the idea of national character, has Howard Mumford Jones's *Theory of American Literature* (Ithaca, 1948), the product of a cosmopolitan mind working in a natiónal context. Also Charles Feidelson's *Symbolism and American Literature* (Chicago, 1953), antithetical yet complementary, is the product of a cosmopolitan mind working in a specifically literary context. The call for an "inside history" was revived by Roy Harvey Pearce's *The Continuity of American Poetry* (Princeton, 1961). Renato Poggioli engages the subject through Pareto's theory of history in *The Spirit of the Letter* (Cam., Mass., 1965), and Claudio Guillén has recently remarked that "to explore the idea of literary history may very well be the main theoretical task that confronts the student of literature today."

4. *Le Dieu Caché* (Paris, 1955).

not poetry is more philosophical than history, it is more formal than history—that is the brute yet elegant fact which we must appreciate without falling into idealistic or unhistorical explanations.

Thus the formality of art becomes a central issue in any literary history. How do we ground art in history without denying its autonomy, its aristocratic resistance to the tooth of time? Is it not a monument rather than a document; a monument, moreover, of the soul's magnificence, and so a richly solipsistic or playful edifice?

To understand the "art" in art is always essential. But it is even more essential today, for we have clearly entered an "era of suspicion" in which art seems arty to the artist himself. The artist, indeed, is often the severest critic of his own medium, which turns against itself in his relentless drive for self-criticism. Artistic form and aesthetic illusion are today treated as ideologies to be exposed and demystified—this has long been true on the Continent, where Marxism is part of the intellectual milieu, but it is becoming true also of America. If literary history is to provide a new defense of art it must now defend the artist against himself as well as against his other detractors. It must help to restore his faith in two things: in form, and in his historical vocation.

TOWARD A THEORY OF FORM

It may seem strange, this suggestion that we suffer at present from a shame of form. But the modern insistence on process, on openness, on mixed media, and especially on the mingling of personal and technological elements indicates more than the usual difficulty with inherited patterns or the desire to "make it new." The older way of achieving a form impersonal enough to allow the new to emerge was to subordinate the individual talent to the tradition. Eliot still thought it possible. Then what is wrong with the old forms? Why do they appear less exciting, less viable— even less pure—than mixed or technological forms? Take the example of a man from whom Eliot learned his craft: no one was more interested in purity of form, or form as such, than Ezra Pound. Yet Pound's *Cantos,* which ransack the high culture of both West and East, remain a nostalgic montage without unity, a picaresque of styles.

We look back at Pound and Eliot,[5] at Bridges and Yeats, and we realize that their elitist view of culture is dead. Though their art aimed for the genuine vernacular, it could not resist the appeal of forms associated with high culture, forms which remained an ideological reflex of upper-class mentality. To purge this ideological stain and to rescue art from imputation of artiness, the writer had to become his own enemy. Today all art stands in a questionable relation to elite modes of thought and feeling. But while the artist moves closer to self-criticism, the critic moves closer to art by expanding the notion of form until it cannot be narrowly linked to the concerns of a priestly culture or its mid-cult imitations.

I want to examine modern criticism in the light of this tendency. Is there a larger conception of literary form in the making? There are four significant theories to be considered. First Marxist criticism, which raises explicitly the issue of elitism; then Frye's theory of archetypes; and finally two kinds of structuralist theory, that of C. Lévi-Strauss and that of I. A. Richards and the Anglo-American critics. I hope to persuade you that an important new theory of form is gradually emerging.

Let me illustrate the Marxist preoccupation with form by a work of art that provides its own critical perspective. Jean Luc Godard's *Weekend* is filmic self-criticism of an extreme kind. The title of the film points to the theme of leisure, or rather of "ignoble leisure"; and Godard engages in the film in a ruthless violation of taboos, especially the taboo of form. Not only are the unities of time, place, and action killed once again, or rather parodied to death, but just about every art-movie cliché—from the films of Antonioni, Fellini, Bunuel, Resnais, Truffaut, and Godard himself—is exposed to massive lyrical ridicule. The result is strangely operatic, since opera tends to be pure superstructure, its form having but an absurd or magical connection with the passions staged. The Antonioni promenade, the Fellini harlequinade, the Bonnie and Clyde relationship, the Truffaut tenderness, the

5. Eliot's dictum in *Notes towards the Definition of Culture* (London, 1948) that "civilization cannot simultaneously produce great folk poetry at one cultural level and *Paradise Lost* at another" is examined by Raymond Williams in *Culture and Society* (London, 1958), pp. 231–32. He points to the contemporaneity with *Paradise Lost* of *Pilgrim's Progress*.

Bunuelian symbols—everything is mocked in this bloody, end-lessly interrupted pastoral.

What remains? The problem of the elitist status of art, expressed in powerful visual graffiti. One scene shows a truck driver playing Mozart on a huge concert-piano that has somehow found its way into a farmyard. Various laborers and old peasant women seem as entranced by that music as the beasts by Orpheus. It is Godard's gentlest scene, but also the most mocking vis-à-vis the Marxist theory of a proletariat pastoral. What reconciliation is possible between Mozart, the proletariat regisseur, and the barnyard set-ting? "What are the conditions," asks Werner Krauss, "which compel a break-through from the base *(Unterbau)* of society and which might rectify its relation to the superstructure *(Überbau)?* In what way can literature belong to the superstructure of so-ciety?"[6] There is nothing that belongs authentically to either the social base or superstructure in Godard's mise-en-scène: we are left with a few lyrical images of old women who seem to listen to the incongruous music and a farmhand walking to its rhythm and yet not to its rhythm. All the rest is—ideology.

If we insert this film into a history of the concept of form, we would have to say that, for Godard, form was less important than its violation. He writes about the problem of form in blood—in the lifeblood of his medium. He hopes that by violating all taboos something deeper than the gratuitous values of a leisure class might emerge. Real pastoral values, perhaps: something from the *Unterbau* or Marxist "deep structure." Yet this movie, which begins as sophisticated pornography, ends with a totally undeli-cious scene of anthropophagy: a progress which suggests that to destroy, through revolution or some radical cleansing, the forms of our high culture will simply result in primitivism, in the naked substructure. We are therefore forced to consider a second rea-son for Godard's violation of taboos. The movie medium, instead of discovering new values, is shown to participate necessarily in the old values, in the capitalistic desire for conspicuous consump-tion. All the totems of movie culture are therefore offered up to

6. "Was sind die Bedingungen die einen Durchschlag aus dem Unter-bau der Gesellschaft erzwingen und damit das Verhältnis zum Überbau richtigstellen? In welcher Weise gehört überhaupt die Literatur zum Uber-bau der Gesellschaft?" (*Perspektiven und Probleme* [West Berlin, 1965], p. 19).

the reluctant viewer in this moveable feast which is like the massacre of matériel in American spectaculars. To go beyond this movie means to go beyond a movie-centered culture and no longer to confuse participation with consumption.

We come away from Godard with two observations about the authenticity of art forms in contemporary society. The first is that the only forms which all classes of society enjoy are primitivistic; the second, that the most we can expect from art is not authenticity but purity—the fissure of the work of art into ideology on the one hand and pure form on the other. Godard's "alienation-effects" are more Mallarmean than Brechtean and substantiate the view that poetry is detachable from a more continuous prose base. Thus form remains a lyrical and dying effect, a falling star in the twilight of taboos.

The theory of form advanced by Northrop Frye is more familiar. He removes the elitism of the art object by pointing to similarities between the structure of primitive myths and the formal principles of all art. The structure of a sophisticated novel by Henry James or Virginia Woolf is like that of any story; and the historical difference between stories is due to what Frye calls the displacement of myth, that is, its accommodation to rules of verisimilitude that differ for different cultures. In a culture, for example, which is realistic, a writer cannot depict supernatural figures directly, yet he invents characters with demonic attributes or with the capacity for violating social norms. Thus Frye can talk of the pharmakos or sacred scapegoat in Virginia Woolf and Henry James, and Ihab Hassan expands that insight to cover a broad range of modern works in *Radical Innocence*.

The virtue of Frye's system is that it methodically removes the one barrier which prevents art from exerting wide influence: the distinction of kind between sacred and secular, or between popular and highbrow. His sense for the commonality of art is radically Protestant: every man is imagination's priest. All art that is good expands imagination; all art that is bad restricts it. Mystery and its brood—secret religion, secret sex, secret government—are simply imagination gone bad. For Frye as for Blake, bad art argues a sick society: one which has the power to block our imagination. And the blocking agent is always a priesthood: some political or religious or artistic elite.

361

It is clear that Frye's theory has affinities with Marxist thought. But the latter is more dialectical and realistic in its view of history. Where Marxist critics confront the individual work and evaluate it according to its struggle with the proletariat-elite, base-super-structure split, Frye's structural observations are developed for descriptive and not for evaluative purposes. His idea of literary history is certainly abstract: not only less sweaty than Marxist literary history, but also less concrete than most scholarly versions. Though he expands our concept of form and redeems individual works from the isolation imposed on them by cult and culture, he may do so at the cost of a false idea of universality and an elite idea of literary history. The illusion that a worldwide culture is already within reach is fostered by evading the question of national difference and large-scale social (East-West) conflict. I suspect that for the Marxist his vision of cultural dissemination is a technocrat's ideal and betrays an American perspective. Werner Krauss would surely commend Frye, as he does other American scholars, for his "radical break with all monopolistic attitudes in the writing of literary history," but he would also criticize a method which bypasses national or ideological differences till literature becomes an "All-Souls, in which Cervantes and Rabelais, Dante and Voltaire, amicably drink tea together."[7] It is, in short, bad comparative literature.

We return later to this problem of how the nationality of literatures is to be respected; but it is important to add that Frye writes about criticism rather than about literature and seems more interested in improving the consumer than in evaluating the product. His whole effort is an attempt to improve the public relations of art. His vision of an expanding cultural universe includes literary works, but they are not the reified apples of his eye. On the contrary, he is less interested in the marmoreal object than in a change of perception from which the object would profit. To Eliot's thesis that the advent of the authentically new work of art

7. Krauss, *Perspektiven und Probleme,* p. 372, translated freely. "Welt-literatur ist dann zu einem Pandämonium geworden, in dem sich Cervantes und Rabelais, Dante und Voltaire zunicken." The specific context is Krauss's attack on a concept of world literature as super-literature, or metahistorical assemblage of masterpieces.

revises our view of all preceding works, Frye adds an important footnote: this change is a change in our consciousness of art and can only occur, therefore, if mediated by criticism. Whatever totemic or elitist elements remain in the literary work, this interplay between art and critic, between product and consumer, expands both and anticipates the Marxist hope (itself a version of Christian communism elaborated around the time of Blake, Ballanche, and Saint-Simon[8]) that the forms of social life dissolve into the form of man—into the expanding humanistic consciousness of a classless society.

It is, hence, a question whether Frye is dealing with form at all: he seems to approach the concept of structure with which structuralism (the third of our theories) is concerned. This structure is a mental fact and supposedly intersubjective: common to every man as man, to priest and peasant, sophisticate and primitive. The shift in linguistics from individual languages (or sign-systems) to language in general (or semeiotics) and from there to structures of the mind parallels Frye's shift from the individual work of art to literature as a totality and from there to a "verbal universe" which exhibits archetypes basic to science as well. Yet the "structures" isolated by Claude Lévi-Strauss differ from Frye's in an essential respect. They are solutions to real social problems, which is why structuralism can call itself a science—a "science humaine." The principles of structure described by Frye solve a problem only in the sense that they free art from the stigma of archaism or elitism and so publish it once again. Tradition is extradition: art must become transitive vis-à-vis its original site in history. Frye teaches us a lot about tradition and handing on, but less about what is handed on. He fails to bring together the form of art and the form of its historical consciousness—which is the ideal of the science we are in search of.

Claude Lévi-Strauss also fails in this, but he does bring together the form of myth and a type of *social* consciousness. Myth, according to him, resolves a societal hang-up or articulates its solution. Since every society has conflicts of interest that cannot be resolved without great mental anxiety, every society will have its myths. If all myths use the same basic method to resolve these

8. See, e.g., P. S. Ballanche, *Essais de Palingénésie Sociale* (1827).

363

social conflicts, then a science of myth would be possible. And this possibility is the claim of anthropological structuralism.

Let us look more closely at the structuralist's description of myth. The form of myth is always twofold: its surface structure reflects local traditions and may be esoteric, but its deep structure is logical and can be formulated in mathematical terms. Myths dealing with the incest taboo, for example, should project in their totality a theory of kinship which makes it clear that the generative problem is how to distribute women fairly—how to pry them loose from father or clan and make them go around. The incest taboo, therefore, is neither absolute nor eternal but a humane and logical institution, part of a system of exchange as complex as the monetary system today.

Here, as in Frye, myth is both story and a principle of structure: a primitive narrative and a functional type of logic. Myth and mathematics join in a mysterious way more reminiscent of Plato than Aristotle. What is lacking in this description is precisely the middle-ground between myth and mathematics which art occupies. Where in this description are the qualities of storytelling that actually involve us—Tone, rhythm, humor, surprises, displacements? A sense of hidden structure or a delight in exotic surface is only a part of this involvement. Surely, even if literature proves to be a problem-solving form, it must be of a more liberal and chancy kind than Claude Lévi-Strauss suggests. And since for Lévi-Strauss, form is totally explained by its social function, we cannot ask which myths are viable universals and which are empty or chauvinistic versions of what Blake called "the Human Abstract." The structuralist science of myth does not allow us to cross over from its theory of form to a descriptive or critical account of the artist's historical consciousness.

Our last theory, and in many ways the one most clearly focused on the literary work, is that of I. A. Richards and the New Criticism. Richards's concept of form is as functional as that of Lévi-Strauss, and it may have a common source with the latter in Malinowski.[9] What ritual, according to Malinowski, does for primitive societies, literary form, in Richards, does for the civi-

9. Cf. Malinowsky, "The Problem of Meaning in Primitive Languages," in C. K. Ogden and I. A. Richards, *The Meaning of Meaning* (1923).

lized (and perhaps over-civilized) individual: it reconciles tensions and helps to unify. Richards, however, does not specify what the basic tensions or hang-ups are: he is content with the common-sense observation that tensions always exist and that the deeper they are and the more complexly respectful of them the reconciling form, the better the work of art or the harmony of the person. We seem to have a very open theory of form which defines neither the contents reconciled nor the exact, perhaps organic, structure by which they are unified.

Open, except for the very insistence on unity or reconciliation, which has become a great shibboleth developed by the New Critics on the basis of Eliot and Richards. Only Empson tried to escape it by postulating types of ambiguity which showed how precarious this unity was, or how rebellious language was. It is important not to be deceived by the sophisticated vagueness of such terms as *unity, complexity, maturity, coherence,* which enter criticism at this point. They are code words shored against the ruins. They express a highly neoclassical and acculturated attitude; a quiet nostalgia for the ordered life; and a secret recoil from aggressive ideologies, substitute religions, and dogmatic concepts of order. Out of the passionate intensity of the post-war period—out of the pressures of politics, press, and propaganda—comes a thoughtful backlash which attempts to distinguish the suasion of literary statements from more imperative kinds. A poem, we learn, does not "mean" but "is"; art, we are told, is pseudo-statement or pseudo-action. Thus the literary work, though nominally democratic—inclusive of anything—is thought of as exclusive by its structure. Art turns out to be a mental purification of the impulses to action: an idea that has eastern resonances in I. A. Richards but is associated in Cleanth Brooks with testing the simplifications by which we live.

Richards's concept of the functional unity of the work of art is far from narrow, of course. By modeling it on the psychology of communication, which includes reader or auditor in the aesthetic transaction, he opened a path to a theory of participatory form and helped to revive the academic interest in rhetoric still important today, when new and sophisticated notions concerning the "entrapment" of reader by writer are emerging. He may also have influenced Kenneth Burke's refusal to equate rhetorical forms with aristocratic or privileged ideas of order and to examine anew both their psychological function and social-participatory (Burke continues to call it "ritual") aspect. Sigurd Burkhardt's emphasis on the "troth-value" of words is a further echo of these explorations.[10]

There is, nevertheless, the distinct afterglow of an elitist idea of culture in Richards's work. The function of art moves closer to that of ordinary language and normal psychological transactions, but it remains reminiscent of Plato's "dialectic." Art's therapeutic virtue is to Richards what the intellectual virtue of dialectic was to Socrates: purging fixed ideas it still leads upward to the one form of truth. The Socratic assumption, moreover, of a basic identity of questioner and questioned evades the issue of class or nationality—it assumes a society of equals whose upward mobility is intellectual in essence. Join Plato's dialectic to communications theory and you get the idea of art as an elite communications medium. What you do not get is a concrete understanding of how this medium mediates: of how it actually, in history, reconciles or unifies different persuasions. For this we need quite another kind of dialectic, which Hegel and Marx tried to develop. We still have not found a theory linking the form of the medium to the form of the artist's historical consciousness.

TOWARD A THEORY OF LITERARY VOCATION

It is time I showed my hand and proposed such a theory. Let us construct it on the basis that literary form is functional and that its function is to keep us functioning, to help us resolve certain hang-ups and bring life into harmony with itself. But let us also agree that art can divide as well as heal, that its healing power may be complicated by its power to hurt. Wordsworth, in the preface to *Lyrical Ballads,* defines the poet as one who "considers man and the objects that surround him as acting and reacting upon each other, so as to produce an infinite complexity of pain and pleasure." Art cannot be expected to "bring us together again" by metaphysic, by an occult virtue of unification.

Since we are looking for a theory of literary as well as functional form, the essential ingredient is whatever makes the theory specif-

10. *Shakespearean Meanings* (Princeton, 1968).

ically relevant to literature. Otherwise we might quote Housman's "For Malt does more than Milton can, to justify the ways of God to Man" and leave it at that. But are there perhaps specifically literary hang-ups? And are we not forced by this question into the psychology of art on the one hand, but also into an analysis of literary history on the other?

Take the contemporary situation. Many artists, today, doubt art to the point of becoming incapable of it. The reason for their extreme self-questioning has already been suggested. The artist has a bad conscience because of the idea that forms, structures, etc. always reconcile or integrate, that they are conservative despite themselves. To create a truly iconoclastic art, a structure-breaking art; to change the function of form from reconciliation and conservation to rebellion, and so to participate in the enormity of present experience—this is the one Promethean aim still fiery enough to inspire. It is the psychic state of art today. But let us think, in addition, about other periods. Is the problem of the present era unique, or is it a special case of a more inherent, perhaps universal, dilemma besetting the writer's consciousness of himself? Were not Keats and Milton, those great formalists, also great iconoclasts, and did they not think about the historical vocation of art?

No great writer is without an identity crisis. The shape of that crisis can be generalized. Though we may not always discern what developmental impasse occurs within the poet's private life, we can describe the vocational crisis that occurs in the poet as poet, in his literary self-consciousness. A great artist has the ambition to seize (and hand on) the flame of inspiration, to identify the genius of art with his own genius or that of a particular age (genius loci). But this exacerbates the crisis of self-consciousness: of emergence and of commitment to being manifestly what one is. In the modern era with its problem of "legitimacy," the artist is especially aware of the need for self-justification.[11] The basic problem, however, is as old as history: how is spiritual authority

11. Cf. Hans Blumenberg, *Die Legitimität der Neuzeit* (Frankfurt am Main, 1966); William Collins, "Ode on the Poetical Character" (1747); Otto Rank, *Art and Artist* (New York, 1932), esp. the chapters on "Creative Urge and Personality Development" and "The Artist's Fight with Art"; Erik Erikson, *Young Man Luther* (New York, 1958).

to be transmitted if not through an elite of persons or communities? There seems to be no recorded greatness without the driving force of an idea of election, or the search for evidences of election.

All societies have rituals for the passage out of latency and into the public light. They seek to guide it and to assure the individual a formal maturity. Van Gennep, who studied these ceremonies, called them "rites de passage." His findings have a complex but real bearing on the function of literature, whether in society or in the individual consciousness of artists. Take Shakespeare's Hamlet, a figure that has fascinated generations. It is widely agreed that an important function of art is to create character types of universal or general appeal and that Hamlet is the type of a man deprived of typical existence: of vocation or role or the possibility of commitment. The paradox, a simple one, is clarified by reference to Van Gennep: Hamlet is "le seigneur latent qui ne peut devenir" (Mallarmé) because he cannot assume his real (regal) self by innocent means—by the formal rite. Ceremony itself, in its legal and ludic aspects, in its justifying and mediating functions, is wounded. Deprived of kingship and shunning the outlaw role of avenger, Hamlet is doomed to remain a liminal person in an action (the play) which is an abortive rite of passage. He becomes the "juvenile shadow of us all" in his psychic struggle with "le mal d'apparaître."[12]

Yet every artist is like Hamlet. The artist must always find his own way to "appear": he has no ritual to guide him. The presumption of his act, the daring of his art, is all. The conventions at his disposal do not lessen the agony of self-election: if he admires the ancients, he trembles to rival them; if he does not admire, he trembles before a void he must fill. No wonder art continually questions the hopes for art; no wonder also that it endures irony and negativity to the point of substantiating Yeats's comment, so appropriate to Mallarmé: "The last kiss is given to the void."

The plea for literary history merges here with that for phenomenology, or consciousness studied in its effort to "appear." Con-

12. A. Van Gennep, *Les Rites de passage* (Paris, 1907; English trans. Chicago, 1961); Victor W. Turner, *The Ritual Process* (Chicago, 1969); Mallarmé, "Hamlet," in *Crayonné au Théâtre* (1886).

sciousness can try to objectify itself, to disappear into its appearances, or to make itself a vocation *as* consciousness. Social anthropology is involved because rites of acculturation and the structure of public life provide many of the collective forms that could allow self-objectification. Indeed, the very multiplicity of terms used to characterize the dynamics of phenomenology (appearance, manifestation, individuation, emergence, being-in-the-world) imply a concern which incorporates the human sciences, or all sciences to the extent that they are humane. This concern centers on the problem of civilization and encompasses both nature and nurture, "those frontiers of biology and sociology from which mankind derives its hidden strength."[13] We have only to look at the crisis point in Keats's *Hyperion* to see this struggle for "appearance" accompanied by all the suggestiveness that hidden frontiers bestow.

In the third book of *Hyperion,* Apollo, the young sun god, attempts to rise—to emerge into himself, helped by the memory goddess Mnemosyne. The sun never rises, however: *Hyperion* begins and ends in twilight. While attempting to dawn, Apollo suffers pangs like those accompanying childbirth or sexual climax or the biomorphic passage from one state of being to another. His "fierce convulse" is comparable to that of the snake Lamia in her transformation to womanhood (*Lamia,* 1, 145 ff). We expect Apollo to become the sun: "from all his limbs/Celestial" a new dawn will break. But the poem breaks off, as if Apollo's metamorphosis had tied itself into a knot and entered a developmental impasse. Though the impasse cannot be reduced to ego psychology —it is clearly related to the Enlightenment assumption of a progress of religion and literature—Apollo, in bringing his identity to light, is also bringing his father to light. In the psychotheology of art, as Keats depicts it here, the ephebe god, under the influence of "knowledge enormous," is about to replace the sun god Hyperion. To bring his identity to light means to bear a father god out of himself. The poem stops on that uncanny yet familiar truth.

To stress the phenomenological dimension is not to transcend the literary aspect. Apollo is the god of art by traditional equation. The knowledge that floods him:

13. Philip Aries, *Centuries of Childhood* (London, 1962), p. 11. Cf. the tendency of Elizabeth Sewell's *The Orphic Voice* (New Haven, 1960).

> Names, deeds, gray legends, dire events, rebellions,
> Majesties, sovran voices, agonies,
> Creations and destroyings . . .

is "epic" knowledge, mediated by literature or by Mnemosyne as mother of the Muses. It signals the change from a lower to a higher mode of consciousness, from pastoral romance to that kind of heroic verse which *Hyperion* seeks to be. Yet Keats does not succeed in passing from pastoral to epic any more than Apollo from ephebe state to Phoebus. What he writes is hot pastoral rather than epic. The very rituals that wing him into a new sphere prove too literary, too magical-archaic, and do not prevent fresh anxieties about the authenticity of his passage. The marble steps the dreamer barely ascends in *The Fall of Hyperion* or Moneta's face "deathward progressing / To no death" are images raised up by his anxiety. Literature is breaking with an archaic mode which has been its glory and remains influential, yet the very idea of ritual transition is part of this archaism and makes the poet aware of his lateness or inauthenticity. His art, a new star, finds itself in the arms of the old by a fatal if fine repetition.

The impasse, then, is that Keats believes in poetry, in its progressive character, yet cannot see an authentic catena between old and new. In a sense he is the catena, and his art the passage. The past masters haunt him: their glory is his guilt. The burden of *traditio*[14] leads to a preoccupation with *transitio,* and transition has two very different aspects in Keats. It may infer a real passing-over, a transcendence of past stages enabled by the "grand march of intellect"—Keats's phrase for the Enlightenment. Wordsworth, he speculates, thinks more deeply into the human heart than Milton, whether or not he is a greater poet. Transition can also, however, infer the obverse of transcendence: transience, or abiding the consciousness of change by "negative capability." That is the real test of the fallen gods in *Hyperion,* by which they become

14. Cf. W. J. Bate, "The English Poet and the Burden of the Past, 1660–1820," in *Aspects of the Eighteenth Century,* ed. E. R. Wasserman (Baltimore, 1965); Harold Bloom, "Keats and the Embarrassments of Poetic Tradition," in *From Sensibility to Romanticism,* ed. H. Bloom and F. Hilles (New York, 1965); and my "Romanticism and Anti-Self-Consciousness," pp. 298–310. Also R. W. B. Lewis, *The American Adam* (Chicago, 1958).

human. All rites lead only to further "dark passages" and not beyond. "We are in a Mist—*We* are now in that state." If the first aspect of the idea of transition requires a philosophy of history, the second elicits the watchword: "The creative must create itself." "The Genius of poetry," Keats also says, "must work its own salvation in a man."

We are close to the era which makes transition a historiographical concept, as in "The Age of Transition."[15] But this concept is a compromise and belies the rich gloom of Keats's verse. While he fails to place us where we can see the historical vocation of poetry, he does somehow transmit deeply, feelingly, an existential or temporal consciousness. Not only by the sensuous or empathetic highpoints of his art. His famed sensuousness exists as one pole in this temporal rhythm, the other being the mind's irritable, positivistic "reaching after fact and reason." A sharp revolution of tempi or moods, the alternation of an overwrought questing with "silence and slow time," is what catches us. In the odes, which traditionally permit bold transitions, this is less remarkable than in the *Hyperion*. Moments before Mnemosyne brings Apollo to the flood stage of recollection, he is steeped in forgetful, even indolent sensation ("Beside the osiers of a rivulet / Full ankle-deep in lilies of the vale"). This direct, precipitous transition from puberty to epiphany, from pastoral to apocalypse—which aborts historical vision proper—puts all progress by stages in doubt.

What remains is almost purely existential: a birth which is a forgetting, and a dying into recollection. But the poetry also remains, as does the question of its relation to this existential metaphysics. There is a metaphysical element because Apollo "dies" into an antelife by a kind of platonic anamnesis. On examination, however, this antelife proves to be Wordsworth, Milton, Spenser,

15. "The doom of the Old has long been pronounced, and irrevocable: the Old has passed away: but, alas, the New appears not in its stead; the Time is still in pangs of travail with the New" (Carlyle, *Characteristics,* 1831). "Our lot is cast in an evil time; we cannot accept the present, and we shall not live to see the future. It is an age of transition" (Thomas Arnold to Clough, 16 April, 1847). The idea has a contemporary source in Saint-Simonianism but older roots in Joachism and a strongly literary sense of *crisis*. Cf. Frank Kermode, *The Sense of an Ending* (New York, 1967).

the Bible, Plato—the *paradise of poets*.[16] Keats is not less a humanist for being visionary: what preexists is not metaphysical, or transcendent of life, but souls that are *logoi*, "sovran voices" mediated by each great poet. So Milton "descends" into Keats: Apollo's birth is predicated on an overcoming of the father gods just as in *Paradise Lost* (itself descended from Biblical tradition) Adam's birth presupposes the fall of the Angels. The fledgling god's dying into the life of recollection is, similarly, comparable to Adam's falling into knowledge or the ambiguous career of the soul in Wordsworth's Intimations Ode, its humanizing passage from a birth which is "a sleep and a forgetting" to the compensating radiance of the philosophic mind. Keats's invention trails clouds of glory. It is itself a recollection, or anamnesis, which either justifies or devours the literary identity of its poet.

GENIUS AND GENIUS LOCI

On the surface there is some naïveté in claiming that literary history should be written from the point of view of the poets or of poetry. It is like saying naval history should be written from the point of view of sailors or ships. Hence it becomes important to stress the relatedness of the literary and the phenomenological points of view, as is implied by the previous section. The artist's struggle with his vocation—with past masters and the "pastness" of art in modern society—seems to be a version of a universal human struggle: of genius with Genius, and of genius with the genius loci (spirit of place).[17]

16. Cf. H. Bloom, op. cit., p. 517.

17. These terms have some kinship with race, milieu and moment, but are free of special sociological meaning and may be as old as Western religion. A study of their history and prevalence must still be made: there are beginnings in Edgar Zilsel, *Die Entstehung des Geniebegriffes* (Tübingen, 1926), W. Lange-Eichbaum and Wolfram Kurth, *Genie, Irrsinn und Ruhm,* 6th ed. (Munich, 1967), chapter 1; and sources cited in note 1 to my "Romantic Poetry and the Genius Loci," p. 311. The *genius loci* concept becomes visible with the nationalization of culture in Roman times and the revival of literary nationalism in the modern period. Whatever credence is given to it as a myth, it was an important structural idea in literature and art from the sixteenth through the nineteenth centuries. In what follows I tend to overburden *genius loci* by having it include "spirit of the age." I hope to work out its relation to that concept as well as to ideas of time as discussed in Kermode's *Sense of an Ending.*

In general, the artist's struggle with past masters corresponds to the struggle of genius with Genius, and his anxiety about the outmodedness of art to his anxiety about the genius of his country or time. To begin with the genius/Genius contest: this opposes or conjoins the personal "ingenium" in its unmediated, forgetful vigor and the starry guide whose influence accompanies us from birth[18] but is revealed mainly at crucial—historical or self-conscious—junctures. The contest is like that of Jacob with the Angel which results in a name (or a new name), one that is generic as well as personal. In the Romantic period Genius appears to genius as memory: as an internalized guardian self or fateful shadow. This is as true of Hegel as it is of Wordsworth and Keats.[19] But in every period something preexists: original sin, the world of the fathers, Plato's Ideas, Husserl's "Ideen," or the mythic forms of *illud tempus.* And in every period there is an *ingénu* to be tested by vision, to be lead out of the state of natural light by a Muse who opens an "everlasting scryne" where the "antique rolles" (roles and scrolls) lie hidden.

To restrict literary or cultural history to the genius/Genius relation skirts two errors. One is that art is seen as a puberty rite or adolescent crisis, localized in personal time even if recurring periodically. The other is that art becomes the story of humanity, in which Genius appears as a hero with a thousand faces (and

18. "Natale comes qui temperat astrum" (Horace). The Genius-genial-genital link, common from Roman times in which Genius personified the male procreative power, apparently helped to establish, in the Renaissance, the connection between Genius and *ingenium* (see, e.g., Rank, *Art and Artist,* chap. 2). Zilsel, in *Die Entstehung des Geniebegriffes,* concludes that genius in the modern sense of the term ("Sondergift der Natur," "Personifikation der Eigenart") became prevalent toward the middle of the sixteenth century as the learned revival of astrological and demonological symbolism joined with a surviving popular belief in genii and guardian spirits. (But J. Burckhardt, *The Civilization of the Renaissance in Italy,* describes astrology influencing the higher classes as early as the thirteenth century.) On the relation between *ingenium* and *vocatio,* see Richard M. Douglas, "Talent and Vocation in Humanist and Protestant Thought," in *Action and Conviction in Early Modern Europe,* ed. T. K. Rabb and J. K. Seigel (Princeton, 1969).

19. Cf. H. Marcuse, *Eros and Civilization,* new ed. (Boston, 1966), p. 232. The modernist conflict between historical memory and "the temptation of immediacy" is scrupulously analyzed by Paul de Man in the Spring 1970 issue of *Daedalus.* He recalls Nietzsche's subtlety and importance.

373

therefore no face, like the ecumenical God) pursuing a gnostic odyssey. Much literary biography or existential criticism falls prey to the first, most myth criticism to the second, error. These errors, however, are fruitful and complementary. We must manage to embrace both; only singly do they lead to an impoverishment in our understanding of art. Apollo's crisis, for example, is clearly that of adolescence. He has left the "chamber of Maiden-Thought" and hovers darkling between ephebe state and godhead. He is at once too young and too old: the middle state is what is obscure, and to emerge from it as a decisive, individuated being may require something equivalent to infanticide or parricide. His metamorphosis can only be toward pure youth (and the mythic figure of the divine child) or pure eld (the divine *senex)* or theriomorphic (and the figure, e.g., of the snake). But these are the very transformations studied by gnostic or myth-critical thought. The philosophers of individuation, from Plotinus through the modern school of Jung and Neumann, reveal how improbable it is for anyone to become truly individual, having wrestled with Genius and received the blessing and curse of identity.

Yet a poet is even more—because more *inobviously*—besieged than they describe. The dramatic encounter of genius with Genius is accompanied by the commonplace quarrel of genius with genius loci: of art with the natural religion or dominant myth of its age. To the burden of vision which rouses the poet's sense of his powers is added a combat with insidious habits of thought. "Reasonings like vast Serpents/ Infold around my limbs, bruising my minute articulations" (Blake). "A weight/ Heavy as frost, and deep almost as life" (Wordsworth). The genius loci can rival Genius as an influence, for it suggests the possibility of a more natural (unselfconscious) participation in a preexistent or larger self. England as Gloriana and America as Virgin Land are visionary commonplaces indistinguishable from an "idol of the tribe" or "collective representation."[20] Though bounded by

20. Myth is expressive of Genius in Northrop Frye, but of the genius loci in Henry Nash Smith's *Virgin Land* (1949). The difference, though significant, is not absolute and shows the need for a unified theory. Is the Old Man of Wordsworth's "Resolution and Independence" a Genius or a genius loci? We have only the sparsest beginnings of a literary iconography on the subject of Genius. See, e.g., C. S. Lewis, "Genius and Genius," in

period and place, the genius loci is as all-pervasive in its domain as a climate of opinion—which makes it harder to confront than a Mnemosyne. What arms does one take up against a spirit? Who will challenge a temperament, tilt with a weather? It is as absurd as the Beatles fighting the Blue Meanies: they try the solvent of music, but their true arms, one suspects, are counter-visionary, obliging the enemy to recrudesce by pop or parody art. One best engages the lurking, many-headed *topoi* or fixed ideas of a culture by sending against them their own image, enlarged and purified. "Bring me my chariot of fire" is still a *topos,* but more than commonplace. We see the spirited form, not the nebulous. The imagery of the tribe is given bounding outline; the imaginative vigor of national prejudices acknowledged and faced.

Should there be conflict in an artist between genius loci and Genius, it takes the form of humanity versus nation or local integrities versus abstract conceptions or art itself versus party allegiance. In the case of Keats, there is evidence that *Hyperion* was meant to depict a geopolitical progress of poetry from Antiquity to modern England. The "beautiful mythology of Greece" was to have been revived or rivaled by "home-bred glory"— by the "Sister of the Island," as Keats calls the muse of his native land in *Endymion* 4. This is the context of the poet's famous, formalistic-sounding statement that "English ought to be kept up." A contradiction remained (as in Blake) between the Genius of poetry and the national genius. Keats thought Milton had shown the way to their reconciliation, and he began *Hyperion* in that belief, but he eventually put Chatterton's "English Idiom in English words" against Milton's "artful or rather artist's humour." There are always, it seems, two genii fighting for the soul of the artist: two stars, or vision of destiny, or Genius and the genius loci.

Starry persons, of course, are an inveterate poetical superstition, and the astrology of genius revives explicitly in Yeats's *Vision,* but all literary judgment, insofar as it is historical, adjudicates the claims of Genius and genius loci. Here is Michelet on the greatness of Rabelais:

Studies in Renaissance Literature (New York, 1966), pp. 169–74; also the analysis of the relation between sense of place and sense of self in my *Wordsworth's Poetry* (New Haven, 1964), esp. pp. 211–19.

Rabelais collected wisdom from the old, popular idioms, from sayings, proverbs, school farces in the mouth of fools and clowns. But mediated by follies of this kind the genius of the age and its prophetic power are revealed in their majesty. Where he does not reveal, he glimpses, he promises, he guides. In this forest of dreams, one can see under each leaf fruits which the future will harvest. The entire book is a golden bough.[21]

Compare this with Bronson Alcott, Thoreau's friend, praising *A Week on the Concord and Merrimack Rivers* as "purely American, fragrant with the lives of New England woods and streams, and which could have been written nowhere else," then because "the sod and sap and flavor of New England have found at last a clear relation to the literature of other and classic lands . . . Egypt, India, Greece, England." Alcott seems more interested than Michelet in harmonizing native and classical genii loci, but when he adds that "especially am I touched by this soundness, this aboriginal vigour, as if a man had once more come into Nature,"[22] he appeals beyond the genius loci to the genius of the artist in its unmediated relation to nature.

The genius loci is especially significant for modern—that is, vernacular—art, for it is then that the assertion of a national genius becomes vital and a Dante, Ariosto, or Milton turn to the "adorning of their native Tongue." Native and national are not always identical, of course, and in the Renaissance this is part of the general problem of constructing a "national universal" from the genius of different localities. In Rabelais, Panurge at one point answers Pantagruel in seven languages, two of which are nonexistent; and Bakhtin has shown how this problematic abundance of linguistic masks fosters a peculiarly modern awareness of concrete historic space.[23] The literary self-consciousness of the

21. *Histoire de France,* 10: 58.

22. *The Journals of Bronson Alcott,* ed. Odell Shepard (Boston, 1938), pp. 213–14.

23. M. M. Bakhtin, *Rabelais and his World* (Cambridge, Mass., 1968), esp. pp. 465 ff. on the birth of modern literature "on the boundaries of two languages" (i.e., Latin and the vernacular). Borges, from this perspective, is a modern Rabelais with a significantly different space-language relation. Cf., for remarks on the birth of a more contemporary literature, Octavio Paz, "A literature of foundations," *Triquarterly* 12–14 (1968–69): 7–12.

modern era is intimately linked to a reflection on the fall of culture
into nationality and its redemption into a new universality.

Finding a more concrete universal, one with truly national or
native roots, proves to be, in the Renaissance, a highly liberative
and creative endeavor. In Rabelais, Cervantes, and Shakespeare,
those vernacular giants, popular culture joins the learned muses.
The neoclassical or purist reaction merely showed how these
giants traumatized later writers. Even before Shakespeare,
Gabriel Harvey had doubts about Spenser—hardly a pop artist,
yet to the genteel he seemed "hobgoblin run away with the garland from Apollo." With the signal exception of France, which
identified culture once more with the purification of language and
the achieving of a new latinity—an ideal that dominated Europe
from about 1660 to 1760—Apollo retrieved his garland by hob-
nobbing with hobgoblin. If literary creativity becomes problematic toward the end of the eighteenth century, it is not because
of a sudden mysterious uncertainty about the vocation of the
artist but, on the contrary, because that vocation, in the light of
the failure of French universalism, is only too clear. An intensely
programmatic consciousness arises which defines the vocation of
literature as Art seeking Pop—art seeking its father figure in folk
culture. Genius merges confusingly with genius loci as Volks-
boden or autochthonous art. We see this most clearly among the
German and English Romantics. In the 1770s Herder writes an
influential essay attributing his nation's literary poverty to the fact
that, unlike England, it had produced no poets to revitalize the
learned muse by bringing folklore into the mainstream of art.
Where are our Chaucer, Spenser, and Shakespeare? he asks. Or,
as Keats will say, "let us have the old poets, and Robin Hood.[24]

24. Herder, "Von Ähnlichkeit der Mittlern Englischen und Deutschen
Dichtkunst" (*Deutsches Museum,* 1777); Keats, letter to J. H. Reynolds,
February 3, 1818. The idea survives into present: "The English language
—that was Shakespeare at the beginning of the seventeenth century—the
English language grew up through the brains and the mouths of English
people as such; I mean the nobility and the common people as well. But
here, here in our country, the educated people and nobility spoke German,
and just the people spoke Czech" (Jan Werich, quoted in A. Alvarez,
Under Pressure: The Writer in Society [London, 1965]). These remarks
differ vitally from an absolutist perspective of popular culture ("let us
have pop art and NOT the old poets"). For a critique of the educational
importance of popular culture, see G. H. Bantock, *Culture, Industrializa-
tion and Education* (New York, 1968).

There is, then, a model which haunts the consciousness of vernacular artists. The "vegetable gold" of great art is to bring Sancho Panza into relation with Don Quijote. Patrician and plebeian are to be fellow travellers, part of the same human family. Genius, in expelling a false or discovering a true genius loci, discovers itself and enlarges us.

In our own day this model is often dangerously simplified. Art, we are told, seeks to revitalize and if need be rebarbarize man. There must be contact with devil or drug or forbidden areas. Thomas Mann's *Dr. Faustus* is the definitive expression—and critique—of that simplification. Yet, simplified or not, this model for creativity becomes an animating force, a psychic silhouette with which the artist strives to coincide. There is also a counter-model, inspired by the French tradition, in which art seeks to purify "les mots de la tribu." Both models, however, are functions of the rise of the national literatures. The nationalization of art is a cultural analogue of the Fall (perhaps a fortunate Fall);[25] and true literary history, like true theology, can help to limit the curse and assure the promise. At least, it makes us honor the paradoxes of an era in which the tenth Muse is Pop.

MILTON AS EXAMPLE: FORM AND THE HISTORICAL VOCATION OF ART

Milton's *Arcades* is a version of pastoral Empson left unexamined and which Godard might enjoy. It is hard to imagine a piece more elite in conception than this courtly interlude. A pastoral in little, it depicts the unmasking of shepherds as noble primitives. An opera in little, it is all opsis, like the tableaux vivants, the staged devices common from Elizabeth's time. A drama in little, its action is a single recognition, complete in the first stanza of the first song and confirmed by the Genius of the Wood. As this sophisticated mixture of genres—pastoral, drama, masque—it tends in its contracted yet leisurely form toward a fourth and undermining genre. Composed of but three songs and the "recitative" of the genius loci, the lyrical form of an ode clearly appears. If genres here, in their very multiplicity and formality, are

25. Cf. "the presupposition of *Weltliteratur* is a *felix culpa:* mankind's division into many cultures" (Erich Auerbach, "Philologie und Weltliteratur" (1952), trans. M. and E. Said, *Centennial Review* 13 (1969): 2.

the superstructure, the deep structure is nothing less than the spirit of song itself, questing like the "secret sluice" of Arethusa for a new country or local form, which turns out to be England—that is, the possibility of a truly native lyricism.

Arcades begins with the fulfillment of a quest:

> Look Nymph and Shepherds look
> What sudden blaze of majesty
> Is that which we from hence descry
> > Too divine to be mistook
> > This, this is she. . . .

The cry practically ends the action: "here our solemn search hath end." It is the formal sign of an epiphany or theophany, of a "present deity" being revealed. It is a show cry, the equivalent of the Lo, Behold, O see. But who is this new god? A lady of seventy, the Countess Dowager of Derby. The whole thing seems to be an extravagant courtly compliment; and after the Genius of the Wood has confirmed the perception of these displaced magi and acknowledged their own "bright honour," the piece concludes by inviting us to attest that a new deity has been found, one who makes England a greater Arcady.

Is there in this spectacle more than meets the eye? Is the compliment all that extravagant, the form all that gratuitous? The setting is not only the estate of a noble Lady but the English countryside, and the masque was probably performed in the open air. Although Milton's literary code is classical and the allusions italianate, the plot, what there is of it, depicts a journey from a southern to a northern Arcadia and the discovery that England, despite its dank climate, has deities worth celebrating:

> Who had thought this clime had held
> A deity so unparallel'd?

In the last song of the masque, the Dowager Countess is directly identified with a transcendent nature spirit, the genius huius loci:

> Here ye shall have greater grace
> To serve the Lady of this place.

These words invite the nature spirits haunting more classical

379

shores to emigrate and grace the English countryside. "A better soil shall give ye thanks." Thus Milton's *Arcades* is really a farewell to Arcades, a "we'll to [Italian] woods no more," or "we'll to Fresh woods, and Pastures new." It is a nativity hymn for English nature poetry, in which Nymphs, Shepherds, and the genius loci make their formal submission.

Milton's simple sooth is never simple. The real discovery here is that of a pastoral within a pastoral. The old gods, the old forms —the elite superstructure—must serve a "rural Queen" identified with the genius loci of England. But is it not ridiculous to make of this septagenarian dowager a new Gloriana? Is what we find here the authentic expression of a national idea of poetry or its misuse as a courtly compliment? Is not *Arcades* at most dirigisme, Kulturlenkung, rather than poetry grappling authentically with the spirit of English history and countryside?

It is a question I want to explore rather than answer. If the Countess of Derby is a personal patron, she is also, not without authority, a patroness of English poetry as a whole, being a distant relative of Edmund Spenser and appearing as Amaryllis in "Colin Clout Comes Home Again." Spenser's homecoming, of course, was bitter: promises of "chere of court" were not fulfilled. He used the pastoral disguise of Colin Clout as a *topos* of modesty but also with secret pride in his resumption of vernacular poetry. Milton's version of pastoral foresees Spenser's redemption and a true homecoming of the spirit of poetry to England. He associates the aristocracy with the poet's game: the unmasking of artificial shepherds as guardians of the realm (nobles) also unmasks the simple sooth of his poetry as not so simple, as having a tutelary function and lineage as old as theirs. Poetry's tutelary function appears even more clearly in *Comus,* Milton's second pastoral masque, which introduces young aristocrats both to society and the truth of fable.

Thus, by glorifying the lineage of the Countess, Milton at the same time glorifies the lineage of vernacular poetry. He honors Spenser all the more because Spenser had first taught English poets how to transfer the Virgilian genres to England and so to increase the honor of the line, revivified rather than interrupted by national ideals. There was schism in the Church, but there would be no schism in poetry. Spenser had more than imitated

Virgil: he had Englished him by understanding how the idea of form merged with that of the historical vocation of art.

Artists may always have had a bad conscience, have always felt themselves Colin Clouts, but Virgil gave his feelings direct expression at the end of the *Georgics* where he accused himself of practicing an art of "ignoble leisure" *(ignobile otium)* compared to the victorious military exploits of Caesar Octavianus. Make war, not poetry. Later commentators saw Virgil's poetry as a conscious progression from pastoral to georgic to epic, a movement which is thought to express a mounting sense of vocation. We go from sheep and the man, to tools and the man, to arms and the man: from the silly arts and competitive songs of rural life, to the more cultic, warlike tasks of agriculture, and finally to those martial and political qualities which extend the empire of civilization. The Virgilian progress was a commonplace in the Renaissance: one may refer to the stanzas introductory to the *Faerie Queene* in which Spenser promises to exchange his "oaten reedes" for "trumpets sterne," or to Marvell's ode on Cromwell which begins:

> **The forward Youth that would appeare**
> **Must forsake his Muses dear,**
> Nor in the Shadowes sing
> His Numbers languishing.

Here Cromwell is a male debutant: to appear or to come out—the humanistic equivalent of epiphany—he must leave the pastoral sphere and exchange plow or harp for sword.

The debut of the Countess Dowager of Derby is somewhat belated (she is seventy years old, the span of human life according to the Bible), but then Milton himself is a belated poet, uncertain, despite the greatness of the poetical era just passing, whether there is true public recognition of the poet as a seeing mouth. Though *Arcades* still looks toward the epiphany of poetry, the courtly culture which could have recognized it is clearly at the term of its life. Seven years later, in *Lycidas,* Milton almost stages his own debut as a poet-prophet who sings independent of any class but his own, the class of all great poets. But he vacillates, returns to swainishness at the end, and does not appear in the Marvellian sense till after Cromwell and the Civil War when he finally passes from pastoral to epic, and to a more than national idea of poetry.

AN OBJECTION

Is not the theory presented here a throwback to nationalistic speculation? That is its danger, yet a lesser danger for us than to remain trapped in the rhetoric of an Esperanto history. Substantive thought about the racial or ideological components in a culture became especially suspect after the Nazis; the American ideal of assimilation then appeared the only pragmatic answer to ethnic stresses in a nation-state. Now that assimilation has proved to be not false but certainly an imperfect reality, we are facing the agony of pluralism all over again—conflicts of allegiance, cultural transvestism, a splintered national identity. Most criticism before the present era was a matter of defining the national genius rather than a particular work of art, and literary history established the native or foreign influences carried forward by an artist. Such determinations could be crassly nationalistic, but they acknowledged that the community was struggling for self-definition and that art played its role in that struggle. No one, of course, wishes to return to the nineteenth century racial calculus, even when practiced by so sensible a critic as Matthew Arnold:

> Science has now made visible to everybody the great and pregnant elements of difference which lie in race, and in how signal a manner they make the genius and history of an Indo-European people vary from those of a Semitic people. Hellenism is of Indo-European growth, Hebraism is of Semitic growth; and we English, a nation of Indo-European stock, seem to belong naturally to the movement of Hellenism. But nothing more strongly marks the essential unity of man than the affinities we can perceive, in this point or that, between members of one family of peoples and members of another; and no affinity of this kind is more strongly marked than that likeness in the strength and prominence of the moral fibre, which, notwithstanding immense elements of

difference, knits in some special sort the genius and history of us English, and of our American descendants across the Atlantic, to the genius and history of the Hebrew people.[26]

It may be needful, however, to take back into consciousness what was too quickly subsumed. "An era comes," said a French contemporary of Arnold's, the philosopher and mathematician Cournot, "which will see the value of ethnic characteristics increase relatively, though decrease in an absolute sense; and Europe seems now [ca. 1860] to be entering that era." The relative increase in the importance of ethnic distinctions he attributed to the very advance of civilization which levels or blunts purely social or historical distinctions and so raises the more ancient or indelible ones. Cournot's anxiety for the organic nurture of cultural forms—an anxiety first arising in the Romantic age—springs from the same insight concerning the advance of civilization. He fears that the expansion and availability of historical forms will burden emerging talents to the point of endangering their growth:

> If it is true that everything living, everything which bears the cachet of native beauty must emerge from a seed . . . how can we conceive of the birth and nurture of a truly original art, a truly innovative style, in an era where all genres, all styles are understood historically, explained, liked, and imitated. . . . When one preserves so well all the dead no place is left for the living. . . . The new type will not be able to sustain the competition with existing types already at a high degree of maturity and evolution. Art will therefore arrive by the very progress of historical criticism at a syncretistic and erudite stage . . . incompatible with conditions favoring its organic development.[27]

A return to Herder and the Romantic historians—or simply

26. *Culture and Anarchy* (1869). Cf. E. Renan, *De la part des peuples sémitiques dans l'histoire de la civilisation* (Paris, 1862).
27. A. Cournot, *Traité de l'enchaînement des idées fondamentales dans les sciences et dans l'histoire* (Paris, 1861), section 543; and *Considérations sur la marche des idées* (Paris, 1872), Bk. 5, chap. 4.

to E. R. Curtius[28]—may be painful. We have tended to forget such "unhappy, far-off things" as the birth struggle of cosmopolitanism and the foundation of the idea of world literature in the cultural effects of persecution, which made the Muse an émigré many times over. Without "racist" events like the revocation of the Edict of Nantes, which "drove the national genius abroad,"[29] we might never have had that cross-fertilization of talents which modernism takes for granted. In reevaluating the prevalence of so many national, religious, or geopolitical ideals—superstitions we still live with despite the universalisms around us—the genius loci concept may help to prevent our collapsing national into nationalistic. It reminds us how necessary the idea of a communal locus is, but also how vulnerable: "From this the poem springs: that we live in a place / That is not our own" (Wallace Stevens).

If art is the offspring of a precarious marriage between genius and genius loci, the place of which it is the genius is not necessarily a nation-state. Art can express a people (an emerging class or suppressed majority), a region (a Galilee whose genius becomes triumphant), or a speech-community (as large as an Empire, as small as a professional body). Hence literary study often combats the premature universalism that urges the institution of a common tongue or perfect language. This ideal of a *caractéristique universelle* has haunted intellects from Leibnitz to Noam Chomsky. Turning sceptical and sensuous, it ends in the aggressive ecumenical utopianism that makes the law go forth from the Zion of

28. "Es wäre eine wichtige Aufgabe der vergleichenden Literaturgeschichte, den Entwicklungsgang der einzelnen Literaturen und ihre Selbstinterpretationen herauszuarbeiten. Was ich das französische Literatursystem nannte, ist eine solche Selbstinterpretation und d.h. eine Ideologie, die bewusst gemacht werden kann. Die Literaturvergleichung würde, wenn sie die bezeichnete Aufgabe ergreift, einen wichtigen Beitrag zur Analyse der modernen Nationalideologien leisten. Diese sind nicht weniger bedeutsam und wirksam als die Klassenideologien" *(Gesammelte Aufsätze zur Romanischen Philologie* [Bern and Munich, 1960], pp. 20–21).

29. Joseph Texte, *Jean-Jacques Rousseau and the Cosmopolitan Spirit in Literature,* trans. J. W. Matthews (London, 1899), p. xiii. Texte, one of our first scholarly comparatists, sees the cosmopolitan spirit founded not by an abstraction from nationality but by a convergence of the "Germanic" (northern) and "Latin" (southern) genius in Rousseau, who consolidated the eighteenth century influence of England on France.

T-groups. But a pentecostal ideal of the plurality of tongues seems preferable to a one-dimensional, deracinated language. "Would to God that all the Lord's people were prophets," was Moses's reply to those who urged him to put down rival sayers. At the end of the eighteenth century Rivarol claimed with elegant contempt that "Leibnitz was seeking a universal language, and we [i.e. the French] were creating it all around him,"[30] but by the middle of the nineteenth—the great period of philological discovery—even a rationalist could defend the secularity of language against ideals of *une langue bien faite:*

> C'est . . . le langage, dans sa nature abstraite ou dans sa forme générale, que l'on doit considérer comme essentiellement défectueux, tandis que les langues parlées, formées lentement sous l'influence durable de besoins infiniment variés, ont, chacune à sa manière et d'après son degré de souplesse, paré à cet inconvénient radical. Selon le génie et les destinées des races, sous l'influence si diverse des zones et des climats, elles se sont appropriées plus spécialement à l'expression de tel ordre d'images, de passions et d'idées. . . . Ce qui aggrandirait et perfectionnerait nos facultés intellectuelles, en multipliant et en variant les moyens d'expression et de transmission de la pensée, ce serait, s'il était possible, de disposer à notre gré, et selon le besoin du moment, de toutes les langues parlées, et non de trouver construite cette langue systématique qui, dans la plupart des cas, serait le plus imparfait des instruments.[31]

CONCLUSION

"I believe in Eternity. I can find Greece, Asia, Italy, Spain and the Islands,—the genius and creative principle of each and of all eras, in my own mind." This confession of a comparatist is Emerson's. Only a century old, it already seems dated in its optimism and deceptively easy in its transcendence of nationality. Yet some such faith has always governed the study of literature when humanistic in its aim. Some such faith makes each national

30. *De l'universalité de la langue française* (Berlin and Paris, 1784).
31. A. Cournot, *Essai sur les fondements de la connaissance et sur les caractères de la critique philosophique* (Paris, 1851).

book a Book of the Nations. Studied this way literature might do what Seneca attributed only to philosophy. It could open "not some local shrine, but the vast temple of all the gods, the universe itself."[32]

The one literary historian, however, who came closest to Emerson's sense of eternity or Seneca's of universality was strangely pessimistic about it. Erich Auerbach's *Mimesis,* written in exile and published after World War II, foresaw the end of western history as we know it—of history as a rich, particolored succession of events with personalities and writers dramatically divided by the pressure of class or conscience. Auerbach looked at this canvas of history, on which he saw consciousness strive with consciousness in the Hegelian manner, with something of Virgilian regret. Like Cournot, he surmised that we were moving toward a *nivellement* which would reduce the autochthonous element and gradually eliminate both local and national traditions; and for him this beginning of conformity augured the end of history. When one sees an airline ad with the motto "Introducing the Atlantic River" or hears André Malraux speak of technology creating an "Atlantic civilization," the forerunner of a worldwide humanistic culture, one is almost inclined to agree with Auerbach that historical time and space may be fading into the uniformity of landscapes seen from the air. But then one remembers the source of Auerbach's own strength as a historian of literature, how he traced the interaction of genius and genius loci, of Latin and the lingua franca, of the vernacular and the high style. Surely in that dubious cultural millennium, in that predicted mass-cult era, a Gloriana will appear once more to a Colin Clout, like another angel to another Caedmon, and say "Sing to me."

32. Emerson, "History," *Complete Works* (Boston, 1903–04), 2:9; Seneca, *Epistolae,* 90.28.

387